Unknown Legends
of Rock 'n' Roll

Psychedelic Unknowns,
Mad Geniuses,
Punk Pioneers,
Lo-Fi Mavericks & More

Richie Unterberger

Miller
Freeman
Books

Published by Miller Freeman Books
600 Harrison Street, San Francisco, CA 94107
Publishers of *Keyboard, Bass Player,* and *Guitar Player* magazines

Miller Freeman
A United News & Media publication

Distributed to the book trade in the U.S. and Canada by
Publishers Group West, P.O. Box 8843, Emeryville, CA 94662

Distributed to the music trade in the U.S. and Canada by
Hal Leonard Publishing, P.O. Box 13819, Milwaukee, WI 53213

Design and Typesetting: Claudia Smelser Design
Editor: Carolyn Keating
Production Editor: Jan Hughes
Front Cover and CD: John's Children, circa 1967; courtesy Andy Ellison
Spine: Poly Styrene of X-Ray Spex, circa 1976; courtesy Maharani Devi,
        © Falcon Stuart
Back Cover: Siren with Kevin Coyne, 1969; courtesy Dave Clague

Library of Congress Cataloging in Publication Data:

Unterberger, Richie, 1962-
Unknown legends of rock 'n' roll : psychedelic unknowns, mad geniuses, punk pioneers, lo-fi mavericks & more / Richie Unterberger.
        p. cm.
Includes bibliographical references, discographies, and index.
ISBN 0-87930-534-7
1. Rock music—Bio-bibliography.   I. Title.
ML102.R6U58 1998
781.66'092'2—dc21   98-11827
[B]   CIP
                                                 MN

Printed in the United States of America
98 99 00 01 02 03   5 4 3 2 1

Contents

Acknowledgments

Unknown Legends of Rock 'n' Roll may bear a single byline, but making it a reality was very much a team effort. If nothing else, it can be considered a triumph of the small but dedicated international network of cult rock enthusiasts. These fans have devoted a large part of their lives to uncovering great overlooked sounds of the past, finding the people who made them, and making sure that these musicians got at least some of the recognition they deserved. That involves not only going to outlandish extremes to find rare records, but also giving vital assistance to those who share the same passions.

Just locating all 60 of the artists examined in this volume within a seven-month span—many of whom had not recorded for years—involved an enormous amount of detective work. This challenging, not to say foolishly overambitious, task could not have been completed without the help of the following roll call of music aficionados, collectors, and even (gasp!) music business professionals. All of them unselfishly gave addresses, phone numbers, or useful advice: Chris Ashford, Simon Aumonier, Jeff Calder, Chris Charlesworth, Irwin Chusid, Dave Clague, Byron Coley, Marty Cooper, Sean Cooper, Jud Cost from *Cream Puff War* magazine, Glenn Dicker, John Dixon, Mark Ellingham, John C. Falstaff, Steve Feigenbaum, Lorry Fleming, Lynne Goodall, David Greenberg, Jackson Haring, Paul Hartman from *Dirty Linen* magazine, Colin Hill, David Housden, Erik Lindgren, Barbara Manning, Mike Mathews, Phil

McMullen from *Ptolemaic Terrascope* magazine, Stephen McParland, David Newgarden, Jack Ortman, Alec Palao from *Cream Puff War* magazine, Archie Patterson, Jan Pavelka, Stephen Peeples, Chuck Prophet, Simon Robinson, Johnny Rogan, Michael Schumacher, Al Spicer, Mike Stax from *Ugly Things* magazine, Christine Freeman Wall, Mike Watkinson, Mike Westbrook, Greg Wolski, Chris Woodstra from the *All Music Guide*, Joseph Yanosik, and Thomas Ziegler.

These friends generously lent or taped rare records that were crucial in preparing many chapters: Todd Barrett, John Dougan, Stephen Thomas Erlewine, Mark Goodman, Ron Nachmann, Pat Thomas, Diane Wallis, and Kurt Wolff. I owe a major debt to the staff of the Flat Plastic Sound record store in San Francisco for allowing me to borrow rare and out-of-print LPs from their vast collection.

Extra special thanks to Jason Gross of the Perfect Sound Forever web site (http://www.furious.com/perfect). Without his indefatigable assistance in tracking down the Plastic People of the Universe—at a time when all possible avenues seemed to have been exhausted—their story could not have been told. Nor could it have been told without the help of Jiri Smrcek, who efficiently relayed my questions to Plastic People founding member Milan Hlavsa, and Michal Stasa, who translated the replies from Czech to English.

Pals Gordon Anderson, Stuart Kremsky, Janet Rosen, and Steve Zeff provided invaluable comments about the book as it evolved from whimsical proposal to finished manuscript. Agent Robert Shepard gave liberally of his time and expertise. My lawyer and friend, Alan Korn, provided vital legal representation and many rare records from his extensive personal collection. Editor Matt Kelsey gave his full support to a most unconventional project, paving the way for the first in-depth treatment that many of the musicians profiled in these pages have ever received in a widely distributed book. Dorothy Cox and Jan Hughes of Miller Freeman did valuable production work for the volume. Thanks to Lenny Kaye, rock scholar supreme and a pillar of the alternative rock community for years, for writing the foreword.

Much love and gratitude is due to my parents, Sue and Elliot, who have been unstinting in their support of my creative and professional endeavors. They should also be hailed for allowing me to listen to the radio as much as I wished from the age of six, and never prohibiting me from playing whatever records I wanted to as I grew up, even if they didn't always understand why I wanted to subject myself to such noise. Believe me, it would have been a much worse racket if I had found all these cult rock records before I left for college.

As best friend and confidante, Dana Mayer helped absorb the emotional ups and downs of my freelance writing crusades through regular transatlantic phone calls and too-infrequent visits. Her advice and steadfast camaraderie over the past few years have been of immeasurable value. The same goes for Susan Mallett, treasured friend, brilliant scientist, and superb hostess, who let me use her Oxford home as base of operations during my first round of interviews in the summer of 1996. She cheerfully endured my five weeks of manic commutes between Oxford and London, and permitted her phone to be used for long-distance calls all over England in comic goose chases after the likes of long-dormant bands such as the Blossom Toes and Tomorrow. She and her friends also gleefully celebrated my successful quest for an audience with the slippery Screaming Lord Sutch, British rock 'n' roll wildman and satirical politician extraordinaire, which was granted a mere 24 hours before my plane took off for California.

Above all, thanks to the many musicians—and various of their associates—who agreed to be interviewed for this book. All were exceedingly generous with their time and memories of events that were often extremely controversial and painful—but, more often, were joyously exhilarating to recount. I had been eager for the opportunity to hear their stories for many years. What I found was fully worth the wait. I am honored to tell their tales, and hopefully widen the appreciation for their very special brands of music.

About the Author

Richie Unterberger has been writing about little-known rock music of all kinds for more than fifteen years. He is a senior editor of Miller Freeman's *All Music Guide to Rock*, the largest rock reference book of artist biographies and album reviews ever published. From 1985 to 1991, he was the editor of *Option*, a magazine devoted to coverage of all types of alternative and independently produced music. He is also author of a travel guidebook, *The Rough Guide to Seattle*, and is currently at work on a travel-oriented guide to the regional popular music of the United States, to be published in 1999.

His research for *Unknown Legends of Rock 'n' Roll* occupied much of 1996 and 1997, bringing him everywhere from hotel rooms in San Francisco's shabbiest downtown neighborhood to Abbey Road Studios in London. Although releases by cult rock artists now form a large part of his music collection, his favorite group remains the Beatles. He lives in San Francisco.

Foreword

Me, I like to get lost.

It's like a labyrinth, these dusty corridors of rock 'n' roll history, walls covered with posters advertising gigs long encored, and record collections consigned to that great garage sale in the sky. If you keep on cruising against the grain, continually reversing and backing over your own tracks, following the windings and the branchings off, the twists and turns and infinite variations of those three chords and a yowling microphone, you'll reach a path with no outlet save itself. Some might call it a dead end. But the brave wayfarers who undertake such a Minos-like journey will know it as an alive beginning, a window into the oversoul of artists who can only be called unique. One of a kind. Cult heroes and villains.

Chances are, unless you are a hardcore rock aficionado, you've never heard of most of the "unknown legends" that make up the cast of Richie Unterberger's characters. Chances are, even if you are a harder-core rock aficionado, you've only listened randomly to the collected works of these UL's, have only a few categorical imperatives to slot these strange mutations and wild cards into your rock family tree, and wouldn't mind knowing more (or indeed, anything) about some oddball visionary whose target audience has trouble enough going pvc, much less platinum.

And yet, for seekers with a taste for the mongrel, each performer in this rogue's gallery is intuitively connected to the instinct for art which helps define our humane sociopathy, beyond the commerce and formats and definitions with which we design our musical personalities. They'll renew your faith in the idiosyncratic as a way of life, performance as psychodrama, career as parable, the unbeaten path to the doorway and the knock that never comes. Until that day when they wake up and find they've become legend.

Which is why, beyond archeology, this book exists. To let all the unknowns—any of us, dreaming our dreams and trying to accomplish our daily tasks—embrace the glimmer of hope that our efforts might someday be heard, passed along, placed in the culturati time capsule to be dug up in an unforeseeable future and seen as an expression of our era on this earth, the true music of myth and memory.

Recognition. At last, and lasting.

—Lenny Kaye

Lenny Kaye is longtime guitarist for Patti Smith, with whom he has frequently collaborated as a songwriter. As a rock critic for the last 25 years in such publications as Rolling Stone *and* Creem, *he was one of the first to champion cult rock artists, and is renowned as the compiler/annotator of* Nuggets, *the first and best '60s garage band anthology. He has produced top-selling, critically acclaimed albums by Suzanne Vega, Kristin Hersh, and Soul Asylum, and recently co-authored Waylon Jennings' autobiography.*

Introduction

I was 17 when I bought the first record that no one—and I mean *no one*—I knew had ever heard. But Love's *Forever Changes* was an album that kept coming up, again and again, as I read more and more rock criticism. Some writers even ranked it ahead of such familiar classics as *Sgt. Pepper* and *Pet Sounds* on their all-time Top Ten lists. In 1979 (or, for that matter, 1997), you didn't hear Love on the local radio stations, even when they programmed special '60s weekends. Could a record so unknown (in the Philadelphia suburbs, at any rate) be *that* good? It seemed worth paying $3.49 for a used copy to find out.

When I finally got to hear *Forever Changes*, I was taken not only by the beauty of its orchestrated folk-rock and inscrutable poetic lyrics, but by its sheer uniqueness. It wasn't easily comparable to the famous '60s bands I loved—the Beatles, the Doors, the Byrds. It certainly wasn't comparable to the pap jamming the airwaves as I finished high school—Fleetwood Mac, Toto, Eddie Money, and the like. Enthused, I played the record to my friend Danny, who dismissed it as low-rent Moody Blues. He then made me listen to two Van Halen albums in a row. Our friendship never recovered.

In *Mystery Train*, rock critic Greil Marcus once described Elvis Presley's "(You're So Square) Baby I Don't Care" as his first "private treasure, a record I loved that no one else seemed to like." *Forever Changes* was my first secret treasure—the difference being that at least everyone knew who Elvis Presley was when Marcus bought that 1957 EP. It took years for me to find anyone else who knew who Love were; it took a few years after that to find anyone who actually owned and liked the record. By that time, Love were just one of dozens—if not hundreds—of "cult" rock acts in my collection. In the absence of airplay, record reviews, or even word of mouth, finding this music was akin to joining an underground cabal. Information was found in fanzines or by talking to fellow record collectors. You often had to take the risk of buying records—which were sometimes expensive imports—without a chance to hear the music first.

These were artists about whom little was known, and little was written. Sometimes they had just one album to their credit; sometimes they had been active for decades. Their music was sometimes so melodic and accessible that it seemed impossible that they hadn't become popular stars. Sometimes it was so defiantly weird and off-the-wall that it seemed impossible that their records could have even been released. Their only common ground was their obscurity and the clouds of mystique surrounding the performers. Who was this Arthur Lee, leader/singer/songwriter of Love, who glared from the LP sleeve with a hoodlum stare while holding a broken flower vase? How in the world did Columbia end up releasing a record by Skip Spence, who sang charbroiled acid-folk in a voice reminiscent, as critic Byron Coley once wrote, of Johnny Cash with a hangover? Did it really only sell 700 copies, as was once claimed? And why did he never make another record?

The more I investigated rock history, the more I came across fascinating enigmas like Lee and Spence. The more I heard and learned, the more I became convinced that their stories should be told—and not just for obsessive record collectors, either. These are artists who have not just made brilliant music, but who have influenced the course of rock history far more than mainstream rock writers and reference books have ever acknowledged. That these musicians didn't "make it" commercially does not mean that they were failures; it was usually due more to their bad management, bad luck, or incompatibility with the trends of their era.

Their records are not musty nostalgic oldies, nor are they interesting chiefly for their oddity. They contain remarkable, ambitious stuff that speaks to today's listeners as much as it did to the listeners of its era. Perhaps more so—in many cases, it's taken decades for this music to find its true audience, after being overlooked at its moment of release. The albums also exude a compelling aura because, in so many cases, there is so little to treasure of a favored lost legend. As Syd Barrett biographer Mike Watkinson noted in the Barrett fanzine *Eskimo Chain*, "Fans have just three albums plus a few bits and pieces to pore over and ponder what might have been. There is something peculiarly enchanting about Barrett's material, something which leaves people panting for more."

Unknown Legends of Rock 'n' Roll presents the stories of 60 of these cult figures. These are some of the best and most fascinating of the rock musicians—from the 1950s through the 1990s—who have rarely or never reached a wide audience. Their careers are full of artistic triumphs and disastrous business transactions; fleeting and not-so-fleeting musical and personal relationships with everyone from the Beatles and Elvis to the Sex Pistols; the exuberant joy of creation, and the pain of internal turmoil and public rejection. About the only thing they all share is a wild disparity between the high quality of their work and the low level of recognition it received.

Some caveats are in order about the actual list of personalities selected. First, this is not a definitive collection of the absolute "best" unknown rockers of all time. I hate making musical "best of" lists because they are so subjective. Taste is a very personal matter, particularly when it comes to such idiosyncratic cult favorites. What I have done is offer a cross-section of some of the best cult rockers, with enough diversity of styles, eras, and regions to hopefully entertain anyone whose interest in rock history extends beyond what they'll read in *Rolling Stone*. You won't find any of these acts in the Rock and Roll Hall of Fame; it's doubtful any will get elected to that institution in the future.

Some (not many) of the artists have had a few hits, but none achieved what you might call true lasting international stardom, although many attracted passionately devoted followings. Exceptions are artists such as Françoise Hardy, Savage Rose, and Sandy Denny, who achieved varying degrees of great commercial success in their European homeland, but are barely known in the United States, the primary (as of this writing) market for this book. I purposely avoided acts that emerged within the last five years, as they are fairly well covered by the expanding network of alternative rock magazines.

Syd Barrett, brilliant visionary and original leader of Pink Floyd, was a useful barometer of sorts. "The-most-well-known-artist-in-the-book-is-Syd-Barrett" became a mantra of sorts when I was trying to convey just how "unknown" my territory was. If people were more famous than Syd, it was a pretty sure sign that they probably out-famed themselves out of consideration, though many of them probably wouldn't agree, particularly if they don't have gold records or paid-off mortgages to show for it.

Virtually everyone I spoke to about this book (including many of the artists interviewed) suggested other musicians as essential additions. Doing a project such as this is bound to provoke controversy, even anger, about the many deserving candidates for cult canonization who didn't make the final cut. You're probably preparing a list of sorts yourself after scanning the table of contents. So many acts with vocal, vociferous constituencies are missing. Where are the Seeds, for example? The Standells? The Germs? Big Star? The Television Personalities? The Residents? The Sleepers? Johnny Kidd? Faust? One noted meticulous scholar of psychedelic music seemed genuinely puzzled—hurt even—than any such volume could fail to encompass Pearls Before Swine. There are reasonable arguments for putting any of these acts, and hundreds of others, into a book like this. But those artists won't be found here.

I can't pretend that the final list was not informed to a large degree by personal taste. I didn't think it would serve anyone's purpose to interview people whose music didn't personally interest me, or worse, whose music I actively disliked. Nor is this perfectly balanced between eras and styles—again a reflection of my expertise, as I feel that it's better to leave genres that are not my bag to other rock scholars. As it is, there is not a single artist covered in the book that I was not eager to talk with and write about.

At the same time, I didn't want to overemphasize some eras/mini-genres to the extent that they dominated the book. There could have been a whole volume dedicated solely to underappreciated '60s rockers. This meant that some worthy candidates were denied inclusion, including some personal favorites of mine, such as the Pretty Things, Tim Buckley, the Fugs, and the Bonzo Dog Band. If there's a volume two of *Unknown Legends of Rock 'n' Roll*, several of these artists—and other, less obvious ones—will no doubt fill in these gaps.

I also heard arguments that some of the acts chosen were too well known for a project like this. Without trying to take the "all things to all people" ethos to extremes, I've included some of the most famed cult icons—Syd Barrett, my early faves Love, Can, Scott Walker, Roky Erickson—as well as bands like Blossom Toes, Judy Henske & Jerry Yester, and the Mystic Tide, whose achievements are known only to those who haunt used record stores and import bins far too often for their own good. When I have written about artists whose feats are somewhat well documented, I've at least tried to talk to associates of theirs that have rarely if ever been interviewed about the musicians, and/or offer some new or rarely printed information.

While space precludes inclusion of complete discographies, there are selective recommendations and descriptions of the most essential points of entry. If the effort and expense needed to locate the records seems exorbitant, take heart. One of the great ironies of the CD revolution is that it's probably a lot easier to find this stuff now than it was when it was first released.

When I first heard *Forever Changes*, I had no idea that there would be enough artists like Love to fill a book—indeed, that pruning the list of deserving acts down to 60 would be a nearly impossible task. I had no idea, either, that when I finally got my chance to write about Arthur Lee, he would be behind bars serving, depending upon what account you believe, a prison sentence of eight or twelve years, or that Skip Spence—once a member of Moby Grape, whose first album I had bought the same month I got *Forever Changes*—would be a ward of the state, nearly incapacitated by years of mental illness and drug abuse.

Stories such as Lee's and Spence's should give one pause before deciding to track down cult rock heroes. It's not just a question of being disappointed with the personalities behind the music—I've never gone in for hero worship, or assumed that great music was necessarily created by great (or even good) human beings. It's also the possibility that the music makers may be uninterested in, or even incapable of, remembering their shots in the dark from decades past. Nonetheless, for each chapter of this book, I determined to locate and interview the musicians themselves for firsthand material, rather than merely relying upon the albums and the scanty printed record. In cases where they were dead, untraceable, or unwilling to speak with journalists, I made sure to speak with at least one key musical or professional associate.

So it was that I scuttled down a busy thoroughfare in a somewhat rundown district of London one brisk morning in late August 1996. Awaiting me at Rykodisc's British office, for the first of the 70 or so interviews I would conduct over the next seven months, was producer Joe Boyd. Joe would, by sheer chance, discuss three figures he worked with that typified the cult-rocker-as-mythological-fallen-angel. There was Nick Drake, mordant folk-rocker, dead at 26 of an overdose that some have thought to be a suicide; Sandy Denny, dead at 31 after falling down the stairs; and Syd Barrett, a mad recluse for a quarter-century, reportedly going blind in a Cambridge hospital. If these kinds of endings were typical of the price one pays for a cult following, the book was going to read more like a *Rock 'n' Roll Babylon* than an homage to the greatest overlooked talent of the rock era.

Those who feel that life on the edge is a prerequisite for rock 'n' roll on the edge would have been disappointed by my very next interview, with Tomorrow lead singer Keith West. The man who once toured with Syd Barrett's Pink Floyd is now the marketing director for Burns Guitars in England, happy to meet me at a pub in suburban London to proudly reminisce about his old psychedelic group, unembittered about their lack of commercial success and recognition, unself-consciously singing along with the Muddy Waters song on the jukebox.

Through the next two weeks, it was the same story, whether getting served tea in the homes of Duffy Power and Blossom Toes guitarist Brian Godding, or quaffing orange juice in the cafeteria of Abbey Road Studios while producer Derek Lawrence spoke about Joe Meek, the mad professor of early British rock 'n' roll. The percentage of raving loonies was going to be a lot lower than many rock fans would have guessed. Even Screaming Lord Sutch—the perennial Parliamentary candidate of the real-life Monster Raving Loony Party in Britain— turned out to be quite an ordinary chap at his London flat, down to the omnipresent tea service which seems a part of every visit to a British home.

When deigning to write about cult legends, the rock press often likes to dramatize the acid casualties and the macabre burnouts. You'll find your share of such figures in these pages, but the great majority of artists interviewed were leading content, responsible, productive lives, whether they were still recording music or not. Only one interview subject had difficulty formulating coherent responses to my questions; more remarkably, only one seemed truly embittered about lack of success. The others, while not absent of regrets about the musical and business frustrations of their careers, seemed genuinely at peace with the way the chips had fallen, and quietly sure that the music they made had been important, though rarely heard by the mass audience. That's not to say that many of the subjects weren't stunned upon being contacted by a stranger who, in many cases, wasn't old enough to buy their records when they were first issued, hailing from a country in which some of those records had never been released.

As is true of any such project, everyone had a different kind of story to tell. When she was interviewed, Judy Henske told me that it's like catching up with your high school class: you'll be astonished by the variety of different, improbable paths taken. And some of the endings are absolutely horrid—Joe Meek, shooting his landlady and then himself when the frustrations of his personal and professional life had gotten the best of him; Graham Bond, throwing himself under a London underground train after years of substance abuse and dwindling creativity; Arthur Lee of Love, reduced to panhandling his former producer on the street, and now serving a lengthy prison sentence.

Yet on the flip side, there are endings that are right from a fairy tale. Ronnie

Dawson, a rockabilly singer who never had more than a regional hit, rediscovered 30 years later, now sells more records than he ever has (to a young indie audience), and gets reviewed in the *New York Times*. Savage Rose, a Danish group that deliberately stopped making records because they were fed up with commercial record labels telling them what to do, played benefits at places like PLO refugee camps instead. They eventually returned to the studio and their latest album is the second biggest hit of their 30-year career. Mayo Thompson of Red Krayola, who started in the psychedelic '60s, had to move to Europe for about 20 years to keep recording music; when he came back to the States a year ago, his new albums suddenly took off with indie listeners, and he's now making his most successful American tours and records ever. The Plastic People of the Universe were harassed, beaten, and even jailed for playing underground rock in Czechoslovakia. Twenty years after the communist government had accused their music of "extreme vulgarity with an anti-socialist and an anti-social impact, most of them extolling nihilism, decadence and clericalism," the group was invited by Czech president Vaclav Havel to play in the Spanish Hall of the Prague Castle—the very spot where the conferences of the Communist Party took place.

Most of the stories fall way in between these extremes of success and failure. What pleased me most about the entire project—negating the frustrations of the occasional unreturned phone calls, unhelpful record companies, and inaccessible business managers—was the sense of validation that many of the musicians are now experiencing. Through reissues and rediscovery of their records by a younger generation—or by peers of their own generation who simply weren't aware of the music the first time around—there was a palpable realization that their efforts had not been in vain. Chart listings, units sold, gross receipts—all are ultimately nothing more than temporary measurements. These musicians experienced a deeper thrill: the satisfaction of crafting art that has endured, and that continues to move listeners in a manner quite outside trends and specific time periods.

As *Forever Changes* co-producer Bruce Botnick says of Love and other groups from the '60s with whom he has worked, "I meet 13-year-olds that are into the music. It quietly has its staying power. Kids today seem to relate to it, and understand what they're talking about, like it's timeless or something. It's not the bubblegum factory."

Glenn Campbell, guitarist for mid-'60s psychedelic unknowns the Misunderstood, was one of the few interviewees to fully articulate the lack of absolute correlation between sales and significance. If anyone had cause to be bitter, one would think, it would be Glenn. His enormously promising group hadn't even made an album before their lead singer got drafted by the U.S. Army, and several other members were deported from their base of operations in London. Campbell had been trapped on a ferry between England and France that wouldn't let him off in either country, was reduced to taking food off other passengers' plates and contemplated jumping overboard in a desperate effort to reach shore. When he finally did make it onto land, he had to sell his precious steel guitar to pay for his return ticket to California. The only Misunderstood album to make it into the shops wasn't released until the early 1980s. Padded out to LP size with unreleased tracks and deteriorating acetates, it has circulated mostly among a small band of collectors. But rather than think of what might have been, Campbell emphasizes what the music has *done*.

"I think it made its point," says Campbell, with firm conviction. "That's basically what we wanted. That vibe and that feeling . . . we wanted people to know that that existed, and there were people thinking that way. And that's happened through the reissue and the cult following.

"Of course, we didn't get rich out of it. We didn't become famous or anything like that, or any of the other trappings that other groups have got. But I think our main objective—what we really wanted to do—was achieved, to some degree, at any rate. That makes me happy."

Think of this book, then, not as a lament for unfulfilled potential, as tragic as some of the stories might be. It's a celebration of the wonderful music that was made. And, I hope, it's a celebration of the human spirit that enables cult rockers to follow their own muse, when it would be so much easier to imitate rather than innovate.

Richie Unterberger
San Francisco

Overlooked Originators

The dawn of the cult rock artist is often thought of as the mid-1960s—the era in which the full-length album began to be utilized as a medium for artistic expression in rock music, and the rock counterculture began to blossom. Yet the pre-Beatles era was just as crammed with talented artists who, for one reason or another, failed to connect with a wide audience. Sometimes the problem was being too offbeat. More often it was simply a matter of distribution, the music business not having fully adapted to the rock phenomenon. Nor did major (and some minor) labels approve of rock 'n' roll, hoping it would disappear, or viewing it as a passing fad, to be supplanted by calypso, a revival of big ballad singers, or the next big thing.

The 1950s were much more than just Elvis, Little Richard, Buddy Holly, the Everly Brothers, Chuck Berry, and the other major early rock icons. Innumerable fine R&B performers and rockabilly singers made hellacious singles, often for small labels, without coming close to even a one-shot national hit. The rockabilly explosion was something of a parallel to the mid-'60s garage rock boom, with thousands of singles—often recorded in primitive conditions—that collectors are still discovering. Even before Elvis had made rock an international institution, dozens of unheralded performers had been laying the groundwork for the music's birth with hillbilly boogie, honky-tonk, electric blues, and R&B vocal groups. Many of these artists are profiled in Nick Tosches' *Unsung Heroes of Rock 'n' Roll*, which takes the unusual revisionist stance that rock 'n' roll peaked in the decade (1945-1955) *before* Bill Haley's "Rock Around the Clock," which is usually considered the first international rock hit.

It wasn't until the 1970s that obsessive collectors—usually European ones—began to unearth the music that had been overlooked in rock's first decade.

Often the performers themselves were tracked down; semi-retired, or working in country music, they were persuaded to make European tours and even return to active recording. In the 1990s, some—such as fuzz/distortion innovator Link Wray, and surf music originator Dick Dale—are more popular than ever, at least as live attractions. Early cult rockers often waxed their efforts for tiny labels, but sometimes outrageous performers would somehow find a place on major label rosters—coffin-entombed R&B wildman Screamin' Jay Hawkins, for example, or Esquerita, an influence on Little Richard with his one-foot-high-and-rising pompadour.

With this section we look at three rockabilly greats, distinguished not just by the power of their music, but also by the originality of their approach. The Collins Kids proved that the attainment of puberty was not a prerequisite for making ballsy rock 'n' roll. Ronnie Dawson, the Blond Bomber from Texas, is emblematic of all those thousands of rockabilly singers who made a couple of great singles before seemingly vanishing from the face of the earth—and, as of the late 1990s, he is perhaps rockabilly's greatest revived-from-the-dead success story. Wanda Jackson, the greatest female rockabilly singer ever, made a lot of inroads for women as a whole in rock that have yet to be fully appreciated.

Wanda Jackson, the mermaid of rockabilly.
Credit: Courtesy Wendell Goodman

The Collins Kids

Look at the photos on a Collins Kids album, play the disc inside, and you could be forgiven for suspecting that the whole thing was a cleverly concocted publicity stunt. The photos show a cowgirl and cowboy barely into their teens, if that. The music is some of the most white-hot rockabilly ever waxed, as Larry Collins' stunningly rapid and dextrous picking backs sister Lorrie Collins' throaty, sexy, and bluesy rockabilly singing. How could two young kids play so well? Were they, perhaps, just a front for the public, with Wanda Jackson and guitarists like Roy Clark and Merle Travis handling the actual recording duties in the studio?

The Collins Kids, though, were for real. And despite their tender ages, they were no mere novelty act. Lorrie Collins, along with the aforementioned Wanda Jackson, was the only game in town as far as female rockabilly singers were concerned. Larry Collins brought the hillbilly stylings of top pickers like Merle Travis and Joe Maphis into the rockabilly era with a harder, more manic, more *electric* edge. With their western outfits and close harmonies, their roots were in the Western Swing era. But the sound of their best records — "Hoy Hoy," "Mercy," "Whistle Bait," "Just Because," "Hop, Skip and Jump" — was pure rock 'n' roll.

Along with Michael Jackson, the Collins Kids may have been the most prodigious sub-15-year-olds in rock history. They were one of the first, if not *the* first, Los Angeles-based rockabilly act; Larry Collins was, without a doubt, the first rock musician to use a double-necked guitar, long before Jimmy Page was causing Led Zeppelin audiences to gasp at his audacity for bringing the instrument onstage. They even recorded for one of the biggest labels in America, Columbia Records. Why is it, then, that they never had a hit, or even merited a footnote in most rock history books?

Lorrie Collins is succinct when I pose the question. "Wrong time, wrong place."

The Collins Kids had gone through a lot of effort, though, to make sure they got as much opportunity as possible to strike it big. The Collins family was living in Tulsa, Oklahoma, when Lorrie Collins began singing at amateur shows. Local Western Swing bandleader and club owner Leon McAuliffe urged her parents to move to Los Angeles, where Lorrie's precocious talent stood a chance of gaining wider recognition. The Collins family sold their dairy farm and took off for L.A. in a '47 Hudson.

"I think my Dad was a little reluctant to go to begin with," admits Lorrie Collins today, when I call her and Larry Collins in Reno, Nevada, where both siblings now live. "He basically was a dairy farmer. Our mother was the one that really was musically inclined. I think she understood the longing to be famous and be a good singer. My Dad — I think he thought we were all crazy. And after the car broke down all that many times [on the way to L.A.], I *know* he thought we were."

While Lorrie was making the rounds of the L.A. amateur show contests, Larry was picking up the guitar at an astonishing speed. When both brother and sister started winning amateur shows, Mom Collins suggested that the pair team up as a duo. By the end of 1954, they were performing regularly on the *Town Hall Party* television show, an L.A.-based program that showcased numerous country and hillbilly artists. Rockabilly didn't even have a name yet in California—Larry Collins remembers that he didn't hear Elvis Presley until a good year or two after joining the *Town Hall Party* cast. There may not have been any musicians even playing rockabilly in the L.A. area in 1955, with the possible exception of Eddie Cochran. Yet rockabilly is what the Collins Kids began gravitating towards.

The Collins Kids, rockabilly singers from teenage to middle age. Larry's still playing the double-neck guitar.
Credit: Courtesy Larry and Lorrie Collins

"I automatically, when I played the guitar, danced around like a maniac," says Larry. "And Lorrie, she moved well, too. We just had a natural Pentecostal beat that followed us in our music. It was rockabilly when we started doing it together. There was no one to learn from. We were just doing what we felt. If the song didn't have a beat and something we could move around to, we didn't do it. They hadn't even coined the phrase *rock and roll* at that time."

Elaborates Lorrie, "I think it was unique inasmuch as it was kind of a combination of country music, of course, because that was our roots. And as Larry said, we kind of grew up in Baptist Pentecostal churches. Church music was a big part of our life, and we all sang. And it was always with a beat." She adds, "It wasn't so much the Elvis gyration type thing that might have been offensive to people. It was more fresh and something they hadn't heard before—two young people who appeared to be having such a good time."

By 1955 the Collins Kids had a contract with Columbia, an association that proved to be a double-edged sword of sorts. Major labels were reluctant to cave into the rock 'n' roll trend at all at this point, when the new music was threatening the soft and safe pop sounds that dominated the hit parade of the time. One of rock 'n' roll's most powerful sworn enemies was easy listening orchestrator Mitch Miller—who, as it happened, was the head of A&R at Columbia.

Given those drawbacks, it's somewhat remarkable that the Collins Kids were signed to Columbia in the first place, and their first singles were not first-class efforts. "We did have a problem finding material that we liked," says Lorrie. "Initially Columbia Records submitted a lot of songs that were kind of novelty, brother-sister kind of stuff." The Collins Kids may have been envisioned at first as a sort of kiddie novelty act, but as Lorrie insists, "We worked hard at our music. We rehearsed many, many hours every day after school. It wasn't a novelty. Finally they realized that these are two young kids that are serious about what they're doing."

The Collins Kids really hit their stride with a blitz of sides in 1957 and 1958. They recorded their best stuff not in the South, where most rockabilly is assumed to have originated, but on Santa Monica Boulevard in the heart of Hollywood, with *Town Hall Party* musicians lending support. "Hop, Skip and Jump" and "Hoy Hoy" are as frenetic as early rockabilly ever got; "Party" was later recorded by Wanda Jackson for her biggest hit; "Mercy" had breathlessly raunchy vocals from Lorrie on par with the most salacious Jerry Lee Lewis. Larry Collins got his own vocal showcase with the similarly exuberant "Whistle Bait." By this time the Collins Kids were writing much of their own best material, sometimes with help from their mother, sometimes entirely on their own. The best of these songs can be heard on the Epic compilation *Introducing Larry and Lorrie*.

All of these sides featured storming guitar by Larry, who really got a chance to strut his stuff on some sparkling duets with Joe Maphis, with whom he recorded four tracks for a 1958 EP. Maphis and Merle Travis both played on

Town Hall Party broadcasts. "Just being around those guys and learning some of their licks, I'd come up with some of my own as well," says Larry. "I've always been a writer from the time I picked up the guitar." Adds Lorrie, "Maphis was primarily country, even bluegrass hillbilly music back then. But Joe went on to do some of the Beach Boys albums. Larry was kind of an inspiration in many ways to Joe as far as putting a little bit of rock in his guitar playing."

"I had the second double-neck ever made," Larry continues. "Joe had the first. A young man by the name of Semie Moseley came down to *Town Hall Party* one night with a triple-neck guitar he had made. He worked for Bigsby. He was one of Bigsby's protégés who built the vibrato and customized guitars back in that time. Semie wanted to go out on his own, and he figured if he could get Joe and I to play one of his custom-made guitars, that would get him started.

"So he brought this triple-neck guitar. This thing had to weigh 30 pounds. I mean, it was solid piece of wood. I think it had a bass, regular six-string, and an octave-higher mandolin neck on it. Joe said, 'there's no way that we can even carry that around onstage. It's something you would have to sit down and play.' So Joe and all of us came up with a way to hollow it out, and cut it down to two necks. He made the first one, the prototype for Joe.

"Then consequently, me being smaller-sized, they made mine two or three months later, and hollowed mine out. Mine was all hollow, I still have it. Matter of fact, I'm looking at it hanging on the wall now. The bottom neck is a regular six-string guitar, and the top neck is a six-string, octave-higher guitar. It's kind of like having a 12-string split apart."

The Collins Kids were plenty busy in the late '50s with numerous TV shows, personal appearances, and showcases at Columbia conventions (Larry: "we were always the country-rock 'n' roll act"). "Being a semi-novelty act did help us inasfar as one direction, but maybe hurt us in the record industry," reflects Larry now. "We did have some support at the company. But it only went so far because of Mitch's position, I suppose, not being a big rock and roll or rockabilly fan."

"I think our age was a drawback in many respects for a hit record," adds Lorrie. "Being so young initially worked for us, and yet worked against us. Then the more we became teenagers—of course everything changed to a certain degree for us, as far as our sound. I think they were looking more to someone like Gene Vincent, or someone like Eddie Cochran, Elvis, Carl Perkins, Jerry Lee Lewis, someone that was appealing to the young girls.

"The first few years that we recorded after our initial novelty songs got out of the way and we started just doing the straight rockabilly songs with the beat that we wrote, mostly—I think that was my favorite time. When they moved us to Nashville and started recording back there with the Jordanaires and doing that kind of thing, I think that our music changed. I think they were trying to . . ."

"—refine it a little," interjects Larry.

"I really feel, like Larry does, that we lost our originality trying to sound like everybody else, like what Nashville's doing now. Everybody's pretty much the same, everybody looks pretty much the same."

"Everybody's got the same damned hat," adds Larry dourly.

By the early '60s, in fact, the Collins Kids were no longer a duo. Lorrie, Ricky Nelson's first steady girlfriend, had married; the act split up not only into solo careers, but different labels. Larry would gain considerable success as a country songwriter, his biggest credit being attached to Tanya Tucker's "Delta Dawn" (which was then made into a huge pop hit by Helen Reddy). But both he and his sister regret that they weren't able to make more recordings as a duo.

"Hopefully, we would have gotten back to where we started, and gone full circle back to the rawness of rockabilly," says Larry. "Now that's what we do on-stage, and it's amazing, it's brand new. That's where I would have liked to have seen our recording career finally evolve back to—the simple raw, three or four-piece group, some good guitar playing, good singing, and everybody [can] hear what everybody's doing."

To this day, the Collins Kids have a lot of musician fans in high places; Elvis Costello and Richard Thompson have even offered to write material for the pair. "You can sit around and lie and say hey, that's enough," notes Lorrie about their reputation in musician circles. "And it *is* a lie, because you do want your peers to feel that way about you, but it's also a disappointment not to have had that hit record, and not to have gone on to other facets as far as the entertainment business. But we achieved an awful lot without having a hit record that a lot of people didn't."

The Collins Kids still give sporadic concerts in the U.S., and are now shopping around an album they recorded with Joel Selvin and Scott Matthews (who also participated in the discs that launched surf rock legend Dick Dale's comeback). And they have a lot of fans that they hadn't been aware of, as they found out when they got together to play a rockabilly festival in England a few years ago. "They kept asking for Lorrie and I to come over to England, and said, you won't believe how popular you are, you just won't believe it," says Larry.

"So finally they talked us into it after about the fourth year, and we got over there, and we *didn't* believe it. I mean, it was 12 bodyguards around us, and kids all dressed in 1955. I mean, they live, eat, breathe, sleep 1955. They know more about Lorrie and my career than we know about it ourselves! It's just amazing."

Recommended Recording:
Introducing Larry and Lorrie (1983, CBS). Twelve of their best cuts, including "Whistle Bait," "Mercy," "Hoy Hoy," "Party," and the Collins-Maphis instrumental duet "Hurricane." A comprehensive Collins box set (*Hop, Skip and Jump*) has been issued on the German Bear Family label, but this is the knockout punch.

Ronnie Dawson

It's early 1997, and Ronnie Dawson, nearing his 60th birthday, is riding a career peak at a time when most of the other original rockabilly singers are starting to cash in their Social Security checks. He's had his picture in the *New York Times*, his records are selling more than they ever have, and the U.S. and European concert schedule for the year ahead is already filling up. I joke that if he keeps on going at this rate, he's going to become too well known to be included in a book dedicated to rock 'n' roll unknowns. "In my case, me being unknown was one of the reasons that I've *gotten* to be known," he shoots back.

Ronnie may be underestimating himself a bit there. Sure, there were dozens, maybe hundreds, of talented rockabilly singers like himself in the 1950s that never had a national hit. Even those that only saw and heard Dawson once, though, were unlikely to forget him. There was that unearthly appearance — the shocking-white brush cut, the ghostly pale complexion. And an equally unearthly, high-pitched voice that made it difficult for radio listeners to tell if he was a man or a woman. The actual singles he managed to release were a mixed lot, but "Action Packed" — with its ceaseless exhortations to "HEAR ME?" — has to be one of the ten best obscure rockabilly treasures of all time. As Chris Dickinson observes in his liner notes to the *Rockin' Bones* reissue, "It's hard to argue with Ronnie's assertion that a car just ain't fast enough to get him where he's going."

Dawson was 19 when "Action Packed" was issued in 1958, but his appearance and voice led some to suspect that he was a good five years younger. These days no one's going to mistake Ronnie for a pre-teen. The brush cut is going grey, and the voice has lowered considerably — in other words, he now sounds like a man in his twenties, instead of a man-child. But where fellow rockabilly oddities have remained the province of manic record collectors and European revival festivals, Dawson has found a whole new audience in the indie/alternative crowd, most of whom weren't born when "Action Packed" was recorded.

For Ronnie, it's not so much a matter of coming back as continuing to do what he's done ever since he started playing electric guitar at his local Assembly of God church. "Rockabilly is a term that we never knew then, really," he claims. "We heard it a little bit, but I didn't ever think it pertained to what I was doing at all. To me it was rock and roll, and it was my music. It's very similar to the Assembly of God kind of church music, and things that I had taken part in in church. Except it was better, 'cause you could do it and nobody would holler at you about it if you got too carried away or anything."

Except for country star Webb Pierce, maybe, who was annoyed enough by the noise of Dawson's rehearsal at the Big D Jamboree to leave before doing his

Ronnie Dawson gets ready to take a bite out of the microphone at the Big D Jamboree in Dallas, Texas, circa 1959. Credit: Courtesy Crystal Clear Sound; photo: Francis Photographers

second show. Ronnie was usually a big hit, though, at the Big D, a kind of Dallas counterpart of the Grand Ole Opry. Big D emcee Johnny Hicks even told the *Dallas Morning News* in 1996, "He's the only one that nobody wanted to follow . . . including Elvis," adding that Elvis had told Hicks, "Don't put me too close to that kid." When asked about the story, Ronnie is diplomatic. "John Hicks, he's a good man. But"—and now Dawson can't stop himself from laughing—"I don't think Elvis ever really was worried about *anybody*."

"The Blond Bomber," as Dawson was nicknamed, got a management deal with Big D promoter Ed McLemore, who also looked after rockabilly stars Gene Vincent and Dale Hawkins. Jack Rhodes, who had penned early Vincent rockabilly classics like "B-I-Bickey-Bi-Bo-Bo-Go," supplied Ronnie with the tune for a debut single, "Action Packed." This was teen rockabilly at its most breathlessly impatient and exuberant; a 1959 follow-up, "Rockin' Bones," was early rockabilly at its bluesiest and rawest. Released on tiny labels, these 45s were only heard regionally, but Dawson caught the attention of a much bigger indie, Swan Records, which took Ronnie and fellow Texas rockabilly performer Scotty McKay on at the very end of the '50s.

"They told us that if they could get the sound that we were getting onstage, they thought they could get some hit records," Dawson remembers. "But lo and behold, when we did sign with Swan and got there, they didn't want me to use the guitar at all. I really couldn't perform those songs [live] with a guitar band, 'cause it was all horn section." Swan seemed bent on trying to transform Ronnie from a rockabilly wildboy into a teen idol; what's more, the promotion of the records suffered when Dick Clark, who ran Swan, got caught in the payola scandal. At any rate, Ronnie wasn't truly cut out for being a teen idol anyway.

"I was just trying to do what everyone else wanted me to do," he notes with regret. "Which was a mistake, basically. I wanted a guitar sound. I would have been happy to have some horns on it, but I still wanted it to be guitar-dominated. I'd kind of exhausted everything and said, 'Well, now I did everything everybody told me to do.' Finally I got to the point where I said 'No, I'm not going to do that,' and just started doing what *I* wanted to do." Dawson got back to the R&B/blues-inflected material he loved with singles recorded for Columbia under the bizarre pseudonym Commonwealth Jones. A young Delbert McClinton played harmonica on a couple of the tunes, which were some of the most unrefined rock 'n' roll recorded for a major label in the early '60s.

However, Dawson would have to wait another 25 years before he was able to resume recording regularly under his own name. He did session work in Texas for stars like Bruce Channel and Paul & Paula. He joined the Light Crust Doughboys, one of the longest-running acts in country music, as their token teen attraction. "I was their teenage star when I went with the Doughboys, because they played a lot of schools and things like this. They wanted me to go on for the young people, because at that time country music was way dead. Fiddle bands were *wa-a-ay* dead," he chortles. "These guys hated to go in schools. But they were one of the few bands that were allowed to do that, so they got me to go on with them."

Dawson spent much of the '60s touring and performing on TV with the Levee Singers, a banjo-dominated act. He recorded a truly eerie version of "Riders in the Sky" with their help that stands as one of the few examples of bluegrass-rockabilly fusion. But most of the '60s, '70s, and the first half of the '80s would find Ronnie inactive on the recording front. He played in a country-rock band called Steelrail, sang commercials (including jingles for Hungry Jack pancakes), and generally kept his craft sharp as much as he could in the face of limited opportunities. "I've pretty much always been a rocker first of all," he emphasizes. "I never really did let it go. I always included it in whatever I did. Even when I was doing country, it had a beat to it."

Ronnie Dawson, still rocking in the 1990s. Credit: Courtesy Upstart Records; photo James Bland

Opportunity knocked in a big way in 1986, when Dawson was tracked down by British rockabilly enthusiast Barney Koumis. Ronnie's old songs were gaining a cult reputation across the water, where fellow Texas rockabilly unknowns like Mac Curtis and Johnny Carroll had already gained recognition. In addition, psychobilly/punk band the Cramps had covered "Rockin' Bones" (although their version was based on a cover, by Elroy Dietzel, that was even more obscure than the original). European cultists have proven to be the professional salvation of many an early rocker, but Ronnie would capitalize on his rediscovery more than most of his counterparts.

"I had never quit performing," he stresses. "A lot of these guys [who were rediscovered] hadn't performed in years. They really couldn't muster up a show. Maybe they could do four or five of their songs. But when you don't do it for a while, man, you lose a little of your fire. A lot of guys too, to be honest with you, were afraid. When you get to be a grandpaw, you go over there and all of a sudden you meet people with blue hair and spiked hair, it could scare you a little bit.

"I never did lose any of my fire. I had kept pretty much staying in front of an audience. So when I got over there and saw all of it, that just ignited me even more. It just happened at a right time for me. I embraced it."

Koumis wanted to record a new album with Ronnie, and here the singer was also at an advantage. Almost all rockabilly comebacks are lame, sad, remake-stuffed affairs. Dawson was still in fine voice and health, and just as importantly, determined to create a product that could stand on its own merits, outside of purely nostalgic grounds. That meant fresh material, and covers so obscure that, Koumis assured the singer, they would only be recognized by the hardest of hardcore rockabilly fanatics. The musicians included guitarist Boz Boorer, who would go on to play in a much different style on albums by British mope-rocker Morrissey.

"I wasn't going to try to repeat anything," says Dawson. "I don't think you can do that. I just tried to think about, how did we get this live, the kind of spon-taneous thing we used to get? I'd come up with the notion that we should do it live. Which I had gotten completely away from, I'm sorry to say. We just found us a little hole in the wall studio in London. When I started hooking up with some of these young cats over there, man, it was like we'd done it before in an-other life or something, 'cause they knew most of my stuff. When [Boz] and I met and locked eyeballs, it was like, 'I know I've known this guy before some-where.'

"As a result, that created a hell of a spark. The first record, we recorded al-most 20 songs in three days. And at the end of that three days, I was actually looking for more stuff to do, that's how good it went." The Cramps, the fussiest rockabilly diehards you're likely to find, enthused in *Incredibly Strange Music Vol. 1*, "A lot of times these old guys put out a new album and it's miserable, but Dawson has a new album out that's great." Dawson returned the compliment by opening a show for the Cramps in London. There may even have been a bit of influence working in the other direction, judging from recent psychobilly-flavored Dawson tracks like "Rockin' in the Cemetery." Never one to waste words, Ronnie had instructed his lyricist, "Just write me something about motor-cycles, graveyards, hot rods, shit like that."

The Dawson revival was slower to take off in the United States, where the first few albums were unavailable domestically for years. Modern day psy-chobillys like Reverend Horton Heat and others, however, created a fresh inter-est in the rockabilly originals. Dawson got deals with well-distributed indie companies in the States that reissued the first comeback efforts and released the newly minted ones; they were backed with table-dancing shows across America that broadened Ronnie's appeal from revivalists to underground rockers. A *New York Times* review exclaimed in the paper's inimitable stuffed-shirt fashion, "Mr. Dawson and his band High Noon made a strong case for rockabilly as a classic folk form that is every bit as pure in its way as bluegrass despite its plugged-in guitars. The set demonstrated what a rich stew of influences—western swing, blues, rock 'n' roll and country—went into a genre that sounds as fresh, sexy and fun-loving today as it did nearly 40 years ago."

Dawson knows that his latter-day success is no fluke. "I think you create a lot of your luck yourself. It hasn't happened to me just sitting here. We've gone out and beat the bushes, and played in every state in the Union in the last two years. Barney Koumis came looking for me in the first place, *because* I was unknown. I was more unknown than Mac Curtis and Johnny Carroll. I'm really an unknown." He corrects himself uncertainly. "I *was*."

Recommended Recordings:

Rockin' Bones: The Legendary Masters (1996, Crystal Clear). A 34-song, double-disc definitive sweep of Dawson's early career, including all of his singles from the late '50s and early '60s, and a wealth of unreleased material (some quite raw) from the same period. It's a bit of a manic ride, trampling through both crude lo-fi demos and sweet teen idol pop, but the best moments—"Action Packed," "Rockin' Bones," and the incandescent "Riders in the Sky"—make it worthwhile.

Monkey Beat!! (1994, Crystal Clear). The best of Dawson's recent efforts is probably the best post-1980 album *ever* recorded by a middle-aged veteran of the original rockabilly explosion. The voice is lower but still supple, and the band and material are raw and spontaneous.

Wanda Jackson, as she appeared in a 1956 Capitol Records publicity shot. Credit: Courtesy Wendell Goodman

Wanda Jackson

As Wanda Jackson remembers it, she was finishing her first album session for Capitol Records in the late '50s. "We had done a country album. But we needed one more song and I just didn't have anything particular that I wanted to do. I said, 'I think I'll just put on this "Let's Have a Party," because people really like it in person, and we'll see how it comes off.'"

What came out was salacious rockabilly of the sort that had never been heard from a female rock and roll singer. Jackson sang about shakin' chickens in the middle of the room with a raw, bluesy growl that anticipated the down and dirty raunch of performers like Janis Joplin by a good decade. Backed by a hard-driving combo that wouldn't have been out of place on a Jerry Lee Lewis record, the choruses were punctuated by exhilarating falsetto whoops more suitable for orgies than your average '50s teenage party. It took a couple years to become a hit single, but in late 1960 it cut through the teen idol pap dominating the airwaves to become her only rock 'n' roll song to make the Top 40.

Jackson made a number of great rockabilly singles in the '50s that do not just boost her credentials as the greatest *female* rockabilly singer. They qualify her as one of the greatest rockabilly singers, period. But the national audience wasn't ready for a woman making rock and roll with just as much abandon as Elvis, Gene Vincent, or Jerry Lee Lewis. By the early '60s she had, like most of her rockabilly peers, turned to recording primarily country music as a means of simple survival.

Listen to "Let's Have a Party," "Mean Mean Man," or "Fujiyama Mama," and you could picture Jackson as a whiskey-soaked hell-raiser, an assumption that could hardly lie further from the truth. In order to uphold her reputation, her father (who also acted as her chaperone) would forbid her to be photographed so much as laying her head on a man's shoulder. At one of her first rockabilly sessions, she was scolded by her producer for drinking milk, which hindered her efforts to get the right kind of growl into her throat.

It wasn't so certain that Wanda would become a rockabilly singer in the first place. After hearing the teenage singer on an Oklahoma City radio show, country star Hank Thompson asked her to sing with his Brazos Valley Boys, and arranged for a contract with Decca Records. The Decca sides, cut in the mid-'50s, are straight, cornpone country, with little hint of the saucy blues feeling that would color her subsequent work. Elvis Presley—whom Jackson toured with, and briefly dated, around this time—helped change that.

"Right after I graduated from high school in '55, even though I was doing country stuff, I began working with Elvis," she remembers. "I worked with him up until the early part of '57, when he went to Hollywood to begin making movies. He encouraged me to try this music. Of course, I loved it. It was my generation's music. I didn't think that I could do it.

"He assured me that I could. He was very influential in helping me. He always took me to his home. He had a big collection of black blues. At that time, he had taken some country and some black blues songs and done 'em his style, with more of a country flair to them. I thought that was real interesting, but I still didn't think I could do it.

"But then when I moved to Capitol, that music had just continued to get bigger and bigger. He said, 'It's going to be the next big music, and you need to get in on it.' I think it took me a couple of years to get the nerve to try it, but I began singing it with my band at dance jobs, the songs that were popular. Especially 'Let's Have a Party.'"

Listening to "Let's Have a Party" today, it's difficult to imagine Jackson lacking the nerve for anything, musical or otherwise. The choice of the song was hardly accidental—Elvis himself had done the original version of the tune, on the soundtrack of the 1957 film *Loving You*. Wanda's cover, it must be said, cuts Elvis' to shreds, introducing a whole new level of untamed glee. The pounding piano on the track comes courtesy of Big Al Downing, a fellow Oklahoman and recording artist in his own right who was sort of a black counterpart to Jerry Lee Lewis.

You could say that the world wasn't wholly ready for an all-out female rocker, but part of the problem was that Jackson was never solely marketed and recorded as a rockabilly singer. Capitol often hedged their bets on her '50s singles by releasing a rocker on one side, and a country song on the other. Jackson, however, never had an easy relationship with the country establishment, causing a fuss on the *Grand Ole Opry* when Ernest Tubb demanded that she cover her arms rather than perform in her tight, sleeveless dress. She never performed there again.

But she did have a key ally in Nashville in Capitol producer Ken Nelson, who had just gotten his feet wet in loose-limbed rockabilly with Gene Vincent. According to Wanda, "Ken wasn't real familiar with that sort of thing. But he understood that it was big music, that I liked it, and that I could sing it. So he just kind of let me have a free hand at whatever I wanted to record. And he enjoyed it. But he really didn't claim to know a whole lot about it. So the musicians and I kind of put the sound together."

Nelson's liberal attitude cleared the way for a series of great country and rockabilly guitarists to appear on Jackson's records, including Joe Maphis, Grady Martin, Buck Owens, Roy Clark, and the lesser-known Vernon Sandusky and Dave Ronson. Those who wince at the mention of Clark and flash on those innumerable terrible *Hee Haw* jokes should be aware that in his early days he ripped off some astonishing rockabilly leads. The solo on Jackson's cover of "Hard Headed Woman" (another tune first popularized by Elvis) is almost avant-garde in its speed-of-light ferocity. Jackson laughs heartily when I tell her how friends refused to concede that it's really *the* Roy Clark they hear on that cut. "He was such a talent that I always just turned him loose too. He'd reach over and grab an ashtray or glass or salt shaker and play wild stuff!"

Jackson had the female rockabilly field almost to herself in the late '50s, despite occasional recordings in the style by such obscure names as Janis Martin, Sparkle Moore, and Lorrie Collins (of the Collins Kids). And although she wasn't scoring many hits, and although she wasn't recording only rock 'n' roll, she waxed a number of great rockabilly classics in her early Capitol days—"Honey Bop," "I Gotta Know," "Mean Mean Man," "Rock Your Baby." The most explosive of all, though, was "Fujiyama Mama," a big hit in Japan. It was only a dozen years after World War II, but apparently the Japanese didn't listen too closely to lyrics promising to cause as much destruction as the Nagasaki and Hiroshima bombs, or to blow her baby's head off with nitroglycerine. Perhaps those same turns of the phrase made the record too hot to handle for American radio stations, in more ways than one.

In 1961, Jackson had a couple of big straight country hits ("Right or Wrong" and "In the Middle of a Heartache") that signaled a departure from hard rocking sounds. "I always liked doing the rock stuff," she makes sure to point out. "But I had been established, at least in America, first of all as a country singer. And by the time the '60s came along, country music was coming back into its own. There was a period there, from, I don't know, '56 through '60–62, that country music just almost went off the air. There just wasn't anyone playing it. Somewhere there in the early '60s, stations began playing all-country formats, which was brand new at the time. And I wasn't getting any more hits in the rock field. They weren't playing me. And the country music people wouldn't play my rockabilly. So I really didn't have a lot of choice, if I was going to continue to get airplay, which I had to have in order to draw crowds."

Jackson had moderate success as a country artist throughout the '60s before falling victim to some record company politics. "There was that one interlude in there when I asked my release from Capitol so that I could do gospel music. I became a Christian in '71, and that's another thing where I fell through the cracks because I'd signed with Word Records, which was the largest Christian label at that time. They were interested in going into country. So they came to me and said look, we can fill your needs with the gospel, and you do country and that'll help us get established as a country label. It looked like an excellent marriage at that time.

"So I left Capitol for that reason. Shortly after I signed with Word, [it was] sold to Dot Records and they brought all of their people that were on their label. I just got lost in the shuffle and all my fans thought that I'd quit recording, or that I'd died, or something," she laughs. "That took about ten years to let people know that I was still around and still recording. That's why there was a break there that a lot of people wondered what happened to me. It would have been very good had it have worked out the way they said it would."

Jackson never intended to leave secular music entirely; the idea was to continue with both country and gospel (she continued to record gospel for independent labels). When demand for European tours began to escalate in the 1980s, though, it turned out that many fans abroad thought of her primarily as a rockabilly singer. Fortunately, Wanda wasn't averse to doing gospel, country, *and* rockabilly, adjusting her repertoire according to the audience. She began recording rockabilly again in the 1980s for European labels. In 1995, she embarked on a five-week tour of American clubs with latter-day country-rockabilly singer Rosie Flores (whose 1995 CD Jackson guested on). It was the first time since the '70s that the born-again Christian had performed secular music in the U.S. What seems more important and ironic to her, though, is that it was her first straight rockabilly tour in the United States, after 40 years as a recording artist.

Jackson sees the influence of her style in such contemporary singers as Flores, Pam Tillis, and Tanya Tucker. Now closing in on 60 years of age, it's still a bit of a shock to her to be gaining fans young enough not just to be her children, but her grandchildren. When I talk with her in late 1996, she was scheduled to go in for knee surgery to repair a torn cartilage. After a winter of recuperation, it's most likely going to mean a return to the road for the country singer who's now come full circle back to rockabilly. "I've been working all summer and fall with this swollen knee. It's kind of hard to rock and roll on one leg!"

Recommended Recording:
Rockin' with Wanda (1960, Capitol). Unfortunately this compilation of early singles may be hard to locate for North American listeners (a European reissue adds a few vital bonus cuts). The title is truth in advertising; this is Wanda at her hardest-rocking, including such classics as "Let's Have a Party," "Fujiyama Mama," "Mean Mean Man," and "Rock Your Baby," some of them self-penned. A couple of U.S. compilations (on Rhino and Capitol Nashville) feature her most well-known early rockabilly sides, although those anthologies mix rockabilly with straight country material.

Lost British Invaders 2

The British Invasion of the mid-1960s was such a massive success—both in pure commercial terms, and in putting the rock revolution into overdrive—that it might come as some surprise to learn that there were dozens of excellent U.K. bands that never had a hit in North America. Those that lived through the era remember how a new sensation seemed to be breaking through the U.S. airwaves every other week or so. With the Beatles leading the way, and the Dave Clark Five, Rolling Stones, Kinks, Animals, Yardbirds, Manfred Mann, Zombies, and Them not far behind, there was already almost too much British rock to absorb. Could there possibly have been room for yet more innovators from the British Isles?

The answer is an emphatic yes. Not on the charts, maybe. But certainly in the record collections of anyone who appreciates assertive blues-rock guitars or captivating harmonies. Or maybe both at the same time.

To generalize somewhat, the rawer end of the British Invasion spectrum got a somewhat raw deal in terms of U.S. success. The Who, people tend to forget, were the definitive cult rock act before the 1967 hit "Happy Jack"; smashes like "My Generation" and "Substitute" went virtually unplayed by American radio, to be scarfed up by the few Anglophiles devoted enough to order import records in the days before specialist rock stores. The Pretty Things took the Stones' R&B attack to an even raunchier level; they would be natural inclusions for a book such as this, except for the fact that their history is so extensive (reaching into early psychedelia as well) that it defies summarization in a few thousand words.

Even less known were the Sorrows, who made some superb singles that fused the Kinks, Who, and bits of mod and Merseybeat, but perhaps lacked the

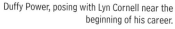

Duffy Power, posing with Lyn Cornell near the beginning of his career.

Credit: Courtesy Duffy Power

distinctive identity necessary to become a major act. Then there were the Action, usually hailed as the best soul-influenced British '60s group bar the Small Faces. The Poets were Scotland's best group, mixing Zombies-flavored minor-key melodies with gorgeous folk-rock-influenced arrangements.

You'd be hard-pressed to find any albums by Duffy Power, Graham Bond, the Creation, and John's Children at the corner chain store. Power and Bond were probably too bluesy for commercial success; John's Children too outrageous; and the Creation simply too unlucky. Yet without them Cream and T. Rex may well have never happened; the Who and Led Zeppelin may well have sounded different. Read on to find out why.

Graham Bond

As Cream stormed the world with "White Room" and "Sunshine of Your Love" in the late '60s, few Americans were aware that two-thirds of the trio had actually played and recorded extensively with another band that had nothing to do with long guitar solos and psychedelia. Bassist Jack Bruce and drummer Ginger Baker had formed the rhythm section of the Graham Bond Organisation, a gritty blues/jazz/R&B outfit whose two albums were never released in the United States. While Bruce and Baker ascended to superstardom in Cream, their erstwhile leader was foundering, drug-addled, and bandless, unable to capitalize on the British music scene he had done so much to develop.

As bad as things were, it would get much worse for Graham Bond before he threw himself under a London underground train in 1974. His associates, however, prefer not to remember the man who could be abusive, cruel, and self-

destructive. They would rather dwell on the contributions of a bandleader who did so much to raise the standards of musicianship in British rock in the mid-'60s, though he proved singularly unable to tailor his work for commercial success.

Long after their demise, the Graham Bond Organisation were touted as something like the first jazz-rock band, and/or the first supergroup. There are elements of truth in both labels, but those are oversimplifications. As jazz musicians adapting to rhythm and blues, the group brought a new level of virtuosity to British rock. Their rough 'n' tumble brand of blues was characterized by Bond's demonic organ, Bruce's fierce upright bass, and Baker's jazzy drumming, with the jazzy touch provided by flights of improvisation and a bit of brass.

Chart hits were necessary for survival in the mid-'60s, though, and Graham Bond had none. His gruff, growling vocals were one obstacle; another was that the band simply didn't *look* like pop stars, what with Baker's ex-convict demeanor, a bald saxophone player, and Bond's own overweight, slightly terrifying countenance. Two albums cut by the Organisation in 1965 held great promise. But Bond missed, by a mere year or two, the era in which albums could sustain a career. Unavailable in the U.S., those LPs are noted these days primarily for the presence of Bruce and Baker, just before they would join Eric Clapton to form Cream.

The music they played with Bond bore little resemblance to Cream's heavy rock, though, which is hardly surprising given Graham's straight jazz roots. By the early 1960s, Bond was acclaimed as one of the most promising rising young British jazzmen, playing alto sax on a jazz LP by the New Don Rendell Quintet. But the British club scene was in the midst of a wholesale transition from jazz to rhythm and blues and rock. Purely as a matter of survival, it made sense for Bond to tap into the exploding R&B scene, and by 1963 he was leading his own group.

The transition was not without its hiccups. An archival recording of a 1963 gig (on Warner Brothers' *Solid Bond*), also featuring a very young John McLaughlin on guitar, shows the band in far more of a jazz mold than an R&B one. For a while they backed

The Graham Bond Organisation, mid-1960s.

Left to right: Jack Bruce, Graham Bond, Dick Heckstall-Smith, and Ginger Baker.

British singer Duffy Power, playing the music on Power's 1963 version of "I Saw Her Standing There," which was only the second Lennon-McCartney cover ever to be issued. McLaughlin's stint with Bond was brief, and by 1964 the group had settled into the quartet—Bond, Bruce, Baker, and saxophonist Dick Heckstall-Smith—that all agree was his classic lineup.

Bond, too, was largely concentrating on the organ by now, squeezing a party-by-the-gates-of-hell swirl of tones from the instrument, in addition to singing most of the act's repertoire. (One of the best examples of his organ playing, interestingly, can be heard on a rare Who B-side, "Waltz for a Pig"; this 1966 instrumental was credited to the Who Orchestra, and recorded because the Who were temporarily unable to enter the studio due to a legal dispute.) Several singles went nowhere commercially, and the group's version of the sappy pop tune "Tammy" was seen as something of a sellout by purists.

The group's best outing remains their debut, *The Sound of '65*, mixing well-worn R&B classics with originals that spotlighted Bond's menacing vocals and the band's hard-boiled arrangements. *There's a Bond Between Us* (also recorded in '65) was a similar but less effective follow-up, though it did include his best blues-rock original, "Walkin' in the Park."

With bands like the Rolling Stones, Yardbirds, and Animals reaching their primes, it was an extremely competitive time to be playing blues-rock in Britain. The Organisation couldn't distinguish themselves with their image; they had to rely almost exclusively on their musical identity. Pete Brown, an aspiring poet/lyricist (and co-writer of Cream classics like "White Room" and "Sunshine of Your Love"), would collaborate closely with Graham in his final years, and offers his own view as to what made the Graham Bond Organisation unique.

"First of all of course, they didn't have guitars, and they were much more jazz-influenced," he notes. "There was a huge Ray Charles influence, but to balance it out there was an enormous Charlie Mingus influence as well. Plus obviously Jimmy Smith and the organ thing. And Roland Kirk as well, which meant that they were much more musically versatile than almost any other group that was around at that time.

"They had better musical chops, and they knew their way around the music probably a lot better than people like the Stones or the Yardbirds. The only other people that were around that were up there with them were probably people like Zoot Money, who also came from jazz and listened to a lot of jazz, and has good jazz credentials." One of Graham's little-credited innovations is his use of the mellotron synthesizer on the band's second LP, *There's a Bond Between Us*, which marked one of the first uses of the instrument on a rock record; Bond even got to demonstrate the equipment on the popular British pop music TV program, *Ready Steady Go*.

Baker and Bruce had yet to reveal the scope of their talents, but Brown is quick to point out that Bond helped his colleagues more than he hindered them.

"Graham in many ways was Jack's mentor. It was the first singing that Jack really did. Graham encouraged people, which was another one of his great qualities. I know the circumstances of Jack doing his first solo singing with Graham on record, which was that he had 20 minutes to do three songs on *The Sound of '65*. But at the same time, Graham certainly must have enjoyed Jack's talent a great deal, and encouraged him to step forward and do some singing. He certainly didn't hold him back.

"I don't think Jack was overshadowed by Graham at all. It was Graham's band, Graham was the frontman. But within that, he featured them a great deal. Because his pride was involved in finding the best musicians, and actually sort of saying, okay, here's Jack doing his thing, or here's Ginger doing his solo. It was really Graham that brought them out and made the public very aware of them."

Duffy Power echoes Brown's words: "He was the guru, he was the high priest. There's no words to describe his enthusiasm. He had a musical philosophy, and instilled it into Jack and Ginger. Jack used to play double bass so hard the bridges would collapse. They just had a great power that nobody else had."

Mind you, Bond's generosity didn't extend to the point of giving Bruce—to most ears, a far more expressive singer—more than an occasional lead vocal in the studio. By the end of 1965, Bruce had been fired—not by Bond, but by Baker (who pulled a knife on him to make his point). The Organisation was obviously not the most stable of outfits, and its prime ended when Baker hooked up with Eric Clapton and patched things up with Bruce, resulting in the trio of Cream. Bond kept the Organisation going for a while with Heckstall-Smith and other musicians (most notably Jon Hiseman) before the act ground to a halt around 1967, hindered by Bond's growing dis-Organisation and, more seriously, heavy substance abuse.

Graham had just over five years to live, and would play and record much music. But he would never recapture the artistic peak of the mid-'60s Organisation lineup and, much worse, launched into a downward spiral of drug abuse. As detailed in Harry Shapiro's fine biography, *The Mighty Shadow* (issued by Square One in the U.K. only), he often made it hell for himself and those closest to him with his irresponsibility, wild mood swings, and increasing obsession with the occult. Worst of all, Shapiro revealed that Bond sexually abused his stepdaughter.

Bond moved to the States in the late '60s and recorded a couple of little-heard LPs, one of which featured only himself and ace session drummer Hal Blaine. By the 1970s he was back in Britain, logging in brief stints with the bands of erstwhile colleagues Baker and Bruce, and recording an album with Pete Brown. His professional activities had come to a standstill, and his health and friendships had seriously deteriorated by the time he committed his grisly suicide on May 8, 1974, at the Finsbury Park tube station.

As to Bond's tailspin, Brown speculates that in the best rock bands "people in long-term musical relationships tended to get the best results. The Stones, Sly, whatever, the best lineups they had were things that worked together a lot, settled into the music, and were able to bring up something a little bit fresh every night and elements of improvisation.

"And Graham never really had that opportunity after the Organisation. Which was a shame. It's the old story—the British business has been notoriously blinkered in its lack of support for things that could have gone on for a great deal of time." Adds Duffy Power, "The thing was, Graham was like a child. He wanted to do everything, he wanted to screw everyone, take every drug. He was his own enemy."

For all that, it's a special man who can elicit this sort of praise from Brown: "I actually do think Graham to musicians is like the Beatles were to the public. As important as that. Everybody went to see Graham. People [like Keith Emerson] that had huge success out of Graham's ideas, presentation, influences. They were probably the most admired group, because of their musical proficiency and their attitude to the conventions of pop, which they obviously didn't subscribe to."

Recommended Recording:
The Sound of 65/There's a Bond Between Us (1988, Edsel, UK). Double LP with both of the albums recorded by Bond's best lineup, at the peak of their powers.

Recommended Reading:
Graham Bond: The Mighty Shadow, by Harry Shapiro (1992, Square One, UK). Very hard to find the U.S., but a good full-length bio of the blues-rock forefather. Plenty of first-hand anecdotes from his key musical associates from the '60s, concentrating on Bond's musical innovations, but not ignoring the sordid aspects of his life and behavior.

"Our show is a premeditated moving picture, nonstop movement."
— Eddie Phillips, Creation guitarist, *Record Mirror*

The Creation

Two British bands of the 1960s could have been described as the rock equivalent of a pop-art action painting. One, of course, was the Who. The other was often tapped as one of the bands most likely to succeed, but rock operas and stadium tours were not in the cards for the Creation. The group boasted a guitarist who did more than any other British musicians except Pete Townshend and Jeff Beck to pioneer feedback and distortion. It's even been reported that he declined an invitation to join the Who as a second guitarist.

The Creation, mod to the max in 1966, as Eddie Phillips (with violin bow) prepares to demonstrate his innovative guitar technique.

But the Creation's series of mod-psychedelic singles fell on mostly deaf ears in the U.K., and were totally unknown across the Atlantic. Their star string-bender had already left the group by the time they disbanded in 1968.

The similarity between the autodestruct pop of the Who and the Creation was hardly accidental. Both groups were produced by Shel Talmy, the American expatriate who did much to boost power chords and fierce guitar leads to unprecedented levels with the Kinks and the Who in the mid-'60s. In early 1966, shortly after the release of the *My Generation* album, Talmy found himself ousted from the Who's production chair by management politics. Around the same time, he began his own label, Planet Records. With the Creation, he found a suitable vehicle to continue shaping his fusion of smart mod pop and searing, experimental electronics.

But the Creation were no novices to this field when Talmy signed them. As the Mark Four, the group had already released a few flop singles (some of which featured future Kinks bassist John Dalton). On the little-noticed 1965 B-side "I'm Leaving," Eddie Phillips tore off what may have been the longest feedback guitar solo ever to grace a rock 'n' roll record at that point. Built around the songwriting team of Phillips and singer Kenny Pickett, the group were clearly on their way to something interesting.

Talmy gave them a needed push, however, taking them into the studio a week after they joined the Planet roster. By that time, Pickett had renamed the band the Creation. On their 1966 debut single, "Making Time," Phillips introduced another element that threatened to outdo even the Who in the weirdness department, playing his guitar with a violin bow. Thus was a fairly ordinary modish power-chord tune given the necessary embellishment to stand out from the pack, as the instrumental break suddenly exploded into groaning and sawing that had little if any precedent.

Talking with me at his San Fernando Valley home in 1985, Shel Talmy still had fond memories of the Creation, nearly 20 years after working with them. "Eddie Phillips deserves to be up there as one of the great rock 'n' roll guitarists of our time, and he's hardly ever mentioned," declared the producer. "He was one of the most innovative guitarists I've ever run across. Jimmy Page stole the bowing bit of the guitar from Eddie. Eddie was phenomenal."

According to Talmy, the violin bow bit came about via the serendipity that often plays a role in rock 'n' roll innovations. "I think he was just fooling around. As I recall, he was practicing guitar at somebody's house and there happened to be a violin bow around, and he picked it up and started messing with it. I heard it, and I said, 'Christ, let's use that. I've never heard that sound before.' So that's how we got into 'Making Time.' And of course Jimmy Page made it his own invention later."

Publicity photos of the time show Phillips somberly chinning his axe and caressing a bow over its strings, with all the poker-faced dedication of a genuine maestro. The gimmick didn't escape the attention of Jimmy Page, who would start using a violin bow to play solos during the Yardbirds' dying days, and take the technique to new plateaus of indulgence with Led Zeppelin. It wasn't enough, though, to take "Making Time" higher than #49 in the British charts.

The second single, "Painter Man," was a more commercial effort, though Phillips made sure to get purposeful squawks out of his guitar throughout. Live, the impact was magnified when Pickett spray-painted a large canvas onstage as the song was being performed; at the climax, it would be set on fire, or Phillips would slash it to bits with his violin bow. The record made #36, but the band would never get that much-needed hit, smash singles being necessary for survival in those pre-album-oriented days. First off, Planet folded. Though they were able to hook up with Polydor quickly enough, in the interim the band suffered several personnel changes. By the time they resumed recording, Pickett was gone, and much of the band's momentum was lost.

Phillips would record three more singles with the group, as well as an album (issued in Germany, Holland, and Scandinavia only). While these were decent enough efforts with thick, crunching guitars, the failure of the Creation to compete with the Who isn't entirely attributable to bad luck. Quite simply, their songwriting wasn't nearly in the Who's league, lacking Townshend's (and, for that matter, John Entwistle's) wit and keen grasp of pop hooks. The cheery harmonies and impressionistic lyrics ("Biff Bang Pow" went one of their B-sides) were firmly in the pop-art tradition. But often one finds oneself waiting for the Eddie Phillips solo, the ingredient that takes the recipe truly out of the ordinary. Put another way, in the Who, Townshend's guitar acrobatics were the icing on the cake; in the Creation, Phillips' guitar acrobatics *were* the cake, and there wasn't as much inside.

Despite a good deal of success on the Continent (particularly Germany), the Creation found Britain a closed market. Phillips left before the end of 1967; the band broke up shortly after that. Almost immediately, however, they regrouped in a different configuration. Pickett rejoined the group, but Phillips had seen enough, abandoning music for, of all things, a job driving a bus for London Transport.

His replacement was Ronnie Wood, fresh from his stint with the original Jeff Beck group. The Creation lumbered on for a few more months, managing to cut some final half-decent tracks in the studio before calling it a day for good. Kenny Pickett became a roadie for Led Zeppelin before entering the songwriting business; Eddie Phillips kept driving the bus, and released a few little-heard singles (one produced by Shel Talmy) in the late '70s. Ronnie Wood, in contrast, went nowhere but up, reteaming with Jeff Beck Group vocalist Rod Stewart in the Faces, and taking Mick Taylor's spot in the Rolling Stones in the mid-'70s—a position he's retained for two decades.

Wood wasn't in evidence when the Creation reunited in 1994. A new generation of fans now revered the Creation as mod icons. One of them, Alan McGee, was sufficiently inspired to name his independent label Creation. The company became one of Britain's most successful alternative rock outfits, and McGee got his chance to record a new single with the band, with both Phillips and Pickett in tow. In the pop-art tradition, the Creation's single was not only produced for the Creation label, but titled, in a mixture of hype and chutzpah, "Creation."

"I am continually surprised at the number of people who actually know who the Creation are," remarked Talmy. "They have a real cult following. They were enormous in Europe, you know, in most of the Continent, except for France. Never quite made it [in Britain] and they went the way of a lot of bands, they decided to break up. I just could not hold them together. I tried. I said, 'Hang on, I think we're just about there.' But Kenny wanted to go off and do his thing. He and Eddie were fighting at the time, too. They had a personality conflict. They have since, of course, become great friends again." Pickett died in January 1997, just after singing a few songs at his local pub with a friend's band.

But maybe the Creation weren't cut out for rock stardom in the first place. "Eddie was typical working class," pointed out Talmy. "He was sort of Cockney, and came from an absolutely 24-karat working class family who were raised to go for security. The fact that he was in a band in the first place was outside the norm of his experience. And when the Creation finally broke up, he became a bus driver of all things. Talk about waste."

Recommended Recording:
How Does It Feel to Feel (1982, Edsel, UK). The best of several Creation compilations, and the easiest to find. Collecting 20 tracks from 1966–68, it contains all the key singles (including "Making Time" and "Painter Man") and highlights from their album. "Making Time" remains their peak, but the droning pyrotechnics of "How Does It Feel to Feel" in particular are still astounding.

John's Children onstage, flanked by a couple of friends. Andy Ellison on vocals; a nervous-looking Marc Bolan (aka T. Rex) tries to concentrate on his guitar on the right. Credit: Courtesy Andy Ellison

John's Children

"They were dreadful. Positively the worst group I'd ever seen. And as the gig sank to lower and lower depths the audience leapt into the pool so that the splashes would fuse the equipment. Eventually the group retreated to a nearby pub. I hadn't the heart to walk off without saying a word, so to help break the bad news that they didn't have what it takes, I went inside and bought them each a drink. Seven beers and 12 whiskies later I told them I'd be their manager."

—Simon Napier-Bell, explaining how he came to manage John's Children, on the sleeve note to the group's *The Legendary Orgasm Album*

For an act that was only together for a little over a year—and that only released half a dozen singles, none of them significant hits—John's Children certainly kicked up a lot more fuss than many bands with truckloads of gold records.

Between late 1966 and early 1968, they managed to record one of the first out-and-out psychedelic singles; get their one and only album banned in the United States before it was even released; have their best shot at a hit single banned by the BBC; upstage the Who on a European tour with an even more assaultive on-stage autodestruction act; and enlist Jeff Beck, Patti LaBelle, John Paul Jones, and Rod Stewart as session musicians on the group's few trips into the studio.

Yet John's Children remain most well known—if their name is recognized at all—for including one Marc Bolan in their lineup, before Bolan would meta-morphose into glam-rocker T. Rex, one of the biggest British rock stars of the early '70s. The irony is that Bolan was in fact with the band for only a few months, and only appeared on a couple of their singles. John's Children were much more than "the band the T. Rex started in." Their calculated sense of mod shock and cutely subversive pop made them as outrageous as any act of their era, even by the standards of mid-'60s Swinging London. "We just looked like four really angelic young guys, but who turned into complete monsters onstage," says singer Andy Ellison. "That was the dichotomy of John's Children, and that's why it worked."

If John's Children were far below the top bands of the day in terms of song-writing talent and instrumental virtuosity, they were second to none in sheer chutzpah. Pure nerve is what got them noticed in 1966, when they were known as the Silence, just one of scores of London mod bands groping to branch out from R&B roots into a more original sound. A brief liaison with Small Faces manager Don Arden came to naught, but on a jaunt to the south of France, bassist John Hewlett and drummer Chris Townson happened upon Simon Napier-Bell in a St. Tropez club.

Napier-Bell at the time was managing the Yardbirds, one of the greatest of all British Invasion bands. Hewlett, it has been reported, wouldn't let the great man finish his meal in peace until Napier-Bell had promised to check out the Silence (so named because they were the loudest band around) in person. After watching a supposedly disastrous gig at a swim club, Napier-Bell agreed to take on the Si-lence—a most inappropriate name given the mayhem that would follow. The band would never have to resolve that particular contradiction, as Napier-Bell quickly renamed them John's Children ("John" being John Hewlett).

In the years following John's Children demise, Napier-Bell denigrated the band's basic competence frequently and bluntly. To hear him tell it, they could barely play their instruments or finish a song. The comments seem odd in light of the fact that the band had been playing professionally for about a couple of years as the Silence, and would write all of the 20 or so songs recorded in the stu-dio by John's Children. "He likes to glamorize everything," shrugs Ellison. "After the band split up, he would then exaggerate how incredibly bad we were and how we were manipulated." But Andy does acknowledge that "in fact, right at the beginning, we were *not* very good."

In any event, Napier-Bell wasn't taking any chances with the group's debut single, an odd ballad called "Smashed Blocked." It might have sounded like sappy teen idol pop if not for the title/chorus, which—accurately or inaccurately—was perceived by some as mod slang for riding high on pills or even more dangerous drugs. (It was most likely retitled "The Love I Thought I'd Found" on its U.K. release for this reason.) Doubtful of his protégés' abilities to cut it in the studio, Napier-Bell arranged to have the backing track recorded in Los Angeles with top session men. Andy Ellison then laid an alluringly shaky lead vocal on top, and the result was credited to John's Children, although Ellison was the only one who actually participated in the track.

Regardless of how authentic a representation it was of the actual group, "Smashed Blocked" was noteworthy as one of the first full-blown manifestations of British psychedelia. That's especially true of the first 30 or so seconds, in which Ellison's heavily reverbed voice drones on and on about getting dizzy and disoriented against a steadily mounting crescendo of blurry, pulsating organ and eerie backup vocal wails. Just as the track seems about to burst into total cacophony, the cheery "Smashed Blocked" chorus kicks in, alternating with Ellison's lonely, forlorn verses, his voice sounding for all the world like an adolescent hippie caught in a tin can from outer space. "Nobody had ever done anything like that—*ever*," says Ellison of the single. "We wanted to be as over-the-top as possible."

As weird a piece of pop as anything on offer in late 1966, it became a small (very small: #98) hit in the U.S., where it made the Top Ten in some markets in California and Florida. That incited demand for a full-length album from the band's American record label, White Whale. Napier-Bell was just getting warmed up with his studio tricks; deeming a bunch of tracks cut by the band as unsuitable, he proceeded to dub massive earfuls of screaming teens on top, taken right from the soundtrack of *A Hard Day's Night*. The result sounded more like a band trying to fight its way out of a vat of tomato sauce than a bona fide live recording.

"Simon never told us that he was going to do that," says Ellison today. "He suddenly arrived one day and said, 'Listen guys, I've made it sound like a live concert!' When we listened to it we went, 'Oh, well, yeah. It *does* sound quite exciting. We'll leave it like that then.' He tried to put it out and say it was a real John's Children manic live concert." At this point Ellison can't stop himself from laughing at the memory. "Obviously it was all going to fall apart at some point, and somebody was going to say, 'Now, come on then?'"

It was something of a moot point, because nobody heard the record for years. Napier-Bell, ever hungry for media controversy, dubbed the album *Orgasm!*, complete with an ecstatic screaming female on the cover. It was reported that the Daughters of the Revolution managed to get the record withdrawn just days before its projected release in March of 1967. Considering the madness of the entire project, it was appropriate that it was finally released in 1971, by which time John's Children—never a household name to begin with—had not existed for three years. (It was reissued in the U.K. as *The Legendary Orgasm Album* in the 1980s.)

The group managed to dent the British Top Fifty with their second 45, "Just What You Want, Just What You Get," with its leering Ellison vocal and disquieting marriage of cheery pop melody with a goose-stepping march beat. (In his liner notes to the compilation *A Midsummer Night's Scene*, Brian Hogg wrote that payola was used to ensure its chart placing, however lowly.) The band ripped off the Who's "I Can't Explain" riff for the B-side, which featured a smoking overdubbed guitar solo by Jeff Beck, a fellow client of Napier-Bell during his tenure with the Yardbirds. The irony of a band of supposed incompetents enlisting one of the world's greatest guitarists for a B-side is delicious, but it did mask a greater problem—namely, the shortcomings of the band's real guitarist, Geoff McClelland. Napier-Bell offered them an apparently perfect replacement with Marc Bolan, a singer-songwriter-guitarist on his roster who was going nowhere as a solo act.

"Marc was a very quiet person when he first entered our band, but he kind of got off on our complete over-the-top energy and madness," enthuses Ellison. "The songs he brought along were absolutely brilliant, and perfect for the band. I prefer a lot of the songs that he did then to the ones that he wrote later for T. Rex, and even the stuff that he did acoustically with the Tyrannosaurus Rex." Bolan's entry into the group was especially timely since the group had just been dropped by EMI after submitting a third single entitled "Not the Sort of Girl I'd Like to Take to Bed." Accounts vary as to whether this was deliberate insubordination on Napier-Bell's part, since Track Records, run by Who manager Kit Lambert, was interested enough in John's Children to quickly sign them.

"Desdemona," a typically buzzing piece of Bolan power-pop—which the songwriter claimed to have written in just 25 seconds— seemed like the band's best hope for commercial success before the stuffy authorities at the BBC shot it down in mid-flight. It seems the organization didn't approve of a line about the song's heroine lifting her skirt and flying. A cleaned-up version was produced for airplay that substituted a more innocuous lyric (although the line had been fairly innocuous to begin with), but it was too late to make up ground. A second Bolan tune, the more psychedelically minded "A Midsummer Night's Scene," was slated for the next release, but a mere 25 copies or so were pressed before it was withdrawn. One of the most collectable British rock singles, original copies have fetched as much as 2,500 pounds, though it's now easily available as a reissue.

Given the band's seeming inability to get on the charts without some calamity or other befalling the release, their chaotic week-long German tour with the Who in April 1967 may have been their finest hour. This was the ultimate battle of the autodestruct bands; John's Children were fresh from an appearance at the 14 Hour Technicolour Dream festival in London where, according to the liner notes of one John's Children bootleg compilation, "Their initial promise to play naked gave way to a more modest 25-minute display of feedback as Bolan spent the entire gig walking round with his guitar on his head, while Ellison emptied sacks of feathers over the audience." Ellison also brought his feather act to Germany, and the group were apparently inciting riots at nearly every venue, even before the Who took the stage.

Was the tour as wild as the legend would have it? "Absolutely," asserts Ellison. "More so. You'd have to have been there to believe it, and when people write about it, it just doesn't really sum up the whole thing. No sooner [than] the first night of the tour, Pete Townshend and Roger Daltrey were already getting angry. We weren't meant to be doing that sort of thing, upstaging any band. We weren't meant to be getting that kind of a response from an audience. We were just one of the support bands. Although we were doing that before—that was our act anyway."

Andy Ellison, caught in the middle of his feather act. Credit: Courtesy Andy Ellison

Andy admits that it was the group's theatrics, rather than their music, that were making the stars of the show nervous, but does take care to point out that "we had these amplifiers that were *louder* than the Who—much louder than we play today. This was banks of speakers, which were on top of each other, and all connected, like walls of sound that went across the back. It was a *massive* sound. Chris [Townson] was a violent drummer with a tribal sort of sound that would set things off anyway." Rumblings from the Who camp grew louder, causing Who manager Kit Lambert to complain to Napier-Bell, who would then "come to us and say, don't worry, just go and carry on, because it's all good publicity. But then things did carry a little too far."

Specifically, Ellison's referring to a show at Ludwigshaven, where the band's set started a riot that brought the police to the venue with water guns. The rest of the show was canceled, and the Who never even got to mount the stage. John's Children's equipment was confiscated by the German police, and the group were deported. Back in the U.K., Marc Bolan, perhaps never destined to be content unless he was the star of the show, left to begin his solo career. Yet at first he played not ferocious power-pop, but hippie acoustic folk with a guitar and bongo. Ellison thinks he may know why it took a while for Bolan to plug in his amp again.

John's Children with bodyguards. Credit: Courtesy Andy Ellison

"All our equipment was confiscated, and there we were sort of being deported from Germany, very sadly shifting our way out through the back roads in Simon's Bentley. On the way there, we dropped off at Luxembourg and spent a couple of nights there, where we saw Ravi Shankar in concert. I always remember that Marc was really taken by just seeing these guys sitting there onstage with sitars and bongos. He was very quiet after that concert, and seeing as when we got back to England we had no equipment, Marc disappeared. He didn't have money—the easiest way to start making music was to sit there, grab his old acoustic guitar again, and things went on from there.

"He started having success that way, but I feel that he really still wanted to do the electronic thing again. Because he had such wild abandon and excitement with John's Children. The seeds had already been sown in the back of his mind. But of course, everybody was wanting him to go out as Tyrannosaurus Rex; he was doing well like that. So that went on for quite a while. I really think that probably John's Children would have been very big indeed had things stayed together." Bolan's experience in John's Children certainly didn't come to naught, as he reworked several tunes from the John's Children days on his early solo records, such as "Go Go Girl," which Tyrannosaurus Rex would retool into "Mustang Ford."

But without Bolan, John's Children was left with a sort of morning-after hangover. For a while they carried on by using some of the Yardbirds' equipment; roadie Chris Colville was drafted in to play drums, and Chris Townson switched from drums to guitar at little more than a moment's notice. The group, too, may have been tiring of Napier-Bell's hype, which had seen them pose in the nude (all the offending parts covered by flowers) for the picture sleeve of their "Come and Play with Me in the Garden" single. Simon had also insisted that the group wear their white uniforms every time they appeared in public. That came to an end when Townson buried his in a field, and Ellison and Hewlett burned theirs before throwing the ashes into the river.

Ellison quickly got going with a solo career, making a variety of interesting pop-psych singles in the late '60s, such as the non sequitur "Cornflake Zoo," recorded over an old backing track that featured former ally Marc Bolan on backup vocals. Hewlett went on to manage Sparks. Ellison played in the '70s with Radio Stars (whom he still plays with periodically). He describes their music as a "mixture of very quirky power pop, lots of very unusual lyrics—the Bonzo Dogs, Frank Zappa, the Who, the Kinks, the Beatles—all mixed together. With a bit of Sparks and a bit of punk thrown in to boot." In 1997 he's still active in music, recording "techno-punk" tracks in the studio with Lift.

One of the bands Radio Stars played with in the '70s was an up-and-coming punk-pop act called the Jam; Jam leader Paul Weller would later cite John's Children as one of his favorite overlooked British '60s groups. So would Noel Gallagher of Oasis, and Morrissey's guitarist, Boz Boorer, who was enough of a fan to join John's Children for a few reunion gigs a few years ago. No less than three John's Children LP reissues hit the market in the 1980s, all with extensive liner notes; there was even a bootleg EP of BBC sessions, and a small book on the band.

The ongoing interest in John's Children is as much of a surprise to Ellison as anybody. "I can only think," he comments modestly, "that the complete madness and enthusiasm that we had at the time must have shone through on some of the records, and people pick up on it." More people, apparently, than picked up on it when John's Children were actually making records—and mostly based on the music, not on the hype. A most satisfying vindication, one would think, for musicians who weren't even allowed to play on their own records at first.

Recommended Recording:
A *Midsummer Night's Scene* (1987, Bam Caruso, UK). This could have been more comprehensive—it doesn't have the wacko Andy Ellison single "Cornflake Zoo," for example, or anything from *Orgasm!* It's got all of the band's singles, though, as well as a couple of late '60s Ellison tracks, one of which ("Arthur Green") is actually a John's Children recording.

Duffy Power

Duffy Power, teen idol-turned-bluesman, 1963. Credit: Courtesy Duffy Power

One of the biggest blues-rock bands of all time, one of the biggest jazz-rock bands of all time, *and* one of the biggest folk-rock bands of all time have one thing in common, though you'd be hard-pressed to find anyone who could name it. But before there was Cream, before there was the Mahavishnu Orchestra, and before there was Pentangle, there was Duffy Power. And John McLaughlin, Jack Bruce, Ginger Baker, Danny Thompson, and Terry Cox were not yet stars, but struggling musicians trying to create a niche for themselves. And while Duffy Power had the luck to sing with all of the aforementioned virtuosos, he was not fortunate enough to follow his former sidemen into international stardom, despite carving his own niche as one of Britain's foremost blues/rock/folk/jazz musicians.

Power is a hard artist to pigeonhole. Before joining the blues-rock underground, Duffy was a manufactured teen idol. He also had the honor of being the second-ever artist to cover a Lennon-McCartney song, though that 1963 single, like virtually all of his other releases, remains unknown outside of record collecting circles.

Underground cachet was not what early British rock 'n' roll manager Larry Parnes had in mind when he signed Duffy in the late 1950s. Parnes changed the singer's name from Ray Howard to the far more dashing Duffy Power, in line with the other obviously fake names in his management stable, like Vince Eager, Marty Wilde, and Johnny Gentle. A bunch of pop-rock-oriented singles for Fontana followed in the late '50s and early '60s.

"With Parnes I never liked anything I recorded," notes Duffy, "and never performed any of it on stage." Duffy's girlfriend convinced him to leave Parnes, and the singer began pursuing a direction more compatible with the blues-folk artists he loved—Sonny Terry, Jesse Fuller, and Leadbelly. Duffy got his real-life hard knocks when he discovered his girlfriend wasn't a singer, but a prostitute. "It sounds corny, but it really sort of grew me up," he says today, without sentimentality. "So I slowly got over that through the music."

Power was now recording for Parlophone, and in 1963 he briefly teamed up with the Graham Bond Organisation. Backing Bond's keyboards and vocals was the rhythm section of Jack Bruce on bass and Ginger Baker on drums. In early 1963 Power was offered a composition by a group just starting to become known nationwide. The songwriters were John Lennon and Paul McCartney, and the song was "I Saw Her Standing There." Duffy's version would mark only the second time a Lennon-McCartney tune was covered on record.

Power had already met the Beatles while touring in Liverpool, and remembers that he was led to believe that the pair had actually written the song with him in mind, although he later learned that wasn't the case. At any rate, he recorded the single with Bond, Bruce, and Baker on backup. "I actually didn't like the song very much," he admits. "But I did it, and I changed it. And Bond played like mad on it, because he wasn't used to it. He didn't know anything about limits. When you're doing a two-and-a-half-minute record, you've got to give it a structure. You can't just go mad all over it.

"People laugh when they think I actually changed the tune of a Lennon-McCartney song," he chuckles, "[putting] all these blues notes here. And they said, 'aw, no, that's not our song!' So we had to go back and do it again. So somewhere there's this weird 'I Saw Her Standing There.' I'm hoping it will come out on the Bond box set that's coming out, they might dig it out. Perhaps McCartney might object to it still!"

After problems developed between Parlophone and Duffy's manager, he found himself without a record deal in the mid-'60s. A brief association with British blues godfather Alexis Korner yielded a rare album before the pair fell out. At loose ends, Duffy arranged to do some informal recordings in a studio managed by a friend. It was these tracks—not even initially recorded with a release in mind—upon which much of Power's celebrity rests, as much because of the sidemen he would employ as for Duffy himself.

For accompaniment, Duffy tapped a variety of friends—who, when you were as well-connected as Power was, included Bruce, Baker, John McLaughlin, and future Pentangle rhythm section Danny Thompson (bass) and Terry Cox (drums). Phil Seamen, one of Britain's top jazz drummers, also appears on some of the cuts. For blues firepower, Power couldn't match fellow Brits such as Eric Burdon and Stevie Winwood, but he brought a pleasing subtlety to the music that drew more from the blues-folk-jazz crossover of Big Bill Broonzy, Billie Holiday, and Josh White than the electric Chicago blues of Muddy Waters. This eclecticism was also reflected in the instrumentation, especially in the use of upright (as opposed to electric) bass. There was also a gutsiness fueled by the British blues-rock explosion, albeit its more sophisticated, subdued side.

According to Power, when he first met with John McLaughlin, "he just played these sort of beautiful but doomy jazz chords. It was an expression of a rather unhappy guy." For the Power sessions, McLaughlin played in a much more gentle, straightahead R&B style, also penning some tunes with Duffy. Power himself played some harmonica and occasional guitar, upon which he unveiled some startlingly eerie, far-out open-tuned riffs on his version of "Louisiana Blues." According to the vocalist, it was the first time he had even sang the song from beginning to end.

The sessions remained at Power's home while he made some other sporadic recordings (most remaining unreleased, though some came out on flop singles) in the late '60s. Fourteen of the songs finally ended up coming out on a 1970 collection called *Innovations* that sold surprisingly well. Of course, by that time most of the musicians who played on the record were famous—with the notable exception of Duffy.

Power's principal regret seems not be his lack of stardom, but his failure to recruit Danny Thompson and Terry Cox as his own rhythm section prior to their tenure with Pentangle. "I was disappointed, because they were there for the asking. If I hadn't have been so ill, I think, psychologically, and had a bit more luck, I could have made them my band, we could have really been successful. I could have kept them myself. I thought, they should have been mine, my rhythm section. After all, they'd taken it and they were doing it with folkies, and they were doing it well. It really upset me, 'cause it's taken me years to get used to using somebody else."

He also maintains that while his sidemen certainly went on to more lucrative financial pastures, that didn't necessarily make for better music. "I suppose in a way, they were all a bit disappointing, what they finally ended up doing. I thought when Jack went from double bass to bass guitar, that was a bit of a shame, 'cause I loved the double bass, the upright bass. He still was one of the first great [electric] bass guitarists, but I didn't like Cream. I thought that was a waste. I didn't think it was well thought-out at all. Then he got into loads and loads of solos and soloing things, and it fell apart where they'd just carry on, playing on and on and on."

By the late '60s, in fact, Power was making recordings featuring only himself and his guitar. The eventual release of these tracks in their unpolished state on the tiny Spark label (now reissued with extra tracks as *Blues Power*) was as much due to circumstance as aesthetics. Originally intended to be embellished with orchestration, the label ran out of money to complete the project, issuing the tapes as they were. Which was hardly a great loss: mixing classic covers with Power's own interesting jazz-blues-folk compositions was Duffy at his most intimate and, in a certain sense, most powerful.

Power became tight with the band Argent in the early '70s, touring and recording with the band, with ex-Zombies Rod Argent and Chris White producing. With their heavier rock feel, these records are generally less impressive than his purer '60s outings, although Power's own talents are undiminished. But the late '70s initiated a rough stretch for Duffy, as acoustic blues-folk fell out of favor, resulting in a shortage of work that found folk acts paying for support slots in a desperate effort to get exposure. Power even recorded some disco tracks in the absence of any other work. In the early '80s he had a mild schizophrenic illness, and was pretty much out of commission as far as musical activities.

The last few years have been much kinder to Power, as he gained an important fan in radio DJ Mary Costello (Elvis Costello's ex-wife). Costello had Duffy on her show for many sessions, and put him back in touch with ex-Graham Bond saxophonist Dick Heckstall-Smith, with whom he played some live shows. In 1996, Power was working on a new album with the London Blues Company.

"Back in 1961, I thought to myself, well, you can't go around singing like a black man, like a field holler or something like that," replies Duffy when asked to cite what's made his music unique in the annals of British blues-rock. "But you could use it in anything, that influence. I never ever settled on being a totally one-way authentic, like a Chicago type, or a folk type. I was always interested in different things. If I listened to some prisoners from Angola State Prison singing something like 'Rosie,' I thought, oh yeah, I want to do that. So when I'd go in the studio, I'd have a go at it. Sometimes that's a mistake, because you can never top these guys. But I always think that if you've got the right feel, this genuine feel, you can always get something of its own. When it came down to it, to be stuck in one thing like that never appealed to me."

Recommended Recordings:

Little Boy Blue (1992, Edsel, UK). A straight reissue of *Innovations*. His best recordings, notable for the assistance of Jack Bruce, Ginger Baker, John McLaughlin, Terry Cox, and Danny Thompson. But the real star of the show is Duffy Power.

Blues Power (1992, See For Miles, UK). Power's late-'60s acoustic sessions are some of the best blues-folk ever to come out of Britain. And some of the most eclectic—check out the cover of the Beatles' "Fixing a Hole."

Just Say Blue (1995, Retro, UK). Although it's not the cream of Power's work, this is a solid collection of rare and unreleased material from 1965-71, most of it unavailable elsewhere. The earlier tracks have more appearances by future stars Bruce, Baker, McLaughlin, Thompson, and Cox.

Out of the Garage 3

It's with some trepidation that I classify the Music Machine, the Remains, and the Chocolate Watch Bands as "garage bands." That's the label that's been handed down to them by mainstream rock critics who have viewed such acts mostly as curiosities. Most listeners (including said rock critics) know of them only via a track or two that have surfaced on compilations. These were the groups, they conclude, that toiled on the farm teams in the mid-'60s, imitating the British Invasion groups and the folk-rock stars, occasionally latching onto a superb piece of one-shot material for a regional or national hit.

But the Music Machine, the Remains, and the Chocolate Watch Band—and numerous others—were not simply "garage bands." They were simply very talented bands that didn't get the success that came to the era's biggest groups, due to ill luck, bad management, the uncommercial nature of some of their music, and other factors. They were also top-notch musicians and composers, recording in state-of-the-art studios, not in primitive garages.

They were at the top of the pyramid of the '60s garage rock explosion—a ball of white heat that encompassed thousands, if not tens of thousands, of American bands trying to grab a piece of the territory opened up by the British stars of the era. Rebellious attitude and an insistence on doing things their own way—including playing their own instruments, and writing their own songs— were their hallmarks. It's true that their aspirations sometimes outweighed their musical abilities, but the best garage rock has a primal (if largely adolescent) energy that little subsequent music has matched.

The Rising Storm and the Mystic Tide are more in line with the garage band stereotype—acts who were barely even known in their home territory, and that only managed to squelch out a few (impossibly rare) records before breaking up. The recording technology they employed was indeed primitive, due to limited funds and studio time. Their imaginations, however, were not, as both crafted compellingly mysterious and melodic material that made the technical limitations of the recordings almost irrelevant. Along with the other "garage rockers" detailed in the section, they offered some of the best subterranean sounds of a time and place in which too much fine music was being made by young bands for even the local charts to accommodate.

The Remains, with fan on Barry Tashian's shoulder. Credit: Courtesy Barry Tashian

San Francisco, 1966.

To most rock fans, those words bring to mind the sound of psychedelia—the mix of electric folk-rock, Indian music, mind-blowing guitar leads, anti-Establishment rebellion, and espousal of free love. Local groups with funny names—Jefferson Airplane, Moby Grape, the Grateful Dead, Big Brother & the Holding Company, and Quicksilver Messenger Service—would bring the message home to Middle America.

The Chocolate Watch Band

Fifty miles to the south of San Francisco, in San Jose, the influence of psychedelia filtered down to other bands with funny names that were just barely out of the garage. For a long time, one of the most outlandishly named of these outfits, the Chocolate Watch Band, were dismissed as something of a joke by serious rock historians. They wrote hardly any of their own songs; they appeared in hippie exploitation movies like *Riot on Sunset Strip*; and the backs of their albums were covered with more ludicrous dedications than any album before or since. Their best-known tune even features lead vocals by a guy who didn't belong to the group.

Time, however, has accorded the Chocolate Watch Band more respect than almost any other garage band of the '60s. Theirs was the ultimate blend of teen frustration and primitive psychedelia, delivered with a Jaggeresque snarl, wonderfully snaky and raunchy guitar leads, and state-of-the-art production that was both sophisticated and experimental. They had the *look*, too: take a glance at shots from *Riot on Sunset Strip*, in which the group make a winning bid for the award of most convincing junior version of the Rolling Stones, American division.

The distance between the Chocolate Watch Band and the psychedelic giants from the city by the bay wasn't as great as you would imagine, according to lead singer Dave Aguilar, who points out that "Moby Grape was physically put together by a group of investors and producers. The same with Jefferson Airplane. We never had that. We were just very excited young guys with an attitude, but no financial backing or investors that were willing to come in and say okay, we'll get you going, we'll set you up with equipment, we'll set you up playing, we'll get you into the studio to start recording. That was the big difference between the groups."

The Chocolate Watch Band, spring 1966. Left to right: Gary Andrijasevich, Mark Loomis, Dave Aguilar, Sean Tolby, Bill Flores. Credit: Courtesy Dave Aguilar

He might have added, as well, that the Watch Band—which had coalesced from veterans of several San Jose high school and college bands—had a much raunchier, bluesier, less folky conception of how a group should sound than most of their more celebrated Bay Area peers. On the other hand, they were no match for gentler acts like the Airplane in the original material department. Which made them ripe for the picking when Los Angeles producer Ed Cobb began looking for vehicles for his songs and studio productions in late 1966.

The Chocolate Watch Band onstage; Dave Aguilar with tambourine, Sean Tolby on his right. Credit: Courtesy Dave Aguilar

Cobb is a pivotal and quite controversial factor in the Chocolate Watch Band story. Formerly a pop star with a folk-pop vocal group, the Four Preps, Cobb had turned his attention to the studio in the mid-'60s. His projects indicated that Ed was far hipper than his whitebread singing career would indicate, as he penned all-time soul classics for Brenda Holloway ("Every Little Bit Hurts") and Gloria Jones ("Tainted Love," revived for an international smash in the 1980s by Soft Cell). He also molded Hollywood combo the Standells into a Stonesy garage band, penning one of the definitive trashy garage-rock staples of the '60s for them, "Dirty Water." By 1966, his gaze had drifted to the San Jose scene, which had produced two of the biggest-selling garage rock hits that year in "Psychotic Reaction" (by the Count Five) and "Little Girl" (by the Syndicate of Sound).

"I think in all honesty Ed Cobb was a performer that had seen his day and realized he could not participate any longer," reflects Aguilar. "He did not want to be shut out of this rock and roll phenomenon that was now happening. He was looking for a band that he could influence and have do his music. The Standells were actually probably a much better band for him to use than us. The Standells, I think, were more malleable, and they were more interested in just being stars. They were probably more interested in doing work in the recording studio. They were much better in a recording studio than we were."

Not that the Watch Band were *bad* in the studio—far from it. Their first single, "Sweet Young Thing"/"It's All Over Now, Baby Blue," paired one of the best Rolling Stones-inspired garage tunes (again written by Cobb) with a tough cover of the Bob Dylan classic. Aguilar's sneering vocals were clearly modeled on British Invasion singers like Mick Jagger, and the psychedelic touch was evident in the imaginative distorted guitar effects and gauzy keyboards on "Baby Blue." But the record died, perhaps because it was unaccountably assigned to Tower's rhythm and blues subsidiary, Uptown—the first of many instances of record company mismanagement of the promising young group.

Cobb, it was clear, was going to be calling the shots in the studio, assigning and/or writing the material. Some of this wasn't to the group's liking—Aguilar makes it clear that he *hates* a lot of what was given to them, like their second single, the "Paint It Black"-inspired "Misty Lane" (which is actually quite a nifty tune, no matter what Dave thinks). Aguilar reveals, shockingly, that the band would play virtually none of the material from their first album onstage. What's worse, their debut LP (*No Way Out*, 1967) had two psychedelic instrumentals that didn't feature any musicians from the band at all; four of the songs that *did* have the band playing were graced by lead vocals not from Aguilar, but from a black session vocalist, Don Bennett.

Ironically, one of these, the swaggering "Let's Talk About Girls," became the Watch Band's most famous cut after it was placed on the 1972 *Nuggets* compilation, the first (and perhaps best) reissue of '60s garage music. The song was actually first recorded in a much more straightforward version by an obscure Tucson, Arizona, group, the Tongues of Truth. It must be conceded that Cobb had excellent, imaginative taste in some of the material he was assigning to the group. In addition to "Let's Talk About Girls," he also gave them a couple of other tasty psych-punk nuggets that had been regional releases for other bands: "In the Past" (by We the People) and "I Ain't No Miracle Worker" (by the Brogues, who played the same circuit as the Watch Band).

Which begs the questions: How exactly was Ed Cobb getting away with putting out Chocolate Watch Band tracks with little or no group involvement? And how exactly did the group refrain from using Cobb's head as a basketball when they heard "their" records?

"We were 16, 18, 19 years old," explains Aguilar. "We'd been picked up by this producer. We were flown down to L.A. We were told on a Thursday that Friday a jet would pick you up and you would go down and record an album and spend a week in L.A. There would be a limo that would pick you up at the airport. Every meal that you ate was catered. We really had no virtual studio experience recording, so we weren't prepared to go into the studio.

"We *hadn't* been writing music. We were stage performers. What we did on stage was what we loved to do. We loved to challenge big-name groups and blow 'em off the stage. *That's* where we got our excitement and our kicks. There wasn't anything better in the world that we loved, going up against a group that had a hit single out on the air with a show that was just so powerful that some of the groups didn't want to come out and play. They were *that* discouraged.

"We were not crazy about the songs that Ed had picked for us, but then again we had no background preparation. We didn't go in with songs of our own that we wanted to record, and so we accepted what he did. We didn't know that he was changing them and adding people to it, and adding stuff to the album, 'til *months* after we'd been in the studio and we were gone. I remember at one point, one of the albums came in, and we took a look at it, played a couple songs on it, and said, 'What the *hell* is this shit?' And somebody threw it in the trash. And we went back to rehearsing for a show that we had coming up. I mean, it bothered us that it wasn't us, but we weren't playing any of Ed Cobb's stuff in performances anyway, and we were right up there onstage with the Yardbirds and the Dead and the Airplane in the Fillmore Auditorium and rubbing elbows and feeling good about it. So that didn't bother us either. We felt that we had arrived, just on a different level. We weren't selling records, but that didn't really matter to us at the time."

Confusing the issue even further is the fact that some of those cuts featuring a less-than-bona fide Chocolate Watch Band are really excellent. The instrumental "Expo 2000," for instance, is a fair bid for an American Pink Floyd, with its spy movie guitar and astral sound effects. On "Let's Talk About Girls," "Are You Gonna Be There (At the Love In)," "No Way Out," and "I Ain't No Miracle Worker," the group achieved just the right balance between garage grit and sinister psychedelia, particularly in Mark Loomis' haunting distorted guitar lines. The garage-psychedelic mix perhaps accounts for why the Watch Band's best material has endured better than both much other garage *and* psychedelic rock.

Cobb's shenanigans, however, didn't augur well for the long-term stability of the group's best lineup (Aguilar, Loomis, guitarist Sean Tolby, bassist Bill Flores, and drummer Gary Andrijasevich). In late '67 Aguilar left in a dispute over the group's direction. Mark Loomis "was the reason why the Watch Band came together," according to Aguilar. "He decided at one point that it was not going in the direction that he wanted it to go. He looked upon it, I think, as his personal band that he had put together, and he wanted to do different music. He wanted to do things more along the lines, I guess, of the Byrds.

"He just announced one day, I quit, and I'm taking Gary the drummer with me. I remember to this day saying, 'You're absolutely crazy. You have no idea what you have here! You have no idea about the potential. Yeah, we've had some problems in these first albums, but eventually we're gonna start recording our own album. We're gonna start doing our own stuff. You have no idea. You don't understand this at all anymore.' And he didn't."

Complicated lineup shuffles continued to afflict the group on their second and third albums. The first side of *The Inner Mystique*, in fact, does not even feature the group at all, but session musicians. By the time the third and final album (*One Step Beyond*) was released (without any input from Aguilar) in early 1969, the group had attained somewhat more control over their studio output. The final irony was that this was by far the least distinguished of the band's efforts, which had by now descended into below-average psychedelic music.

Few people outside of California had been aware of the Watch Band in the '60s. It took new generations of listeners in the 1980s and 1990s to raise the Chocolate Watch Band to somewhat mythic status. Reissues of their work in the U.S. and numerous European countries probably rate as some of the best-selling '60s garage catalog items around. Aguilar has recently recorded some tracks with a reformed Watch Band (minus the late Sean Tolby), and says he'll still get calls from 13-year-old boys in Ohio who have tracked him down and are "absolutely in love with our stuff." The fans on the other end of the phone are in for a shock as well—Aguilar went on to become a professor of astronomy in Colorado, and then into high-level scientific work in the aerospace industry. When I talk to him in late 1996, he was launching plans to start his own multimedia company. It's not exactly the kind of resume you'd expect from an ex-garage rock singer.

Aguilar himself continues to keep abreast of contemporary rock, mentioning Nirvana, Smashing Pumpkins, and Stone Temple Pilots as some of his current faves. "I think it's hard for people to understand what garage bands were about sometimes," he muses, "because today it *is* so commercial. And there are so few places for kids to play. But it was an era where every Friday and Saturday night, there were bands playing everywhere, all over town. That's what was so exciting, and that's why people had so much opportunity to play. Nobody had told us we couldn't do it, nobody told us we needed a manager, nobody told us that it was too difficult, so everyone *did* it. And I think that's something that we've lost today. I wish there were more kids out there playing music."

Recommended Recording:
The Best of the Chocolate Watch Band (1983, Rhino). Still the best of the several Watch Band compilations, including all the key singles and album cuts ("Let's Talk About Girls," "Sweet Young Thing," "Are You Gonna Be There," "I Ain't No Miracle Worker"), and bluesier songs from the *Riot on Sunset Strip* soundtrack that give a closer approximation of their live sound.

"My social life's a dud, my name is really mud!" snarls Sean Bonniwell on the Music Machine's "Talk Talk," the most radical single heard on Top 40 radio in late 1966. Against a succession of grinding two-note fuzz riffs and key changes that rise and rise until they hit the ceiling, Bonniwell spews and growls a rally cry to social alienation with a mixture of sarcasm, rebellion, self-pity, and paranoia. "Talk Talk" was one minute and 56 seconds of garage psychedelia at its most experimental and outrageous. "Chinese jazz," Bonniwell has called it, perhaps because *nobody* knew what to call it when it first came out.

Bonniwell wrote a bunch of other great songs for the Music Machine, but most of the world never got to hear them. Gross mismanagement and a series of bad breaks broke the spirit of the band after a year or so; by the beginning of the

The Music Machine

1970s, a disillusioned Bonniwell had quit the music business. Most galling, though, is that the Music Machine have now been tagged by many rock historians as a one-hit wonder, a garage band that said all they had to say in two minutes. Careful examination of their repertoire reveals them to be more properly classified as one of the top experimental-punk-psychedelic groups of all time. Their relentless invention in the studio was matched only by the restless metaphysical probing of Bonniwell's compositions.

As was the case with many other notable California rock bands of the time, the Music Machine's roots were not in tough rock 'n' roll, but in the commercial folk boom of the early 1960s. Bonniwell was part of a folk trio, the Wayfarers, that made a few albums for RCA, crossing paths with future stars like Cass Elliott, Bob Dylan (who told Sean never to be intimidated by the recording studio), and Byrds leader Roger McGuinn. Once he and McGuinn shared a ride

The Music Machine in their dressed-in-black, one-black-glove glory; singer and leader Sean Bonniwell in center.
Credit: Courtesy Sundazed Records

from San Francisco to L.A., singing Beatles songs along the way; McGuinn told him about a band he had started called the Jet Set, which would soon evolve into the Byrds. "He said folk-rock is what I want to do," remembers Bonniwell today. "I said, 'well, I don't know. I want to go to the hard stuff.'

"I really didn't think much of the Beatles. I enjoyed their musicianship, and I thought they were marvelous harmony singers, and of course great writers. But I really didn't think they were hard enough. They were a different standard for the direction that I was going in. All I knew is that I wanted to do something completely unique."

To pursue his lofty goal, Bonniwell enlisted drummer Ron Edgar, and Keith Olsen, who had played bass with folk-pop singer Gale Garnett (famous for "We'll Sing in the Sunshine"). Organist Doug Rhodes, who had played with soft-rock stars the Association, and guitarist Mark Landon made the group a quintet. By this time they had changed their name from the Ragamuffins to the Music Machine, in honor of the nonstop blast of originals they cranked out onstage. It was an unlikely cast of characters for the baddest rock group on the block, clawing their way up the intensely competitive L.A. scene through hotel lounges and bowling alleys.

What was behind the metamorphosis of Sean Bonniwell, clean-cut commercial folk balladeer, into a black-clad harbinger of complex messages of love and doom? "The idea of simply plugging folk instruments into electricity was an idea whose time had come. I think early rock 'n' roll was really electrified folk music, which explains the lyrical content of so much of the songs. Aside from the pop commercialism, the majority of the push or the motive for the songs was really a need to express the changing times. The conservative musical style of the times built up in me a frustration that I could really do nothing to stop from releasing."

From the outset, Bonniwell ensured that the Music Machine sounded like no one else by having the band tune their instruments down from the standard E to a D flat, giving them a bottom-heavy, ominous sound. Important contributions were also made by the screeching, buzzing, wiry tone of Landon's guitar, and the stop-start, cymbal-punctuated drumming of Edgar. Olsen produced the hardest, thickest, and most reverberant bass sound of his day. Tying this all together was engineer Paul Buff with his innovative production techniques (he invented a ten-track recording machine when most studios had four), as well as Olsen, who created a fuzz box that gave the band's records the fattest fuzz tone of the period.

"At the time, the recording technology, and even the speakers, didn't produce that thump in the chest from the bass and the bass drum," elaborates Bonniwell. "It's a hallmark today, it's something we all take for granted. But at the time, you really couldn't capture it on tape. And I really wanted that bottom power punch. I had Doug play way up on the Farfisa, so that the sound was spliced and separated as much as possible. I told [Ron], never play the cymbal. We used them only for accents." Of course, there were also Bonniwell's vocals, which could vary from a larynx-stretching gravel-growl to a quivering, sweet croon as the mood warranted.

It wasn't enough for the band to *sound* like nobody else; Bonniwell also made sure they *looked* like nobody else. To a man, they dyed their hair black, wore only black clothes, played black instruments, and wore one black glove at all times—even in public. After a few concerts the gloves would shrink into use-lessness from perspiration, and it got to the point where each musician was churning through three or four pairs a week. But to the group, it was more than a matter of keeping up appearances. As Bonniwell says, "We figured if we wore all black and played all original music, we wouldn't have to suffer the indignity of playing lounges and trying to pretend like we were a cover band."

Onstage the Music Machine segued nonstop from song to song for an hour or more, at a time when hardly any unknown bands were playing original mater-ial, and *no* bands were performing sets without as much as a few seconds of inter-ruption between tunes. The Hollywood Legion Lanes bowling alley became their regular gig, Bonniwell paying the club owner—who was nonplussed by packed houses that listened, rather than danced—$50 a week to keep the residency going. A couple of weeks after producer Brian Ross saw the band there, they were in RCA studios, cutting "Talk Talk" in two takes ("Come on In," originally planned as the A-side, was completed in just one pass). The whole session cost a mere $150. "I rehearsed the Music Machine mercilessly," admits Bonniwell now. "The songs were so finished by rehearsal and live performance that by the time we got into the studio to record them, we could do them backwards, literally."

For Bonniwell, the band's unity and dedication in the studio were features that set them apart from some of their more celebrated peers. "Like with the Buf-falo Springfield," he adds by way of illustration. "What an incredible band. I re-gard their work as far superior to mine in almost every way. But those people did nothing but fight in the studio. I mean, they spent a fortune recording. Because they experimented and they arranged, they'd sit there and get high, they'd argue, and they'd jam. I didn't want to have anything to do with that, because I knew that there was no clear vision there."

After getting picked up by Art Laboe's independent Original Sound label, "Talk Talk," after being a smash in L.A., crashed into the national Top 20 by the end of 1966. The band's first album, *Turn On*, served notice that Bonniwell was a songwriter of unusual complexity by 1966 standards, writing about alienation, frustration, and internal struggle with seductive, ambiguous dark mystery. Like every other male songwriter of the day, much of his angst was woman-related, but his romantic dilemmas were usually psychological rather than biological. His was not a one-sided, narcissistic rebellion; his anger was tempered by a sense of self-doubt and self-questioning. Bonniwell did not simply rail against prob-lems, as many punks from decades later would; he tried to make sense of the confusion surrounding him, with an empathy and compassion that invited the listener to share his struggle.

In these respects—as well as the band's use of high organ riffs and clear hi-low instrument separation—the Music Machine's material bore some similarity to that of the Doors, who would release their debut album slightly after "Talk Talk" became a hit. As to whether the Music Machine actually influenced the Doors, Bonniwell muses, "I have no way of knowing. My intuition tells me that [what the Doors played was] electrified folk music. Morrison's writing style is based on three- and four-chord passages utilizing relative minors, very much like folk music did. And he was a storyteller, very much like the folk era glorified. I think in that way, there were some similarities."

But the band's innovations were not wholly appreciated by their record company and managers, who, according to Bonniwell, seemed bent on mishandling their career from the word go. "Nobody gave a *damn* about how I wrote my songs, how we recorded them, the longevity of the band—nothing," he relates, with an anger that still simmers after 30 years. "I mean, we recorded the *Turn On* album after a 30-day tour. Mark's fingers were literally bleeding. I could hardly even speak, much less sing. We recorded the bulk of that album at three o'clock in the morning, after having pulled into town about seven that night, after [playing] every single night in a different town."

What especially infuriated Bonniwell, however, is that Original Sound insisted that almost half the album be Top 40 covers, although the band had a wealth of strong original material in reserve. Bonniwell did like the band's cover of "Hey Joe," the first slow rock version of that oft-interpreted '60s standard, recorded a few months before Jimi Hendrix also did a slow version on his debut single.

More serious problems were in store. "The People in Me," a strong follow-up single to "Talk Talk," stiffed at #66 when the band's managers angered a powerful radio honcho by giving the record an exclusive airing on a rival station. This, says Bonniwell, effectively killed the record's chance on the biggest Top 40 stations nationwide, and also damaged the prospects for other Music Machine singles (none of which so much as made the Top 100). The group's managers turned down an offer for a British tour, and more crucially, a spot at the pivotal Monterey Pop Festival in 1967. Instead of playing at the first major rock festival or in Europe, the Music Machine were zigzagging across the country on a series of one-nighters that were planned with little regard for the band's career or well-being.

Bonniwell agrees that the Music Machine should have been allowed to concentrate on albums geared toward the mushrooming market for long-playing records and serious, ambitious rock, rather than the Top 40. He had in fact envisioned Music Machine albums as nonstop segues of music with no interruption between individual songs, but Original Sound would have none of it. "They wanted me to write another 'Talk Talk'. They wanted us to pump out hit records. There was *no* thought given to the vision, or to the industry evolution, or the evolution of the audience into album rock and album concepts."

So it was that fine singles like the boiling "Double Yellow Line" (written on the way to a recording session, with one hand on the steering wheel and the other penning lyrics) got lost in the shuffle. "The Eagle Never Hunts the Fly" is the Music Machine's tour de force, and one of the great unsung moments in psychedelic music as a whole. While Bonniwell mixes concerns about both ecology and personal liberty into his most tortured vocal, compelling organ and bass riffs fight it out with epic fuzz guitar riffs and shock wave reverb. Bonniwell's scream/duck call in the instrumental break is one of the eeriest vocal sounds to be heard on *any* rock record ("my face got three shades of red" he proudly declared in an interview with the *Ugly Things* fanzine). Original Sound only released the single, he laughs, because label chief Art Laboe thought, for some unfathomable reason, that it sounded like the Count Five's dissimilar garage rock classic, "Psychotic Reaction." The song, he adds, is "little-understood today, and was even less understood back then."

But by the time of the single's release, the original Music Machine were splintering. Fed up with low royalties and a grueling tour schedule, they had had enough. Keith Olsen eventually became a mega-successful producer; 1975's Top Ten *Fleetwood Mac* album is his most famous credit. Bonniwell kept the Music Machine going with other musicians in a confusing period that saw his contract transferred to Warner Brothers, and some of his releases credited to "Bonniwell Music Machine."

The band's one Warner Brothers album, a mixture of tracks recorded by the original lineup and ones done by Bonniwell with other musicians, actually had its share of good-to-great moments. "Talk Me Down" and "Bottom of the Soul" were as hard-hitting as '60s pop-punk got; "Discrepancy" was extremely far-reaching even by Bonniwell standards, employing two different vocals singing two different lyrics *and* two different melodies. But Bonniwell readily concedes that he missed the original incarnation of the group terribly.

"I brought in so many different players when I was auditioning players for the Music Machine," he sighs. "That's why the Warner Brothers album has such an eclectic approach, not only with my songwriting so different in every aspect, but the approach to recording. Each [track] was a studio invention. That's why it's such a collection of potential singles, with the exception of a few songs.

"I also knew that the seven or eight people that I used in the recording studio really had no notion at all what they were doing. They played the right notes and tolerated my unyielding pursuit of excellence, for the most part. But I would have to go back in after they recorded, and I spent hours remixing and dubbing, just doing things that were joyless, because you're trying to capture something that isn't there. For the most part, I made them presentable, and there is some inspiration on a lot of those songs."

Had the original Music Machine lasted longer, he speculates, "I think Keith and I would have formed a partnership. He would have become the producer of the Music Machine, we would have produced other people, I would have written for other people, and we would have experimented. There's no telling how far we would have gone, because Keith and I had a creative energy and enthusiasm that was just unmatched. With our penchant for experimentation, and the way that I saw no limitations on songwriting—and never have—there's no telling what we would have gone into. I think it would been radical, I know that. It would have been unique."

After a commercially and artistically unsuccessful, heavily orchestrated solo album in 1970, Bonniwell retired from active recording. He went "into my transcendentalized western guru period, where I renounced capitalism, dropped out, and sold everything I had, got a 1948 Volkswagen bus, piled everything up that was important into it, and started off across the United States." Journeys into various kinds of mysticism, including astral projection ("I almost didn't get back a number of times"), ended when he embraced Christianity. "I finally realized that it was God who saved my life, and I'd better write it down, better give myself a reason for having gone through everything I did. Which is what started me writing the autobiography."

When we talk, Bonniwell is finishing revisions for the second edition of his book, living in, of all places, a converted garage. The 500-page volume, for that matter, is titled *Beyond the Garage*. Its scope includes—but is ultimately much wider than—the Music Machine story, also reflecting "my having been a teenager in the '50s, a rock celebrity in the '60s, a guru in the '70s, and a Christian from the '80s on. My life has paralleled the decades of American change." (*Beyond the Garage* is available from Christian Vision Publishing, P.O. Box 409, Porterville, CA 93258.)

In the last 15 years, Bonniwell has finally received his due as an important innovator by '60s rock aficionados, and most of the Music Machine catalog has been reissued. "Rock and roll was a teenager in the '60s, and I used that climate to express my confusion, my anger, at the injustice of the world, as expressed in the music," he theorizes. "Basically, it was art rock before there was such a thing as art rock. It's not so much that I'm the grandfather of punk. This isn't my own designation—this is given to me by people who now recognize a genre, or the early beginnings of a genre, that I was definitely a major contributor to. I never saw it before. I see that now."

Recommended Recordings:
The Best of the Music Machine (1984, Rhino). Superb 14-track distillation of their best tracks, including the best Original Sound singles, and some of the better cuts from the more obscure late '60s sessions. Bonniwell himself provides comments about each song in the liner notes.

Beyond the Garage (1995, Sundazed). The finest material from the Warner Brothers era, the best of which measures up to anything the band did, whether played by the original lineup or not.

The Mystic Tide

Joe Docko of the Mystic Tide, live at a teen club in the Plainview Shopping Center in Plainview, New York, 1966. Credit: Courtesy Dave Brown

Those of us too young to experience the '60s blues revival firsthand read the stories of the rediscovery of blues legends like Skip James with a touch of envy. How exciting was it, we wonder, to track down a legend who had been nothing more than a name on a record label? And how did those musicians react to the news that, unbeknownst to them, a growing cult of collectors revered the rare singles they had cut decades ago?

It's an element of mystery that's gone out of music scholarship, so I relish the chance to call Joe Docko, lead guitarist, singer, and songwriter for the Mystic Tide, one of the greatest garage bands of the '60s (and certainly the most obscure act detailed in this book). Calling them the pride of Woodbury, New York—a Long Island suburb—would be somewhat of an overstatement, given that the Mystic Tide even had trouble selling records in their own tiny hometown. That despite the magnificence of some of the material on the four singles they managed to release on their own labels in 1966-67, some of which anticipated the sound of underground acts with a much higher profile, such as Pink Floyd, the Doors, and the Velvet Underground.

We forget, however, that undiscovered legends like the old Delta blues musicians did not sit by the phone for 25 years, waiting for their rediscovery. They got on with their lives, sometimes continuing to play music, and sometimes giving up out of frustration and disinterest. It was the latter case with Joe Docko, who still resides in Woodbury, and who didn't pick up a guitar for some 18 years at one point. As he talks in his heavy New York accent, it's obvious he still hasn't quite gotten over the shock of getting calls— nearly 30 years after the band split up in the face of massive disinterest—from fans who weren't old enough to buy records when the Mystic Tide were recording. One gets the feeling that he's still more bewildered than flattered, and certainly not yet accustomed to giving interviews to the media.

Docko may also be puzzled because, truth to tell, there are no grand mysteries at the heart of the Mystic Tide legend. No missed opportunities with Columbia due to personality conflicts with producers. No bottom-of-the-bill encounters with visiting stars like the Stones or the Byrds. No wild electronic inventions. No violent breakups due to death or misadventure. No food fights. The group played their innovative material to mostly deaf ears, and split in the face of commercial indifference. What mystery remains is mostly contained on those excruciatingly rare singles.

And that is mystery aplenty for inquisitive ears. Playing his Fender Jazzmaster through a Fender Super-Reverb amp, Docko created shimmering, echo-laden psychedelic guitar leads that sounded like a collision of the Ventures and the Yardbirds. There were occasional upbeat, poppy tunes, but usually the songs explored dark and disturbing themes that distinguished them not only from the local bands working Long Island, but from most of the thousands of garage bands throughout the United States. "Mystery Ship" and "Mystic Eyes," with their eerie guitar glissandos and mysterious lyrics, sound like primitive antecedents to the Doors. "Psychedelic Journey" is a nearly ten-minute-long instrumental that sounds like a rawer take on Pink Floyd's legendary "Interstellar Overdrive." And "Frustration" is an all-time garage classic, with two different lead vocals singing simultaneously, grinding doomy chord progressions, and frenzied strangled leads from Docko that echo Lou Reed's similar "ostrich" guitar breaks with the early Velvet Underground.

What makes these songs all the more fascinating is that the Mystic Tide—a quartet in their teens—could not have been overly familiar with, and most likely were totally unaware of, the Doors, Velvet Underground, and Pink Floyd when they made their handful of 45s. Like numerous other young American musicians, they were having their heads blown by the Beatles, Stones, Yardbirds, Zombies, and Them. Unlike most Long Island bands, though, the group were determined to play their original material, crowd expectations—even those of audiences they played for at local dances and colleges—be damned.

Docko takes pains to explain that, contrary to what some people might think, the mid-'60s was not an era of unlimited freedom. "When you look back at that time, a lot was happening musically, especially with the British stuff coming on. But on the local scene in Long Island, it was very Top 40. There was also a lot of bad music being played. If you wanted to play local places, you had to do a lot of terrible music, which we refused to do. We did originals and stuff that we liked, and sort of bluesy stuff. That helped us in the long run, but in the short run back then it sort of hurt us. Some people flipped over it, and some people wanted Beach Boy music or soul music or just whatever the Top 40 [was] at the time. We refused to sell out.

"There was great stuff happening at that time around the world, like in England and Texas and different spots. But in Long Island it was really sort of a dead place as far as that music coming in. Maybe in a way, that added to the darker sound of our music—the frustration of what we had to play against around here."

That frustration not only spilled over to the title of one of their best songs, but to their experiences in the recording studio (where they had just three sessions). Engineers were not used to musicians playing at window-rattling volumes; nor were they receptive to young kids insisting on capturing that energy on vinyl. Compounding the conflict was the length of the Mystic Tide's original material, which often ran between five and ten minutes a song—an unheard-of duration in 1966. And, as Docko points out, they improvised and played their compositions differently every time—not an approach that was readily adaptable to the studio.

"You'd go in there trying to sound like the Who live in concert, and they had the Kingston Trio in mind," recalls Docko with amusement. "At that time in the studios there was no such thing as distortion overdrive. We turned up the amplifiers *way* up. The songs were longer than three minutes—at that time, there *were* no songs longer than three minutes! The engineers told us, 'Make the songs much shorter, put up baffles, turn the amps down.' They'd say, 'The tracks are bleeding from one instrument to another.' That was sort of a battle, getting the sound down. You'd [get] the records back, and it was *really* toned down from what you expected [it] to sound like."

What did end up on the records was pretty neat, even if a bit lo-fi by major label standards. The over-limited distortion on the guitars on cuts like "Frustration" give them a grab-you-by-the-throat immediacy that would be pretty impossible to re-create with today's super-sophisticated equipment. The discerning listeners of Woodbury, however, were not unduly impressed—the four Mystic Tide singles, pressed in small quantities by the band themselves, were not played on the radio and barely sold at all, even at their own gigs.

The creepy lyrics of "Running Through the Night" and the all-out improvisation of "Psychedelic Journey" (which had to be split into two sides of a 45 due to its mammoth length) showed that the band weren't exactly preoccupied with commercial success anyway. They were more into the kind of bluesy psychedelic improvisations of one of their favorite tracks, the Paul Butterfield Blues Band's landmark 13-minute instrumental "East-West." Although the group, according to Docko, came close to a major label deal a few times, nothing came of it. By 1967 the lack of a commercial breakthrough, as well as Docko's self-confessed dominant John Fogerty-like role in writing and singing all of the band's material, had led to internal friction in the group.

As impressive as some of their recordings were, the group were clearly still more a diamond in the rough than a major act at this point. One is tempted to speculate how much further they could have gone with more support and opportunity to hone their songwriting and instrumental craft (a few Docko originals, in fact, never made it onto tape). It wasn't to be—after briefly reducing to a three-piece, they split, unnoticed. Docko gave up playing guitar for almost 20 years. In a scenario guaranteed to cause heart failure among seasoned record collectors, he even threw out the original master tapes of the Mystic Tide, as well as most of the remaining original 45s.

That was before, of course, he learned that the original singles were fetching up to $500 on the collector's market. The tracks did come out on a weird unauthorized French reissue that put some Mystic Tide singles on one side of an LP, and rare 45s by a totally unrelated folk-pop-rock band from San Jose (the E-Types) on the other. In 1994, the entire Mystic Tide oeuvre—both sides of the four singles, three demos, and some newly recorded material by Docko—came out on CD on the Distortions label. Over 25 years after splitting up, the Mystic Tide had their first bona fide album.

One suspects the belated recognition is bittersweet for Docko, who had to phone his sister in Indiana and have his brother-in-law tape the Mystic Tides tracks for Distortions to use on the reissue, as he had no singles left himself. He can't locate two of his former Mystic Tide bandmates; the third seems totally disinterested in the group's cult status, failing to return phone calls even after receiving a copy of the CD. "I guess it was maybe too little, too late or something. The fact that it finally did find its audience is really, really surprising to me. It really just blows your mind. I thought it was ahead of its time. But not *that* far ahead," he laughs.

"The stuff we were playing and our sound actually would probably fit in very well today, like with the, whadayacallit"—the way he awkwardly searches for the right words makes it clear he's not simply parroting a trendy phrase—"alternative rock, that sort of stuff. Nowadays everyone improvises and jams and goes on and on. At that time, that's what we did. Groups like Yes, Emerson, Lake & Palmer—they had, like, jazz musicians coming in and classical musicians playing rock. We didn't fit with that. But with the current period, with the alternative rock, we would actually fit right in, right now, today. Maybe that's why we're popular."

Recommended Recording:
Solid Ground (1994, Distortions). The *only* Mystic Tide album, in fact, has all 11 of their surviving tracks from the 1960s, as well as a few much less impressive Docko outings from recent years.

'60s Garage Bands

The Music Machine, the Remains, the Chocolate Watch Band—all are, to some degree, heart-breaking tales of groups that got to the brink of big success before their dreams were shattered by record company politics, petty in-fighting, or bad luck. And just think—these were among the most *successful* of the so-called "garage bands." Far more typical were the experiences of the Mystic Tide or the Rising Storm. A few singles on a local label, a privately pressed album, and a few devoted listeners at the small-scale gigs and parties they played were their only material rewards before the musicians scattered.

The garage band phenomenon was so widespread throughout the United States that it wasn't until the 1980s that the explosion was properly appreciated, quantified, and (as is inevitable) catalogued and collected. To begin with, the term "garage band" wasn't even in common use when '60s garage bands were at their peak. The transformation of American, (mostly) male youth into long-haired teenagers bent on impersonating the Rolling Stones was too sudden and omnipresent to give rise to handy classification. And so few of the garage bands had national hits

Joe Docko at the Mystic Tide's last recording session, June 9, 1967, in Ultra Sonic Recording Studios, Hempstead, New York. Credit: Courtesy Dave Brown

that even when rock histories began to be written in the late '60s, most critics remained largely or wholly unaware of the sheer tonnage of wild and interesting sounds that had been recorded. Most of these records sold in quantities of a few thousand at most, and often only in the hundreds or dozens, making the task of finding the true gems a considerably difficult one.

The British Invasion was the match that started the fire of this distinctly American style. Overnight, bands were growing their hair and picking up guitars in attempts to emulate the Beatles, the Dave Clark Five, and (within a few months) meaner, bluesier groups like the Rolling Stones, Animals, and Kinks. The first garage bands began to appear in 1964, though most were still coming to grips with the responsibilities of writing their own material. Some notable acts made an impact that year. Minnesota's Gestures did a superb Mersey-surf hybrid called "Run, Run, Run" that almost made the Top 40. The much-loved Sonics stormed the Pacific Northwest with their crude pastiches of R&B, frat rock, and night stalker mayhem on regional singles like "The Witch" and "Psycho." But the garage scene didn't peak until 1965 and 1966, when the innovations of the Beatles and (to a somewhat larger degree) the Rolling Stones had been fully absorbed by adolescents and young adults.

These groups were on the average several years younger than their idols. Their music was understandably more juvenile and immature, not to say rawly executed. Their attitudes and energy—nasty and exuberant at once—are what the thousands of garage aficionados treasure. The guitar attack of bands such as the Yardbirds was exaggerated into thick fuzztone riffs, embellished by snarling vocals and cheesy Farfisa/Vox organ runs. Frequently the sneer was enough to cut through the often incredibly primitive recording equipment used to preserve their efforts on wax, though many would argue that these tracks were actually enhanced by the overamped guitars and needle-in-the-red vocals. At least these groups were playing, for the most part, live—with a rowdy flair that on many recent releases has been smothered by much modern technology and overdubbing.

The odds were heavily stacked against the garage bands becoming stars on the level of the Beatles or even the Byrds. There was just too much competition: there were only so many places on the charts, far less than could be accommodated by the average slew of garage releases in a typical week in 1966. This gave rise to dozens of regional scenes that were, in a way, precursors of the punk/new wave communities of the last 20 years. Bands played mostly for audiences in a 50-100 mile radius (sometimes more, frequently less). They also cut mountains of records, because even if they had no shot at the national hit parade, there was always the chance that they might be played on the local radio station—and sometimes even become big hits there, played alongside Herman's Hermits and Nancy Sinatra, while remaining unheard just a few counties away. Los Angeles, Boston, Minneapolis, Chicago, Pittsburgh, and Texas were home to particularly thriving garage band scenes, yet just about every mid-sized town (and some smaller ones) had one as well.

Many of the garage band rarities were mediocre, or excruciatingly awful: monotonous sub-Stones riffs, asthmatic vocals, woefully inept instrumentation and songwriting. Quite a few, however, were great—and not merely because of their excessive pre-punk energy. Many garage bands were not so much primitive diamonds as genuinely overlooked talents. Twenty or so years after they had vanished, they would claim international cult followings that far outweighed the recognition they had achieved during their youth. Many would argue that they deserved full-length treatment in a book such as this, rather than a scant sentence or two in a sidebar. But even this is much more than they've gotten in most other rock reference books.

Such a roll call would probably include the Seeds, famed for "Pushin' Too Hard" and Sky Saxon's inexhaustible (if monotonous) stoned ramblings; the Standells, a typical Hollywood club act who ingested the early Rolling Stones and came up with "Dirty Water"; the New Colony Six, who tempered the organ-driven R&B fury of Them and the Animals with clean-cut Midwestern pop harmonies. There were the Shadows of Knight, Chicago's answer to the Rolling Stones, who got a national hit with a cover of Them's "Gloria"; and Zakary Thaks, one of the most accomplished teen bands of all time, capable of both kamikaze-paced fuzz-blues stormers and intricate early psychedelic guitar riffs.

There were bands who landed one-shot hits when their singles were picked up for national distribution, like the Syndicate of Sound ("Little Girl") and the Count Five, with their glorious Yardbirds rip-off, "Psychotic Reaction." There were bands that crossed the garage band ethic with early mind-bending psychedelia, like the 13th Floor Elevators and the Electric Prunes. There were the Barbarians, the band with the hook-handed drummer, Moulty, who somehow landed a slot alongside the Rolling Stones, James Brown, Smokey Robinson, and other superstars in the legendary *T.A.M.I. Show* movie. There were the Lemon Drops, who crossed garage band pop with Donovanesque folk. We haven't even mentioned one-twentieth of the groups that have been exhumed by lengthy, loving fanzine retrospectives.

By 1968, the garage band era was largely over. The original musicians had moved on to more sophisticated music, had broken up to go to college or were drafted. Homogenizing trends in radio and the music industry meant less opportunities for such acts to record. Rock historians generally ignored the garage bands until the early '70s, when future Patti Smith Group guitarist Lenny Kaye compiled the *Nuggets* double album, featuring the very best (and most famous) garage band classics. In the mid-'70s, the garage bands were belatedly recognized as an influence on the primal fury of the early punk rock groups.

Yet *Nuggets* was just the tip of the iceberg. The past 20 years have seen a growing waterfall of literally thousands (no exaggeration) of reissues, extending from major-label acts to bands that weren't even aware of the recordings themselves. Stacks of fanzine reviews raving uncritically about generic batches of clumsy two- or three-chord wonders can be daunting for the newcomer, who just wants to get a handle on how to dig into this immense body of work. It's best to start with the *Nuggets* series (although it sounds like a sleek Mercedes in comparison with the average garage reissue), or the imperfect but extensive *Pebbles* compilations (several dozen volumes and counting), and pursue some individual favorites from there.

The Remains

On the inner sleeve of the Beatles' *Anthology Vol. 3* album, there's a small strip of type in the bottom left-hand corner reading simply: "The Remains." Unless you're a serious Beatleologist, you'd have a hard time deducing that it's not some enigmatic in-joke, but a fragment from the poster that advertised the Beatles' final live performance at San Francisco's Candlestick Park on August 29, 1966. The Remains, along with the Ronettes and the Cyrkle, were one of the warmup acts for the Fab Four's final American tour. Unlike those two other names at the bottom of that poster, they didn't even have a single national hit record to their name, and to this day are mostly known, if at all, for their brief association with the world's most popular rock group.

To those rock fans coming of age in Boston and New England in the mid-'60s, though, the Remains were much more than a trivia question. They were the best and hardest-rocking of the bands from the region, and indeed one of the two or three most unjustly overlooked American groups of the mid-'60s. At a time when U.S. acts had barely begun to grapple with the concept of writing their own material and growing their hair long, the Remains were one of the few American ensembles to meet the British Invaders on a level playing field, with a largely self-penned set that combined American rock/R&B raunch with the melodic finesse of the Zombies and Lennon-McCartney.

"Mention the Remains to anyone who lived in Boston during the golden years of 1965/1966," wrote Patti Smith Group guitarist Lenny Kaye in his liner notes to the *Nuggets* compilation, "and the result is likely to be the moans of pleasure that only accompany the truly great." But despite a quick major label deal, an appearance on the Ed Sullivan Show, and that prestigious gig with the Beatles, the Remains were rarely heard outside of New England and New York City, breaking up shortly after that Beatles tour, leaving their one and only album to flounder unpromoted.

Partly as a result of that *Nuggets* anthology—the first project to collect so-called "garage/punk" singles of the 1960s—the Remains are also remembered, rather inaccurately, as a garage band. If garage groups could be defined as longer on raw enthusiasm than talent, the Remains do not fit the bill. They offered both enthusiasm *and* an extremely tight, highly professional sound heavy on Rolling Stones-ish guitar, hard electric keyboards, and wild song-ending accelerations that were sort of U.S. counterpoints to the Yardbirds' more guitar-based "rave-ups." Penning most of the material was lead singer and guitarist Barry Tashian, who infused his compositions with the major-minor chord blends and tempo shifts that were characteristic of the best mid-'60s British Invasion groups, although the Remains—sometimes billed as Barry & the Remains—added a distinctly American sensibility.

There was little precedent for the Remains to follow on their home turf when they formed at Boston University in 1964 with a lineup that also included bassist Vern Miller, electric pianist Billy Briggs, and drummer Chip Damiani. "It seemed like most of the bands in Boston wore matching red waistcoats and clip-on bow ties," remembers Tashian. "They played cover tunes exclusively. Very good musically, but not much in the way of creativity. But the Remains began writing our own songs from the outset. I identified my cause with what the Stones were doing, making cool re-creations of great rhythm and blues records. I was young and going through a rebel phase, proclaiming my independence.

"My cause was, 'Let's get a group together and really listen to what one another is playing.' Rather than just mindlessly perform our particular functions, we created an interactive band machine. After a while, our rhythm patterns got very tight, like a four-headed, eight-armed creature, throbbing to a common

The Remains in New York City, 1966. Left to right: Vern Miller, Barry Tashian, Chip Damiani, Billy Briggs.
Credit: Courtesy Barry Tashian

wave. In time, this pulse became my obsession. It had to be reached in every performance, like a climax."

By early 1965 Epic Records had signed the band, but, to Tashian's frustration, "It was very hard to perform that climax that I mentioned earlier in the studio." To other ears, their first batch of singles actually sound pretty great, but the Remains felt they didn't capture the intensity of the group onstage, where a state-of-the-art sound system ensured that no matter how loud they turned the amps, the vocals would still be audible. Initially recording in New York City, in the summer of '65 they tried cutting tunes in Nashville under the direction of Billy Sherrill, later to become famous as the producer of mushy country hits by Charlie Rich, Tanya Tucker, and others.

There was nothing countrified about the Sherrill sessions, but the group remained somewhat frustrated about both their studio sound and their lack of a national hit record. In May of 1966, after four singles had gotten little attention outside of the Northeast, the group recorded a live-in-the-studio demo for Capitol. The label passed on the band, but Tashian feels that the results came a lot closer to the onstage frenzy of a Remains club gig in New York (where the band were playing much of the time by 1966).

All but one of the songs on that tape (now available on Sundazed's *A Session with the Remains*) was a cover, though. If the band were to break out of the major leagues, it would have to be with less shopworn material. Their sessions for Epic in New York in the summer of 1966 saw them exploring a number of directions, whether a wild guitar raveup of Petula Clark's (!) "Heart," or the tense soul-rock of "Don't Look Back," written by young songwriter and blue-eyed soul vocalist Billy Vera (who would top the charts in 1987 with "At This Moment," an MOR pop song from the *Family Ties* TV show). The most solid clue to Tashian's future direction, however, was a cover of Charlie Rich's "Lonely Weekend," as well as his own countryish ballad, "Thank You."

Before more progress could be made in the studio, however, that tour with the Beatles beckoned, N.D. Smart having now replaced Damiani on drums. Between shows, Tashian would listen to tapes of Indian music with George Harrison, who also took Barry to Hollywood parties featuring such luminaries as David Crosby and Roger McGuinn of the Byrds. With enough material in the can for a debut album, and very positive reviews for their slot on the bill (some reports even inferring that the Remains put on a better performance than the stars of the show), a breakthrough seemed imminent. But actually, a *breakup* was imminent.

"55,000 people make a lot of noise," reminisced Tashian. "It was a very thrilling experience for me. The low points were being accepted by the audience only to a limited degree compared to the Beatles. Duh!" he laughs, fully aware of the futility of competing with the group that were, as John Lennon had let slip shortly before the tour, now bigger than Jesus. "The lowest point was when the tour was finished and the low emotional backlash began. I decided, purely on an emotional basis, to dissolve the Remains."

Barry's decision was motivated to some degree with impatience for that all-important national hit, so important in the days before groups could survive via albums alone. In any case, the one Remains Epic album—patched together from singles and various sessions—was not released until *after* the tour, wasting the group's best promotional opportunity. The sheer logistics of keeping the Remains together and touring the Northeast were daunting in light of the fact that Smart was living in Ohio. By the time the LP came out, the Remains no longer existed, ensuring that the record became a rare collector's item (in 1991 it was reissued by Epic on CD, with plenty of extra tracks).

"In hindsight, I think Epic did all they could do," avers Tashian. "It wasn't enough, though. You can't shove a record down the public's throat and make it a hit. They could have probably pushed our singles harder. But Epic's priority at the time were the Yardbirds, Bobby Vinton, Ed Ames, and Mike Douglas. Sure, sometimes I wonder if we'd stayed with it, what would have happened. But there's no telling. We may have never had a hit."

Perhaps some sort of progress could have been made, he acknowledges, by "merely sticking with it longer and trying to achieve some sort of balance of the live, raw intensity we had and the more muted studio techniques. If the Remains had stayed together, we would have stayed with traditional-based music, meaning rock and roll, rhythm and blues, and blues styles. I never got into psychedelic music. It was not for me. I expect our original tunes would have tried to keep within that framework, and yet try to be commercial enough to garner us a hit."

In any case, Tashian's interest was now drifting, somewhat unexpectedly, to country music, partly as a result of his friendship with the International Submarine Band, Gram Parsons' first group. Tashian had met Parsons before the Beatles tour, when he and Bill Briggs would stay at the ISB's house in the Bronx, where the fledgling country-rockers would play Buck Owens songs. The International Submarine Band moved to Los Angeles soon afterwards, and in early 1967 Tashian and Briggs followed, playing in an embryonic version of the Flying Burrito Brothers with Submarine Band bassist Ian Dunlop. The name was adopted by Parsons and Chris Hillman for their own country-rock band, although Tashian and Briggs had gone back to Boston and tried to start their own Flying Burrito Brothers as a rhythm and blues group. "That didn't work, so it didn't last that long," admits Barry, although they were still billing themselves as the Flying Burrito Brothers when the Parsons-Hillman group bearing that name came through Boston. "So there were ads in the paper for the Flying Burrito Brothers East and the Flying Burrito Brothers West," he chuckles. "Sounds ridiculous now."

Tashian hasn't done too badly for himself in the ensuing 30 years, although it hasn't been as a rock 'n' roller. In the early '70s, he contributed guitar and vocals to Gram Parsons' *GP* album. In 1980, he joined Emmylou Harris' band as a replacement for future country superstar Ricky Skaggs, staying for nearly ten years. In the 1990s he's concentrated on country and bluegrass duets with his wife Holly. As I talk with him in late 1996, he's in the studio in Nashville (where he now lives), where they're working on their fifth album together. He's not reluctant to talk about the rock 'n' roll days, however; in fact, he's just published a book about his experiences on the 1966 Beatles tour, *Ticket to Ride*.

"Time brings about changes," he philosophizes. "I believe in the evolution and development of the individual. And my path led me to meet Gram Parsons, and to be struck by the country music he was singing. The work he did with the International Submarine Band, the Byrds, the Flying Burrito Brothers, later with Emmylou Harris and myself, really changed my taste from pure rock music to a quest for the true nature of country music. The trick at that time was to do a country song with a rock 'n' roll attitude. To do this, you'd have to know how to sing rock and roll songs, and know how to sing country songs. You'd then cross-pollinate. I've been interested in country music and traditional acoustic music like bluegrass, country blues, and old-time music for years now. I think that as I got older, a lot of the rebellious anger that fueled the great rock and rollers had dissipated.

"But I always have that rock 'n' roll attitude just hanging in the wings, easing out on stage now and then for a cameo appearance. I am quite proud of the work that the Remains did. Those recordings really sound great today. They *have* stood the test of time."

Recommended Recording:
The Remains (1991, Legacy). All the tracks from their 1966 album, plus almost a dozen non-LP singles and demos. Barry Tashian doesn't view the Remains' recordings as especially British Invasion-inspired. But this is nonetheless some of the best British Invasion-inspired rock recorded on either side of the Atlantic, with an equal footing in both the raunchy rock and melodic pop styles of mid-'60s British rock.

The Rising Storm

Phillips Academy in Andover, Massachusetts, is not the place you would expect to breed one of the most revered cult garage bands of the '60s. The prep school counts among its graduates George Bush, Oliver Wendell Holmes, and Edgar Rice Burroughs. It's a place where the affluent send their offspring to prepare for careers as respected doctors and lawyers, not to play rock 'n' roll.

The Rising Storm, who graduated from the institution in 1967, *did* go on to the professional careers for which they had been so assiduously groomed. Before they left, however, they found time to cut one of the most esteemed garage records of all time. *Calm Before*, pressed in a quantity of 500 and distributed primarily to fellow pupils, friends, and family, now fetches over $1,000 in mint condition. The revival of interest in the band has now become something of a story in itself, with National Public Radio reporting on their reunion gigs, and—unbelievably enough—serious interest from a major studio in filming the band's life story.

Somewhat lost in the shuffle is the music itself, which largely lives up to its reputation. The Rising Storm were not the only band of their ilk in the mid-'60s; there were enough vanity pressings of the sort, at Phillips Academy and similar places, to generate a mini-genre of "prep school rock" among hard-core collectors. Usually these LPs were jammed with cover versions of hits, and half of the Rising Storm album indeed features renditions of songs by "real" bands. It's the half devoted to self-penned songs that truly elevates this record from the pack, particularly the delicate, haunting folk-rock originals. These songs radiate an aura of innocence as mysterious as the cover, which shows the sextet perched on a rickety bridge over a desolate beach.

Tony Thompson, lead singer, rhythm guitarist, and leader (as he is described on the back of the LP), sets the scene: "We were all boarding students. We were away from distractions that most kids our age had, although we wished we weren't. We weren't around girls, it was a boys' school. We weren't around family. Our weekends were, for the most part, ours. Life was pretty simple.

"We used the time to practice our music. We would eat all our meals together and talk about music. The tables at school in the dining hall were perfect for our band, because they would seat six people in a fairly small space, and we would just talk music the whole time. My roommate was the bass player, Todd Cohen, for two years. He and I just thrived on putting the needle on the vinyl and working out the parts together. There was music always playing in our room, and other band members were also nearby, so that we would visit with each other. It's kind of hard to describe how integral music was to our lives. We were in classes together and walking between classes together. Every spare moment we had, we were talking about what song we were gonna practice next, what music we were listening to on the radio, what we liked, and what we didn't like."

The term "garage" band is an anomaly in a situation where there were no garages to be found. "We even had to be somewhat surreptitious about practicing. It was almost as if we were the bad boys. The kids who were in rock 'n' roll bands were not appreciated by the faculty, the administration. The music building was not set up to allow us to practice in any profitable manner, so to speak. We had to kind of scrimp and save our money for equipment, and we weren't allowed to make a lot of money—$50 a dance was the maximum. The school, I think rightly, was not interested in having us make a lot of money and become

Rising Storm, posing for the cover of their only album. Credit: Courtesy Erik Lindgren

popular outside the campus. They wanted us to concentrate on our studies. Can't blame 'em for that—that's what we were there for.

"But, as a result, when we wanted to practice, we found ourselves in closet-sized spaces, basements. We often were stopped from practicing by faculty members on Sunday mornings or on Saturday afternoons, or when they discovered us and we weren't supposed to be there. It was really very much part of our lives, practicing on the fly, finding a place to do it, and wheeling our equipment there and doing it."

Fueled by the Beatles, Stones, and more esoteric faves like Love and the Mothers of Invention, the Rising Storm were just one of several bands at Phillips Academy. It was, according to Thompson, almost a rite of passage for the groups to make a vanity pressing before graduating. So during spring break of 1967, the group gathered in the Boston area to record their one shot at immortality. It was cut for $1,000—out of funds the band had saved from their $50 gigs—in a mere week.

Calm Before, however, would be remembered as more than a mere vanity piece. Even as they prepared their (successful) applications to such hallowed institutions as Harvard and the University of North Carolina, they were determined to do something out of the ordinary on what unkind souls might call a class project of sorts. That's apparent even on the covers, which largely opt not for three-chord standards like "Gloria," "Hey Joe," or "Satisfaction," but for little-known tracks by Love, the Remains, and the Rockin' Ramrods, the last two of whom were primarily known only to Boston-area residents.

But it was the original material—to which the whole band contributed, but which was largely penned by Thompson and lead guitarist Bob Cohan—that was most memorable. "I'm Coming Home" and "She Loved Me" were acceptably R&B-tinged stompers, but the melancholic folk-rock cuts were something else altogether in their dreamy, melodic haze. As you might expect from adolescents on the verge of a massive upheaval in their somewhat insulated lives, there is a pervasive sense of about-to-be-lost innocence on Rich Weinberg's "The Rain Falls Down" and Cohan's mysterious "To L.N./Who Doesn't Know." Most mysterious of all is Thompson's "Frozen Laughter," which quotes from T.S. Eliot's "The Waste Land," backed by a mournful acoustic, drumless arrangement that winds down with a swirl of backward tapes. Apocalyptic is not exactly the word—it's more like a soundtrack for someone gazing out of a deserted seashore house that's inhabited by too many painful memories.

"The music was fairly unusual," notes Thompson with pride. "It was not copycat kind of lyrics, or copycat kind of chord progressions, for the most part. We tried to make statements about what was going on in our lives at the time, and how we felt about the world. The originals [were] for the most part slow, melodic music, and the lyrics were important. I think that was what distinguished it from other bands at the time." "Frozen Laughter," with its enigmatic references to orange shadows in the nighttime, "was very much about a state of mind that was not healthy, really. It was a drinking song. It was about having a relationship that went bad and what that does to you, how it makes you feel when you want it to end."

The Rising Storm took their music seriously, but took their budding professional interests much more seriously. No one expected to make a career out of music, and upon graduation, the band scattered to four different colleges, keeping in touch to varying degrees. And that was that for *Calm Before*, until 1981, when the group became aware of how hot an item the LP was among '60s collectors.

"When I first heard about garage music," laughs Thompson, now an attorney in Washington, D.C., "it was the late '70s, and I didn't know what it meant or what it was. I frankly thought that there was a misspelling and it was really 'garbage' music. And I'm not kidding. I thought people were making fun of it."

As for the revival of interest in the Rising Storm, "We didn't believe it, really. We thought that it must be some kind of mistake. There was a lot of skepticism about whether this was all cynical enthusiasm or real enthusiasm. On the other hand, as we began to realize that there were people who really were taking our music seriously, we decided to go with the flow for the most part and started bragging to all our friends about it."

The group even reunited for a class reunion in 1982, with Andy Paley (now a successful producer) on bass, even though by this time the members had long settled into careers in law, journalism, academia, medicine, and ski instruction. That reunion gig was released as an album, rather to the band's embarrassment, as they hadn't practiced much and weren't expecting the show to be recorded. Still, all six of the original members reconvened for a short "Ain't Dead Yet" tour in 1992, which included another class reunion at Andover, some new studio recordings, a feature story in the *Washington Post* magazine, and, in the strangest twist, the stirrings of interest from a classmate who had become an independent film producer.

Warner Brothers has now purchased an option on the band's story. Thompson tells me that the producers are considering such modifications as changing the character of Erik Lindgren (the producer who instigated the Rising Storm reunion) to a woman who becomes romantically involved with two of the band members, marrying one of them. Apparently, Hollywood treats the '60s garage band phenomenon with as much attention to accuracy as it did in such rock docudramas as *The Buddy Holly Story*.

Thompson, though "euphoric" about the latter-day acclaim for the band, keeps his expectations in perspective. "The kind of stuff that we were doing was very similar to alternative music now. I've always felt what has not shone through this for the most part, in all the publicity surrounding the Rising Storm since we were 'rediscovered,' is the music. People aren't focusing on the music. They're focusing on the story. It's kind of a snowball effect—we're famous because we're famous, not because of anything else.

"Warner Brothers wants to do a movie because, gee, this is a neat story about a band that was rediscovered. Not because the music's good, but because it's a neat story. It's kind of a circular, very weird phenomenon, where success breeds success, and relates very little to the music."

What's it like, then, for a group to start playing together a good 15 years or so after they thought they'd played their last note? "It's very difficult, I should tell you, at this stage in our lives as a band, to get together and to do something good. Musically, we're all fine. I feel that I've gotten a lot better. I think others in the band have gotten a lot better. But musically, it's been so long since we were sitting around that table, talking together and being together day after day, month after month, year after year. We're not there anymore. We're all leading different lives, and our musical tastes have diverged, our philosophies about life have diverged, our goals in life have diverged. Our closeness and our willingness to put up with each other's quirks, our patience with each other, our tolerance for each other, has dissipated.

"I don't mean that to sound like it's a bad thing, or an unhealthy thing. It's a very natural thing. I think we're all smart enough that we can put those differences aside to a point. But we don't have the congruence that we had in 1967. I don't think there's any way we ever could have that again, unless suddenly we were back in an environment where we really were playing and communicating on a spiritual level again all the time. That's what makes bands good, is that there is that philosophical oneness, that group sense. We all would love that to be possible, but it's not realistic."

Recommended Recordings:
Calm Before (1967, Arf Arf). After years of floating around only as a collectible with a sky-high price tag, or as a French bootleg, the legendary 1967 album is now readily available on CD. The disc also includes their 1982 reunion show, *Alive Again at Andover.*

Psychedelic Unknowns

On the radar screen of rock history psychedelic music was little more than a blip—a flurry of activity in the late '60s that only lasted for a few years before musicians came to their senses and retreated into more conventional sounds. Only a few psychedelic acts became truly huge—the Beatles in their *Sgt. Pepper* era, Jimi Hendrix, the Jefferson Airplane, the Doors, Pink Floyd (who soon became prog rockers anyway), and a few others. But the years 1966–1969 saw a truly vast assortment of reckless experimental efforts devised for public consumption on both sides of the Atlantic. The LP format had taken over from the 45 as a prime vehicle, its increased space offering far greater freedom for length, variety, and conceptually linked works. Major labels, for a brief time, were receptive to sounds and notions that would have been stopped at the door just a year or two previously.

Many of these records were indeed truly self-indulgent, or even dreadful, as groups took advantage of their freedom to engage in bloated jams or half-assed pretensions inspired by a breeze through Tolkien's *Lord of the Rings*. But—as is the case with every genre that is slowly milked to death—there were also quite a few truly inspired outings that explored intriguing directions that not only were little traveled in their time, but have been little traveled since. By their very nature, many of these ambitious works were uncommercial. They were also often too weird, or too long, for radio to comfortably program, or labels to sensibly market.

It's thus unsurprising that many of the most interesting psychedelic groups lasted for a mere record or two before blowing apart in frustration; several of the psychedelic bands that managed only one album (Tomorrow, the United States of America, Judy Henske/Jerry Yester) are written about in the section on one-shot artists. To them could be added such intriguing one-offs as Clear Light, which sounded like the Elektra Records roster (the Doors, Tim Buckley, Love) being tossed into a blender; J.K. & Company, who made a beautiful, mysterious album of sedate folk-psychedelia that blended some of the better aspects of Donovan and George Harrison; Faine Jade, who sounded like a dead ringer for an American Syd Barrett; the Lollipop Shoppe, who sounded like a rawer version of Love with their punk-folk-rock-psychedelia; and the C.A. Quintet, who wrote songs about cold spiders and trips through hell, backed by martial trumpet fanfares and guitars that squawked like outboard motors. A two-shot group of note, though their debut far outshone their second effort, were H.P. Lovecraft, who sang haunting science-fiction-influenced songs with unison folk-rock harmonies that nearly matched those of the Jefferson Airplane.

As befits the diverse nature of the style, the four acts profiled here illuminate very different sides of the psychedelic experience. The Deviants took their cues from the scathing satire of the Fugs and the Mothers of Invention, as well as bone-crunching blues-rock; the Blossom Toes were British psychedelia at its most carefree before they suddenly plumbed into the darker aspects of the Love Generation. The Great Society came tantalizingly close to a national breakthrough with their fusion of jazz, Indian, and rock music before lead singer Grace Slick left for the Jefferson Airplane. And the Misunderstood's stranger-than-fiction transatlantic misadventure—which knocked the wind out of one of the '60s most promising bands—rates among rock's greatest tragedies of unfulfilled potential.

Mick Farren of the Deviants sings on left; woman on right not sure whether dancing is appropriate response. Credit: Courtesy Mick Farren

The Blossom Toes

The British psychedelic scene of the late 1960s was littered with dozens of ridiculous names, along the lines of the Orange Seaweed, Mandrake Paddle Steamer, and the Glass Menagerie. Often the music these outfits created was as tutti-frutti as their monikers. You could be forgiven for dismissing the Blossom Toes out of hand for those very reasons, in the unlikely event you should come across one of their records.

But the London band—which, for one thing, hated their name, which they didn't pick themselves—are the most notable exception that proves the Rotten Name rule. Perhaps no other British group of the era, psychedelic or otherwise, recorded such fine music with such little recognition to show for it. Of all the bands in rock history that have recorded just two albums, few can match the Blossom Toes' rare feat of producing albums that were not only first-rate, but totally different from each other. The first was orchestrated pop-psychedelic English summer-day whimsy; the second was all heavy guitars and March of Doom lyrics, closer in tone to Captain Beefheart than the Kinks. Within years the records had built up a tremendous mystique in hardcore collector circles, frequently cited as the psychedelic relics most worthy of being reissued (which they were, finally, in the late 1980s).

The group's idiosyncratic achievement could have hardly been foreseen in the mid-1960s. At that time they were the Ingoes, one of the zillions of British R&B bands trying to get a foothold in a country where supply exceeded demand. They were fortunate enough to become clients of British impresario Giorgio Gomelsky (manager of the Yardbirds and mentor of numerous other innovative U.K. acts), and an 18-month residency in France bolstered their chops. Signed to Gomelsky's Marmalade label, the Ingoes were assigned

The Blossom Toes in their late-1960s psychedelic finery.

the Blossom Toes name against their will, and set about writing material for their first LP in 1967.

Their debut album, *We Are Ever So Clean,* is remarkable for its wealth of strong original material, since the band, less than a year previously, had been mostly doing R&B/soul covers. Guitarist Brian Godding, the most prolific and probably most talented composer in the group, had in fact been writing songs for a while. But these tunes were not soul/mod derivations. These were eccentric, oh-so-British character sketches about watchmakers, balloonists, frozen dogs, and being late for tea, delivered with a euphoric, druggy spirit well in keeping with the ambience of London 1967. Intricate, brass-heavy orchestration embellished the basic guitar-bass-drum arrangements of the band. The whole effect was something akin to the Kinks jamming with the Salvation Army on the village green on Sunday afternoon.

Godding denies that the group were unduly influenced by, or even particularly big fans, of the Kinks. In fact, while he's reasonably proud of the album, he takes care to point out that it wasn't exactly a project over which the Blossom Toes had 100% control. "It was a very hard record to make, because A) we weren't very experienced in the recording studio, and B) in those days, because of union rules and things like that and the limitations of tape recording—there was only four-track machines—you tended to have to do everything at once. So if Giorgio said, 'Well, we'll have a 20-piece band on this,' you had to do it with them. You couldn't say, 'Right, we'll put it down, and you can get him to overdub it.' You had to actually go out there and perform everything with these

Credit: Courtesy Brian Godding

guys, who were all professional session musicians, good musicians. We were learning to play, and these guys were professional, top-shit musicians. It was very intimidating sometimes.

We would demo those tunes, and then give them to the arranger, mainly David Whitaker, who's good and imaginative. And then he'd come up with the arrangement. But by the time he came up with it, that was it. We didn't talk about whether we liked it or not, he just went and did it. Fortunately, I can listen to it and think, 'yeah, I do like it,' but there was no discussion. Apart from that, David Whitaker is a man you don't discuss things with. He's a very nice guy, but if you say 'I don't like that,' he throws an artistic moody like you've never seen in your life.

"The first album, it wasn't our product. It was kind of like a joint venture between us and Giorgio and the arranger. We never felt that was our record, even when it was finished."

Another major frustration for the group was that due to the complexity of the arrangements, little of the material could be played live. A bootleg of a 1967 Swedish performance confirms that what they were playing in concert bore little relationship to what they had done in the studio. In fact, it's a downright sloppy gig, with chaotic improvisation rather than droll songwriting being the order of the day. Not that the offers for live work were pouring in, as the album sold little in the U.K., and there were no hit singles.

Thus it was that, after a couple of personnel changes, the band, in Godding's words, "vowed after making the first record that if we made another, we'd never do it the same way. We wouldn't go through that again, with all these arrangements, orchestration, that stuff. We thought, we've got to make a record we can play. All the stuff on the second album became our stage music."

Blossom Toes play all the music on the second album, *If Only for a Moment*, which is notable for some of the classiest proto-progressive rock dual guitar leads (between Godding and Jim Cregan) you're likely to come across. The group's wistful vocal harmonies are also intact, but make no mistake—this is a hard-rocking,

Brian Godding onstage with the Blossom Toes. Credit: Courtesy Brian Godding

sometimes downright *heavy* band, and the chirpy chamber orchestra of the first LP is gone for good. Most surprising, however, is the somber lyrical tone of the extended compositions, dealing with bombs, war protests, and tortured uncertainty. Bassist Brian Belshaw does a Lurch-like vocal on "Peace Loving Man" that makes Captain Beefheart (one of their big influences at the time) sound like Tony Bennett. It's almost as if the smiley face of the debut album has been inverted into a puzzled frown.

"Lyrically, the second album is a much more serious record," observes Godding. "It's like deaths and bombs and killing people and all that sort of stuff, and brain damage. I don't want to say that we were druggies or anything, but LSD was quite influential. Also we were touring in areas like Czechoslovakia and places which were having pretty heavy-duty political scenes, with the Russians moving in and Dubcek rushing out. All this influences you, it kind of makes you sort of look at life slightly differently. That second one bordered on a protest album."

Unfortunately, the Blossom Toes themselves went over much better on the European continent (where they played quite a few festivals) and in places like Prague (where they were able to fill amphitheaters seating over 10,000 people) than at home. In Britain they continued to slog it out on the club circuit, where they were sometimes threatened by physical violence at miner's clubs and workingman's clubs not inclined to listen to songs like "Love Bomb" and "Peace Loving Man." The final straw arrived at the end of 1969, when the group's van overturned on the way back from a gig. No one was seriously hurt, but combined with the continual strain of limited success and the touring grind, the group never ended up reconvening. Godding, bassist Brian Belshaw, and Kevin Westlake, who was the drummer on the first LP, did make an album under the name B.B. Blunder in the early '70s. Westlake's successor, Barry Reeves, moved on to the most unlikely gig of drummer with the James Last Orchestra, one of the longest-running easy listening outfits in Europe.

Godding has kept busy with many rock and jazz projects since. These days he plays in British jazzman Mike Westbrook's band, which tours their avant-garde take on the Beatles' *Abbey Road* (in fact, Godding lives in St. John's Wood, just a ten-minute walk away from Abbey Road Studios). Still proud of his tenure in the Blossom Toes (if a bit bemused by this American writer sipping tea in his flat who's gone to so much trouble to track down a member from a band that is totally unknown in the U.S.), he nonetheless has few regrets about the group's demise. He points out that the act had run its course in the face of strained financial circumstances and little record company support.

"By the time the Blossom Toes split up, we were playing all the stuff from the second album, and we could do it in our sleep. You could go on stage pissed out of your head and it wouldn't make the slightest bit of difference. It gets to the point where once you lost that edge in your head, then you lose your direction, then you lose your interest, and other things start taking over. You start thinking, I've got to do something else 'cause I'm just becoming like the Swinging Blue Jeans. Which is not an insult to them, because that's what they want to do, which is fine. They just want to go out and have a good time, make people dance, and they're happy. But if you want something else out of it, then it goes."

Recommended Recording:
Collection (1988, Decal, UK). A double LP with most of the first album, all of the second, and a non-LP single. Almost everything is here, and it's much easier to find than the original releases.

"When it was noised abroad that the Deviants were to record an LP I hoped that it would be good but feared that it would not be so . . . they were loud, enthusiastic, repetitive, manic and not very good."

— John Peel, from the liner notes to *Ptooff!*, the first album by the Deviants, 1967.

The Deviants

That's not the sort of ringing endorsement an up-and-coming band is hoping for when the top underground rock radio personality in Britain writes the liner notes for their debut record. But between the time Peel—who is still, incidentally, the top underground rock radio personality in Britain, 30 years later—first saw the Deviants in London's legendary Marquee club, and the time *Ptooff!* was released, a minor miracle had occurred. The scruffy underground act were only minimally competent instrumentalists; they had only worked up a bare handful of original tunes. But they had managed to synthesize their wildly diverse plate of influences—Frank Zappa, the Who, Charles Mingus, the Velvet Underground, the Fugs, and more—into an album that transcended the group's limitations and became something of a minor masterpiece.

Was it psychedelic music, blues-rock, avant-rock, proto-punk, or comedy? All of the above at times; none of the above all the time. What *Ptooff!* offered was a combination acid trip/horror show. The roller coaster ride went through maddeningly repetitive metallic bone-crunchers, beautiful flower-power ballads, Cagean experiments in musique concrete, deliberately offensive comedy, solemn poetry, and sound collages that referenced Jimi Hendrix, Bo Diddley, and Swinging London nightlife. The Deviants may have been aligned with the hippie/underground movement. Yet if this was flower-power and free love, it was delivered with a sneer that had no patience for a mindless flight from reality, with an anarchic energy that looked forward a full decade to punk.

The mainstay of the group was lead singer Mick Farren, a "just ex-art student" when the band formed in 1966. The pounding British Invasion R&B of fellow art-school acts like the Rolling Stones and Pretty Things was the Deviants' heritage. The group—first called the Social Deviants, then shortened to just the Deviants—were, according to Farren, "trying to push it in simultaneously a more demented and more intelligent direction. 'Cause we couldn't really be spending our time recycling old Jimmy Reed tunes . . . . There was a certain happy-go-lucky, pill-taking attitude to it all."

The Deviants performing in front of St. Paul's Cathedral, London, late 1960s, at an anti-apartheid event lobbying for the freedom of Nelson Mandela. Mick Farren on vocals. Credit: Courtesy Mick Farren

For inspiration, the Deviants looked to the radically uncommercial music of New York bands like the Fugs and the Velvet Underground. The relatively primitive instrumental skills of these groups was no drawback in the Deviants' eyes; they themselves couldn't play that well in conventional terms. And in any case, limited finances meant that massive speakers and PAs were little more than wishful thinking. "We were trying to blend it all into something that made sense, without very much money," notes Farren. "The Fugs had a certain kind of jug-band appeal, which fitted our income at the time."

Through Joe Boyd, a London-based American who was producing and staging shows by underground groups such as Pink Floyd, the Deviants came into possession of some early unreleased, drummerless tapes of the Velvet Underground. Farren was beginning to think he'd dreamed the tapes' existence before these exact tapes surfaced as the first disc of the Velvet Underground box set in 1995; the Deviants even covered an unreleased Lou Reed composition from that reel ("Prominent Men"). The Deviants were striving for the fusion of avant-garde ideas with elemental rock, and listening to the Velvets' sparsely arranged demos of "Venus in Furs" and "All Tomorrow's Parties," Farren felt the VU were arriving at a "similar kind of synthesis."

The Deviants wouldn't get a chance to commit their visions to vinyl until late 1967. A rich acquaintance of the band had inherited a fortune when his father committed suicide. He kindly redirected a few thousand or so pounds to the Deviants, who took the money to fund the studio sessions that gave birth to *Ptooff!*

The results were difficult to compare to much else in either the London or U.S. underground, with the possible exception of the early albums of Frank Zappa and the Mothers of Invention. This was particularly evident in the longest, most ambitious cuts, which were multi-part suites of sorts that craftily juxtaposed blues-rock, pulsating guitar feedback, poetry, found sound clips, and satire. The satire got especially gross on "Garbage," with over-the-top retches and simulated on-mike vomiting, followed by Farren urging his listeners to buy, stroke, and fondle refuse. "Deviation Street" was a nine-minute audio collage of Swinging London, segueing from cliched blues-rock and Pretty Things-styled R&B to screaming audiences, stoned partygoers, blissed out sitar-backed mysticism, and Farren's snide remarks about CIA agents and hippies.

The social criticism/satire got particularly vicious on "Nothing Man," where doom-laden percussion effects, faint howling choirs, and eerie tape manipulations provided the backdrop for Farren's spoken attack on the contemporary Nothing Man. The Nothing Man seems to be a symbol of all that the Deviants were pissed off about, incapable of any emotion but hate, able to think but not to feel. Much of the credit for the unusual effects on this track is due to a friend of the band, J. Henry Moore, who had been a pupil of John Cage. Moore would use unusually placed tape recorders to devise musique concrete effects, which (again, aside from Zappa's early work) had rarely been heard in a rock context.

Farren admits that this type of inventiveness was impossible to successfully recreate onstage. In order to construct the lengthy experimental tracks in the studio, the band had to extract the best 45-second excerpts from what they could perform live, "and collage it in with a lot of other stuff. Which was too unwieldy to do live. I mean, even Zappa had problems with [doing such things live]. We wanted to do bits of this, bits of that, lay backing vocals on there that we really couldn't reproduce in a live context. But as a recording entity, it really just fell into place."

The best representation of what the Deviants could sound like live may be "I'm Coming Home," wedding an insistently repetitive hard rock riff to Farren's lustful lyrics. Farren compares the track to the Velvet Underground's similarly bludgeoning "Sister Ray," "because the big thing we did was the 'Sister Ray'-style, endless, monotonous guitar thrash thing. We were one of the first bands doing it. Then about a year later, we heard the first Stooges record, the MC5's 'Kick Out the Jams,' and thought, ah, kindred spirits. But no way were we as tricky, tight, and together as the MC5. The Stooges jumped in, and sort of did what we were doing live on a record."

Although *Ptooff!* only contained seven songs, it covered yet more territory with a couple of beautifully melodic, acoustic flowery ballads, one of which ("Bun") was a Spanish/classical guitar-styled instrumental. Farren passes the responsibility for these to guitarist Cord Rees, who was only a Deviant briefly—"I always felt they were kind of a sop to the worst kind of Donovan fey hippie Incredible String Band mentality in the audience." His feelings are unchanged; when *Ptooff!* was reissued on CD in the States recently, Farren deleted these two tracks, as well as the routine blues-rocker "Charlie."

Issued in a Roy Lichtenstein-inspired pop-art/comic book foldout cover, *Ptooff!* did brisk business for a self-pressed release, with many of the sales coming from underground head and poster shops. For all its underground credibility, there were few other indie releases in the London psychedelic scene. "It's a pity there weren't more indie labels back then, because there was a lot of good stuff going on. The only claim to fame the Deviants had is we managed to persevere and actually get some stuff down onto vinyl. 'Cause there are other bands, like the Brothers Grimm and the Giant Sun Troll and the whole list of them you see on posters. But they never actually got to record. And back in those days, you didn't tape the shows, because we didn't have the technology. So a lot of that stuff was lost. Fortunately, we weren't. That was an incredibly lucky break, or we would have just been a name on a poster."

In retrospect, Farren feels the original Deviants may have played all their cards with *Ptooff!* "We heavily immersed ourselves in the *Freak Out* album [by the Mothers of Invention] and cut-up techniques. All that was really shoveled into the first one, which I think really exhausted a lot of the ideas, and a great deal of the spirit. The subsequent records were much more what we were doing on the road. In hindsight, I'm self-depreciating and say there's more luck than judgment. But I think we had something going, a kind of spirit of adventure that you can only have when you really don't know there are any rules to break."

Before their split at the end of the '60s, the Deviants would issue two more albums. I'm thinking how to broach the subject gently, as *Disposable* (1968) more than lived up to its name with its sub-Fugs sort of satirical rock. #3 (1969) found the band going into a much more straight rock direction; guitarist Paul Rudolph wrote most of the material, and Farren contributed nothing songwise. But although a couple of the cuts approach the sort of guitar-oriented psychedelia identified with the Yardbirds in their Jimmy Page days, the Deviants didn't have the straight rock chops to compete at that game successfully. I needn't worry; Farren feels the same way.

"The first album, we didn't really know enough to be daunted by what we were attempting to do," he theorizes. "On the second one, we learned a bit more, which was just enough to make it bad. Much the same applies to the third one."

There were still some good times to be had on the road. Never one to shirk from taking risks onstage as well as in the studio, the Deviants played sit-ins and other politically charged events in Europe that sometimes developed into riots. Fires and explosives often left the stage a mess. Even the hippies could find the group hard to handle. "There was a definite kind of Beefheart and the Magic Band weirdness about the Deviants that really upset people. They'd be there with their beads and bells, and really not understand why we were snarling at them and setting fire to our arms. All this sort of smoke and mayhem—they thought that was all a bit aggressive."

Nor were they particularly loved in the British provinces, where long hair was still an invitation to have one's manhood questioned. Opening for the newly formed Led Zeppelin, "We played the Exeter town hall, and all those farm boys showed up. Some girls were watching us at the front, and the farm boys said, why are you watching them faggots? These fistfights started, the cops came, and we scurried back into the dressing room after beating our way off the stage, the roadies sort of fighting a rear guard. Physically fighting any people with microphone stands. Plant and Page are laughing their heads off, going, god, you must have been awful. And they went on to exactly the same reception. It's hard to really grasp how little it took to offend people back in 1968."

The Deviants remained unknown in the United States, although Seymour Stein of Sire Records became a fan and arranged for *Ptooff!* to be released stateside. Ironically, it was their one and only tour of the U.S. that proved to be the straw that broke the back of the original Deviants. After some rough gigs in the Northwest, Farren left the group. When Stein got wind of Farren's departure, he withdrew tour support, which effectively ended the band. In retrospect, Farren wishes the Deviants had concentrated their American gigs around New York, the area in which he thought they were most likely to be appreciated.

Farren went on to make a solo album; the rest of the Deviants mutated into the Pink Fairies in the '70s (with occasional contributions from Farren). Farren reactivated the Deviants for a spiffy EP on the new wave-oriented Stiff label in the late '70s, delivering punkoid satires like "Screwed Up" and "Let's Loot the Supermarket" with savage humor. "It was a way of getting people into the studio with me, but they were on my dime rather than their own," points out Farren. "So they could leave their conflicts at the door. There's nothing so good as getting a bunch of musicians who are at odds with each other, and putting them in a studio where they're not responsible, they just have to do what they're told."

These days Farren is much more well known as a writer than a musician. He'd actually been writing since the Deviants days, and after their demise made a name for himself as a noted rock critic, working on books about Elvis Presley and the British beat boom, and contributing to *Trouser Press*, the top new wave magazine in the U.S. By the 1980s he was living in the States, and had embarked on a series of successful science fiction and vampire novels. He's currently also working as a screenwriter in Los Angeles; two recent projects include a treatment of the life story of Latin American revolutionary Che Guevara, and a fictional study of a late-'60s British rock band (not, however, based on the Deviants). He also periodically records and performs with new versions of the Deviants, his scathing, nasal style and poetic delivery still intact.

Although relatively few people heard the Deviants, Farren thinks that "certainly the spirit of what the Deviants were doing translated absolutely to people like Jones and Strummer and Rotten. McLaren, basically, in the early days of the Pistols, was using the same kind of schtick that I'd been beating people with ten, nine, eight years earlier. When Patti [Smith] was first going up with Lenny [Kaye], that was really our formative sound, except that Patti was a lot more self-consciously poetic. The Ramones and the Pistols played much shorter songs, 'cause we'd keep that thrash thing going for 20 minutes. And we didn't play it quite as fast. But beyond that, it was the same electric razor."

The day of recognition for *Ptooff!*, however, may be around the corner. "I keep getting these fanzines in the mail where they're cross-referencing it with lo-fi industrial music by bands that I've never heard of. But it seems to strike some kind of resonant chord with the youth of today, which is kind of mind-boggling." He giggles, with a mixture of pride and bewilderment. "It's also very satisfying. After all those years, the damn thing starts to make sense to *somebody!*"

Recommended Recording:
Ptooff! (1967, Sire). The essential Deviants album is a circus of '60s underground rock styles, delivered with a punkish attitude and relentless imagination that belies the band's rudimentary skills. If possible, try to find the original poster cover edition. The mid-1990s reissue is a truncated version that eliminates the softer songs, a couple of which, Farren's opinion to the contrary, are melodic psychedelic meditations that add to the diversity of the record considerably.

The Great Society

It was September 11, 1966, and the Great Society—one of the most promising up-and-coming psychedelic bands in San Francisco—were headlining the esteemed Fillmore over the Jefferson Airplane and the Grateful Dead. Vocalist Grace Slick brought the show a frenzied climax by screaming "Feed your head!," the crowning line of her own composition, "White Rabbit." Along with "Somebody To Love"—written by the band's lead guitarist, Darby Slick, who was also Grace's brother-in-law—it was the most popular song in the still-young band's repertoire.

"We seemed unable to do anything wrong," wrote Darby Slick about that night in his autobiography, *Don't You Want Somebody to Love.* "It felt like the audience was worshiping us, and we played with more emotion than ever before . . . . Certainly, this show has remained one of the performance highlights of my life."

The glow was short-lived. As the band were packing up, drummer Jerry Slick, brother of Darby and husband of Grace, broke the bad news. The Jefferson Airplane, wishing to replace their original female singer (Signe Anderson), had offered the spot to Grace Slick. With encouragement from Jerry, Grace had accepted. With only one poorly distributed single to their name, the band's career was over. They were almost as short-lived as the ambitious program of liberal social measures that president Lyndon Johnson had introduced under the "Great Society" umbrella shortly before the band took that name as their own.

For the past 30 years, the Great Society usually have been remembered only because Grace Slick added those two showstopping numbers, "White Rabbit" and "Somebody to Love," to the repertoire of the Jefferson Airplane. In 1967, the Airplane's own versions became monster Top Ten hits, spreading the hippie gospel into Middle America and beyond. By the time the Airplane recorded those songs for their second album, Darby Slick was several continents away, immersing himself in the study of Indian music. Were it not for some live tapes of the Great Society that were posthumously issued to capitalize on Grace Slick's fame, the band's recorded legacy would be virtually nonexistent.

The Great Society were much more than a trivia question, however. They were one of the best and most innovative psychedelic outfits, doing a great deal to incorporate Indian influences and jazz improvisation into a rock format. "Somebody to Love" and "White Rabbit" were but two items from an impressive catalog of original numbers that broke some genuinely new ground in rock songwriting. Mid-'60s rock and folk-rock were fused with raga-ish modal jams and unconventional lyrics about free love, with more surrealistic tunes (such as "White Rabbit") fueled by mind-expanding drugs. The band walked a razor's edge between raw basic rock and ambitious experimentation, rarely over-indulging themselves or losing sight of their knack for haunting melodies. The key ingredients in the attack were the piercing alto vocals of Grace Slick (who also played guitar, bass, organ, and recorder) and the surf-psychedelic aura of Darby Slick's Silvertone guitar.

The decision to go for a Silvertone guitar was economic as well as aesthetic. The model was cheap, and before the Great Society formed, Darby had been playing Silvertones that belonged to a friend before purchasing his own at Sears. He liked the sound well enough to stick with the Silvertone in the Great Society, especially as "that particular one had a sort of a raunchiness added to the surf thing, which I really appreciated—a little bit of distortion coming out of the guitar itself, rather than out of the amplifier." As he learned electric guitar, Darby's musical horizons were being expanded by his eclectic interests in rock, folk, jazz, and Indian music (he saw Ravi Shankar live well before the Beatles made the sitar player a household name). By the mid-'60s, Darby, his drummer brother Jerry, and Jerry's wife Grace were beginning to jam and rehearse together, with the intention of forming a band to make a mark on the then-embryonic San Francisco rock scene.

About a year or so of rehearsal finally led to the Great Society's first public performance in October 1965, with David Miner on guitar/vocals and Bard Dupont on bass. It was this quintet that auditioned for Autumn Records, the small San Francisco-based indie that had recently landed a couple of national hits with the Beau Brummels. In a few weeks they were recording demos for Autumn, mixing rather standard, sub-Rolling Stones-ish guitar rock with numbers that attempted to draw from a far more radical canvas, particularly in the use of

An early lineup of the Great Society. Left to right: Grace Slick, Jerry Slick, David Miner, Bard Dupont, Darby Slick.
Credit: Courtesy Sundazed Music

Eastern music. As Darby puts it, compared to the other San Francisco groups that were forming in late 1965—Jefferson Airplane, the Grateful Dead, Big Brother & the Holding Company, and Quicksilver Messenger Service being the most famous—"we had more direct jazz influence. All of us had listened to a lot of jazz, and we were directly trying to put some of it in there. I also think that the Indian influence was stronger in our band than any of those other bands."

The Indian influence was *extremely* strong in one of the songs they recorded for a single in late 1965 under the direction of producer Sly Stewart, soon to become much better known as Sly Stone. "Free Advice" is downright radical for the era, with insistent raga-derived guitar lines underlying Grace Slick's shrill, wordless, banshee-like sing-chants (which all but obliterate the actual lyric of the tune, sung by David Miner). It was once reported that this number took 200 takes to perfect, exhausting Sly's patience; the actual figure turns out to be 53, still an astronomic quantity by the standards of the period.

Bound for greater glory was the other side of the single, an ominous, minor-keyed song that Darby had written just after an acid trip. If there was to be a hit to be found in the group's erratic early repertoire, "Somebody to Love" (initially titled "Someone to Love") was the obvious contender. But when it was released (backed with "Free Advice") in February 1966, Autumn Records was in its death throes. The single was barely distributed at all, except to some close friends of the group, who could get it at the Psychedelic Shop on Haight Street.

By this time the band was rapidly evolving beyond their primitive Autumn recordings (which were issued in 1996 on Sundazed). Dupont was replaced by Peter Vandergelder, a bassist who could also play sax and flute, adding some unusual versatility to the group's sound. The Great Society were particularly anxious to improve both their musicianship and arrangements after opening for the Blues Project, the noted New York blues-rockers, at a show in early 1966.

"We were on the bill with them at the Avalon, they just blew us off the stand," remembers Darby. "They were so much better than we were. They were *technically* better than we were—that is, the drummer was a stronger drummer than our drummer, and each instrument like that, they were stronger than we were, except probably Grace was as good as their singers, or as powerful, at least. So that really inspired us to dig into a new level of work, and a new level of improving ourselves as musicians.

"But beyond that, and at least as important, their arrangements were a lot better. Until that gig, we did a lot of things where whole bunches of us would be kind of playing the same rhythm. You know, if there were two guitars, we would both be kind of just strumming along and playing very similar kinds of stuff. Now, listening to the Blues Project, we started to make stuff where it would be like, okay, if this person's playing on this beat, then this person is going to play on this other beat, and we're going to get this kind of syncopated counter thing going. So our music started to get a lot more sophisticated.

"And in the same way, we also started to build up the sections where we would maybe not have everybody playing at the same time, which was a new concept to us." He laughs modestly, although it should be considered that it was unusual to find such a level of sophistication in *any* rock group at the time. "We would sort of add instruments as this section would go along, or even like, 'You play on this note, and then you play an octave higher, and you play an octave higher than that, but you wait two bars, and you wait four bars.' Or whatever, to make the thing build as it went along. We got more directly conscious of all those kinds of things, so it became more sophisticated."

In Barbara Rowes' *Grace Slick: The Biography*, Grace and husband Jerry observe the effect the Blues Project had on the band in somewhat more negative terms. "She went crazy," Jerry told Rowes. "She wanted to sing with a tighter band and better musicians. She wanted to work with other vocalists to weave intricate harmonies into the fabric of the songs." Added Grace on the same page, "After I heard the Blues Project, I knew what I wanted to do, but it wouldn't be possible to cram five years of musical knowledge into two months in order to open up our band with intricate harmonies and improvisations."

But in reality, as the musicians began to intensely apply themselves to rehearsing, arranging, and songwriting in 1966, they were evolving into something truly special, and something that couldn't be measured by musical chops alone. Songs like "Grimly Forming" and "Arbitration" illustrate what Darby means by building songs in sections, as odd (even apocalyptic) verses trade off against concise instrumental passages that neatly balance rock dynamics with elements of jazz improvisation and Indian-Eastern modes. The Indian-jazz meld is even more prominent on the instrumental blowout "Father" and the original version of "White Rabbit," which is dominated by several minutes of exhilarating interplay between Ornette Coleman-inspired raga-ish guitar lines and snake-charmer sax before Grace's vocal even enters the picture.

At the same time, the group also had a knack for blending major and minor chords into fetchingly haunting, more or less straight rock songs like "Didn't Think So" and "Darkly Smiling." Grace's buoyant "Often As I May" had genuine hit potential, though its lyrical advocation of free love was quite controversial for 1966. The group's restless experimentalism even extended to their covers, such as the tense, circular riffs on their cover of the girl-group classic "Sally Go Round the Roses."

Darby agrees that the band favored a dark and haunting sound that leaned toward blends of minor and major modes, as opposed to the cheerier, bluesier items that David Miner had penned for the group in their early days. "I think it matched our personalities more, for sure. We did 'Nature Boy' [a pop standard popularized by Nat "King" Cole], which is kind of a dark and haunting song, even though it's pretty and about love. But that sort of bittersweet quality is something that's always been present in the artists that I've liked."

Fortunately, much of the Great Society's material was preserved on live tapes—recorded at the Matrix club in San Francisco in mid-1966—that were issued in the late '60s (and have usually remained in print in one form or another). Although the performances are not as polished as they might have been had the group had the opportunity to record them in the studio, the double album's worth of tracks enshrines the Great Society as one of the most inventive groups of the era, contrary to the impression that Grace Slick has given in some of her comments about the band.

"Obviously, this is a very personal kind of interpretation of the circumstances," notes Darby diplomatically. "Grace has said negative things about the musicianship of the people in the Great Society, from the time that she left the Great Society. I think if you listen to the Grateful Dead's first album and the Jefferson Airplane's first album and compare those with the Great Society . . . many people come up to me and say we were as good as musicians as those people were. To me, it's not a real important issue. But I think that it would be possible for Grace to have specific motivations for saying those things, self-serving motivations, let us say. I leave it to you or anybody else to decide who were the best, and who were the worst. "

By the late summer of 1966, different interests were beginning to unravel the group. David Miner left, and then asked to rejoin; the group refused to let him back in, preferring to work as a smaller unit. Darby Slick and Peter Vandergelder became increasingly serious about their desire to study Indian music. But the biggest threat to the Great Society's long-term stability, ironically, was their biggest asset. As the band matured, Grace Slick took over almost all of their lead vocals; her striking beauty was also the visual standout onstage (amplified to an even greater degree by the rarity of a female rock musician in any band whatsoever in the mid-'60s, let alone one that fronted the group). With her star quality, first-rate songs, and ice-clear vocals, she was more essential to the act than any other member. The Jefferson Airplane took notice of her potential, and were quick to ask her to join their lineup as a replacement for Signe Anderson (who sings on the Airplane's first album). From their first performance to their last, the Great Society had lasted for only about a year.

As they were on the verge of signing with a major label, the group, had they survived, would have most likely soon been in the studio recording their debut album. Yet in Darby's opinion, "There's no reason to think it would have been a masterpiece. Maybe if we had started and begun a thing, like the Beatles did, of a record every eight months, or something like that, maybe after three or four they might have started to get to be pretty good."

But Darby concedes that the Great Society's days were probably numbered anyway. "Our personalities were certainly in conflict, in one way or another, for that year. I was mad when Grace quit the band. But really it was [because] *I* wanted to be the one that quit. I was just mad that she quit first. Peter and I were already talking about stopping to study Indian music full-time. Because once we ran into that and really sort of got how wonderful it was, how evolved and just what a great music it was, then it seemed like the only logical thing was to learn as much as possible about it."

Indian music was not a flavor of the month for Darby. When the Great Society disbanded, he almost immediately sold his equipment and his car to finance a trip to India to study with world-renowned sarod player Ali Akbar Khan. After a few months in Calcutta, Darby learned that "Somebody to Love"—which he had given permission for the Airplane to use—was climbing the charts. The irony was that, as the songwriting credit read simply "Slick" on the Airplane's *Surrealistic Pillow* LP, most listeners logically assumed that it was Grace's composition.

Darby returned to the United States in time for 1967's Summer of Love, but remained serious about Indian music and has played little straight rock music since, studying with Ali Akbar Khan for 12 years. For the past few years he's been playing in a band (and has recorded an album) with his son, with whom he invented a fretless guitar that, in his words, "was able to combine all that I could do with the guitar and the sarod in one instrument." He's glad to patiently recount the Great Society days in his Marin County apartment, but it's clear that his mental and musical energy is focused much more on the present.

With no bitterness, he adds that he's just read that Grace has signed a book deal for a reputed $1 million advance. The advance for his own autobiography (issued by a small publisher in 1991), he smiles, was but a tiny fraction of that. Grace's celebrity continues to overshadow the rest of the Great Society, it seems, 30 years after the band's paths diverged.

Recommended Recording:
Collector's Item (1990, Columbia). Although the performances are occasionally raw and tentative, this is a 67-minute collection of early San Francisco psychedelia at its best. Recorded live at the city's Matrix club in 1966, it includes thunderous pre-Jefferson Airplane versions of both "Somebody to Love" and "White Rabbit."

The Misunderstood

It was late 1966, and and Fontana Records had assembled several dozen members of the press to hear the label's newest and most adventurous act at its London headquarters. The Misunderstood had just blown the audience's mind by running through a set of songs that took the psychedelic explorations of the Yardbirds to new heights. Monstrous feedback dovetailed with shimmering Indian-flavored melodic passages; Glenn Ross Campbell coaxed all manner of dive-bombs and eerie tidal-wave sustains from his steel guitar. But the band had one last trick up their sleeve.

"We pulled out an envelope," remembers Campbell. "We said, 'There's a piece of paper in the envelope with a word written on it. What we want you to do in this next song—if you want to call it that—we'll play for approximately six minutes, and then we're gonna ask you questions about what you heard. And what we want is, basically, your feelings—what the song made you feel like, or makes you think of. We're not interested in whether you think it was too loud or too long. We're not interested in a critique. We just want to know what you were *feeling*.

"At the end, we asked three or four people. One person goes, 'I kept getting flashes of when I was a kid in my father's apple orchard or something.' The next one goes, 'I had a craving for applesauce.' We did about three or four, and they were all spot-on. So we open the envelope, and of course the word in the envelope was 'apple.' One way or another, everybody we talked to, their feelings or thoughts were centered around apples. Oh, man—the flashbulbs went off, and some women started screaming, yelling out, 'They're witches! They're witches!'"

If the Misunderstood were indeed witches, they were sorcerers of the most benign and progressive sort, using their extraordinary powers to smash the outer limits of psychedelic rock, expounding a message of love and possibility. Their supposed supernatural powers, however, could not prevent a few external Blue Meanies from breaking up the party almost before it had started. In early 1967, the Misunderstood should have been standing alongside Jimi Hendrix, Pink Floyd, and others as the greatest newcomers of the just-blossoming psychedelic scene. Instead, the group had suddenly and irrevocably dispersed, unable to keep playing together in the face of insurmountable obstacles placed in their paths by both the American and British governments.

Just two years before they seemed poised to become underground heroes in London, the Misunderstood were a struggling American garage band, finding what work they could in Riverside, California. Evolving from a surf combo

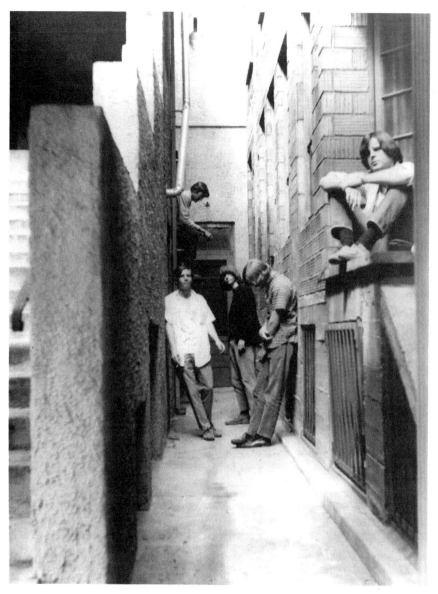

The Misunderstood, in the alley, mid-1960s. Left to right: Rick Moe (sitting on ledge), Greg Treadway, Glenn Ross Campbell, Rick Brown, Steve Whiting. Credit: Courtesy Glenn Ross Campbell

called the Blue Notes, by 1965 they had added lead singer Rick Brown and begun writing material in the spirit of blues-based British Invasion heroes like the Yardbirds and the Rolling Stones. An acetate from around this time (some of which can be heard on the *Before the Dream Faded* reissue) shows them to be an above-average garage act, caught in the transition between surf music, Del Shannon, and the Animals. There was little to indicate that they were any more special than hundreds of other similar bands across the U.S.; being based a good 50 miles of so from Los Angeles meant that they were unlikely to attract any attention from the music industry.

The arrival of Glenn Campbell (no relation to Glen Campbell the pop star) helped the band find a much more startling direction. Campbell had already played the swooping, ear-catching steel guitar leads on an instrumental single by the Goldtones, "Gutterball," now considered a cult classic in its own right by surf collectors. Always looking for new sounds—"the steel for me was just a big experimentation," to be used "in every way conceivable"—Campbell was asked to audition for the Misunderstood, who were looking for a replacement for their recently departed guitarist George Phelps. Used to getting physically beaten up for bringing a steel guitar to rock group auditions, Campbell made sure he was heard by bringing along eight or so of his own friends to stymie any threat of physical attack. He needn't have worried—after just one song, he was in.

Campbell brought not only a new instrument into the group, but new influences as well. His eclectic tastes extended beyond rock and blues to Indian ragas, Library of Congress recordings of tribal New Guinea music, and African songs with cycles that wouldn't repeat for minutes on end (as opposed to the usual four-bar or eight-bar repetitions found in much pop music). "Usually I would meet with resistance from most bands I'd been with," says Campbell. "But with Misunderstood, there was none of that. They were fascinated, much as I was. They were willing to try anything. There was never any of the usual sort of ego paranoia. They'd take a chance of looking like a fool just to try something new."

While remaining fairly blues-based, the group began to improvise and experiment with amplification and guitar effects in a manner reminiscent of the Yardbirds, who were, Campbell noted, "almost to us like a kindred spirit." An obscure single of blues numbers recorded by the Misunderstood in their Riverside days betrays relatively little in the way of daring approach. Unreleased demos of "I'm Not Talking" (based on the Yardbirds version), however, are startling even today, with their shrieking-banshee steel guitar leads, blistering raga runs, and extended bouts of feedback. Campbell points out that it was all but impossible to find old blues records in the States in those days, meaning that they had to be learned by playing them over and over at the house of a friend who had a big collection. "That's also partly why we never copied anything exactly. Because we didn't *have* it to copy. That's another thing that led us to be a little more original, because we didn't have any choice. Our memories weren't photographic enough to copy 'em directly."

Southern California didn't know what to make of a group that would literally leave the stage for extended periods to let their instruments feed back on their own. Even on rare trips to Los Angeles, says Campbell, "The audiences just didn't know how to take it. They came to a standstill, would stare, mouths hanging open." Part of the thrill was the sheer novelty of seeing a steel guitarist set up his equipment in a hard electric rock combo—"it looked weird, sounded bizarre, and added greatly to the uniqueness of the band. Most kids didn't know what it was. I used to hang sort of joke packets of potato chips and those little beef sticks off my guitar on strings and sell them at gigs."

Campbell pushed things into a different dimension by asking some engineers he knew to construct a light show of sorts, well before such accoutrements were common at rock concerts. "I wanted to make a unit which, as you play, would be assigned three primary colors. It would divide the musical frequencies up to those colors, and pulsate the lights accordingly. We were told it was impossible to make at that point. But I refused to give up, so I got some motorcycle light bulbs and car tail lights, hooked them up with guitar jacks, and stuck them into the external speaker connections of our amps.

"And lo and behold, they worked like a charm. They weren't color, but they were white, and as you played and got louder, they would ebb and flow with the volume and frequency range. We tried it at rehearsal with the lights out at my mom's house in the living room, and it was great." When it came time to debut the contraption in front of an audience, "We got the instruments feeding back, and left the stage. The way we did it, they would just go on indefinitely. The feedback would go into harmonics and octave changes and so on. It was quite eerie in itself. But when you combined that with these lights, it was a really bizarre effect. The lights were going up and down, [the audience's] faces would come into focus and stuff, and they were absolutely hypnotized, stunned, just standing there. We thought, man, we've stumbled onto something here. From that time on, we were considered the sort of alchemists of the music scene."

But Riverside—where the band were regularly hassled, sometimes physically, merely for wearing their hair long—was not exactly the most sympathetic climate to boldly take rock groups where none had gone before. What they were doing was more in line with British groups such as the Yardbirds and the Who. The arrival of a certain British DJ into San Bernardino confirmed an inkling they were starting to toss around in their minds. Radio personality John Ravenscroft—soon to change his name to John Peel and become Britain's most influential rock announcer/programmer (as he still is three decades later)—became a big fan of the band, helping them to arrange demo recordings. When the Misunderstood mused how they might stand a better chance of acceptance in England, Peel encouraged them to make the move. Unlike most young men with little cash, less name recognition, and no work permits, the group decided to go for it.

Not ones to accept what could or couldn't be done with their music, the band scrapped together enough money to make the journey. Some of the funds were raised by winning several Battle of the Bands competitions that Campbell cheerfully admits "were virtually fixed—but, I mean, we probably would have won it anyway." They had to smuggle their equipment off their boat through U.K. customs with help from a sympathetic crew, and soon found themselves riding into London, a couple of impressed females in tow. As Campbell remembers it, they were riding in the same sort of baggage compartment that the Beatles used for a famous scene in *A Hard Day's Night*. As far as the band knew, John Peel's parents were expecting them at a house in London, where the Misunderstood planned to stay until they got settled. So far, so good, but the screenplay would soon be hijacked by the likes of Fellini and David Lynch.

"We're riding high," recounts Campbell gleefully. "We got off and get a taxi to John's place. We thought they were all informed and knew we were coming. There's *nobody* there. I mean, we've got a mountain of equipment—amps, drums, all in cardboard boxes. We're sitting there, it starts raining on us, and we're pulling out raincoats and putting it over the equipment and getting soaked. Pretty soon the neighbors get curious, 'cause we'd been there overnight. They come the next morning and bring us cups of tea and more blankets. We're all wrapped up like Indians on a reservation.

"We're there, literally, for a couple of days. Finally, John's parents come home. And they walked straight by us, didn't even *look* at us. We went banging on the door and said, 'Excuse us, but we're the Misunderstood.' And they go something like, 'Yeah, we can believe it!'" The band had to wait yet another eight hours before Peel's parents got hold of their son in the States to confirm the story and let the Californians in. Their hearts sunk when they found unsent promo packages in one of the closets, and realized "there was nobody waiting to see us or any interviews set up or anything." But they did call a manager from a list that Peel had supplied, and through that contact got a deal with Fontana Records.

Rick Brown came over a couple of weeks later than the rest of the group, and had somehow been led to believe that the Misunderstood were already famous in England. Instead of mobs of screaming fans, he was met by bandmates so strapped of cash that they'd had to jump subway barriers just to make the trip to the airport. Ending up on the wrong side and running late, they then had to run across a landing strip as a plane was taking off overhead. Getting back into London meant crashing the subway barriers again; "The cops were chasing us and jeez, this wasn't what Rick had in mind at all!"

The band were by now getting more "unsettled" than "settled"; bassist Steve Whiting got a job at a hospital carrying body parts down to the incinerator that lasted about one day and, more seriously, rhythm guitarist Greg Treadway was drafted and had to return home to join the Navy. The band were living in a rat-infested basement that was so cold that ice cream wouldn't melt, although Brown managed to share a flat with Yardbirds guitarist Jeff Beck. Yet in the midst of this Keystone Cops-gone-Kafka routine, the band actually began to make some headway.

With a new English guitarist, Tony Hill, the band recorded material for Fontana that stands as a high point of early psychedelia. The guitar work was thrilling, Campbell's especially, recalling Jeff Beck's most experimental work with the Yardbirds, with the unusual super-amplified steel guitar runs adding textures that were (and still largely are) unheard of within a rock context. While the songs could be recklessly cosmic, they were delivered with a mix of aggressive raunch, hypnotic raga-rock, and sudden shifts into meditative passages of glistening beauty. Best of all was "I Can Take You to the Sun," which shows the band at its most tender and Indian-influenced, moving from a Yardbirds-ish rave-up to an exquisitely delicate acoustic classical/raga guitar arrangement, devised and played by newcomer Hill. "I Can Take You to the Sun," backed with "Children of the Sun," would be their debut single; four other tracks from the sessions, thankfully, surfaced in 1982 on the *Before the Dream Faded* reissue.

"When Tony was in the band, we virtually had no limits," exclaims Campbell. "We could do umpteen different styles or colorations. We were approaching it like a trio, much like Hendrix did later, and Cream, even though there [were two guitar players]. But the way Tony and I were playing, it was almost like one instrument. We kind of weaved and ducked and twisted around, but quite often, we were taking solos at the same time. And we were sort of dancing together as soloists.

"I actually had an advantage over the guitar in the sense that I had this huge fat sound, and I could sustain it as long as I want. [With] regular guitar players, there wasn't a whole big choice of pickups, and their strings are thinner; I had huge, heavy strings. I could get quarter-tones, eight-tones, anywhere in between, where guitar players can only get half-steps, except when you bend strings." Campbell also used a fuzz box that "made all these horrendous noises. We cranked it up like screaming and squawking and feedback, which was exactly what we wanted."

The single wasn't a hit, although Fontana had been excited enough about the group to actually bump established artists' studio time to make room for the Misunderstood's sessions. And the band weren't entirely pleased with the coverage surrounding the "apple" incident at Fontana's press launch. "I had a book that was about two and a half inches thick," says Campbell. "It was a notebook of various chords and rhythm combinations and all sorts of stuff, inversions, harmonies that would seem to produce certain effects, so that we could write songs with these various already researched combinations, and expect a certain response from an audience. The idea was not to control an audience. The idea ultimately was that we could set up healing centers to use music and lights in a sort of holistic kind of way, and also to communicate our experiences.

"But we all got a bit worried, and we actually took the book and destroyed it. We might have been maybe giving ourselves a little more credit than we were due. We felt we stumbled onto something we didn't really want to get in the wrong hands, and it kind of spooked us a bit. So that book just got torn up and burned."

The Misunderstood would never get a chance to implement their still-futuristic notions (and before you laugh too hard, consider that Jimi Hendrix has also been said to have considered the use of music as a healing mechanism). Their gigs were infrequent due to lack of work permits, though those that saw them were impressed, including Pink Floyd, who had yet to make records—"we kept getting reports from people that were seeing Pink Floyd that they were copying a lot of our stage act." From Campbell's perspective, the Misunderstood were truly ready to assert themselves once drummer Rick Moe heard Mitch Mitchell's drumming on Jimi Hendrix's first single, "Hey Joe." "I wanted another soloist in there, coming from the drums. I go [to Rick], '*That's* the kind of drumming I'm talking about.' And he goes, 'Now I see what you mean!' To me, that was the last awkward link in the group. From then on, we could have just skyrocketed. That probably saddens me more than anything, because he knew what I was talking about. I can't even remember now if we ever even got a chance to rehearse again after that."

Soon after, Rick Brown returned to the United States to sort out his draft problems—unsuccessfully, as it turned out, since he was briefly drafted before going AWOL in Haight-Ashbury. With the FBI on his trail, he returned to London briefly, managing to slip out of England just before the authorities caught up with him there; he went on from there to India to join the Hare Krishnas for a time, after which he eventually established himself as a gemologist. Meanwhile the rest of the band had unsuccessfully auditioned for a replacement vocalist. In keeping with the larger-than-life adventures that seemed to be dogging them at this point, they found themselves stranded in France in early 1967 after being sent to nonexistent gigs. Whiting managed to get back into England with the help of an elite London call girl, on the pretense that she would marry him. Moe and Campbell got shuttled back and forth on the ferry between France and England for three days; immigration refused them entry to either country, and they were reduced to stealing food off of other passengers' plates. They were even considering jumping overboard to reach England before they were dissuaded by the crew.

Finally they were allowed into the U.K., on the condition that they leave within 24 hours. Campbell had to sell his steel guitar, and Moe his drums, to pay for their tickets back to California. It was suddenly over, although Glenn would soon return to England to front an entirely different lineup of the Misunderstood that played a much different sort of blues-funk-rock. Campbell hadn't wanted to use the Misunderstood name for this venture, but was pressured into it by his record company.

Says old friend John Peel of the Misunderstood's peak lineup today: "If they'd managed to get themselves sorted out in London, I really think they would have done quite extraordinarily well. Even if they hadn't been influential up to that point, I do think they could have certainly taken their place amongst the more notable bands at the time. They were barely getting started. It's one of the great disappointments of my life, really, that Rick got drafted, and it all fell apart."

Amplifies Campbell: "I think we would have achieved quite a bit. I think it would have been a major group. It would have been like a symphonic rock band, really. Not that we'd have done that—what I mean is, there would have been a lot of colors, a lot of shades, and lots of ideas thrown in there. The only thing that really stopped it was the bloody Vietnam War. I'm not saying that just [in] a selfish respect. For such a useless war, its tentacles just reached everywhere."

Campbell went on to experience a bit of success in the U.K. in the early '70s with the bluesy hard rock band Juicy Lucy. He's now living in Auckland, New Zealand, where he does a lot of session work and TV/radio ads, and plays with New Zealand country artist Al Hunter. Not that he's stopped experimenting—he's recently built an archtop nine-string semi-acoustic guitar with special blues and jazz tunings, using an old Hofner body. "Everybody said it couldn't be done—it's really revitalized my interest in music."

Trying to summarize a one-of-a-kind band like the Misunderstood is nearly impossible, but Campbell gives it his best shot: "It wasn't that we were so much overlooked when we were around. It was just that nobody knew we existed! The people that heard us *couldn't* overlook us. We were just too different.

"The Misunderstood might have some powerful, rough sections that were anger. But we'd always balance it off somewhere in the song with something soft, and more serene. It's like a good book. It takes you through ups and downs, but in the end, it all balances out."

Recommended Recording:
Before the Dream Faded (1982, Cherry Red, UK). Half of this disc contains interesting cuts from the band's Riverside days in the mid-'60s, illustrating their evolution from a decent garage band to a Yardbirdsy blues-psychedelic one. Pretty good, but what you really need to hear are the six tracks they recorded in London in 1966 (all contained here). This is not just overlooked psychedelia, but a tantalizing glimpse into directions that were never fully explored in rock music as a whole before the Misunderstood's tragically premature demise. Believe it.

Mad Geniuses & Eccentric Recluses

Perhaps no cult rockers inspire greater fascination or devotion than those who died young, lost their marbles, or avoided the public eye with a zealous passion bordering on obsession. A big part of it has to do with the sheer mystery surrounding their affairs. The artists profiled in this section are either dead, not talking to the media, or not really capable of expressing themselves coherently in an interview situation. This in turn gives rise to a constant buzz of rumors—sometimes true, more frequently false—surrounding the figures that, in a vicious circle, only serves to enhance their mystique.

These artists were at once the most interesting, and the most frustrating, to research in the entire book. In the absence of personal access, in each case I've spoken with people who knew them well and worked with them closely. This approach must inevitably lead to a great deal of speculation—Nick Drake, Scott Walker, Roky Erickson, and the other musicians featured here were/are such enigmatic characters that even those who collaborated with them intimately can only guess at some of their motives and inspirations. It is at least fairer to the artists involved to get some observations from people who knew them well, rather than continuing to add fuel to the rumor fire with poorly educated guesses surrounding their behavior, warranted or otherwise.

The Greta Garbo-like Scott Walker and the inscrutable Lee Hazlewood aside, these are not only among the most tragic stories to be found in this book—they're among the most tragic stories in rock history. Whatever demons and chemicals drove Syd Barrett and Skip Spence into madness and worse, it should be remembered that behind the insanity, or appearance thereof, lurks a very human person whose story deserves sensitive appreciation by an ever-growing

Joe Meek, a genius at producing outer-space sounds with primitive equipment is shown here at his studio on Holloway Road.
Credit: Courtesy RPM Records Archive

coterie of fans. If we cannot communicate with them in "normal" terms, we at least have their music, which conveys joy and complex emotions in strikingly vivid terms that few of the sane among us can match.

Syd Barrett

"Syd Barrett was offered 200,000 pounds by Atlantic Records to record any new material, however basic, according to the new edition of Syd Barrett: Crazy Diamond *by Mike Watkinson and Pete Anderson . . . . Tim Sommer, a senior A&R executive at the label, declared that 'his entire involvement could be limited to strumming a few songs in his living room. The songs could be of any nature, could reflect any state of art Syd is capable of achieving—fragmentary, covers, a cappella, non-pop, even entirely instrumental or, for that matter, spoken word.' He also suggested Peter Buck and Mike Mills of R.E.M., or Robyn Hitchcock as possible collaborators. Sommer claims all are 'good friends of mine, and would most certainly do this in the blink of an eye.'*

Barrett has so far shown no interest in the offer."

—Vox *magazine, January 1994*

"In a private ward at the Adenbrookes' Hospital in Cambridge, where a Barrett Room is named in honor of his late father, the respected pathologist, Syd Barrett lies resting. He is now almost totally blind, following complications arising from diabetes. The prognosis isn't good if he does not routinely take the prescribed insulin, and Barrett seems either incapable or unwilling to do so by himself. Since the death of his mother Winifred in 1991, Syd has often lapsed into diabetic coma, apparently unconcerned about his health. However, he is watched over by a tight network of understanding relatives and neighbors."

—MOJO *magazine, September 1996.*

And so the psychodrama of rock's most fascinating cult figure continues. It may be that a good 90% of the customers that fill stadiums to watch the 1990s version of Pink Floyd have no idea who Syd Barrett is. Many would find it incredible that he was their lead singer, chief songwriter, and lead guitarist when the band first exploded upon the British psychedelic scene in 1967. For a short, exhilarating time, Syd was not just the leader of Pink Floyd—he *was* the Pink Floyd, certainly in terms of establishing the band's unique astral vision.

One brilliant album and a couple of brilliant singles later, Syd was out of the band he had founded, unable to either work with the group or, equally importantly, be worked *with*. A couple of erratic but periodically fascinating solo albums followed. And then—for the next 25 years and counting—there was silence. Not just retirement, but a near-total withdrawal from the "real" world, in which he was rarely spotted in public even in his hometown of Cambridge. His old band carries on, more financially successful than almost any rock act in the world. But in the eyes of Syd's hardcore following, they've never matched the playful genius of their Barrett-dominated 1967 debut, *The Piper at the Gates of Dawn*.

It's been a long and, for the most part, frightening trip since Syd founded the band in Cambridge in the mid-'60s. The Pink Floyd rapidly evolved from the usual R&B knockoffs to a fiercer, more experimental, electronic sound that incorporated elements of improvisation and the avant-garde. By late 1966, they were darlings of the London underground, playing freaky original material at the UFO club, the base camp of the movement.

It wouldn't have meant much to the larger public, however, without the imaginative songwriting of Barrett. He began to devise songs that married the Floyd's outer-space arrangements with charming, hook-happy, pop-conscious vignettes with a distinctly English slant. "Arnold Layne"/"Candy and a Currant Bun" was their electrifying debut single (and small British hit), Barrett delivering

Syd Barrett, at far right with Pink Floyd, was the band's indisputed leader in their early days, writing and singing most of their material, and playing lead guitar. Credit: Michael Ochs Archives

the tale of an innocuous transvestite on the plug side, and an eerie, almost free-associative ode to psychedelic pleasure on the flip. It was the sound of young life on the edge, its appetite for experimentation leavened by a slightly mad glee. What few realized at the time was that the madness was becoming very real.

The producer of that single was Joe Boyd, who has for three decades enjoyed a hugely successful career, working on recordings by Fairport Convention, the Incredible String Band, R.E.M., Nick Drake, and many others. As producer in the studio, and as the musical director of the UFO club, Boyd had the opportunity to observe Syd and the band at close quarters in late 1966 and early 1967, in the months before they landed a deal with EMI records.

"All during that period, Syd was a delight," he remembers. "He was absolutely fine to work with. He was a little spacey, but not much. He was witty and funny and energetic, and really the centerpiece of the band. Roger [Waters, bassist] was a kind of anchor, the one who would organize the group's thoughts in a way. But Syd was the spark." Although "Arnold Layne" (which had been produced independently) immediately established the Floyd as a major new contender, Boyd was ousted from the producer's chair by EMI in favor of Norman Smith, a veteran who had engineered many of the Beatles' early sessions.

But the band's debut, *The Piper at the Gates of Dawn*, was one of the core classics of psychedelic music. Barrett's genius was to tap both the innocence and fear of childhood as the sources of his imagery. Most of his songs could pass for fairy tales, if not for the vague menace lurking underneath the surface—the toy-store crashes of "Bike," the witches and satanic cats of "Lucifer Sam," the mother telling bedtime stories who breaks off abruptly to leave Syd desperately hanging on her words in "Matilda Mother."

Despite Pink Floyd's space cadet image, Barrett's songs were usually very much in the British pop tradition. Boyd relates the little-known fact that Syd had actually written additional material for a much lighter, whimsical band with whom the producer was also involved. "One of the great sorrows in my collection is that I don't have the demo tape that Syd gave me of six or eight songs that he hadn't recorded," he reveals. "I was recording a band called the Purple Gang and we were looking for material, and Syd gave us this tape. There were some terrific songs, very different from [what he ended up putting on his solo albums]. Strong, melodic, good songs."

The contributions of fellow Floydians Waters, keyboardist Rick Wright, and Nick Mason can't be overestimated. Along with Syd's own swooping, fourth-dimension guitar playing, Wright's ethereal, black mass organ work gave the material the texture (and melodicism) it needed to truly sound not-of-this-earth. "Astronomy Domine" gave full vent to the band's spaciest concerns, as did the crunching instrumental, "Interstellar Overdrive." Executed with a freshness that has not dated, the album made the British Top Ten, as did a concurrent single, "See Emily Play."

In retrospect, most agree that by the time these records were released, the Syd who wrote the songs was no more. Whether massive LSD consumption, the pressures of oncoming rock stardom, or some previously dormant psychological instabilities were to blame could never be determined; most likely it was a combination of all of the above. What's for sure is that by mid-1967, Syd's behavior was becoming most alarming.

Joe Boyd saw Syd at close range for the last time in June of 1967, when Pink Floyd played the UFO club for the last time. "It was absolutely packed. You couldn't move. The band kind of elbowed their way through the crowd, and I had to sort of push them in the backs to make room for them to get in because there was no backstage entrance. And that was when I saw Syd for the first time in three months. I guess I'd seen him from a distance and people had told me that he'd taken a *lot* of acid. He looked completely changed, he just looked like there was nobody home. He just stopped playing on stage."

Over the next few months, Syd's deterioration was astonishingly rapid, as related in a series of incidents that have since passed into Pink Floyd legend. Standing on stage all night in a catatonic state, playing one note, or playing nothing at all. Giving television host Pat Boone the silent treatment when interviewed during the Floyd's brief, disastrous 1967 American tour. Locking a girl-friend in an apartment, shoving food under the door to keep her from starving. Feeding LSD to his cat. Crushing Mandrax tablets into his hair to create an impromptu mod hairdo just prior to taking the stage, during a late '67 tour in which the band appeared on the same bill as Jimi Hendrix. But what was most worrying to friends and associates was that the Syd Barrett they knew had vanished, leaving a shell with whom it was impossible to communicate.

Keith West was the lead singer of another prominent British psychedelic band, Tomorrow, which toured briefly with Pink Floyd in Europe. "I'd seen him at a club two or three months before and we were all buddies. Three months later he was almost comatose, just sitting and not talking to anybody, acting very strange, staring people out, being obnoxious and arrogant. Everybody just thought he was just being arrogant. But he wasn't. We never realized what he was going through. People would talk behind his back and say, you know, 'He thinks he's so cool,' but we didn't know how serious it was."

A late '67 single ("Apples and Oranges") flopped, and as the band struggled to maintain some semblance of professionalism onstage and in the studio, they began to realize how difficult it would be to carry on with Barrett. "You could see the effect that he had on the rest of the group," continues West. "They didn't know what to make of it at some point. Everybody could see that they were getting fed up with the situation. We did a couple of tours with them in Europe, and people would be writing notes out and passing them because Syd wasn't talking that day for some reason. It was really sad to see."

The upshot was that Syd was eventually forced out of the band he had founded. For a while guitarist Dave Gilmour made the Pink Floyd a five-piece, but the situation lasted only briefly before Gilmour became Barrett's replacement in 1968. Most of their second album, A *Saucerful of Secrets*, was recorded without Barrett, and Pink Floyd's management were so doubtful that the band could exist without Syd—who, after all, wrote their songs, sang them, and was the lead guitarist—that they left the remaining Floydians to their own devices, opting to manage Syd as a solo act.

Pink Floyd, of course, proved them wrong—*Saucerful of Secrets* made the Top Ten, and five years later, with *Dark Side of the Moon*, they became one of the very biggest rock groups of all time. To a significant minority of Floyd fans, though, the post-Syd incarnation of the band—all 25-plus years of it—has never matched the heights of the Syd Barrett lineup. As Boyd explains, "Syd wrote three-minute pop songs. Slightly weird pop songs, but they were three-minute compositions. The group, in live performance, would also do these long instrumentals, and they would extend songs of Syd's by these long solo sections. I've heard them doing a ten-minute version of 'Arnold Layne.' But still there was a structure, and a song.

"When Syd stopped being the man who wrote all their material, the whole structure of things changed. They became much more of an instrumental group, with the lyrics and the singing like an introduction to the instrumental work. I think Roger as a songwriter, and Dave Gilmour for that matter, don't have the wit that Syd had. Syd was a very funny and inventive songwriter, and they don't really have that. But they do have something that probably may be more commercial than what Syd had, a kind of particular type of almost Wagnerian chord progressions that give their instrumental stuff a unique sound. You can tell a Pink Floyd chord progression a mile away; there's something about it which is absolutely characteristic of them. The fact that it was primarily instrumental is one of the reasons why they can be as famous in Malaya and Brazil and Russia as they were in the United Kingdom and the United States."

Syd's eccentric behavior would never reverse itself, but his recording career wasn't finished. After keeping a low musical profile at the end of the '60s, he emerged with two solo albums in 1970, *The Madcap Laughs* and *Barrett*. Ragged but charming, with bare-bones arrangements (his ex-bandmates lent considerable assistance, particularly Dave Gilmour, who produced most of the sessions), the songs nonetheless suggest sketches rather than fully developed artworks. The off-the-cuff feel, as it turns out, was hardly deliberate. Syd's accompanists would sometimes settle for a take that approached completion, as Barrett often proved unwilling to rehearse the arrangements, or even divulge what key the songs were in.

"That's true," admits Robert Wyatt, then a member of the Soft Machine, who drummed on some of Barrett's solo sessions. "But I mean, I was brought up, musically, in the '50s. If you want eccentricity, and that kind of non-verbal world and those kind of weird signals that you have to pick up, you can't beat jazz musicians, you know." In comparison, he states, "Working with Syd Barrett's a piece of cake, I think. I found him courteous and friendly."

So Syd wasn't difficult to work with? "Absolutely not, no. Very easy. Almost too easy. He was very, very easygoing. So easygoing that you didn't necessarily know what he wanted, or whether he was pleased with it or not, because he seemed quite pleased with what you did. Possibly he may have suffered from moving into the world of commercial culture. It might have been very confusing for him. I just think that not everybody fits into the business. I know from personal experience, it's not that easy."

Barrett's solo work is treasured by the faithful in spite of its erratic nature, partially because there was nothing else to come. After moderate sales, critical acclaim, and a few BBC and live appearances, Barrett all but disappeared from the face of the earth. An attempt to form a trio with Twink (drummer for British underground bands like Tomorrow and the Pretty Things) and bassist Jack Monck was nothing short of disastrous, as the fledgling outfit made it through only a few public performances before falling apart. By the mid-'70s, Barrett had already started to acquire mythic status, enhanced by occasional sightings, as when he showed up unannounced in the studio in the hopes of contributing to Pink Floyd's *Wish You Were Here* album. Incredibly, his ex-bandmates at first could literally not recognize the now overweight and balding figure.

Attempts at a third album in 1974 came to nothing, and at any rate Barrett seemed disinterested in music. Or little else—he became a recluse in his native Cambridge, incapable of working, looked after by protective relatives who respected his wishes for limited contact with the outside world. A 1990 photo that appeared in Nicholas Schaffner's Pink Floyd biography *(Saucerful of Secrets)* was nothing less than shocking. Even if Syd cultists that made the pilgrimage to Cambridge in hopes of tracking down their hero had met him face to face, few would have recognized this decidedly average-looking, dumpy middle-aged man, who looked a good five or ten years older than his 45 years.

The Syd Barrett cult continues to grow bigger and bigger, partly because of the unique magnificence of his work, partly because of the mystique around his reclusion, and partly because of the pervading sense of disbelief that there is so little of his work available. A "lost album" of sorts, *Opel*, was collected in the late '80s from solo outtakes, and unveiled some fine previously unreleased material. Following that was a box set that presented all three solo albums and alternate versions that were essentially outtakes of outtakes, Syd's ravenous cult being happy to find whatever it could. Bootlegs of early Floyd radio broadcasts, alternate mixes, and more outtakes, with fidelity ranging from stellar to horrible, continue to make the rounds as well. A fine biography of Barrett appeared (*Crazy Diamond*), and various Syd fanzines have kept the flame burning for two decades.

Iain Smith, who edits one of those fanzines (*Eskimo Chain*), speculates as to why the Syd Barrett legacy continues to exert such a compelling fascination, over 25 years since Barrett last recorded. "As Nick Mason once remarked, it's very much the James Dean syndrome of someone exceptionally talented not fulfilling his potential. People find it hard to believe that Elvis Presley or Jim Morrison are actually dead, so with Syd the fact that he's still out there somewhere in the Fens makes him even more fascinating. Plus, of course, although his body of work is so limited, what there is has a unique otherworldly brilliance. Add that to the myth and you have an exceptionally potent combination."

Recommended Recordings:

By Pink Floyd:
The Piper at the Gates of Dawn (1967, Capitol). One of the great psychedelic albums, and the one record in which Barrett's talents were in full flower. Also check for the early Pink Floyd single tracks "Arnold Layne," "Candy and a Currant Bun," "Apples and Oranges," and "See Emily Play," available on several compilations.

By Syd Barrett:
Crazy Diamond (1993, EMI). Once you're hooked, you're hooked. So although a three-CD set of both the official albums, the *Opel* outtake collection, and yet *more* outtakes may seem excessive, this is the definitive compilation of Barrett's solo work, missing only some BBC tracks (issued on *The Peel Sessions*).

Magnesium Proverbs (bootleg). The best compilation of unofficial material: 1967 BBC Floyd sessions, alternates, acetates, solo live performances, and the like.

Recommended Reading:
Crazy Diamond: Syd Barrett & the Dawn of Pink Floyd, by Mike Watkinson & Pete Anderson (1991, Omnibus). Fine, straightforward bio with plenty of anecdotes from friends and associates. Jammed with fascinating stories about Barrett's eccentricities, but the respectful treatment gives most priority to his wonderful music. The Pink Floyd bio *Saucerful of Secrets* (Harmony), by Nicholas Schaffner, also contains a good deal of interesting information about Barrett in its early chapters.

Nick Drake

Publicity-shy Nick Drake turns the tables on his photographer.
Credit: Courtesy Hannibal Records

If rock has an equivalent to the romantic poets of the early nineteenth century, Nick Drake may fit the bill as well as anyone. The brooding wistfulness, the bittersweet longing for the past, the cloud of despair at ever quite fitting into the imperfect material world—the singer-songwriter delivered all of the above in a low-key, melodic fashion that disguised the turbulence of his musings. Tragically, he fulfilled another tenet of the romantic myth by dying at a young age, in circumstances that indicated a possible suicide.

There's still much debate about whether Drake's death in 1974 at the age of 26 was indeed by his own hand. But almost all would agree that the folk-rocker was ill-equipped for a contented existence on this earth, let alone survival in the volatile industry of popular music. Unable to effectively communicate with other human beings except through his music, he made three brilliant albums in the late '60s and early '70s that found few listeners during his lifetime. In the manner of another tormented British genius, Syd Barrett, these have generated a cult following among old and new generations that simply grows and grows without leveling off. There are probably many more times as many hardcore Drake fans now, over two decades since his death, than there were at his prime.

Early home recordings by Drake in the late '60s (now bootlegged) show a promising British folkie in the mold of Donovan and less celebrated British guitarists such as Bert Jansch, mixing covers of '60s warhorses like "Let's Get Together" with his own more idiosyncratic compositions. After seeing Drake support Country Joe McDonald at the Roundhouse in London, Ashley Hutchings of Fairport Convention recommended the Cambridge student to producer Joe Boyd. Via his work with Fairport Convention and Incredible String Band (among others), Boyd, a young American based in London, had already built a resume as the top producer on the British folk-rock scene.

Drake was signed to Boyd's Witchseason Productions company, and Joe was in the producer's chair for Nick's first album, *Five Leaves Left* (1969). This was an astonishing debut for a 21-year-old, with a far greater compositional and musical sophistication than the acoustic-oriented tunes on his home tapes. Debts to Donovan, Tim Buckley, and Van Morrison were obvious, but run through a peculiarly British filter and Drake's distinctively jazzy, breathy vocals.

Working with a floating cast of session musicians including bassist Danny Thompson (moonlighting from top British folk ensemble Pentangle) and (on one track) Richard Thompson, Drake sang with a smoky, measured tone that didn't suggest detachment nearly as much as a sort of foggy melancholy. Read on their own, the lyrics had a downbeat longing verging on despair. But combined with the lovely, baroque orchestration (fellow Cambridge student Robert Kirby, who had never worked in a studio before, did most of the arrangements), the songs grew into something more complex and intriguing. Rarely had such a bitter pill been served in such a soothing package.

Boyd takes care to praise an oft-overlooked facet of the singer's music: "When you put aside the singing, lyrics, the arrangements, and everything else, and you just listen to the guitar playing, you can hear that Nick was an extraordinary musician with very, very strong technique, big strong hands. The guitar playing was incredibly clean and accurate and inventive. The way he developed his tunings, some people still haven't figured out some of his tunes."

Although Drake's career encompassed only three proper albums, his discography is remarkable in that all of the full-length works were quite different from each other. What's more, if you gather a roomful of Nick Drake devotees together and ask them to choose their favorite recording, the votes would most likely be evenly split among the three albums. Critics thus identify Drake's "peak" at their peril, but it may be that *Bryter Later* (1970) was his most accessible work. From a purely musical standpoint, it's his most diverse work, with Dave Pegg and Dave Mattacks from Fairport Convention providing most of the rhythm section, and appearances by John Cale and Richard Thompson. Female soul singers Doris Troy and Pat Arnold even do backup vocals on "Poor

Boy." Robert Kirby again adds some beautiful classical-influenced orchestral arrangements.

The bemused, melodic grandeur of Drake's peculiar melancholia remained unfettered. The singer-songwriter took a most unusual chance by dispensing with lyrics and voice altogether for a few orchestrated instrumental tracks, which rate among the most appealing selections on the record. Joe Boyd—a man who has produced records by Pink Floyd, R.E.M., Richard Thompson, and several other legends—goes so far as to say, "It's one of those albums that I can listen to without ever thinking, 'I should have done this better.' I enjoy it every time I hear it."

Drake had left Cambridge to pursue music full-time in London after *Five Leaves Left*, but it was soon apparent that he was rather too introverted to play the pop star game. He rarely played live to support the record; he probably gave no more than a dozen concerts after his debut LP, and never played at all in public after 1970. There would be only one unrevealing interview in the music press. In an effort to make Nick's songs more widely known in the industry, Boyd even engaged Elton John—then a struggling singer-songwriter himself—to sing demos of several of Drake's songs. (The results, along other John-sung demos of songs by John Martyn and the Incredible String Band's Mike Heron, have since been bootlegged.)

Oddly enough for such an uncompromising artist, Drake placed a high value on commercial success, and when *Bryter Later* sold in very modest numbers, he became severely depressed. The already introverted musician moved back to his parents' house and began withdrawing from most forms of social contact. His mental illness took a more subdued, less flamboyant form than that of Syd Barrett, another legend of the era who withdrew into seclusion. Drake would sit motionlessly for hours on end or wander about aimlessly. In her biography, French pop singer Françoise Hardy remembers how Nick sat in a corner, never saying a word, when he watched her do a session for an album she was making in England in the early '70s. Drake, in Hardy's words, "was truly the champion of inhibition." And, perhaps worst of all, he wasn't able to write more songs.

"When we were doing Françoise's album, Nick Drake came up and sat next to me in the control room," remembers guitarist Jerry Donahue. "I was just making some friendly conversation. He was very quiet in between questions; there would just be a gap. Then I'd ask another question. And each time I did, his eyebrows would raise way up, his eyes would widen, and it was like an effort to kind of get the answer out to satisfy the situation at hand—'I've gotta deal with this—somebody's putting me on the line, they've actually addressed me and asked me a question. I will do my best to get an answer out.'

"Then having successfully managed to crank an answer out, he would withdraw again into silence, until which time I might feel inclined to ask him another question, and the same sequence of events would take place. It was *very* bizarre. I've never known anybody like him. And he wasn't unfriendly. But you just really felt like you were putting the guy on the spot when you'd ask the most simple harmless questions. I thought he had a real rough time with himself. It was impossible to get to know him, certainly in that brief encounter."

Boyd knew Drake about as well as any of his musical associates—which is to say, he only knew him up to a point. "He was expressive, but very quietly and very shyly," he observes. "He'd never behave as what you would call an extrovert. Sometimes you'd do something in the studio and I'd sort of look around and see what Nick thought of what somebody was doing as an overdub, or something like that. He'd be looking at his shoes, he'd kind of stutter a couple of times— 'well, uh, I'm not sure I like this.' He was very clear, but the texture of the behavior was never extroverted. It was always very quiet and sort of self-contained, hesitant about voicing."

Boyd himself was no longer available to work with Drake after *Bryter Later*, having moved to Los Angeles to work for Warner Brothers. "The reasons he wasn't successful during his lifetime were a combination of fairly simple things," he adds. "First of all, he didn't build up a live following or tour. The example of someone who I guess could be a kind of parallel to Nick in some ways and did do well [was] Leonard Cohen. His records were released in North America at the height of the boom in FM radio, when people were playing a lot of album tracks. He didn't tour either. He didn't perform until well after he had become famous.

"Because Nick's records weren't released in America until the early '70s, it was really down to England to make him a star. He fell, unfortunately, in the period [of] the demise of [pirate radio]. All you had was BBC Radio One and there wasn't really much room for album tracks or for artists like Nick on radio in Britain. Eliminate live performances, radio exposure—I mean, there isn't a lot there to get what he did across. But at the same time it's also true that I think the music doesn't reach out and grab people by the lapels. It takes a bit of getting used to, and it's also very English. I think for America at that time, a kind of unassertive introspective English musician wasn't necessarily going to get a lot of attention."

Drake did rouse himself out of his depression to record his final album, *Pink Moon* (1972), with John Wood, who had engineered the first two records. The ten songs were recorded in just two sessions, and often in just one take. Featuring only Drake and his guitar (there was a piano overdub on the title track), it was not just Nick unplugged, but utterly naked. His previous work could not exactly have been described as happy-go-lucky, but this was certainly his bleakest effort. Writing as though each word cost a shilling, Drake chose to say more with less: the lyric of one song ("Know") is only 18 words in its entirety. The least commercially viable of Drake's albums, it is also the one that is championed the most among his fans.

Drake himself probably suspected that *Pink Moon* wasn't bound for Top of the Pops, delivering the tapes to Island Records' receptionist without a word (Island didn't realize they had the album until they opened the package after Drake left). Shortly after its release, he checked himself into a psychiatric hospital for five weeks. Thereafter he wrote little music and rarely ventured out, except to see friends like fellow British folk-rock guitarist John Martyn, who has added to the chorus of describing Drake (in *Record Collector*) as "the most withdrawn person I've ever met."

Drake did manage to put down four more songs (since issued on the *Time of No Reply* collection), but the sessions for a prospective album went into limbo. Françoise Hardy once asked him to write for her, but nothing came of it. On November 25, 1974, with the fate of the fourth album still undetermined, Drake was found dead in his bedroom in his parents' house after taking an overdose of antidepressant medication. He left no note, and it was ruled a suicide by his coroner, although the verdict was disputed by his friends and family.

Yet Drake's cult has now grown to the point where he has sold more records since his death than he did in his lifetime. Famous musicians such as Jackson Browne, Peter Buck of R.E.M., and Tom Verlaine have cited their admiration for Drake's work. But the bulk of his acclaim may come from the alternative rock underground, which has found an instant affinity with Drake's inability to fit in to the world as we know it, even if few are able or willing to specifically emulate his solitary sound.

"The reason why it's successful now is because it's too good *not* to be," summarizes Boyd. "There are a lot of things which feel like they're a part of their time, and they have a fascination for that reason. But I think Nick's music doesn't really feel that way. His songs were very rarely covered, which I think is partly due to his uniqueness and the fact that what he did was completely outside all trends and movements. It feels kind of outside of time in a way, so it doesn't date. People, once they sit down quietly and listen to a Nick Drake record, very rarely lose interest after that."

Recommended Recordings:
Fruit Tree (1985, Hannibal). It may seem excessive to recommend a four-CD box set as the definitive release. But Drake's body of work was so strong that once any single album is digested, nothing less than everything else will do. This has all three of the albums he released during his lifetime, as well as a worthy collection of outtakes and demos, *Time of No Reply*.

The Complete Home Recordings (1996, Nixed). With such a slim oeuvre to choose from, Drake fans are eager for evidence of anything else that the man recorded. This bootleg collection of over 20 home recordings, made in the late '60s before he had signed a record contract, doesn't match his studio work in either songwriting or performance, but it's a nifty and enjoyable document of his folk-based roots.

Recommended Reading:
Nick Drake, by Patrick Humphries (1997, Bloomsbury, UK). It's something of a miracle that a 280-page biography could be fashioned from the life of someone who only gave one interview, and rarely talked at all during his last few years. This does a commendable job, however, of fleshing out his story as much as possible, with numerous interviews with friends and associates dating back to Drake's schoolboy years. Inevitably many gaps remain, yet this manages to clarify many mini-myths which have sprung up around Drake since his death, and offers lucid, passionate analysis of his recordings and compositions.

Mad Geniuses

Syd Barrett, Roky Erickson, and Skip Spence may now, to various degrees, be incapable of communicating effectively with the outside world, or even of totally caring for themselves. This disassociation from reality has to some extent lit the fires of the extraterrestrial glow of their music. Syd, Roky, and Skip may be some of the most extreme examples of talent gone so awry it's taken them straight outside the music business. Yet they're not even the most famous of rock icons who have attracted a cult due, in part, to their form of mad genius—not by a longshot.

By far the most renowned of the '60s acid casualties was Brian Wilson, leader, principal songwriter, and producer of the Beach Boys' greatest work. As is the case with all "acid casualties," drugs were most likely only one of the factors involved in Wilson's emotional breakdown. Years after the Beach Boys' commercial peak, stories began to emerge about Brian's abusive father, Murry; it's been speculated that the deafness in one of Brian's ears may have been caused by a childhood beating. There was also the tremendous artistic and financial pressure bearing down on Brian as the one who supplied and produced the group's hits, especially as the fortunes of two of his brothers (Beach Boys guitarist Carl Wilson, and drummer Dennis Wilson) and one cousin (Beach Boys lead singer Mike Love) were directly tied to the eldest sibling. Boasting one of the most clean-cut images in the industry, the Beach Boys were actually one of rock's most dysfunctional families.

None of the public knew this when Wilson guided the Beach Boys through *Pet Sounds* (1966), which regularly appears on critics polls as one of the best 20 or so albums of all time. That record was the optimum balance between magnificent songs and experimental production, but with his proposed follow-up, *Smile,* Brian began to move into densely constructed tone poems that sometimes approached musique concrete. A lot of this music (much of which is now widely available on bootleg; excerpts appear on the Beach Boys'

Good Vibrations box set) was beautiful, but it probably wouldn't have been nearly as commercial as their previous hits. Business and family pressures—as well as Wilson's own mysterious inability to finish what he'd started, as he endlessly tinkered with tracks and compositional ideas—meant that *Smile* was never released.

Wilson descended into depression and rarely ventured out of the house by the 1970s; his physical health deteriorated. He was eventually placed in round-the-clock care of a psychiatrist, Eugene Landy, whom some have scorned as an opportunist for his unconventional methods and financial practices. Recent attempts to place Brian back in the public eye—via a glossy Don Was-directed documentary, for instance—project a cheerful desperation in their insistence that everything's fine now, really. Everything's probably *not* fine. On a ballyhooed 1995 comeback pairing with Van Dyke Parks (Wilson's songwriting partner during the *Smile* era), Brian did not write any of the material.

The worst of Wilson's problems, at least, were largely shielded from the public eye. That wasn't always the case for Peter Green. Green was the leader, lead guitarist, principal songwriter, and principal singer of Fleetwood Mac, which had just become one of the most popular groups in England and Europe when Green decided to leave in 1970. The reason was not just to pursue a solo career, which he did with little success. It was also because he'd become extremely uneasy with the wealth and fame attached to pop stardom. Lots of rock stars give lip service to such sentiments in their dashes from the limo to room service; Green was one of the very few, or perhaps even only, musician in his position who apparently meant what he said. Even before his rather sudden exit, Green had proposed that the band donate their profits to charity. The rest of the group couldn't agree to do this, no matter how much they sympathized with Peter's altruism.

Fleetwood Mac in those days were not playing the sunny Californian pop that brought them international stardom in the mid-'70s. They were a gritty, moody blues-rock band, and Green wrote their best songs, which were soulful and eloquent statements with a strong hint of despair. A lot of despair apparently seeped into Green's spirit during the 1970s, when, after an unfocused solo debut album, he largely retired from the music business. He moved to Israel to work on a kibbutz, and upon returning to England worked at menial jobs as a cemetery gardner and a hospital orderly. He gave away all his equipment to Thin Lizzy guitarist Snowy White; then he asked for it back. Following a still-fuzzy 1977 incident in which he was reported to have threatened his former manager with a gun, he was diagnosed as a schizophrenic. He made an unimpressive return to recording, but by the end of the 1980s, tabloids were reporting that the former guitar god was sleeping without a roof over his head.

Circumstances improved for Green in the '90s, when he actually returned to playing music in a low-key fashion, although years of medication and bouts with mental illness had obviously taken their toll. Sometimes his struggles are blamed on bad acid from the Fleetwood Mac days, particularly on an occasion in early 1970 in Munich, when Green was taken (some say virtually kidnapped) to a nearby commune where drinks were spiked.

Peter told Mick Fleetwood he wanted to live in the commune; Mick and the group's manager had to drive there to convince Green to resume the tour When he gave a rare interview for *MOJO* in 1996, his manager warned reporter Cliff Jones, "He's great on the '60s. Last week's more of a problem." (Fleetwood Mac had more than their share of instability in their early days, incidentally; guitarist Jeremy Spencer bolted from the band in California during an American tour to join the Children of God sect.)

There are some performers who have been labeled as "mad geniuses" although, on closer inspection, they seem not to fit anyone's definition of madness at all. One of the most notorious cases is Scott Walker, profiled in this book. Walker's extreme reclusion—when set against the standards of behavior expected of pop stars—led some to conclude that he must be locked up comatose somewhere. After all, he was only making albums once every ten years, never giving interviews, and never showing his face (let alone singing) in public. One of Walker's associates told me that, over the course of a career that has brought him into contact with numerous famous musicians, Walker—a close collaborator—is the only one who has never given him his phone number. Yet interviews by the man himself in 1995 (after a rare album release) confirmed that Walker was very much in control of his senses, even if he maintained a Garbo-like mania for privacy.

The disappearance of Peter Perrett, leader of the new wave cult group the Only Ones, from the music business for a decade or so can be chalked up less to eccentricity than a more mundane factor—heavy drug use, as he's detailed since he resumed a solo career in the mid-1990s. But long absences from the business, combined with reports (true or unverified) of behavior that deviates from the showbiz norm, has been enough to fuel rumors of bizarre withdrawal from society. That was the fate that befell Poly Styrene of X-Ray Spex after she joined the Hare Krishnas—although, as she now takes pains to clarify (see the X-Ray Spex chapter), she wasn't making music because she couldn't get a record deal, not because she'd vanished into the netherworlds of mysticism.

Sometimes the madness in mad geniuses is only for show, as with Screaming Lord Sutch's satirical political campaigns, or Arthur Brown's fire-coated helmets, underneath which lay reasonably ordinary Englishmen. Sometimes it explodes all too violently into real life, as in the suicide of Joy Division's Ian Curtis, or producer Joe Meek, whose tortured life ended after he murdered his landlady and immediately turned the gun upon himself. Many are classified as "mad" only because they are willfully eccentric, like Julian Cope, who does concept albums about the destructive power of the automobile and writes books about German '70s progressive rock. What gives the lives of Syd Barrett, Skip Spence, Roky Erickson, Nick Drake, and Joe Meek a special fascination is that the madness seems genuine—the barriers between their life and their art proving to be all too fragile.

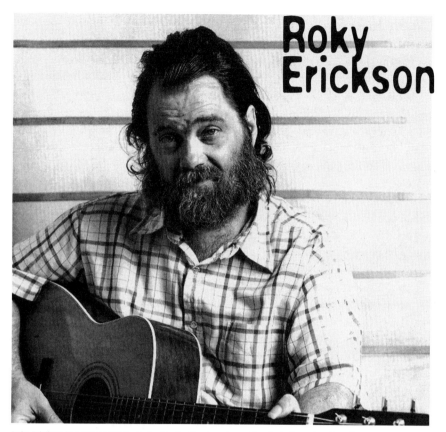

Roky Erickson in a 1994 publicity photo. Credit: Courtesy Trance Syndicate Records; photo Scott Newton

"*I consider him one of the best straightahead rock and roll singers.*
  —Stu Cook, Creedence Clearwater Revival bassist, and producer of two Roky Erickson albums

"*Stu Cook and I thought that he was the most interesting lyricist, writing about the most interesting stuff, that anybody in rock was at the time.*
  —Craig Luckin, ex-manager of Roky Erickson

"*Only a Captain Beefheart or a Roky Erickson could write something like 'Click Your Fingers Applauding the Play.' Mick Jagger couldn't come up with something that brilliant. Yet he'll make $47 million this year, while Roky lives in a dump.*"
  —Henry Rollins, *Rolling Stone*, April 20, 1995

"*He's the greatest rock and roll singer in the world, to my way of thinking. Still is.*
  —John Ike Walton, drummer for the 13th Floor Elevators

Clearly Roky Erickson is not the sort of cult legend that inspires lukewarm testimonials. He's what those in the know call a musician's musician. In his native Austin, Texas, he's more than that—he's an institution, revered on the same level as his old friend and one-time Austin resident Janis Joplin.

This innovator of psychedelic music may have escaped the early grave that was Joplin's fate. But some feel, he's been condemned to a far grislier destiny. After a one-shot garage psychedelic classic, "You're Gonna Miss Me," Roky's '60s band, the 13th Floor Elevators, ran aground in a tangle of drug problems and personnel conflicts. Sent to a mental hospital near the end of the '60s for several years, Erickson has never recovered from the ordeal or his various chemical excesses. When profiled by *Rolling Stone* in 1995, the cult legend was living in a one-bedroom house behind a porn store on the fringe of Austin. He was spending his days cranking half a dozen sound systems simultaneously—"a rock station, gospel music, a police scanner or CB radio, a monster movie on the VCR, white-noise static," Don McLeese reported. He may not have died, but his mind, to most outward appearances, was fried.

How much remains of the Roky who fronted Texas' first all-out psychedelic band is uncertain. In the mid-'60s, the teenage Erickson had recorded a promising but underproduced local single with the Spades, "You're Gonna Miss Me"/"We Sell Soul." Even at this point, there was no mistaking that inimitable voice—equal parts Buddy Holly, Little Richard, and pure dementia that veered off into hair-raising yelps and fire-engine screams. Erickson was persuaded to join a more experienced band, the 13th Floor Elevators, who cut a remake of "You're Gonna Miss Me." The song became a big regional hit, and a small national one—to this day, the only bit of widespread commercial success that has come Roky's way.

"You're Gonna Miss Me" retained a fair amount of garage raunch, but the band was pursuing more avowedly psychedelic directions by the time of their first album in 1966. "Roller Coaster," "Reverberation," "Don't Fall Down," and "Fire Engine" all reflected the mania of the acid-rock experience. The Elevators' guitar-dominated rush was given a strange, exotic flavor by Tommy Hall's odd jug percussion runs. "Splash I," perhaps the best song Erickson has ever sung, also gave evidence of the sturdy, tender, melodic folk-rocker underneath. "Roky was a ball of fire, man," exclaims original 13th Floor Elevator drummer John Ike Walton. "He played lead, rhythm, sang, played harmonica, and ran the whole band by himself."

Ex-Texan Chet Helms was instrumental in setting up dates for the Elevators at the Avalon Ballroom in San Francisco. The group played there so often that they're sometimes mistakenly identified as an early San Francisco psychedelic act. For a few months in early 1966, Janis Joplin even sang backup vocals with the band, though she would shortly establish herself as a solo singer with Big Brother & the Holding Company. Yet chemical enlightenment was soon getting the better of some of the band's more enthusiastic drug consumers.

Walton was a non-acid-taker who would eventually leave in frustration over the band's drug excesses, particularly those of Erickson and Hall. "Those guys would take a whole bunch of acid before they'd go play. After a few concerts at the Avalon, it got so bad that Roky wouldn't even sing. He'd go out there and turn on his amp, turn towards his amplifier, and try to get feedback through his guitar. And he would just sit there.

"So [guitarist] Stacy [Sutherland] and [bassist] Ronnie [Leatherman] and I didn't know what to do. We just decided, well, let's just play some blues, let's just jam, play some double shuffles. We did that, and Roky would just continue to sit back there with his back to the audience and his amplifiers squealing. Too much drugs, man. I don't know how much is too much, but it was too much for Roky, because he forgot to sing . . . he forgot that he was our lead singer."

Around this time, Erickson found time to lend a hand on the recording of the first album by the Red Krayola, another Texas band on the International Artists label whose wall-of-acid weirdness made the Elevators sound almost normal. "He was one of those people who just never had any doubts about what direction he was going in," claims Red Krayola mainstay Mayo Thompson. "One could look at Roky and knew that he knew exactly what was going on, that he knew what we were talking about, he could hear the music.

"My impression of him was that he was an extremely sensitive person and extremely talented, with a great deal of energy, power, charisma, all those kinds of things. But in a certain sort of sense, somebody who needed somebody to take care of other kinds of affairs for him on some level, that's all. He didn't seem to me to be debilitated in any way." Thompson takes care to add, "Taking seriously the idea of taking acid every day is questionable. Even to me at the time, being wild child or whatever, you look at that and you go, boy, that's extreme."

Personnel shuffles midway through the Elevators' second album (*Easter Everywhere*) may have resulted in the creation of a similar but less impressive effort than their debut. By the time of the band's final studio LP, Stacy Sutherland was writing most of the material. Erickson would soon face a far more troubling dilemma than the disintegration of his band. Busted for marijuana in the state of Texas—notorious at the time for meting out harsh sentences to drug offenders—Erickson pleaded insanity. In the opinion of some of his friends, that might have been the worst mistake of his life.

For three years, Erickson was confined to Rusk State Hospital for the criminally insane. With the help of family and friends, Roky eventually gained his release in the early '70s. As part of the effort to prove himself fit for society, Erickson wrote his first book, *Openers*, much of which deals with Christian religious themes, although opinions are mixed as to how much of the text reflects Roky's actual views of Christianity.

The electroshock treatments and medication administered to Erickson at Rusk, however, exacted a heavy toll from which he has never recovered. He was making music again soon enough. Walton was one of several musicians with whom Erickson worked shortly after his release, but John confirms that Roky wasn't all that together, especially when he drifted back into drug use. Erickson was increasingly prone to forgetting the words to his songs, and in Walton's view, Roky's guitar playing had deteriorated.

"He came to me and said, 'I don't want to play in a band with somebody who doesn't like my lead guitar playing.' Well, Roky's the worst lead guitar player on earth!" Walton laughs affectionately. "They don't come any worse. He can play rhythm. But when he'd start taking that lead, it wouldn't matter to him what key that was in. He played the same notes no matter what. It was awful, it was just horrible."

Vocally Erikson's talents remained intact, and as a songwriter, he was more far out than ever. His focus, however, was shifting from levitation and chemical spirituality to an odd mixture of tunes about demons, monsters, and disfigured creatures that owed more to comic books and horror movies than LSD. Some live gigs with cult Texas roots-rockers the Sir Douglas Quintet in the mid-'70s resulted in Craig Luckin, manager of Sahm's group, handling Erickson's affairs as well. By the end of the '70s, Roky had been shepherded into the studio for a proper album, with ex-Creedence Clearwater Revival bassist Stu Cook handling production.

The sessions, however, would not turn out to be run-of-the-mill affairs, and not just because Roky was wont to be singing about two-headed dogs at the time. First, Luckin and Cook had to get him out of a Texas State mental hospital in Austin, to which Roky had been committed during one of his down cycles. "I took the approach that, since Roky was so, shall we say, unpredictable—mercurial is a good word—there's no telling where he was going to be at in terms of his desire to work on any given day at any given time during the day," explains Cook. "When he takes his medication, as bad as that stuff is in the long term, it definitely works in the short term. He was cooperative, inquisitive, alert. But not really focused on the recording.

"I finally figured out, the way to do it is just get him in the studio and just keep coming at him. Don't let him have a chance to start talking about his apartment or dinner. Just keep him flooded with musical paths. That way, I found I could keep his attention. And whenever he started to lose it, I'd use my bag of tricks. Once it started to slow down, he would start to wander.

"So I developed a plan where I just had to strike when the poker was hot, at all times. Had to have everything ready to go for him, and when he got tired of doing one song, I'd have to immediately move on to another song. I'd have to have an assembly set up to maximize the amount of time that I had with him."

Leaving nothing to chance, Cook adds, "Whenever that red light was on, I'd let him go. When we'd get to the end of the song, I'd rewind it, and we'd just do another take. I would fill up every track practically on the tape with Roky's singing. When I ran out of tracks, I would just run another tape—always always

always record anything Roky said or did. We'd be in the control room talking, I'd have the button on the talkback mike—I'd have it taped down so that anything that was said in the control room went to tape. So that anything he said, any inspiration he got, any comment he made, we would always have it to refer to or in fact edit it in, use it, in a song. So I ended up with reels and reels and reels of wild, unsynced Roky stuff. A lot of which, later, when he wasn't in the studio, I'd sit there with the engineer, and we'd fly it onto the tape."

It wasn't always certain what Roky had in mind as far as the final product. "I think he's a tremendous songwriter myself. I think he has this vision that's unlike any other artist that I've worked with or even many that I've heard. But he would not be organized at all in his approach. Every time he'd sing a song, he'd sing it differently—different lyrics. He had an idea of what he wanted to do, but because of his condition, he was not able to repeat himself. [With] most singers, each take is the same, you're just looking for a special performance, or you're trying to correct the flat singing, the sharp singing.

"With Roky, it was much more abstract than that. I would have to help him write the song in the sense that from everything that he said or sang, I'd have to assemble it into verses or choruses. How I thought, if I was writing a song, this is how I'd do it. The real test of the whole thing was when Roky heard the album when it was done," he chuckles, "to watch his reactions to how his songs had come out. But he liked it."

Roky Erickson & the Aliens, however—picked up by CBS in Britain—was not a success. It wasn't just because Roky could barely manage to utter more than five words at a time when he was interviewed in London by Nick Kent (the subsequent article is reprinted in Kent's anthology of pieces, *The Dark Stuff*). It was also because Roky's stuff was too strange for a mass audience, even as songs like "Two Headed Dog," "Creature with the Atom Brain," and "I Walked with a Zombie" guaranteed a cult following among both '60s acidheads and punk/new wave-types. It's not quite accurate to say that Erickson had abandoned psychedelia, as he in fact did not even write most of the 13th Floor Elevators' lyrics to begin with; he was usually responsible for the melodies on the Elevators songs that he contributed to, not the words.

Cook agrees that Erickson's vision had changed considerably since the Elevators days. "The particular set of material that he presented to me is more along the lines of a comic book nightmare in subject matter. He's very concerned about aliens and things like that, other life forms, interplanetary invasion. A lot of times, you really couldn't tell—the way Roky'd look at you, he'd give you one of those looks—and wonder, well, is he putting me on? Or is he *too* serious? I wanted to keep it light, even though the subject matter was at times kind of nightmarish, ghoulish."

If Roky was indeed putting people on, he didn't help his case by declaring in 1982 that he was inhabited by a Martian, going as far as to get the statement notarized. Craig Luckin maintains that this was never meant to be taken seriously. "He never wanted to talk about the mental hospital or arrest or anything. So when the interviewers would ask 'what have you been doing since the Elevators' or whatever, this was his response to the pain. He knew that [pretending to be an alien] was the only way to turn a tragic situation into a humorous situation. In most of his later interviews, he explained to the press that he really knew he never was an alien."

But by the early '80s, Roky's image as a brain-damaged idiot savant of sorts had been cemented in the media. Any ground he might have gained on musical merits was negated by his tendency to work with slipshod bands and ignore existing record contracts, resulting in sub-standard, hastily conceived live and studio albums that sounded more pedestrian than extraterrestrial. One acoustic, unplugged album was even recorded in a Holiday Inn hotel room—and it actually turned out to be one of his better solo efforts. Live, Roky could be an ordeal, often unable to make it through an entire set without forgetting his material or losing interest.

Roky's done little recording since the mid-1980s, experiencing psychological problems and occasional run-ins with the police related to the cycles of his medication. In 1990, he was prosecuted for stealing mail from a neighbor. Erickson's many fans rallied to his defense, crafting a tribute album on Sire (*Where the Pyramid Meets the Eye: A Tribute to Roky Erickson*) that was probably the only project that could have united R.E.M., ZZ Top, and the Butthole Surfers in service of the same cause (the charges were dropped). Henry Rollins' 2.13.61 Publications has published *Openers II*, a collection of Roky's lyrics.

Roky made a fairly effective, folk-flavored return to the studio in the 1990s for material that ended up on *All That May Do My Rhyme*, which had cameos by Charlie Sexton, Paul Leary of the Butthole Surfers, and Roky's brother Sumner Erickson, a member of the Pittsburgh Symphony. A 1997 episode of the cult TV series *The X-Files* even wove a screenplay called *The Truth About Aliens* into the plot that was attributed to a character named—Roky Erickson. Clearly he has some friends in high places.

"The most appreciative audience for Roky seems to be, in any particular era, the hippest rock songwriters and musicians," says Luckin. "The fact that it hasn't reached a bigger audience is something that befuddles most of those people, as well as myself."

Whether that matters so much to Erikson is a matter of speculation. He may be unable to make it through his songs in his rare live appearances these days. But he's out of the hospital for the time being, aided by a network of friends that tolerate the electronic madness in his Austin shack. The cacophony of sound, perhaps, is a reflection of his own inner confusion—and at this late date, it's doubtful whether he'll be able to sort out all the voices, musical or otherwise, for the comeback that he may or may not even want.

Recommended Recordings:
The 13th Floor Elevators:

The 13th Floor Elevators (1966, Collectables). The first album remains the group's strongest, featuring "Splash I" and "You're Gonna Miss Me," though it is perhaps not as mind-blowing as Elevators fans may have you believe. A domestic best-of consolidating the several albums' worth of Elevators material is overdue, though one did appear on the French Eva label in 1994.

Roky Erickson:

The Evil One (1981, Pink Dust). Erickson's sessions with Stu Cook in the producer's chair are generally considered his most focused and worthwhile solo work; the results, confusingly, were spread across a UK-only LP (*Roky Erickson and the Aliens*) and *The Evil One* LP, which combined five of the *Aliens* tracks with five others. The Pink Dust CD reissue combines the contents of both albums into one disc.

All That May Do My Rhyme (1995, Trance Syndicate). Roky's folkier, more romantic side comes through on this rootsy combination of sessions from the mid-'80s and mid-'90s, although the singer himself is not as demonically inspired here as he is on his harder-rocking efforts.

Lee Hazlewood

"Poet, Fool or Bum?" That was the question Lee Hazlewood posed with the title of his 1973 album. Britain's *New Musical Express* answered the query with a one-word review worthy of *Spinal Tap*: "Bum."

For a growing cult of listeners, the answer isn't that simple. How can you judge a man who sounds like Johnny Cash might after gargling with razor blades? Who can't seem to decide whether to be a Nashville cornball or a brooding desert Leonard Cohen? Who experienced immense commercial success producing pop stars like Nancy Sinatra and Duane Eddy, but regularly churned out oddball solo albums that could only have appealed to the most narrow of audiences? Who invested a great deal of time and effort in the sessions he produced for others, but seemed to make many of his own records as if he were in a race with the studio clock? Who only made the charts under his own name by cutting incongruous duets with the daughter of the most famous American pop singer of the twentieth century?

No one's sure if Hazlewood was trying to make deep statements or was constructing some kind of lengthy, inside cosmic joke. Perhaps Lee wasn't even sure himself. Hazlewood refuses to clear up the mystery, avoiding the media like a patient evading his next dental appointment. Of all the artists researched for this book, none proved to be a more slippery eel than Lee Hazlewood, his present whereabouts varying wildly according to the source. He was in Sweden. He was in Spain. No, he was in Las Vegas. No, he wasn't in Las Vegas, but he was back in the United States. Where? Don't know. Try his publishers. (Calls to them were not returned.)

Even Lee's associates seem unable to grant concrete insights into his songwriting and general weltanschauung. What did he have in mind when he wrote songs about velvet mornings and mystical women named Phaedra? Couldn't tell you. Was he as strange a guy to work with as rumor would have it? Yep (no elaboration forthcoming). "That doesn't surprise me at all," says Billy Strange, who worked extensively with Lee as an arranger in the 1960s. "He was slippery even when he was in Hollywood and we were working together. There are things in his mind that nobody else knows."

Hazlewood is most acclaimed/notorious for his recordings from the 1960s and early '70s, as well as the hits he wrote and produced for Nancy Sinatra between 1966 and 1968. (His LHI label also released the sole album by the International Submarine Band, Gram Parsons' first country-rock group.) However, he'd been an active player in the music industry since the mid-1950s, when he was a country DJ in Phoenix, Arizona, moving into production with a country-flavored rockabilly smash, Sanford Clark's "Fool, Fool, Fool," in 1956. He made his first true mark with a series of instrumental smashes by guitarist Duane Eddy, who employed the revolutionary approach of playing bigger-than-life twangs on his bottom strings on hits like "Rebel Rouser."

"There used to be a piano player, Eddie Duchin, out of New York," remembers guitarist Al Casey, who played on many Hazlewood productions in the '50s and '60s. "He would always play the melody real low on the piano, which was unusual. [Lee] asked Duane, can you do that on guitar? Then they worked in the tremolo on the guitar, and the echo chamber and all that, and there it was." "It" was a massive low, growling guitar sound that would be featured on virtually all of Eddy's hits until the run finally exhausted itself in the early '60s, though Lee would continue to favor such low guitar sounds on his many subsequent productions.

By the 1960s Hazlewood had gone Hollywood, where he kept busy producing, songwriting, helping to run small labels, recording as part of a folkish group called the Shacklefords, and making his own eccentric country-folk-pop-rock records. He got some pop hits by producing (and writing some material for) Dino, Desi & Billy, which featured the juvenile sons of Dean Martin and Desi Arnaz. Had it not been for one song, Hazlewood might be remembered today only for such interesting but relatively minor accomplishments.

In the mid-'60s, Lee began working with Frank Sinatra's daughter Nancy, who was on the verge of being dropped from Reprise (Frank's own label) after a series of flops. Nancy came across a demo of one of Lee's songs, "These Boots Are

Lee Hazlewood, reunited with Nancy Sinatra onstage in the mid-1990s. Credit: Tom Erickson

Made for Walking," which she wanted to make her next single; Lee argued that it was meant to be sung by a man, not a woman. Sinatra got her way, singing in a much lower register than usual. The famous descending quarter-tone bass run, a variation on the sound Hazlewood had devised for Duane Eddy, was a big part of the appeal of the record, which was half-menace and half-camp. Sprightly go-go horns also helped the single get to #1, and the song established a partnership whereby Hazlewood would write and produce most of Sinatra's hit singles.

"Nancy had been recorded by people such as Jimmy Bowen," notes Billy Strange, a major contributor to her records as arranger. "But they'd all been big pop records with strings and horns and all that mess. I think what made those particular records that Lee and I did on her unique was that it was the first time that anybody had ever taken a rather country approach with Nancy. And, in order to save it from being totally hillbilly, we added some horns. Here she was, the daughter of a famous pop singer, and she was in fact neither pop nor country. We sort of filled in around her with a little country, slightly pop base that made it very different for the marketplace. Plus I think that 'Boots,' being as odd-ball a piece of material as it was, was just the icing on the cake."

Hazlewood and Sinatra were two very different talents that nevertheless needed each other to make a splash. Hazlewood had the songs—hooky, slyly silly country-pop songs with enough rock 'n' roll to make the hit parade—and the production acumen, tapping the cream of L.A.'s session players, like Glen Campbell, guitarist James Burton, and drummer Hal Blaine. Lee's sandpaper growl of a voice could have never put the songs over to a big audience. Sinatra, with her sex kitten peep, could do that with an ease that made it easy to overlook the occasional strange lyrical twist.

And some of the songs *were* strange, although their subversive structures went overlooked by rock cognoscenti at a time when *Sgt. Pepper,* the Doors, and Jimi Hendrix were blowing minds left and right. "These Boots Are Made for Walking" itself had some odd sadistic undertones; "Friday's Child" and "Love Eyes" were forlorn, even bluesy numbers with a downbeat mysterioso vibe quite at odds with Nancy's chirpy Hollywood image. Hazlewood would contrast the slick, Tijuana Brass-like professionalism of the horn and string charts with grungy fuzz guitars and touches that seemed oh-so-faintly psychedelic.

Never was this more apparent than on "Lightning's Girl," a 1967 hit that paired a crunching fuzz guitar riff with violently ascending violins that were as dissonant as the orchestral crescendo on the Beatles' "A Day in the Life"—all underlined by Sinatra's bitchiest vocal. Yet underneath all of this was a cowboy love triangle ballad, with hokey vocal choruses for emphasis. Few producers and songwriters have managed to combine such disparate elements *and* make the Top 40. But because Hazlewood was far more pop-oriented than the emerging psychedelic rock stars, he wasn't considered at all hip at his peak.

Hazlewood reserved his strangest productions with Nancy, however, for a series of duets that contrasted Sinatra's high, girlish voice with Hazlewood's lo-o-o-w, off-key grumblings. They were the Mutt and Jeff of pop, yet they had a series of hits with some of Hazlewood's most evocative, mysterious compositions, usually boasting unforgettable minor-key melodies. "Sand" was notable as Lee's tangent into psychedelia, with a gonzoid backwards electric guitar break that was far-out even by 1968 standards.

"'Sand' was Lee's 'Norwegian Wood'," Sinatra told Al Quaglieri in an interview reprinted in the liner notes for Sundazed's CD reissue of her 1966 LP, *How Does That Grab You?*. "A running theme in his songs from that point was the young girl with the older guy. That was his fantasy and he captured it beautifully in song. But you have to remember that he had already done those songs. I was the second woman to sing them with him. Suzi Jane Hokom was the first. Suzi Jane's interpretations were good, but different. With me, he took the little girl quality and put it with adult ideas and something very interesting happened."

Yet the pinnacle of their collaborations—and probably the pinnacle of Hazlewood's entire career—has to be "Some Velvet Morning," a strong candidate for the strangest song ever to enter the Top 40. Beautifully mournful violins introduce rolling, doomy riffs, over which Hazlewood sings about a velvet morning when he'll be straight, and open up someone's gate into some sort of paradise. A drug hallucination? From someone who looks like a taller Sonny Bono turned cowboy? Just as we're weighing that possibility, Nancy intercedes in her most la-la sort of voice, singing angelically of flowers and daffodils—and just as suddenly, we're back into Lee's spooked-out ruminations about an occultish life-giving force named Phaedra. Nancy and Lee could have been singing two entirely different songs; their merging into a single, inscrutable tune was as mesmerizing as any acid trip.

The Hazlewood-Sinatra collaborations of the late '60s are Lee's most accessible and, justly, famous work. Yet true Hazlewood aficionados don't stop there. Whether due to luck, perseverance, or the kind of freedom that comes with producing massively successful hit singles, Hazlewood recorded a bizarre series of albums for several different labels that could not possibly have been marketed successfully in the 1960s. There was, of course, the matter of Lee's voice, which defied most conventional notions of holding a tune. So did Bob Dylan's, but Dylan was targeting a specific alienated youth market with his increasingly surrealistic poems. Hazlewood's songs, to most appearances, were as wacko as his voice.

There's the acoustic *The N.S.V.I.P.'s (Not So Very Important People)*, which intersperses Lee's rambling monologues about American weirdos with folky tunes that manage to be political without assuming any kind of political stance, like "Have You Made Any Bombs Today." There's *Trouble Is a Lonesome Town*, a concept album of songs about a quasi-Western town called "Trouble," again linked together by rambling monologues; it's akin to listening to Johnny Cash (who was recording concept albums of his own about trains and prisons) without the talent. On *Love and Other Crimes*, Hazlewood sounds like Cash turned drunken lounge singer. The sloppy, afterhours ambience of the session suggests that the album was recorded as an afterthought at the end of a Nancy Sinatra date, in about as much time as it takes to listen to the LP itself.

My vote for the best Hazlewood album would be *Lee Hazlewoodism: Its Cause and Cure*, which contains ten compact, melodramatic pop-folk tunes that veer between shameless TV movie-of-the-week sentimentality and utterly ridiculous camp. One moment Lee can toss off an epic mariachi ballad about a bullfighter, "Jose," in the most deadpan of narrations; the next he's doing a cheery sing-along ditty about some lucky couple (who've won the lottery? inherited a fortune?) wallowing in their freedom to do nothing but sit at home; following that is a self-pitying lament to a bartender who isn't listening; then there's a hokey near-striptease to announce that "Suzy Jane Is Back in My Town."

Any success at presenting a balanced individual is destroyed by the self-penned liner notes ("if the United States would allot just a fraction of the monies it spends on the Vietnam War to liver research for ball point pens, what a happy old world this could be"). That, by the way, is one of the "causes" of the "Lee Hazlewoodism" of the album's title; the bottom of the sleeve announces, in headline type, "THE CURE: BUY THE DAMN ALBUM." On most of his records, in fact, Hazlewood's disconnected liner notes more often than not gave the impression that the records were off-the-cuff in-jokes rather than serious statements. Even the relatively straight notes on *The Very Special World of Lee Hazlewood* were signed by "Pencil Pusher J-431M."

"I don't think he really even cared if those albums were hits, to tell you the truth," offers Al Casey. "I think that just kind of gave him a chance to do what he really wanted to do. Some of those songs, they're great songs, but they weren't that commercial. I think he just wanted to get those out there, let people hear what he could do." Was that sardonic, throat-stretching delivery deliberate? "Lee always sang that way," responds Casey, who should know, having worked with him since the '50s, and featured Hazlewood as a guest singer on a recent solo album. "His first songs that I heard were just kind of simple, basic country songs. Then he just seemed to progress as a songwriter, and start writing deeper stuff."

"I think Lee probably was not striving for anything except to be different," says Billy Strange, who arranged some of Hazlewood's solo material. "He was a country boy at heart, and that's the way he wrote." Were these Johnny Cash imitations, or even Johnny Cash satires? "I don't know that he was trying to emulate anyone insofar as their writing and/or performances were concerned. He just sort of did his own thing."

The Johnny Cash-isms had largely disappeared by the early '70s. *Forty* and *Poet, Fool or Bum* were somewhat more serious attempts to plug into the singer-songwriter scene, though the blend of MOR pop and still-eccentric lyrics effectively precluded Lee from the mainstream. *Forty*, a song cycle of sorts about middle age, was the more effective of the pair, although it actually contained no Hazlewood originals. *Poet* was Leonard Cohen-as-easy-listening; in fact, Lee covered a Leonard Cohen song on the LP, as well as one by a then-unknown Tom Waits. Yet also in the early '70s, he seemed determined to play up the most clownish aspects of his image via a duet album with Ann-Margret, *The Cowboy & the Lady*. Its gatefold cover found Ann-Margret dressed in nothing but a hat, boots, and umbrella covering the naughty bits. Lee stood next to her wearing nothing but boots, a bandana, and a gunbelt, the last of which was hung exactly where you'd expect.

Hazlewood spent most of his post-1970 career living in Europe, making sporadic recordings that were heard by few. He participated in Nancy Sinatra's comeback tour in the mid-'90s, but resolutely refused to be interviewed. It's difficult to ascertain whether he's aware of his growing following among underground types, who are attracted both by his uncompromising individuality and his, well, general weirdness, which makes him fit into the burgeoning "Incredibly Strange Music" cult quite well. Even as early as the mid-1980s, he was attracting such unlikely fans as punk diva Lydia Lunch—who covered "Some Velvet Morning" as a duet with Australian post-punker Roland Howard—and Sonic Youth. Sonic Youth?

Yep, in 1986 Kim Gordon described Hazlewood in *Option* as "a genius. One of the most radical lyric writers in the history of American songwriting." Elaborated husband and bandmate Thurston Moore, "Lee Hazlewood wore all black, cowboy kind of stuff, sang songs like 'Jackson' that used these clichés, but they were really perverse . . . I think Nick Cave really borrowed a lot from Lee Hazlewood. I can't tell if he was a false cowboy or just some kind of Hollywood songwriter. He's like the exotica of country and western."

Recommended Recordings:

Nancy and Lee (1968, Rhino). The principal Hazlewood-Sinatra duets, including "Some Velvet Morning," "Jackson," "Sand," "Lady Bird," and "Summer Wine," now reissued on CD with bonus tracks. Most of the aforementioned songs are included on Nancy Sinatra's *Greatest Hits* (also on Rhino), which is also essential listening for any fan of Hazlewood's, although that disc is unfortunately missing "Sand."

The Many Sides of Lee (1991, Request, Italy). An expensive 25-track import CD, probably unauthorized. But Hazlewood's original solo albums are long out-of-print, command expensive collector prices, and are ultimately harder to find than this compilation. It does a good job of bringing together highlights from his '60s releases, including "Jose," "Home (I'm Home)," and "Dark in My Heart." It also has his own, excruciatingly self-mocking version of "These Boots Are Made for Walking," and several singles with Suzi Jane Hokom (his pre-Nancy duet partner), including a different version of "Sand."

Love

Big rock magazines like to shake out their cobwebs every few years or so by running critics' polls of the best 100 or so albums of all time. There's been a steady changeover in the content over the last two decades, with a few hardy perennials occupying more or less constant places on the list. Most of them will be familiar to listeners—the Beatles' *Sgt. Pepper*, the Rolling Stones' *Exile on Main Street*, Bob Dylan's *Blonde on Blonde*, the Beach Boys' *Pet Sounds*, the Velvet Underground's *The Velvet Underground and Nico*, the Sex Pistols' *Never Mind the Bollocks*, and in recent years, Nirvana's *Nevermind*. One record that keeps reappearing, though, seems to have been heard mostly by the critics themselves rather than the general public—Love's *Forever Changes*. Perhaps the most durable "cult" album in rock history, its fusion of folk-rock and psychedelia was very much of its time, 1967. But more than any other record of its period, it carries an unworldly, dream-like air that transcends its era. Some writers have gone as far as to name it the most timeless rock album ever made.

If *Forever Changes* was the ultimate cult album, Love were in some ways the ultimate—and perhaps the very first—cult group. Though their prime era stretched over a mere three LPs and two years, they chalked up a number of firsts. They were the first notable interracial self-contained rock group; one of the very first to generate an avowedly underground following, in both America and England; and the first top-notch act, aside from the Mothers of Invention and Bob Dylan, to cover an entire rock album side with one track. Their eclecticism was unsurpassed, drawing from British Invasion, folk-rock, flamenco, pop crooners, free jazz, soul, and mariachi brass. They influenced the Doors, Pink Floyd, Jimi Hendrix, and the Rolling Stones. In their local L.A. stomping grounds, they were stars. Elsewhere they were barely known, except for a couple of singles that rose to the middle of the charts in the mid-'60s.

Love were also a band of contradictions that might have been ultimately just too hard to balance or compromise to qualify for commercial success. The group initially set out to pattern themselves after both the Rolling Stones *and* the Byrds. Arthur Lee was a black man who sang not like Otis Redding but Mick Jagger; on the band's finest album, he tempered his British Invasion influences into a Johnny Mathis-like mode. Their stock-in-trade was light, melodic folk-rock tunes, yet their only two hit singles were an atomic pre-punk tirade and a cover of a Burt Bacharach-Hal David composition. They refused to tour outside of their Southern Californian base. And just at the time when they should have been asserting themselves as one of rock's top acts, the core of the group imploded, leaving a subsequent trail of albums that many feel to be Love in name only.

While the editions of Love that recorded three albums for Elektra in 1966 and 1967 were fully operative bands, their vision was very much that of Arthur Lee, chief songwriter and vocalist. Even from their album sleeves, you can tell that Lee was the ultimate rock enigma—a black man caught in the white-boy world of L.A.'s Sunset Strip, peering from behind Granny glasses with an unsmiling stare that could bore through bank vaults. When the British Invasion hit, though, he was just another musician scuffling at the edge of Los Angeles' young rock biz, cutting a derivative soul-rock single as a member of the American Four, and writing and producing a single for Rosa Lee Brooks in 1964. Helping out on the latter session was a young unknown guitarist named Jimi Hendrix, who would later follow in Lee's path as one of the few black musicians to make a mark in the world of psychedelic rock.

Love's publicity photos were as enigmatic as their songs. Left to right: Alban "Snoopy" Pfisterer, chief songwriter and singer Arthur Lee, Ken Forssi, Bryan Maclean, and John Echols. Credit: Courtesy Rhino Records

With guitarist and ex-Byrds roadie Bryan MacLean, Lee formed the Grass-roots; the name was changed to Love when another Los Angeles group called the Grass Roots got a pop hit in 1965. Elektra Records, one of the top folk labels in the U.S., had been making tentative forays into rock with a single by the Beefeaters (soon to become the Byrds) and early demos with the Lovin' Spoon-ful. Love's self-titled album, which appeared in the spring of 1966, was probably the first out-and-out rock LP on Elektra, with the possible exception of the 1965 debut release by the Paul Butterfield Blues Band.

Love was an impressive debut, but a little too derivative of their main influences, recycling variations of ringing, circular Byrds riffs a bit too often, played and sung with a rawness more akin to the Rolling Stones ("Can't Explain," in fact, lifts some words wholesale from the obscure Stones track "What a Shame"). The best half of the album was truly special, though: the delicate balladry of "A Message to Pretty," the garage rant "My Flash on You," the heartbreakingly acoustic paean to nuclear holocaust ("Mushroom Clouds"), and the moody instrumental "Emotions" (used as a recurring theme for filmmaker Haskell Wexler's 1969 classic leftist political tract, *Medium Cool*). Also acoustic was the bluesy, morbid "Signed D.C.," one of the most down-and-out songs in all of pop, inspired by the drug abuse of Love's first drummer, Don Conka.

Bryan MacLean served notice that Lee wasn't the only composer of note in the group with "Softly to Me," which showcased his precious, almost effeminate sense of melodicism; he also sang the cover of "Hey Joe," one of the first versions ever released of that oft-covered '60s standard. But the track that became a hit (#52 to be exact) was the raucous "My Little Red Book," a cover of a Bacharach-David composition originally recorded by Manfred Mann (whose vocalist, Paul Jones, was one of Lee's models). Pink Floyd's early manager was so impressed by Love's version that he attempted to hum its descending guitar line to the band's first leader, Syd Barrett; Barrett mutated the riff into the berserk early Floyd psychedelic instrumental "Interstellar Overdrive."

Even before the first album, Love had shown signs of the instability that was to plague the group throughout its brief time in the limelight. Early drummer Don Conka had been replaced by Alban "Snoopy" Pfisterer; bassist John Fleckenstein (later to join the Standells) was replaced by Ken Forssi. Bruce Botnick, who worked as an engineer on Love's first two albums and co-produced *Forever Changes* with Lee, emphasizes that Lee, "basically, *was* the band. He could play any of the instruments, and would show the guys what to play. Depending on who could keep up with Arthur is who was there."

Keeping up with Arthur was a major task in 1966, as *Da Capo*, released in January 1967, finds Lee's musical palette expanding at a furious rate. Tjay Cantrelli was added to the lineup for this record only to provide jazzy colorings, with Pfisterer (who would be gone after this album) switching to keyboards with the addition of drummer Michael Stuart. Side one of the record is one of the most impressive rock LP sides ever crafted up to that point, and probably the most diverse, with each of the six cuts exploring a different tangent. "Stephanie Knows Who" is jazz-punk-psychedelia with restless, twisting tempo changes, Lee's grunt 'n' holler vocals, and Cantrelli's free-jazz sax solo. "¡Que Vida!" sees Lee's Johnny Mathis inclinations start to flower in a series of rhetorical question-and-answer lyrics; "The Castle" is a charming flamenco-rock hybrid; and "Orange Skies" (MacLean's lone *Da Capo* composition) is blissful flower-pop. Yet the most popular track (which had already been released as a single) was the relentless, vicious "7 and 7 Is," with its grinding fuzz riffs, bass guitar solo, nonstop 100-mile-per-hour drum rolls, and simulated atomic bomb explosion (recorded by a friend of Botnick in Nevada). The cut inched inside of the American Top 40 in September 1966.

"She Comes in Colors," colored by harpsichord and Cantrelli's flute, may be Lee's most melodic and graceful song; he (and others) believe that it may have provided the inspiration for the Rolling Stones' rather similar "She's a Rainbow" (in which the phrase "She comes in colors" is a prominent part of the lyric). Side two, the 19-minute suite "Revelation," was an experimental jam that stomped through basic blues-rock, crazed harpsichord runs, jazz improvisations, and a drum solo, but it was a real letdown after the concise wall-to-wall gems on side one. Lee, characteristically, claimed that the Rolling Stones saw Love doing the song in a club and ripped it off for their own 11-minute blues-rock jam, "Goin' Home," which appeared on the Stones' *Aftermath* album in 1966.

Da Capo, which charted at #80, is not merely notable for the sheer gorgeous textures of the songs, but also for Lee's relentlessly probing, metaphysical lyrics. He evoked more questions than answers; the lyrics didn't strictly make sense, but were constructed and phrased with a lilting, surrealistic beauty, or a thinly veiled, socially conscious anger. "I think the two American quintessential bands that really had something to say from that period were Love and the Doors," says Botnick, who worked on all the classic Doors albums as either engineer or producer. "I thought Arthur was one of the funniest people I'd ever met. His sense of humor in his lyrics was unbelievable. Arthur was very anti-war—that's what '7 and 7 Is' is all about. And he didn't talk about 'girl, I'm gonna love you,' or 'you're the coolest thing that's ever happened in my life.' That wasn't his thing. He didn't use the word 'baby.' He came from a different place, like [Jim] Morrison did."

But Botnick also takes care to point out that Bryan MacLean's contributions were very important, even though the Brian Jones look-alike only wrote one or two songs per album. "He was incredibly valuable. Love was really the two writers, Arthur and Bryan. And Bryan brought another sensibility to it, as deep as what Arthur was writing, but coming from a different direction. He was very sensitive; I didn't know it at the time, but a lot of things affected Bryan religiously, and caused him to go out and become a born-again Christian." MacLean's sensitive nature couldn't have made it that easy to share space in the same band with the more caustic Lee, who remarked in the liner notes to the Love box set *Love Story*, "I was writing more about real life. 'Orange Skies' was a good song, but I had to go to Bryan and ask him, 'Why don't you write about things that are real? Why are you always writing about ice cream?' But I truly admire him. I think he's a great songwriter."

MacLean actually wrote quite a few songs in the mid-'60s that were never recorded by Love, due at least in part to Lee's reluctance to put many of them on the group's albums. MacLean's belated 1997 Sundazed release *ifyoubelievein* included ten previously unissued solo acoustic demos from 1966 and 1967 of MacLean originals, eight of which were never recorded by Love; it also has additional solo acoustic demos, from 1972 and 1982, of songs that were written during the mid-'60s. This material, though only available in skeletal form, is the only clue as to what Love's records might have sounded like if MacLean had been allowed to wield greater influence over the group's repertoire.

The Lee-Morrison comparison is apt considering that both the Doors and Love were on Elektra, and that Jim Morrison named Love as one of his favorite groups. The Doors had signed to the label in the first place, in part, because Lee had recommended the band to Elektra chief Jac Holzman. By mid-1967, in fact, the Doors were making a lot more national headway than their one-time idols, as "Light My Fire" scorched its way to #1. In a 1991 article in *Goldmine*, Lee claimed, "Elektra didn't promote me like they did the Doors . . . the Doors did a tour up and down the East Coast so they could get out of L.A. They ate shit and were getting paid to play all these funky little places up and down the East Coast. I wasn't gonna go eat puke. I wasn't gonna go eat garbage like the Doors did. Why should I do that when I already had my cake and was about to eat it?" Lee and Love could be their worst enemies when it came to promotion, though, refusing to tour nationally, appear at the Monterey Pop Festival, or go to England, where they were attracting an underground following. When Holzman cajoled them into making a publicity jaunt to New York, the band stayed for one day, doing no concerts or interviews before they returned home.

When Love assembled for what was to become their crowning achievement, there was some doubt they would even survive the *Forever Changes* sessions. "It's well-documented that I took them into the studio to produce this album, and they couldn't play, basically," states Botnick. "[Arthur] was going a lot faster than they could. He was quite upset about it." To prove his point, Botnick recorded a couple of tracks using "The Wrecking Crew," Los Angeles' A-team of pop session musicians, including drummer Hal Blaine and guitarist Billy Strange.

"I did it intentionally, to shock the band into getting serious, which did work. I remember Bryan sitting there crying, and a couple of guys were crying during the session. As it turns out, two of the songs that I did with the Wrecking Crew did wind up on the album—Arthur played live rhythm guitar, he overdubbed his voice, and that was kind of it." But "all of the rest [of the album] was all the band playing."

It was fortunate that Botnick had helped save the day, as *Forever Changes* was one of the masterpieces of '60s rock. Lee delivered an armful of opaque, shimmering compositions that could play like a midsummer night's dreams of light psychedelia ("Andmoreagain," "The Good Humor Man He Sees Everything Like This"), boast a hard-nosed, somber raunch that critiqued war ("Live and Let Live"), or expand into movie-length epics ("You Set the Scene"). More often, the strains of sardonic realism and wishful fantasy mingled to the point where they became inseparable. Arthur sang the songs with a gliding restraint that sounded like nothing so much as a psychedelic Johnny Mathis. MacLean stole some of the leader's thunder by penning the album's most popular cut, the enchantingly wistful "Alone Again Or." This song, like most of the album, was given an unearthly sheen by glistening strings and horns — sometimes sounding like the Tijuana Brass on acid — that are among the most successful arrangements of their type ever employed on a rock record.

"I brought the stuff in," admits Botnick. "You gotta look at music in that period. Radio wasn't narrow like it is today. In those days, you would hear Love followed by Frank Sinatra, going into Herb Alpert and the Tijuana Brass. There was an amalgamation, a synergy, between all the different styles.

"I brought in this arranger [David Angel]. I think I might have found him through my mother, who was a music copyist working for Sinatra and Nelson Riddle at the time. He sat down with Arthur, and Arthur really warmed to it. He sang all the lines to Angel — all the string lines and all the brass lines, everything. It's a really weird mix of Tijuana Brass and the rock 'n' roll he was coming from. At that time, it was the thing to do, to legitimize yourself in some respects, to have strings on your record — [to show] that you'd grown up, and to make rock 'n' roll legal in some respects. Some of it is a little dated, but I really enjoy it."

Interestingly, Neil Young was at one time supposed to co-produce the album with Botnick, but backed out at an early stage. "I thought it would be a real good idea, because I had worked with him with Buffalo Springfield. The more he got into it, he was realizing that he had things he wanted to say and do, and producing wasn't one of them. He basically just said, 'I'm sorry I said yes, I made a mistake. I gotta go do my thing.' But I'm certain had he been involved, it would have different; I'm sure he would have played guitar [as well]."

This edition of Love lasted for only one more, rather marginal single before it broke up in 1968. Thirty years later, the reasons for the split remain unclear; MacLean says he left, while Lee maintained he fired the band because they couldn't cut it. In the liner notes to *Love Story*, Lee is quoted as follows: "We used to work every night. After we started making money, the less we worked, the less we were a unit, and Love deteriorated. People's personal habits started to come before the music . . . each member of Love had a style of his own. I mixed it all together. When they couldn't follow the changes in my music, I had to make changes." MacLean, the half-brother of country-rock singer Maria McKee, largely dropped out of the rock scene to concentrate upon Christian music. Forssi and guitarist Johnny Echols, unfortunately, would only make news when they were convicted for armed robbery of several doughnut shops in the L.A. area.

Forever Changes had peaked at a mere #154 in the United States, but did significantly better in the U.K. More importantly, the mystique around *Forever Changes* just grew and grew, picking up new listeners from subsequent generations over the next 30 years. The most avid fans were fellow rock musicians; Botnick even recalls the Clash being "just over the top about *Forever Changes*" when he was introduced to the British punk stars over ten years later. Lee, sadly, was unable to capitalize on his masterwork, forming various different incarnations of Love with different musicians in the late '60s and early '70; old friend Jimi Hendrix even made a guest appearance on one track on the 1970 *False Start* album. Critical opinion regarding these records diverges wildly; some dismiss them out of hand, others insist they are criminally underrated. It seems fair to say, though, that those who treasure Love for the incandescent glory of their first three albums will be surprised, and quite possibly disappointed, at the rather routine hard rock that typifies the band's subsequent releases.

Observes Botnick: "If you look at all the albums that Arthur did after *Forever Changes*, Love really wasn't a part of the thing anymore; he was just using the title. There isn't the kind of growth that there was—explosively—on the first three albums." What might the original Love have achieved if they had been able to stay together? "It's kind of hard to say where they would have gone. But the band had gotten to the end of the road," Botnick concludes somberly. "*Forever Changes* was really Arthur and Bryan's record. The [other] guys were just sidemen."

After the mid-'70s, Lee was rarely able to cash in on his growing renown, recording only sporadically. Botnick remembers being approached by a panhandler outside an L.A. club around 1980, discovering to his shock that the man was Arthur. By the early 1990s, Lee had gotten his act together to some extent, embarking on a grinding series of tours at small venues in North America and Europe—an ironic outcome, to say the least, for the man who refused to tour outside of California when large audiences were there for the plucking. In 1992, he recorded an album for the French New Rose label that included "Five String Serenade," which was given an effectively haunting reworking by popular neo-psychedelic '90s brooders Mazzy Star. A comeback single on the tiny Distortions label in 1994 showed some of the spark of the old "7 and 7 Is" days, and garnered a few favorable reviews in the rock press. It would be nice to conclude the story on a somewhat optimistic note, but the anvil was about to fall on any dreams of a comeback.

Accounts of the incident differ, but in the autumn of 1995, Lee apparently was blasting the stereo at his apartment in the L.A. suburb of Van Nuys, eliciting complaints from a neighbor. Arthur, reported *MOJO* magazine, responded by "brandishing a handgun and firing shots in the air." With two prior felonies to his credit, Lee fell victim to California's infamous three-strikes-you're-out law by landing a 12-year sentence (also, confusingly, reported as eight years) for illegal possession of a firearm.

Dave Brown, owner of Distortion Records, has little sympathy for Lee's current predicament. "I met Arthur when he began playing live shows again around the fall of 1993. I always admired the man and his music, and asked him if he wanted to do a record. He said he wanted to put out a single and wanted $1500 in advance, which was a *lot* for a single, but I went ahead with it only because I wanted to do a Love single very much.

"When 'Girl on Fire' was released in early '94, I sold about 1800 copies, which is OK. But Arthur thought that it was still 1966 and he could sell half a million copies of 'My Little Red Book' and be number one in L.A. When I sent him more money to record more tunes for an EP, he decided to keep the money instead, telling me that I owed him for sales of the 45 which I didn't break even on.

"In his live shows he was singing John Lennon's 'Instant Karma.' Well, his own karma has got him eight years in jail—you can't keep burning people and expect to get away with it, and I'm not the first guy he burned either. His music is great, but I can't say too much for his dishonest character."

Lee had eloquently pined for freedom on *Forever Changes'* "The Red Telephone," singing poignantly about being locked up by jailers that threw away the key. He had warned in the same song that tomorrow, any one of us could find ourselves in the same predicament. Art has now imitated life in a tragic fashion that no one could have anticipated when Lee was at the top of his game in 1967.

Recommended Recordings:
Love (1966, Elektra). Raw but satisfying folk-rock, the delicate acoustic-oriented cuts demonstrating more of the uniqueness to come than the more straightahead rockers. Also includes their garage-rock classic, "My Little Red Book."

Da Capo (1967, Elektra). Side one (or the first six songs of the CD) features some of the most beautiful, wide-ranging psychedelic rock of the '60s; only the tedious 19-minute jam "Revelation" keeps this from being a stone classic.

Forever Changes (1967, Elektra). An album whose spellbinding eeriness has been canonized by an untold number of rock critics, with an organic, consistently magic flow matched by few other recordings, obscure or not.

Love Story 1966-1972 (1995, Rhino). Double-CD box includes all of *Forever Changes*, everything from *Da Capo* except "Revelation," much of the debut LP, and a selection of Love/Lee's better post-*Forever Changes* recordings. Well-assembled, with a detailed history of the band in the enclosed booklet. But it's missing a few decent cuts from the first album; a package that included the Lee–MacLean-era recordings in their entirety might have been a better idea.

Joe Meek

The saga of Joe Meek has not only the makings of an essential chapter of cult rock history, but of a cult cinema classic as well. At the core of the plot is the story of a maverick producer taking on the whole of a stale British record industry, becoming the nation's first renowned independent producer, refusing to work within an entrenched studio system, preferring to devise and record all manner of far-out pop sounds in his tiny London flat. For personal color, there's his obsession with outer space and the occult, which served as twin inspirations for the inimitable electronic sound effects that decorated many of his most successful records. For a bit of titillation, there's his homosexuality, which had to be repressed at a time when to be gay in England was to be a criminal.

Joe Meek, at ease in the 1960s, giving little indication of the demons that would drive him to homicide and suicide in 1967. Credit: Courtesy The Official Web Site of the Joe Meek Appreciation Society

Few if any Hollywood studios, however, would give the green light to a film ending in such a blaze of senseless violence. The real life Joe Meek story, however, came to its close in such a fashion on February 3, 1967, when, beleaguered by personal and financial problems, Meek shot his landlady and, several moments later, turned the gun on himself. It was the eighth anniversary of the death of one of his heroes, Buddy Holly.

Less than five years earlier, Meek had been at the top of the world when his crowning achievement—the Tornados' instrumental "Telstar," which he wrote and produced—topped the British charts. Shortly afterwards it duplicated the feat in the United States, over a year before the Beatles would launch the British Invasion. With its outer-space whirs and bleeps, "Telstar" has been perceived by many as a one-shot novelty. But in fact it was just one of hundreds of tracks on which Meek pushed the technology of early-'60s studio equipment to the limit, generating unearthly sounds that were not just years ahead of their time, but have proven virtually impossible to duplicate.

Meek had been striving to create an extraterrestrial ambience ever since, as a teenager, he put speakers in his family's cherry orchard to drive away the birds, and built the first television set in his hometown. By the 1950s he was working in London as a balance engineer, upsetting the traditional safeguards of British studios by experimenting with distortion and sticking mikes inside bass drums. By 1960, he was ready to strike out on his own, founding his own record label, Triumph. When Triumph couldn't keep afloat, he went the independent route whole-hog by starting a production company of his own. He would record music in his own apartment at 304 Holloway Road in North London, above a leather goods shop, and lease the masters to British labels.

In order to fully appreciate the extent of Meek's innovations, one has to realize how radical it was to operate outside of the established studio hierarchy in 1960. This was long before the word "indie" was commonplace. Records were made in professional studios, overseen by the staff members of Britain's few established, major labels. In this respect, Meek was the British equivalent of Phil Spector in the United States. Too eccentric to work within the strictures of mainstream music, both opted to craft the sounds they heard inside of their heads by doing their own thing on their own terms. Nowadays the term "independent producer" is commonplace; although they were not the only ones, Spector and Meek were the first of the major independent rock producers to live by their own rules.

While some would also draw comparisons between Spector's Wall-of-Sound methods and Meek's own larger-than-life productions, the similarity only stretches so far. Spector was concerned with embellishing his soulful pop-rock songs and singers with symphonic instrumentation. The production and arrangement were important, but no more so than the words and music, often supplied by top-notch Brill Building songwriters (such as Spector himself). To

Meek, the ornamental effects often *were* the essence of the record. Generic teen-idol pap, tame instrumental rock tunes, Buddy Holly pastiches, even the odd hard R&B—the material didn't matter as much as the *sound*, and the futuristic effects in which it was dressed up.

To achieve this end, Meek made voices and instruments sound like nothing else on the planet. Backup female choruses sounded like wind-driven ghosts. Drums sounded like marching armies (and in fact, this percussive effect was often created by having the musicians and whoever else was around stomp on the studio's floors and stairs). He put pins in piano hammers to create a warped honky-tonk sound. He put vocals through vari-speed processes to make his singers sound like outer space munchkins. Organs had a mutant wobble-tone that resembled circus calliopes. Electric guitars became swarms of stinging bees. And everything was compressed and limited like hell, giving the final product a twenty-first-century kind of electronic sheen.

Most of Meek's records, however, were not experimental exercises. They were pop tunes, aimed squarely at the teenage market, with little of the guts or blues/soul influence that would characterize the British Invasion of the mid-'60s. Meek's own taste ran to gloppy ballads or saccharine pop-rock, sometimes in the Buddy Holly mold. Hits by various instrumental groups and teen idols (most notably John Leyton) gave him a solid track record, but Meek didn't become an industry giant until "Telstar" in 1962. With its buzzing and humming electronic intro and outro, and a tune dominated by harpsichord-like glissandos and the keening pre-synthesizer tones of the clavioline, "Telstar" anticipated aspects of psychedelia by a good four or five years. Meek had been experimenting with outer-space effects for years; indeed, in 1960 he recorded an entire (and silly) LP of such material, based around a loose concept of life on the moon (remember, this was about ten years before Apollo 11). "Telstar," though, brought the futurism to the public in a melodic fashion that remains riveting today.

Tony Dangerfield, a singer-bassist who worked with Meek both as a solo act and as a member of Screaming Lord Sutch's band, confirms that the producer poured the heart and soul of his efforts into sonic effects rather than the actual song. "Musically, he actually worked quite quick, but he would spend hours, *hours*, just trying to create sounds for intro and outro." These sound effects were often inspired by Meek's fascination with space exploration and the occult; the hellish combination of coffin squeaks and vampire squeals on Screaming Lord Sutch's "'Til the Following Night" is an especially effective example.

But the effects weren't necessarily created by state-of-the-art technology. "The intro to 'Telstar,' those rocket-taking-off-sounds—it was like a plank of wood about that long." Dangerfield spreads his hands about two feet apart and laughs. "Two six-inch nails with a rusty spring! He just kept twanging this, playing it backwards, speeding it up." On another occasion, Dangerfield was present on a session for a tune called "Three Coins in a Fountain," which Meek wanted to embellish with the sound of—what else?—a coin dropping in a fountain. After dropping a penny into a bucket didn't work, Meek had the drummer pop his mouth into the mike for a good three hours. The poor musician's face was black and blue by the time Meek got the office boy to create the particular mouth pop the producer was looking for.

"Joe made great records *despite* the studios," agrees Derek Lawrence, who assisted Meek for a time, before going on to become a successful producer himself, working with Deep Purple, Wishbone Ash, and Quiet Riot. "Joe was inventive *because* he didn't have a lot of equipment. That's the only way you can describe it. He would get the string section in, and they'd be all over the place. On the stairs, in the bathroom, in the toilet, in the kitchen. Wherever there was space, there was a musician. You'd get this really thick snare drum sound [with] the telephone book."

Meek also wrote the material for quite a few of the records he produced, which was rather remarkable considering that he couldn't hold a tune. Compounding the horror was his method of demoing a new composition over an existing rock 'n' roll record that had a rhythm or feel he was seeking; the problem was, it would usually have a totally different melody (some gruesome examples of this can be heard on RPM's *Work in Progress* CD of Joe Meek rarities). "Musically, to be quite honest, he was tone-deaf," confirms Dangerfield. "When you got a Joe demo, he'd be humming on it, trying to sing it. And he was way off what he really wanted. So you had to try and interpret that melody."

Lawrence is even blunter in his assessment: "I maintain that the bands wrote most of the songs. What Joe would sound (like) on those demos, no one would ever know." He adds, "Joe Meek made some of the worst records ever made. He made five or six of the *best* records ever made. I think he never actually differentiated between the music he liked and the blokes he fancied. A lot of blokes would come in that Joe just fancied. And he made records with them."

So it was that the careers of singers with modest or less-than-modest vocal talents, such as Heinz, got a big push from Meek. For all the lack of consistent quality control standards, though, many of even the least distinguished Meek outings were made more palatable by the presence of some of the finest instrumental talent on the budding British rock scene. Nicky Hopkins, Jimmy Page, and Ritchie Blackmore are among the virtuosos who made some of their first appearances on Meek productions. Meek restrained himself more than usual on the early-'60s singles by Screaming Lord Sutch, which were some of the first genuinely hard-rocking R&B-influenced records to be issued in Great Britain. Buried among the dross of the hundreds of tracks in the Meek discography are some astonishing guitar leads. Blackmore's solo on the Outlaws' otherwise generic 1964 single "Shake with Me" is Hendrix three years ahead of schedule, for instance, and even the most limpid Heinz cut is usually elevated by some scorching R&B guitar riffs (by Blackmore and others).

The British Invasion, with its harder sound and groups that penned their own material, curtailed Meek's success. He would still have some hits (most notably with the Honeycombs, whose "Have I the Right" entered the Top Five in America in 1964), and would even make some respectable sides with harder-rocking groups like the Syndicats (with a young Steve Howe on guitar). Meek had once been way ahead of the industry, but by early 1967, his sound, once futuristic, was dated. Compounding the lack of hits were financial problems, pill-fueled paranoia, and impending investigation as a suspect in the murder of a teenage boy. Meek's tantrums were the stuff of legend—Dangerfield remembers him throwing telephones at musicians with whom he was displeased, and Lawrence recalls how he'd go into fits and lock the doors to his studio for a week or so. With hindsight, the double murder scenario that ended his life was the culmination of his increasing psychological instability, although no one suspected it would manifest itself so violently.

Meek was hardly a hip name to toss around in the ensuing two decades. But in the past few years he's undergone a remarkable rehabilitation of sorts, as both '60s collectors and general enthusiasts for offbeat pop began to appreciate the uniqueness of his recordings. A full-length biography, *The Legendary Joe Meek*, appeared in 1989; an acclaimed BBC documentary was made in the early 1990s. In 1996 a long-overdue CD collection of his work was released in the U.S. All of which made it less shocking to read the following praise from the most unlikely source: former Dead Kennedys singer Jello Biafra, in the book *Incredibly Strange Music, Vol. 2,* stated "You can tell a Joe Meek record a mile away."

Recommended Recording:
It's Hard to Believe It: The Amazing World of Joe Meek (1995, Razor & Tie). A 20-song compilation of Meek's most famous and most creative work: "Telstar," "Have I the Right," and a mixture of hits and flops by Screaming Lord Sutch, John Leyton, Glenda Collins, the Outlaws, and others. Those who want to dig for more Meek are advised to be selective among the dozen or so compilations of his work clogging the market. If you want to take the plunge, you're better off going for a single-artist collection (by the Honeycombs, Tornados, Screaming Lord Sutch, or Heinz) than the far more erratic various-artist compilations.

Recommended Reading:
The Legendary Joe Meek, by John Repsch (1989, Woodford House, UK). Entertaining, detailed 300-page-plus biography of the producer that gives weight to both his musical breakthroughs and his personal demons.

Skip Spence

Ask people to name the premier acid casualty of the 1960s, and most will name Syd Barrett, the original Pink Floyd leader, who drifted off into madness after 1967. If Barrett has a counterpoint in America, it would have to be Skip Spence, the Moby Grape guitarist who released one brilliant acid-folk album in 1969 before disappearing into the bowels of the California state mental health system. Like Barrett, Spence conveyed a magical sense of childlike wonder with his one-of-a-kind songs, which fascinate with their eerie tightrope walk between coherence and madness.

If Skip was a psychedelic cousin of Barrett's, he drew upon bedrock American blues, country, and folk influences to a far greater degree than his British counterpart. Tragically, his only solo album, *Oar*, passed unnoticed upon its release in 1969, the victim of both underpromotion and unfashionability. The much greater tragedy is that the madness that *Oar* hints at was a very real hell that's prevented Spence from making a living as a professional musician ever since—and has, basically, prevented him from functioning in society as well.

Spence was never the most organized guy, but no one could have pictured him as the axe-wielding man who would end up in New York's Bellevue mental hospital when he joined the Jefferson Airplane in 1965. The story goes that Marty Balin, when he was organizing the first version of the group, picked Spence to be his drummer simply because Skip *looked* like a drummer, although Spence was actually a guitarist who had never played the drums in his life. "I remember how frustrated, or excited at the same time, he was about having to learn drums," remembers Dave Aguilar, who was on the San Francisco psychedelic scene as a lead singer for the Chocolate Watch Band. "When he was in the Airplane, he was pretty happy-go-lucky and very talented, and excited about what was happening."

Spence played on the first Airplane album, and helped write a few of the better folk-rock originals in their early repertoire. But he was kicked out and/or left, so the story goes, because of unreliability. Skip at any rate may have welcomed the chance to return to his favored instrument, the guitar, and got that opportunity when Matthew Katz (who had managed the Airplane in their early days) built a new group around him called Moby Grape.

Every member of the five-man outfit wrote the songs on the Grape's classic 1967 debut album, a critical favorite for its blend of blues, rock, country, folk, and psychedelia. The most exuberant and, probably, popular of these tracks was Spence's "Omaha," a rousing call to love and unity. According to Peter Lewis, one of the Grape's three guitarists, Spence's compositions differed from those of his bandmates in how "they dealt with the situations he found himself in. They weren't songs about girlfriends and stuff like that as much as they were about

Skip Spence in concert with Moby Grape. Credit: Michael Ochs Archives

what was going on, in terms of the relationships he had with the rest of us. He, probably more than any of the other writers, was able to write for the *band*."

Almost before they were out of the gate, Moby Grape's career was crippled by over-hype (Columbia released five singles at once) and scandal (three members, including Spence, were arrested for consorting with underage girls the night of their press party for their debut). By early 1968, the band were in serious trouble. In order to record a follow-up album, the musicians relocated to New York City, away from their familiar environment of friends and family. Drugs, internal friction, and a general shortage of quality material were wearing their spirits down. It was in this uneasy atmosphere that the happy-go-lucky Spence underwent a frightening change in personality that would land him in a mental institution.

It seems that Spence, after a gig at New York's Fillmore East, went off with a woman—sometimes described as a witch of sorts—who fed him some particularly potent acid. Spence flipped out, and took a fire axe to the Albert Hotel in search of Moby Grape drummer Don Stevenson (whom he thought was possessed by Satan), breaking down the door to the room Stevenson shared with Grape guitarist Jerry Miller. Finding it empty, he went into the studio, where producer David Rubinson disarmed him. The incident culminated in Spence being committed to New York's notorious mental institution, Bellevue Hospital, for six months.

"I think he did some blue cheer or something, and it took him completely over the top," remembers Rubinson. "He became very irrational and very destructive, and was very upset with the members of the band, with the engineer— he really just got completely beside himself. We had to have him physically removed from the studio area. He was threatening people, and he was very self-destructive, he could have really hurt some people in the group and himself.

"He just wasn't himself. He was a very mercurial person, but not a nasty or angry person. But he was really beside himself in the hospital, too. I think that caused long-term damage, that whole episode."

Peter Lewis wasn't in New York at the time, having returned to California briefly. But he remembers being told how, in the space of three days, "instead of being Mr. Love he was Mr. Hate," wearing upside-down crosses and carving devil's horns into his Strat Cutaways. It wasn't necessarily the acid itself, Lewis theorizes, but "the stuff in your body that it releases. If there's no more of it, then it kind of acts like speed on you. I think that's what happened to Skip. The only thing he was really hanging by was this preconception people had of him as a rock star. Once he was in the tombs of Bellevue and people could only think of him as this paranoid schizophrenic . . . he just took on that lid. I don't think he ever relinquished it. To say it's tragic is an understatement."

Although Spence didn't have a guitar in Bellevue, he did begin to accumulate ideas for some of the songs that ended up on his solo LP. According to

Rubinson, after the Moby Grape had gone on to complete their second album without Skip, "I went down to the Bellevue Hospital prison ward, and I got a defense lawyer. We got the money together and made a case. I put up some bail, and we bailed him out. But he was kind of in my charge. I had to sign the papers that I would make sure that he was okay.

"What he wanted to do when he got out was, he wanted a motorcycle and to go down to Nashville and record an album. And Columbia generously at that time, considering what had happened, said okay. They gave him a budget, and he went on down to Nashville, I believe by motorcycle, and went to work in the studio."

Within the space of about a week, Spence finished writing all the material and recorded the album. What's more, he played all the instruments himself, and acted as his own producer. Which perhaps accounts for both the very personal nature of the material, and the bare-bones feel of the arrangements, which have a spooked-out, one-man-alone-in-a-bare-light-bulb-hotel-room ambience. The results were not psychedelia in the San Francisco sense, but a sort of summit meeting of Delta bluesmen and the spirit of Haight-Ashbury. Spence's deep, whispery, almost wraith-like vocals imbued the songs with a compelling, at times painfully transparent, honesty.

This was music without artifice, but of considerable depth, particularly in the witty and humorous wordplay that is the strongest similarity between Skip Spence and Syd Barrett. At times Spence's cracked vocals were applied to lyrical concerns of almost biblical resonance, such as "Books of Moses" and the weary "Weighted Down (The Prison Song)." Yet there's also considerable humor, as well as punning phrases, in songs like "Lawrence of Euphoria" and "Dixie Peach Promenade," where Spence muses how he could use some yin for his yang. If Spence's vision had been informed by excessive drug use and his debilitating experiences at Bellevue, they certainly hadn't dimmed the childlike lightness of his spirit.

Oar's tapes were shaped into something more accessible by Rubinson and several engineers. "The task we had in mixing was to make his ideas more clear to somebody listening to the record," says Rubinson, who compares the project to extracting the tablets from the Rosetta Stone. "To clarify, to distill, not to make it more perfect, not to smooth out the rough spots, not to try to make it more like everybody else's record. To bring out the essence.

"At that time *Sgt. Pepper* had come out. Even Moby Grape wanted things backwards on their albums and orchestras and stuff. What was happening (on *Oar*) was totally against (that) grain. It was completely from the heart and completely raw. It was like sitting down and listening to an authentic blues recording, a field recording almost." Rubinson would go on to compare the record to old blues 78s in the liner notes, and adds, "If there's such a thing as a naif movement in rock and roll, *Oar* would be the first of its kind. It's guileless.

"There was nothing between him and his art, there was no 'gee, I'm going to try and make a hit record, I hope the critics like this, I bet I could make some money if I do it this way, what's the budget like, are we over budget, do we have enough this time?' It was never a consideration of anything like that. It's like Grandma Moses. He would basically sit on the front porch and create a master-piece—boom. There was no 'How do I do this, what's the best chord here.' It was totally intuitive. He was, in his earlier incarnation, a very witty, whimsical, light-hearted guy, full of laughter. And not a poet of darkness. The drugs took that. But this album is very personal and *very* witty."

But not very commercial. *Oar* was rumored to be one of the lowest-selling albums ever released on Columbia. The *Rock Family Trees* reference book, for instance, quotes a sales figure of 700, which looks like a misprint—but maybe not, considering that hardly anyone even saw a copy of the original release. "Co-lumbia, when they heard the finished product, were bemused," notes Rubinson. "But at that time, they had no aspirations for this commercially. They didn't think it was going to sell, and they barely pressed it up and basically buried it. They never really serviced it properly, and it was never promoted." As a conse-quence, *Oar* has probably sold considerably more copies in its reissued editions (on the British Edsel label as an LP in 1988, and as a Sony Special Products CD reissue in 1991) than it did in its original incarnation.

Lewis remembers going with Spence to an L.A. record store to buy *Oar* and Neil Young's self-titled debut LP (also released around that time), playing the records, and judging *Oar* as the clear winner of the pair. He also concedes that *Oar* "was scary, to me, when I heard it . . . not that it wasn't organized. It was. But there was this part of it that delved into the darkness of the soul."

After the *Oar* sessions, Spence returned to his family in Campbell, Califor-nia. There would be no solo follow-up, and only a couple more brief stints with Moby Grape. And Spence would begin a long journey through mental difficul-ties and bouts of homelessness that continues to the present. Assorted stories of his eccentricities would eventually be publicized, like the time he was declared dead of a drug overdose by a coroner in Santa Cruz, only to get up and ask for a glass of water. Lewis remembers a particularly frightening incident at a Big Sur monastery, in which Spence was literally trying to strangle him as Lewis drove down the mountain back to civilization.

By the time he was tracked down by the *San Francisco Bay Guardian* in 1994, he was living in a San Jose residential care home, a diagnosed paranoid schizophrenic taking anti-psychotic drugs, given to hearing voices and talking to himself. The accompanying photo flashed teeth whose state of decrepitude would have been far more appropriate on a man 30 or 40 years older.

In late 1996, Lewis tells me, Spence is "living in a trailer in Santa Cruz. He hasn't got any money, 'cause the state gets all his royalties. He drinks a lot of beer and sits there all day and rolls his own cigarettes, and sits and waits for something to happen. But he's sick. His liver isn't that great.

"They have to beg this asshole guy that's his conservator for money to pay the phone bill, and get the right herbs for him to take so they don't just keep pumping him full of psych meds, which are ruining his liver. Skippy was never totally figured out, even though he was scrutinized by a lot of people with Ph.D.'s and stuff. For a guy like him to have become answerable to the bunch of people that he ended up being controlled by was maybe the worst thing that could happen." It should be added that Spence was not the only member of the Grape to have a tough go of it after the 1960s. Lewis discovered bassist Bob Mosley living homeless by the side of a San Diego freeway several years ago. The band lost the ownership to their own name for many years, and only recently won back the right to play as the Moby Grape for reunions.

An unexpected bright note was sounded for Spence in early 1998, when a tribute album of *Oar* covers was reported to be in the works, featuring such alternative rock icons as Robyn Hitchcock, Wilco, Mudhoney, the Flaming Lips, and Son Volt. It would also be appropriate for eclectic folk-rock-rap star Beck to contribute to the project, as his unnaturally low vocals and screwball ruminations, intentionally or not, betray clear similarities to the *Oar* album.

For all that he's been through, Spence still inspires almost holy reverence from those who know him well. Lewis, who is helping to produce recordings of some of Spence's songs, contends that many "see nothing but the paranoid schizophrenic. But he can also be like the Maharishi, where being around him for a day is totally energizing. I've seen him get in a cop car and tell the cops to drive him down the block and let him off where he wants to get off, like they were taxi drivers. He has certain power over people that are objective realists. It's really cool. I love going to play with him, because he's still that innocent young guy that, if you play something he likes, he jumps up and down and squeals. To see him suffer like he does, it's almost unbearable."

"I don't know anyone who ever saw the world the way he did," summarizes Rubinson. "I think it's a horrible tragedy that drugs did to his mind what they did, because he was a really phenomenal poet and energy source. A lot of people have difficult psychological problems. It's just the degree to which they can socialize them and function. And unfortunately, he took the route of toxic material and drugs. It completely ruined his life. I can't think of a more salient example of the ill effects of psycho-pharmaceutical chemicals than Skip Spence. It did not have to be that way."

Recommended Recording:
Oar (1969, Sony). *The* acid-folk experience—haunting, inspirational, and unique. The CD reissue adds a few previously unreleased bonus tracks, although these are just half-formed ideas and sketches as opposed to songs. Several of Spence's songs are also available on *The Jefferson Airplane Takes Off* (1966) and Moby Grape's first two albums (most of which are compiled on the *Vintage* double-CD reissue).

Idiot Savants

The Deviants, the Holy Modal Rounders, the Monks, the Red Krayola—none were gifted with what most listeners would term extraordinary instrumental or songwriting talents. Their genius was their ability to make extraordinary, original music with pure inspiration that overcame the limits of the gifts God gave them. For every near-masterpiece like the Deviants' *Ptooff!* or the Monks' *Black Monk Time*, however, there are hundreds of similar cult rock acts who possess similar eccentricity, but little or none of the even rudimentary talents needed to make records that most people would consider even remotely listenable. These are the idiot savants of rock, whose hopelessly meandering songs and out-of-tune caterwaulings would get them barred from most open-mike nights. Nevertheless, a lot of them manage to get onto record—and, perversely, become championed by small cliques of rock critics and collectors who are convinced that such artists represent musical expression at its purest and least diluted.

You can go all the way back to certain rockabilly cavemen for idiot savants if you're so inclined. The most notorious of these would be Hasil Adkins, a one-man band who's been recording in his West Virginia shack since the 1950s. In the words of rock critic Cub Koda (writing in the *All Music Guide to Rock*), Adkins combines "a three-octave voice that can go from sub-glottal Elvis moans to blood-curdling screams with an overamplified guitar that sounds like a gigantic rubber band." Match these with lyrics about chopping women's heads off and eating peanut butter on the moon—along with the Haze's perennially unsteady timekeeping abilities and limited canvas of chords—and you can see why he didn't exactly give Elvis any sleepless nights.

Tellingly, Adkins didn't really find a wide audience until the 1980s, when the thirst for trash culture and ironic primitivism had become a serious quest. As one critic once pointed out, however, listeners expecting some outer-space fusion of Gene Vincent, Jimi Hendrix, and the Cramps after reading various rave reviews are apt to come away distinctly underwhelmed. Marginally more pleasing, perhaps, were the proto-cowpunk ravings of the Legendary Stardust Cowboy (the "Ledge" to his friends). His late '60s single "Paralyzed" presents a mutant hillbilly, whose brain has fried in the desert sun, playing psychedelic Western swing at 78 revolutions per minute.

The first self-conscious *artistes* who played at the idiot-savant game may have been the Godz, who recorded some of the most way-out records for the most way-out label of the 1960s, ESP (see separate sidebar). Lester Bangs once wrote in *Creem* that the Godz "are a pure test of one of the supreme traditions of rock & roll: the process by which a musical band can evolve from beginnings of almost insulting illiteracy to wind up several albums later romping and stomping deft as champs." Their 1966 debut (*Contact High*) was recorded, apparently, *before* the band had ever played their instruments; the drums were relentlessly plodding, the guitars squalled like cats in the microwave, the vocals were out of tune, and the songs were nothing more than droning baby-talk patter. I could not force myself to listen more than twice to the copy I found at the Berkeley Flea Market in 1984; a then-friend and fellow critic sniffed, "I'm not sure you really know what's going on there." Which is the fail-safe position on any idiot savant discovery: the sheer unpleasant amateurism of the music counts for nothing next to the boldness of the attitude, and the subversion, whether deliberate or not, of pop and rock norms.

It's doubtful, however, that the Shaggs had self-conscious subversion on their minds when they entered a recording studio in the late '60s. The Massachusetts sisters were advised by the recording engineer to come back when they had improved, but their dad insisted on seeing the session through. The results were issued as *Philosophy of the World*, treasured for almost 30 years by those who worship naiveté at the expense of rhythm, tune, harmony, and melody. The Shaggs were important, gushed one friend to me, "because they have no influences!"

But, ironically, the Shaggs themselves *became* influences on acts that raised their no-chops-necessary ethos to new extremes. The champions in this regard would be Half Japanese, whose debut album—a three-record box set—was as subtle as their music, which prided itself on maximum cacophony and irritability. Noted musicians like Velvet Underground drummer Maureen Tucker and progressive rock guitarist Fred Frith were sufficiently intrigued to become guest stars on some of Half Jap's many records of the 1980s and 1990s, which have resolutely shied away from anything conforming to conventional notions of entertainment.

Frank Zappa—by many standards, an actual *savant* with no idiocy involved—made his own contribution to the genre by championing the career of Wild Man Fischer, an ex-mental patient who strummed his loony tunes on a broken guitar with just-post-tonsillectomy vocals. Zappa was intrigued enough to produce *An Evening with Wild Man Fischer* on his Bizarre label in the late '60s; listeners were unsure whether Frank was genuinely convinced that Fischer had something to offer, or whether the whole thing was a cruel joke. If nothing else, it was a sure-fire missile for inciting the wrath of mainline rock critics such as Dave Marsh, who was barely able to contain his rage in *The Rolling Stone Record Guide*, calling the album "a particularly vicious example of Zappa's penchant for sadistic social commentary. The results are brutal, not funny except to the emotionally immature and the socially callous, and would constitute a deleted embarrassment in recorded history if the record industry had any shame."

Marsh may have been overreacting, but his rant did bring up a legitimate point: were fans laughing with or, perhaps more likely, *at* the likes of Wild Man Fischer? The latter-day counterpart to Wild Man Fischer may be Daniel Johnston, against whom I've borne a grudge since a record executive kept me and a whole houseful of music fans up for hours by inserting tape after tape of the Texas singer-songwriter's cloying kiddie rock. Johnston, who based himself in Austin, is no Roky Erickson. But he found an immediate niche in the alternative rock world, eventually landing on a major label and recording with buddies like Sonic Youth. The problem was, Johnston was not just an eccentric; he was actually mentally ill. While acclaim from the alternative press has been constant, there's also a suspicion that he would have never even gained a recording contract had he not been marketed as a novelty of sorts—a mental incompetent who thinks he can sing and play, isn't he funny? Which might be considered cruel and unusual punishment, rather than positive reinforcement.

The same syndrome has resurfaced with the fledgling career of Wesley Willis, a chronic schizophrenic who spent much of his adulthood as a homeless man in Chicago. That didn't stop American Recordings from signing him, and Willis at last notice was still busy singing rants about McDonald's and incessant, rambling tributes/diatribes about rock bands ranging from the Rolling Stones to Urge Overkill. Greg Workman, former manager of Alternative Tentacles (which released a Willis collection in 1994), told Irwin Chusid (in the July 1996 edition of *Pulse!*): "I've warned Wes that not everyone has his best interests in mind. But part of being mentally disturbed is that he thinks he's going to be the biggest rock star in the world. Lots of people are feeding that delusion. He's the sweetest guy in the world, but it's disgusting the way some people are taking advantage of him."

When it comes to idiot savants with mystique, no one can beat Jandek, the Houston eccentric who has self-released over two dozen albums featuring spooky, slightly demented stream of consciousness ramblings and guitar playing which rarely strays from set notes and chords, none of which pick out anything close to a melody. His voice can range from a hushed whisper to a Janovian primal scream; unsettlingly, he hardly ever mines the wide territory between those extremes. Sometimes the guitar is acoustic, like a deathbed Neil Young; sometimes he sounds like the 13-year-old who's just gotten his first electric for his Bar Mitzvah. Occasionally a woman adds gospelish moans in the background. The albums are issued in plain sleeves with no liner notes, and enigmatic cover photos with all the attention to framing and focus of the do-it-yourself stalls at Woolworth's.

"How to describe Jandek?" asked Irwin Chusid rhetorically in *Pulse!* "Like most amateur rock crits, start by comparing him to the Beatles. Then strip away melody, catchy hooks, rhythm and harmony. Next toss out vocal and instrumental ability, along with any trace of human emotion other than pain. Aside from these deficiencies, he's *exactly* like the Fab Four. Or maybe the Velvet Underground—after taxes." Presumably the records aren't shifting in great quantities; at one point Jandek was offering a "special" of 25 LPs for $55. It hasn't helped that he seems to view the merest concession to self-promotion as unacceptable. When I contacted him to propose an interview in 1986, he responded, "Questions etc. can't be arranged. Also, we think your article will be better without them. At least we hope so." And then the kicker—"Anything else, just ask."

When I ring up Scott Walker's management to request an interview, I'm curtly informed that Walker never speaks to the press unless he has a new album out. Which, these days, is a once-a-decade or so event. There was an eleven-year gap between his last two albums, *Tilt* (1995) and *Climate of Hunter* (1984). Would I have to wait until 2006?

Scott Walker

A few days before, I had called his British record company—a large, major label. Walker, the voice on the other end of the line maintained, had not done an album with them for years. (*Tilt* at this point had been on the shelves a mere 15 months.) Why didn't I call the label's American office instead, she asked. I hadn't the nerve to tell her that the record had never even been released in Walker's native country.

The runaround is entirely in keeping with the mystique of the leading candidate for oddest trailblazer in pop music history. Scott Walker found fame as the lead voice of the Walker Brothers, who were marketed as part of the British Invasion, although they were neither British, nor actual brothers, nor even named Walker. At the height of Beatlemania, while everyone else was cranking up their guitars, he attained stardom by crooning soulful pop-rock ballads in the manner of his heroes Tony Bennett and Jack Jones. When his contemporaries were experimenting with psychedelics, he was watching Bergman, flirting with socialism, taking a two-week cultural trip to Moscow, and checking himself into a monastery for ten days. Breaking off from his fellow Walkers at the end of the '60s, he became a huge solo star in Britain by covering risqué Jacques Brel songs and writing morbid, introspective odes to gloom that made Leonard Cohen seem like the class clown. An American who became a star in Britain after moving to London in the mid-'60s, he was (and is) virtually unknown in his own nation, where few of his solo records have even been released.

Scott Walker, British Invasion heartthrob, in the mid-1960s.

Walker hasn't sold large quantities of records since around 1970, but in a sense the story got even more interesting. Always shy of the limelight, Walker become something of a recluse, recording only every few years or so, when the mood suited him. After a lackluster reunion with the Walker Brothers in the mid-70s, he took a left turn into avant-garde electro-pop—music that was bound to alienate most of his old fans, and pick up few new ones. Despite good critical notices, recording became a rare event, as, seemingly, did public appearances of any kind, musical or otherwise.

Most of his '60s contemporaries started out as fiery innovators, eventually mellowing into predictable bland pop singers. Walker—along with rare exceptions like Marianne Faithfull—has traveled in exactly the opposite direction, from bland teen idol to arty songsmith to art-rocker whose musings are so oblique and impenetrable as to be inaccessible to all but an extremely small cult audience. His reclusion and almost defiant uncommerciality have given rise to the usual mad genius rumors. Yet when he did grant a precious few interviews in the mid-1990s, the picture was that of a very sane, if very private, person. "Don't

knock the boy," warns Brian Gascoigne, who has collaborated closely with Scott as the arranger and keyboardist on Walker's last two albums. "He's a very good egg in a pretty stale omelette. Really it's as Laing said about mad people. They think they're sane and everybody else is mad, and who's to say they're wrong?"

There was little that was arty or oblique about the early career of Scott Walker, born Noel Scott Engel in Ohio in 1944. In fact, when he started to make records as a teenager under the name of Scotty Engel in the late '50s, he was mostly just horrible. Already the owner of a gorgeous voice, he ground out

Scott Walker, avant-garde auteur, 1990s.

numerous vapid teen idol pop singles before taking up bass and playing on some raunchy Californian rock instrumentals in the early '60s. By late 1963, he was working with another singer, John Maus, in Hollywood. After the British Invasion took off, they were approached by drummer Gary Leeds, who had just backed American singer P.J. Proby on a British tour. Proby, unknown in the U.S., was a star in England. If they would team up together, Leeds insisted, he, Engel, and Maus could do the same thing.

It was an incredibly nervy, perhaps foolhardy, move—three Californians in their early twenties, without a hit, a place to live, or even the right haircuts (although the hair would grow shaggy soon enough), flying to London to join the British Invasion. It wasn't planned for Walker to take most of the lead vocals, but his honeyed baritone was the group's greatest asset. "Love Her," an orchestral ballad that they had already issued in the States to no reaction, became a modest hit in Britain after their arrival. Philips UK was encouraged enough to get the Walker Brothers, as they were now calling themselves, into a British studio to record a Bacharach-David ballad, "Make It Easy on Yourself." The record made #1 on the British charts in September 1965. The trio's gamble had paid off; though at times they were on the verge of flying back to the States during their first few months abroad, they were now receiving media and fan adulation almost on the order of Beatlemania.

"Make It Easy on Yourself" set the formula for most of the Walkers' hits between 1965 and 1967—big, booming ballads whose soaring melodies, operatic delivery, and resonant production bore a distinct resemblance to the hits of the Righteous Brothers (an American duo who, as it happened, were also not brothers, nor named Righteous). "My Ship Is Coming In" and "The Sun Ain't Gonna Shine Anymore" were also huge British hits for the group in early 1966. "Make It Easy on Yourself" and "The Sun Ain't Gonna Shine Anymore" also made the U.S. Top 20 in a sort of sneak British Invasion attack, although the Walkers never attained anything close to the same level of success in their homeland as they did in Britain.

Walker's voice quickly came to dominate the group musically, a circumstance that Gary Leeds says "happened by accident, really. He was just basically the bass player and did a bit of harmony. It happened he had the good voice and it worked better here." Most of the hits were supplied by outside songwriters, yet Walker's own compositions for the group—mostly confined to albums—were starting to exhibit a darker, more complex tone. "Archangel" had a refrain built around a Bach fugue; "Mrs. Murphy" was a hint of his later preoccupation with middle-aged wallflowers; "Deadlier Than the Male" viewed romance in ominous, almost paranoid terms.

These songs weren't terribly suitable fare for the Walkers' mostly female, mostly adolescent, audience. By 1967, the Walkers themselves were getting out of step with the British pop scene, which was hurtling into hard rock and psychedelia. (Oddly, the Jimi Hendrix Experience, who had just released their first singles, made one of their first tours with the Walker Brothers in early 1967.) Prevailing trends and his burgeoning songwriting/solo vocal talents made Scott's decision to opt for his own career unsurprising.

It's worth considering, however, what the girls who had swooned over Scott in the Walker Brothers thought when his self-titled debut arrived in the shops. This was not easygoing pop-rock, though the beautiful symphonic arrangements remained intact. Walker was now singing about brooding loners, or characters that seemed to come straight from the Ingmar Bergman films he loved. He also covered three songs from the great French songwriter/social ironist Jacques Brel. The album, and the solo records that followed in the late '60s, presented music to listen to, alone, sitting by the window at a desolate apartment, with the lights out. The beauty of the melodies, and Walker's increasingly supple and operatic baritone, only enhanced the complex appeal of the material. It wasn't rock, perhaps, but it was way too far out and morbid to find an easy listening audience with fans of Scott's vocal inspirations, Jack Jones and Frank Sinatra.

Gary Leeds for one is unsurprised that Scott's solo work took such a dark and serious turn. "We used to go see all the Bergman films. He was really into all the existential stuff. He used to take me to see *War and Peace*—it lasted about 35 days.

"Half the management thought he was the next Sinatra. His voice is, I would say, better than Sinatra's in a different light—I don't think anybody can come near his singing. Then when he writes that type of deep stuff . . . of course, you couldn't do a concert with that, unless everybody was wearing black."

This was seriously *adult* pop music, but the problem was that it wasn't being heard by serious adults—the older rock audience was into progressive rock. Walker had enough straight pop and teenybopper fans (who, presumably, did not always listen hard to the lyrics) to ascend to solo stardom. *Scott 2*, in fact, made #1 Britain in 1968, a remarkable feat at a time when Hendrix, the Beatles, and Cream were at their peak. *Scott 3* also made the Top Ten, despite the inclusion of uncommercial-as-all-hell numbers like "Big Louise" (about a hefty prostitute) and "We Came Through" (a cavalry charge with spaghetti western production that would do Ennio Morricone proud). One person who was probably listening was David Bowie, who certainly sounds influenced by Walker's drawn-out, emotive vocal style, fascination with the macabre, and haircut (look at photos of Bowie circa 1967-68 for proof). The records fell on deaf ears in the United States, where they were virtually unknown, if they even gained a release at all.

Walker's albums from the late '60s and early '70s (now mostly available on CD in the U.K.) are inarguably his artistic peak, and a source of inspiration for subsequent generations of doom-and-gloom rockers. *Scott 4* is probably his best, featuring entirely original material; "The Seventh Seal" (based upon the Ingmar Bergman film of the same name) and "The Old Man's Back Again," rumored to be about Josef Stalin, are two of his most ambitious works. "Time Operator," from 1970's *Til the Band Comes In*, is his most sublime lyrical triumph: an entire song about a man so lonely that he's fallen in love with the voice of the automatic phone operator, whose periodic recitals of the time punctuate the mournful arrangement.

But by the early '70s, Walker had begun to fade commercially. The subsequent decade was characterized by sporadic, slipshod recordings in which he often didn't even write much of his own material, offering pointless covers of tunes by Neil Diamond and Jimmy Webb. A reunion with the Walker Brothers in the mid-'70s yielded a Top Ten British hit ("No Regrets"), but was predictably uninspired. Walker had permanently abandoned his native U.S. for residence overseas; his chapter in pop history seemed over.

Sharp ears, however, found something interesting brewing in his contributions to the Walker Brothers' final reunion LP, *Nite Flights*. These had a stark electro-pop feel totally unlike his earlier work. The bleak "The Electrician" in particular recalled the '70s collaborations between Brian Eno and David Bowie on such albums as *Low*. Bowie and Eno themselves, in fact, have been reported to have expressed an interest in working with Walker based on that one track. It would take six years for Scott to harvest that seed. When *Climate of Hunter* finally appeared in 1984, the Scott Walker of old was gone, except for that familiar voice. He was now singing abstract poems against bleak, almost amelodic electronic textures. Some critics were mightily excited, but the public took little notice.

Brian Gascoigne, a key architect of Walker's new sound as arranger and keyboardist, postulates: "I think he started out feeling the need to redefine, for himself, regardless of his audience, the relation of lyrics to music in contemporary song. That sounds pompous, which he isn't at all. But the presiding ingredients in 'pop' songs—hook, groove, traditional chords, predictable instrumentation, rhythm section and overdubs, etc.—seemed stale to him, and unable to convey the degree of passion, complexity, or ambiguity that he was after. Each of the songs had an extensive sub-text, not always extractable. The sound palette he was seeking had to reflect the particular mood, usually agony.

"Having one of the richest baritones in the history of popular song, he associated using it to its full with the pelvic-thrusting ego-tripping of most other pop icons. And although he knows how to use his voice and how to accompany it, he refuses to do any proper conventional 'singing'—long notes, controlled vibrato, crescendos, or just reveling in the vocal sound. Which we all miss, but which he would feel to be a concession to showbiz, and a distraction from the purpose of the song."

Walker by now was more interested in composers such as Mahler, Messiaen, Penderecki, and Copland—as well as free jazz and hip fusion—than rock. "But the important thing about these sources for him is not to copy them, but to take a mood, a chord, an orchestral texture which triggers an emotional response in him, and to use it as a starting point for a particular texture that he needs at a given point in a song. By the time this has been experimented with, altered, retried, and altered again, you would be hard put to identify the original item, although the mood will have stayed the course . . . . He operates on the same principle as the serialists in that as you get used to the musical vocabulary, a regular major chord sounds like a dissonance. This is where he likes to be."

In other words, Walker was getting too uncommercial even for the likes of Brian Eno fans. Eno and Daniel Lanois were slated to produce *Climate of Hunter*'s follow-up, but the project was abandoned after some work due to, in Gascoigne's estimation, "clash of personalities. Scott won't be dictated to by conventional—and that includes Eno/Lanois'—musical processes. He is happy to listen to suggestions, the more the better, as long as nobody tries to insist on one that has been sidestepped. And they, as hired producers, never understood that, or if they did, they had decided to override that process. I find Eno much more interesting as a writer than a musician, and could see that Eno hadn't the faintest idea of what Scott was up to. Their instincts were leading them in different directions, and had it been finished, it would not have been as interesting as either *Climate of Hunter* or *Tilt*."

When it finally emerged in 1995, *Tilt* boasted operatically sung, unfathomable lyrics and minimalist song structures. No verses, no choruses. The mesh of classical motifs with imaginative timbres and instrumentation owed more to serious contemporary composition than anything that could be construed as "pop." It made *Climate of Hunter* seem positively commercial. Wrote Stephen Thomas Erlewine in the *All Music Guide*, "It's arguably the most inaccessible, difficult album ever recorded." An *NME* reporter described the staff reaction to the album thusly: "Within three minutes of opening track 'Farmer in the City,' they are banging their heads on the desks and pleading for *Tilt* to be ripped off the stereo and tossed into the Thames." The writer relayed the story to Walker himself, who was sitting for one of his rare interviews, and "Scott looked pleased."

But Gascoigne paints a picture of a thoughtful worker in the studio, not a lunatic. "Scott will wander into the studio with a smile and a frown together and innocently start inspecting the instrument—hurdy-gurdy, Mongolian nose-flute, or whatever—and ask about some bit of it. This will encourage the musician to produce the range of standard jokes and rude noises of which all instruments are capable, and which so enliven boring rehearsals and sessions. But he will then realize that Scott really is interested in these outside sounds for real. And it is at that point that the session starts in earnest . . . . Although I'm allowed to write the melody on the lead sheet, for the purpose of alerting Scott if his experimentations with the accompaniment should take him somewhere that the melody won't fit over, I'm not allowed to play or hum it in the studio, as the musicians have to work without knowing it, to prevent them from having a conditioned response."

Gascoigne reports that Walker's option has been extended for another album, and that Scott may be working on a film score—which might be a fruitful avenue to pursue, given Walker's current aversion to conventional pop melodies and lyrics. Why, however, is this former golden boy of '60s pop—the one who, in Gary Leeds' words, "could just snap [his] fingers if he wanted to be a success, and go on right through Vegas and really do some damage"—determined to be so uncommercial?

"He had reached a point where he had decided to only do what he wanted," explains Gascoigne. "No producer with his own agenda, no interference from the record company, and nobody involved to hear any of it until mixed. I think this was partly because he knew that what he was trying to do would induce cardiac arrest in the suits, and partly because he wasn't even sure it would work. He knows that the mass audience will not venture down such a spiky path, and he must be gratified, as I have been, by people coming up and saying that it meant a lot to them.

"Perhaps he isn't even sure himself if what he's doing is more than just therapy, although enough people seem to like it. He freely admits to having been traumatized by the sort of adulation he received in the '60s, and is widely read, and aware of contemporary art and poetry. His cultural frame of reference is miles wider than any other songwriter I've ever met. That makes him, as it makes me, extremely schizophrenic about the genre limitations of songwriting. After all, he knows he's only in a position to spend months making an uncommercial album because of the success of the historic commercial ones. I'm sure he wants to make sure that he doesn't blow the opportunity."

Recommended Recordings:
By the Walker Brothers:
After the Lights Go Out (1990, Fontana, UK). Excellent 20-track compilation of the Walker Brothers' best material, including both the massive hits and the most interesting tunes Scott wrote for the group, such as "Mrs. Murphy," "Archangel," and "Orpheus."

By Scott Walker:
Boy Child: Best of 1967-1970 (1992, Fontana, UK). The ideal counterpart to *After the Lights Go Out*, with 20 of Scott's best original tunes from his solo heyday. This does not include any of his renowned Jacques Brel interpretations, which are spread throughout his first four solo albums. Those four records (all

available on CD on Fontana UK) are also worthwhile for fans with an appetite for more, *Scott 4* (containing entirely original songs) being the best of these. There is also a compilation in the U.S., *It's RainingToday*, which contains tracks from Walker's 1967-70 period.

Tilt (1995, Drag City). One of the most daring albums ever made by a middle-aged former pop star; too weird and challenging, in fact, to even make the *alternative* radio charts. It will not, however, appeal to many fans who treasure his early work.

Recommended Reading:
Scott Walker: A Deep Shade of Blue, by Mike Watkinson and Pete Anderson (1994, Virgin). Exhaustive and entertaining biography, covering everything from the '50s through the early '90s with great detail. No firsthand interview material from Scott, but plenty from key colleagues like Gary Leeds, John Maus, and various producers and arrangers.

From the Continent 6

Rock music is a very Anglo-centric medium. Those of us who live in the United States, Canada, and the British Isles can tend to forget that there are several hundreds of millions of rock listeners who do not think or speak in English. When they form bands, they are at a twofold disadvantage. If they want to make a wide international impact, they must sung in a second language, English. And if they want to compete in the international marketplace, they're largely overlooked in the crush of the zillions of acts that American and British companies can sign in their own backyards.

Nevertheless, almost since its mid-'50s beginnings, rock 'n' roll has flourished in non-English-speaking countries. On occasion, these countries have spearheaded movements that have proven to have real international influence, particularly in the world of progressive rock, which by its very nature relies less upon lyrics and singing. There are also superstars like ABBA and a-ha, who achieved international success by sounding as transatlantic as possible with their lowest-common-denominator washing machines of British and American mainstream pop.

Behind the seemingly irresistible urge to homogenize and anglicize, however, lie hundreds of intriguing bands from the European continent who took inspiration from British and American rock stars, but came up with hybrids of their own. Just within the five acts selected for this chapter, there's a great deal of stylistic diversity. The Outsiders took the British Invasion R&B of the Pretty Things and made it even punkier and stranger; Savage Rose were possibly the most eclectic and interesting art-rock group of their era, and almost certainly the only group to both open for James Brown at a major music festival and play at P.L.O. refugee camps; Can probably did more than anyone else to establish German electronic/progressive rock as an international influence. All of these groups sang primarily or wholly in English, which couldn't be said of Françoise Hardy, who mixed rock and girl-group influences into the best of the French chanteuse tradition, or the Plastic People of the Universe, one of the few rock bands who truly changed the world with their role in the Czechoslovakian dissident community.

I would go out on a limb and rate these as the five most interesting rock artists to hail from Continental Europe, in spite of the many who would vote for Faust, Tangerine Dream, Q65, or what have you. Those that disagree, or have their appetites whetted for more, will find plenty of honorable mentions in the sidebar overviews of Kraut rock, Eurobeat, and rock behind the Iron Curtain. And we're not even getting into the numerous bands from South America, Japan, and other far-flung regions that have generated cult icons of their own. The world's a much bigger place than pop radio would have you believe; it's time to start exploring.

A recent publicity shot of Annisette, lead singer of Savage Rose.

Can

When the group thatwould call themselves Can began playing together in 1968, it would have been hard to imagine a more unlikely cast for a progressive rock group. The four core members had hardly ever played rock music before, for one thing. Jaki Liebezeit had spent most of the previous decade as a jazz drummer, logging a stint in Chet Baker's band. Bassist Holger Czukay had studied composition with avant-garde giant Karlheinz Stockhausen; guitarist Michael Karoli, who had studied with Czukay, was still deciding whether to pursue a career in law or music. Conductor, composer, and keyboardist Irmin Schmidt had also studied with Stockhausen. Except for Karoli, all of them had just entered their thirties. Schmidt, according to Czukay, had problems musically counting to four in the beginning (he hastens to add that "every one of us" had such weaknesses). And all were from Germany, a country that had thus far produced no rock bands of international influence.

"When I founded the group, I wasn't really thinking about a rock group at all," admits Schmidt today, speaking from his home in France. "My idea was to get a bunch of people together from all kinds of directions—new music, jazz, classical. I wanted one of those guys who could play kind of a rock beat guitar. I wanted somebody like Jaki, who was a jazz musician. This 'new music' cliché got too narrow for me. I wanted something wider. Above all, what I wanted was to make some spontaneous music which was created by communication between people, and not composed by me [alone]."

Can were one of the very first rock groups more concerned with mood and sonic textures than conventional "songs" with verses, choruses, and lyrics. The experimental, almost "chance" nature of their compositions, with rare exceptions, militated against mass acceptance. As if this wasn't enough to guarantee a specialized audience, they chose to work with two of the oddest lead singers in rock history: an African-American painter/sculptor who improvised raw rants over Can's throbbing pulses, and a Japanese wanderer who could hardly speak English (the language in which Can chose to compose). Yet today, Can are venerated as one of the most influential and relevant groups of the 1970s, pioneers of today's ambient, techno, and electronic rock with their jagged, oft-dissonant statements of insistent, repetitive riffs and jarring audio collages.

Although the musicians may have been schooled in serious composition, the zeitgeist of the late '60s was pushing them towards rock. The Beatles and Jimi Hendrix were incorporating avant-garde ideas into hugely popular rock records anyway. More consciously experimental acts like the Velvet Underground and the Mothers of Invention were borrowing themes and approaches from contemporary composition. All of the aforementioned artists were influential in Can's blend of Stockhausen and rock. But the final ingredient wouldn't be supplied until a black American artist named Malcolm Mooney visited the band in Cologne.

Mooney, as Schmidt remembers, was visiting a composer friend of his in Paris, where Schmidt's wife Hildegard (who eventually became Can's manager) invited him to Cologne. "He didn't come to join the group," says Schmidt. "He came to the studio, and spontaneously just sang. We said, look, why don't you just stay and go out singing with us? He stayed. His singing put the whole thing more to the rock side. One of the first members, David Johnson [who played flute], left because he felt uncomfortable, because for him it was becoming too much rock."

Mooney's appearance was especially fortuitous in that his spontaneous approach to singing, and lack of anything resembling a solid background in rock music (in fact, Mooney had no singing experience whatsoever), fit in well with the modus operandi of the group. "We didn't want to read music off papers," says Czukay, recalling the Can days in his San Francisco hotel room, at the end of his very first American musical tour in early 1997. "We really tried to make instant compositions from the very beginning. Malcolm was a great rhythm talent. He was a locomotive!

Can in the early 1970s. Left to right: Damo Suzuki, Michael Karoli, Irmin Schmidt, Holger Czukay, Jaki Liebezeit.
Credit: Courtesy Mute Records

"That was the right singer from the very beginning, as this was our weak point. Maybe we were creating rhythms, but you could say we were not very stable in doing that. That means [we needed] someone who was pushing us into the rhythm, and giving us the feel that this is the right thing to do. This was Malcolm Mooney, and he got integrated very much into what all the other musicians did. I think he was the right singer in the right place at the right time."

Can's first album, *Monster Movie*, has been described as a sort of raw Velvet Underground, a somewhat misleading tag, as Can were far less conscious of constructing songs in which the words and vocals were crucial. It's more appropriate to note that Can followed the Velvets' lead in creating drone-like clusters that could be simultaneously hypnotic and dissonant. The limited abilities of the players on rock instruments—Czukay often stuck to repetitious two-note riffs, and Schmidt learned to play rock on a broken keyboard—ensured, to a certain degree, that the music would be at once minimalist and experimental. Mooney's atonal vocals, it must be said, are found by many to be less than an acquired taste, as they're much more colored by energy and rhythm than conventional pitches.

Mooney's behavior had become very erratic by the end of 1969—he would sometimes disappear from gigs mid-show, or not show up at all. On the advice of a psychiatrist, he returned to America. For months the group was without a permanent lead singer, a dilemma that was solved in May 1970, when Czukay spotted a Japanese busker at a Munich cafe. That very night, 21-year-old Damo Suzuki gave his first concert with Can.

Suzuki was, if anything, an even more unusual frontman than Mooney. He sang in English, but didn't seem to know the meaning of the words, mumbling and humming the lyrics as if singing to himself. In almost any other band this would have been a serious liability. But to Can, who thought of the vocalist more as another instrument than a dominant voice, he was heaven-sent. Mooney and Suzuki were both, in their separate ways, appropriate for Can's mission, although probably neither could have joined any other band of a similar profile. Czukay agrees that their crossing paths with the band were particularly inspired accidents: "You can say, if you're a religious person, they were given by God."

Most fans regard the next few years as Can's finest period. Suzuki's voice was like a hallucinogenic element in the mix, floating in and out of the songs in ways that were both evocative and nonsensical. On *Tago Mago* (1971), the group established trance-rock grooves with tracks like "Oh Yeah," "Aumgn," and "Halleluhwah" (described by *The Rough Guide to Rock* as "a shotgun-wedding of the James Brown band and the Velvets playing 'Sister Ray'"). *Future Days* (1973), by contrast, was modern psychedelic music with its languid, shimmering vibes. Can's music was especially well-suited for film, and in their early career they contributed to numerous soundtracks. American audiences may be most familiar with this aspect of their work via their music for Wim Wenders' 1974 film *Alice in the Cities*, which actually only features Karoli on guitar and Schmidt playing directly on the strings of a grand piano. Unfortunately, the tapes of that particular soundtrack are now lost.

Most Can fans find it hard to stop with two or three albums because, being apt to work via "instant composition" in the studio as well as onstage, each record was an unpredictable departure from the group's previous efforts. Given their preferred working methods, Can were fortunate to be able to record at their own pace in their own studio. During their first few years this was a two-track, which, the members believe, if anything enhanced their creativity, forcing them to create complex sounds from limited facilities. "We played together live in the studio as we would do it on stage, without an audience," notes Czukay.

"It always turned out that when we started on a new record, it took a totally new direction," chips in Schmidt. "We wanted to be surprised *ourselves*—onstage, on record, and by each other."

The group was actually at its most unpredictable in concert, where they might play a 90-minute piece nonstop ("like a big symphony," according to Schmidt), and improvised in a manner much more identified with free jazz ensembles than rock bands. When a power outage interrupted a show in Brussels, Liebezeit filled in the space with a 20-minute drum passage. "When it came to making a big performance of nothing, Can was very important," asserts Czukay with pride. "I think it had something to do with football or sports. You can't really say in the next minute, where is that ball going to? A team which is playing with such a ball knows very well about strategies, but actually you can't say, by definition, when the ball is in this or this area. It's the same with Can music. We knew how to build up the whole thing, but the actual sound and development was not foreseen."

In Czukay's view, multitrack recording may have worked against the group's strengths. "I regard the very first albums being the most important, as Can was most innocent at that time. If a group is new, young, and starting from the very beginning, actually you can't do anything wrong. You do something wrong when you try to learn. When you get older and experienced, this is the time when you can have some errors.

"In the beginning, we were recording on two tracks. Then we had a hit in Germany, and we were able to afford a multitrack machine. From this moment on, you can say it was the beginning of the end of Can. In such a group, everybody has to criticize the other one about what he's doing wrong. But when the multitrack machine came out, it was, 'I want to hear the guitar,' or 'I want to hear the bass, who has made this wrong?' The musician was getting a little bit afraid, and said 'Okay, I do my part now and play it as good as I can.' The others shouldn't be in there because it makes him nervous. The group was suddenly not so strong."

The group lost a more tangible asset in September of 1973, when Suzuki left Can after marrying a German woman and becoming a Jehovah's Witness.

"We tried a hell of a lot of singers," laments Schmidt. "Then we found out how rare it was that a singer fit into Can. This [Suzuki and Mooney] both had in common, however difficult it is to explain why. They had the same kind of mystery."

Czukay: "The problem was, when Damo disappeared, Can was now without a singer. Suddenly we felt a hole in our music. Michael was singing, but he is not . . . a guitar player actually should not sing, except like Jimi Hendrix or something like that. A guitar player should play guitar. We tried out so many singers at that time. And nobody really fitted into the group again."

Commercially, if anything, Can were beginning to make big strides. They were signed by Virgin, a label that in its first few years issued quite a few German rock releases; they even got a British hit with "I Want More." They were getting deeper into funk and ethnic rhythms. In the States, where several Can albums were never even released at the time, they remained so underground as to be invisible. Ironically, Czukay says, "I always thought, if Can makes it, it will make it in America. I thought the way the rhythms were done, the way we played live — it was a hell, actually, of rhythmic impact. I thought that would fit far more into America than Europe."

When I relay that observation to Schmidt, he seems dubious. "Our rhythms were much nearer to, say, Sly Stone live, than to any European band. But I'm not sure the Americans would have been ready for such avant-garde craziness. Whenever I was in the States and listened to any concerts in universities and big halls, it was much more civilized than we were. All the people that came from the States and listened to us in England or Germany or France, even people from the business, didn't think it would work in the States."

In the late 1970s, Czukay left the bass to take a nebulous role as "sound editor." He surmises: "I knew where the weak point of Can was. They were dealing too much with themselves; nothing came from outside. So I looked [to use] radio, telephone, and all these sorts of devices. That means you suddenly get information from outside, get off your routine, and get fresh again. But, maybe, the other members didn't like this idea very much. That was the reason why I got out and started on my own, towards the end of Can."

The split, in 1978, was hardly acrimonious, considering that members of the band have continued to record and play with each other on numerous solo/side projects. Czukay has assumed the highest profile, collaborating with David Sylvian and Jah Wobble, and pursuing ethnic-world-music-pop-experimental fusions. Schmidt has been very active in film work; he, Karoli, and Liebezeit continue to record. A steady stream of Can material emanates from the archives, and in the late 1980s the group even did a reunion album with Malcolm Mooney. "Sometimes it was difficult because we hadn't played for such a long time together," says Schmidt, who often works with Karoli and Liebezeit on non-Can projects to this day. "Making this kind of spontaneous music, it's very dependent on this kind of telepathy. Most of the time, it was quite fun. It's always beautiful to play with them."

Can's music—with its spooky, electronic eclecticism—sometimes seems more appropriate for today's scene than it did for the 1970s. Several influential new wave musicians—including Julian Cope, Pete Shelley (of the Buzzcocks), and Mark E. Smith (of the Fall)—have been extremely vocal about their appreciation for Can, even if it's not always evident in those artists' music. Holger Czukay also sees a link between Can's experiments and today's ambient-techno scene:

"This open-minded conception which Can established is a good way to master the future. I can see that now, working with young people from the electronic scene. They understand me perfectly. They are able to interact right away. [Their] music, with all these devices, is perfectly designed for the electronic world. This is very living electronic music. Nothing is wrong with that."

Recommended Recordings:
Anthology: 25 Years (1994, Spoon/Mute). Can's extensive discography isn't easily boiled down to a two-CD anthology. At the same time, if you haven't heard them before, this is the only way to get a survey of their diverse accomplishments.

Tago Mago (1971, Spoon/Mute). The most energetic document of the Suzuki era, including the favorites "Oh Yeah," "Halleluhwah," and the relatively concise "Mushroom."

Future Days (1973, Spoon/Mute). The favorite Can album of many psychedelically oriented listeners. Spoon/Mute, incidentally, have issued most of the band's discography on CD.

Recommended Reading:
The Can Book, by Pascal Bussy & Andy Hall (1989, SAF, UK). A good primer of the band's complex history, including individual chapters on each member, a chronology/history, and separate sections on the group's studio work, live shows, and reunion.

Krautrock

While Can are probably considered the most influential of the German progressive rock bands that emerged in the early 1970s, there's an entire phalanx of groups from the same movement that can claim cult followings of their own. Faust, Neu! (exclamation point always included), Amon Düül II (not to be confused with Amon Düül I), Ash Ra Tempel, and the early works of Kraftwerk, Tangerine Dream, and Popol Vuh—all were merging psychedelic rock with avant-garde/contemporary classical compositions, as well as cutting-edge electronics. The emphasis was not so much on tightly constructed, singable songs as relentless cosmic exploration, often instrumental and/or jam-like in texture. When the music began to make an international impact in the early '70s, it was dubbed "Krautrock" by the English-speaking press.

The "Krautrock" label may smack of political incorrectness to some. We do not, after all, call Japanese rock "Niprock" or some such thing. In fairness, it must be pointed out that one of the biggest groups of the genre, Faust, didn't seem to mind that much, or else they wouldn't have recorded a 12-minute track entitled "Krautrock" themselves. Some may prefer the term *Kosmische Musik* (cosmic music), an appropriate handle given the group's unceasing quest to set the controls for the heart of the sun. It was as if *Star Trek*'s mission to explore new worlds had been entirely hijacked by the Vulcans, replacing Dr. McCoy's sarcastic humanism with a deadly serious purpose—occasionally letting its guard down for a chuckle, as Mr. Spock does on rare occasions.

The peculiar character of Krautrock may be in large part due to German youth's intense struggle to create an identity of their own in the 1960s counterculture. They had to buck the enormous historical weight of the atrocities committed by the Nazis of the previous generation; the postwar occupation of Germany by American and British forces had amounted to a sort of cultural imperialism that inundated the country with Anglo popular culture, especially rock 'n' roll. It would be difficult to beat the Beatles, Jimi Hendrix, or the Doors at their own game. Something that was in a sense even more radical would be needed to carve an identity for German rock.

As the chapter in Can makes clear, the avant-garde compositions of Karlheinz Stockhausen were a key influence on that group's mix of rock with contemporary classical music. To varying degrees, the ideas of Stockhausen and similar composers also informed the music of other German bands that were struggling to create their own vocabulary in the rock idiom. Also influential was the experimental rock of bands like the Mothers of Invention, Velvet Underground, Fugs, 1967-era Beatles, and Jimi Hendrix Experience, who were incorporating elements of avant-garde music, sound collage, and poetry into their records. Few of the German groups would abandon "songs" as such completely, but the emphasis would often be on lengthy improvisations that used then-futuristic devices such as synthesizers. Krautrock, like the progressive rock movement in England, was an extension of psychedelia; it differed from Anglo prog rock, however, in that it was less concerned with either lifting from the classics, *or* bothering with conventional pop hooks. Mantra-like moods would often be a guiding principle, along with unconventional bouts of freakouts that made many of the prog rock groups across the water seem tame.

"In hindsight, Krautrock was not remotely 'hippy' in its modern post-punk definition," writes Julian Cope in his *Krautrocksampler* book (the best available survey of the genre). "It was soaringly idealistic and hard as nails. This *Kosmische Musik* was played by painted freaks and longhairs whose attitude had never left the idealism or the communes/collectives of the mid-1960s. Krautrock's heart was still in the MC5's guitars and the White Panthers' civil insurrection of 1969 Detroit, and the sheer moment of Andy Warhol's 1966 Exploding Plastic Inevitable . . .

"Many of the groups were only intent on capturing the Moment. There are more classic extended true 20-minute freakouts within the sleeves of Krautrock LPs than in the British & American music of all time. And all in space-punk gatefold sleeves, too. Albums were impossible to judge as they came out because they defied analysis alongside anything else but other Krautrock. And for all its '60s idealism, the West German scene was never in a stasis—it did not yearn for some lost undefined Golden age, but constantly dipped into the new music forms that arrived and adapted them as its own."

Those who find Can's work impossibly uncommercial should be advised that you ain't heard nothin' yet until you get to the likes of Faust, who used pinball machine-activated synthesizers onstage and inspired tongue-twisting reviews such as "distorted drone-guitar mantras jump-cut to studio-concocted caprices to cathedralized organ music to idyllic lulls of plangent pastoralism" (the *Spin Alternative Record Guide*). Ash Ra Tempel played crazed heavy rock with electronics, eventually recording an album that featured vocals by Timothy Leary, then a fugitive from American justice hiding out in Switzerland. Electro-rock pioneers Neu!, when they ran out of money to complete their second album, filled an entire LP side by remixing tracks at 16 rpm *and* 78 rpm.

Amon Düül I and Amon Düül II emerged out of the same late '60s commune, and hardly anyone but aficionados have managed to keep them straight. Amon Düül II's ridiculously eclectic take on post-psychedelia would come to totally overshadow their less inventive sibling band, especially when they featured the witchy warbles of Renate Knaup. Bands like Cluster, La Dusseldorf, and (let us not forget) Guru Guru were even more obscure in presence and intention, finding foreign ears mostly via fans who probably used little discretion in what they bought at the import bins.

Krautrock bands were fortunate to emerge during an era in which German record labels granted them freedom that would have been unimaginable in the U.S. (though it may well have been that it was the German bands themselves that forced the record business to adapt, not the other way around). 20-minute freakout jams? Double albums with gatefolds?

Outlandishly surrealist/psychedelic cover illustrations? No problem. It was in those sleeves—with images like a can of vegetables (for Can's *Ege Bamyasi*, natch) or Faust's debut, which impaled an x-ray of a fist onto a transparent sleeve—that the bands' sense of humor found its greatest (or, sometimes, only) outlet.

By the early '70s, interest in Krautrock had spread across the European continent and into the British Isles. A then-fledgling Virgin Records signed so many German progressive bands that the label was to a large degree identified with the sound during its early days. But Krautrock would never make much of an impact in the States, even among underground audiences. Partly this was because the music was just too strange for audiences weaned on a constant diet of commercialism. Also, to put it bluntly, much of the music was just too damned serious in its tenor, though champions of the form are always quick to unearth hundreds of examples of the groups' (very subtle) wit.

Krautrock's heyday was approximately from 1968 to 1974. Thereafter, the impetus of the leading bands began to wither, and their personnel to splinter. Klaus Schultze, Hans Roedelius, Manuel Göttsching, and other Krautrock vets inaugurated prolific solo careers that would emphasize their "serious" side more than the rockist tendencies they were prone to fall into in their early projects. The minimalism and sheer anti-commerciality of much Krautrock appealed to early punk rockers such as Johnny Rotten, who as John Lydon would guide Public Image Limited through deconstructions that owed considerable debts to the Germans.

Some diehards kept the faith. A number of them ended up as programmers at my college radio station, where the prime-time progressive slot continued to program Krautrock and its offshoots well into the 1980s. The Krautrock/Eurorock spaceship, they were convinced, was the music of the future, just as surely as the Kremlin was convinced that communism would soon take over the world. Neither of those developments came to pass, of course. Yet Krautrock did find its belated audience among the techno/ambient crowd of the 1990s, who recognized the Germans' repetitive beats, electronic screeches, and trance-inducing jams as forerunners of the icy futurism of . . . well, today.

Francoise Hardy

When the Beatles came through Paris on their 1965 European tour, they declared that there were two people they wanted to see: Brigitte Bardot and Françoise Hardy.

When Bob Dylan went through the French capital on his own European tour the following year, he also announced his wishes to meet two people. One was Brigitte Bardot. The other was Françoise Hardy.

While the summit meetings that followed were not exactly epochal events, they were a testimony to the mystique of the only Frenchwoman to rival sex symbol Brigitte Bardot as an international icon, if only on a cult level. All Americans know who Bardot is, but if they've seen Hardy at all, it's only been a fleeting glimpse of her in the definitively silly '60s comedy *What's New Pussycat?* Bardot's film credits may have been far more extensive than Hardy's, but there is no question as to who is the better singer—and the more creative artist.

Despite her remarkably photogenic visage, Hardy's forte was not acting, but writing and performing music. And when she sang, it was almost always in French, which guaranteed that her recordings would pass unnoticed in the U.S. during the '60s, despite her belated acclamation as perhaps the finest French pop/rock singer of all time. Today Hardy has one of the most rapidly expanding American cult followings of any musician, with her sumptuous French picture sleeves rating among the fastest-moving items at many a U.S. record convention.

She's always been far more than a cult item in her native land, though, where her debut 1962 EP, featuring the hit "Tous Les Garçons et Les Filles," sold over a million copies. Throughout the '60s, she would be one of France's most popular celebrities, recording (and, usually, writing) a thrilling series of suave heartbreak ballads as well as perky, Spectoresque rockers. Her superstar status waned a bit with her decision in the late '60s to stop touring extensively. But she's remained perennially popular and beloved in France, a nation in which—as the late Serge Gainsbourg and the French Elvis, Johnny Hallyday, could tell you—it's far easier to remain a pop music star into middle age than it is in the States or the British Isles.

Hardy, now approaching her mid-fifties, broke a musical silence of nearly a decade with the unexpectedly hard-edged 1996 album *Le Danger* on the large Virgin France label. That doesn't mean that interviews of the woman whose 1986 biography was titled *Superstar et Ermite* are necessarily easier to come by these days. Seven months of continual phone calls to Virgin's Paris office resulted in no definite yes or no answers, but plenty of rationales for indecision. She was in the midst of shooting a video. She was going on holiday. She was *on* holiday. She was going on holiday (again). In mid-1997, she was too stressed to grant interviews, I was told, pending the verdict regarding a proposed duet with

A recent publicity shot of Françoise Hardy. Credit: Courtesy Virgin Records, Paris

Iggy Pop (whom the skinny Hardy slightly resembles today physically). And then she was away on holiday again . . . perhaps, in accordance with her well-publicized interest in astrology, the stars would need to align themselves just so before any decision could be made. Fortunately, her legacy on record, stretching over 35 years, is rich enough to speak for itself.

Born into a Parisian family of humble means, Hardy taught herself a few chords on the guitar, and was already singing her own compositions in French clubs by the age of 17. Successfully auditioning for Vogue Records in 1961, her debut EP appeared the following year, featuring the teen-idolish ditty that, depending upon which figure you believe, would sell in the neighborhood of one, two, or three million copies. Hardy's opinion of "Tous Les Garçons et Les Filles" apparently isn't that high: in the French-only *Superstar et Ermite*, biographers Étienne Daho and Jérome Soligny relate that the session was completed in three hours, according to the singer, "with four of the worst musicians in all of Paris."

The record was, however, effective in introducing the 18-year-old's still-maturing but already fetching blend of sultry, breathy sexiness and reserved-yet-emotional vulnerability. The material and arrangements—at the outset an obvious mimic of lightweight late '50s/early '60s American teen pop—was already drastically improving by the second EP, especially on the snaky "Le Temps de L'Amour," with its spy-movie guitar and splendidly film noirish vocal. (The song, which Hardy has never bettered in her whole career, was co-written by future long-running romantic partner Jacques Dutronc, himself a French pop star, and eventual father of Françoise's son.) French pop/rock from the 1960s has never traveled well to the English-speaking audience, in part because of the language barrier, but also because of the extreme sentimentality of the melodies, vocal delivery, and arrangements. Hardy was almost unique in her ability to transcend these problems by combining the best of American and British contemporary pop with the seductive grandeur of Continental epics.

Much of the credit is due to the erratic but often superb Vogue productions, which backed her voice with gorgeous and varied orchestrations. Sweeping strings, melodramatic female choruses, devious jazzy organ licks, grand pianos, dainty harpsichords, thundering drums, British Invasion-like fuzz distortion, menacing reverbed guitar: all could be used to great effect, sometimes in the same cut. None of this would mean anything without Hardy's own superb songs. She wrote most of her own material, employing, despite her disclaimers about knowing only three chords or so on the guitar, captivatingly dramatic chord progressions with a beguiling mixture of sweetness and sadness. Those same qualities held true for her lyrics, which could occasionally be upbeat to the point of ebullience, but were usually melancholic ruminations on the disappointments of young love, whose misery was made to sound far more entrancing than depressing. Hardy was also clever enough to deliver the songs in an understated yet moody fashion that was somewhat akin to the early work of Marianne Faithfull, yet with far greater melodic power and emotional impact. When journalists of the era criticized her for not singing loud enough, she would explain that she conceived of her voice as one instrument among others.

Her Vogue recordings, especially those from 1962 to 1967, are usually esteemed by collectors as her best. Yet Hardy herself was surprisingly dismissive of them in her biography, noting that an artistic director of the rival Fontana label had expressed an interest in working with her, and "I often wondered since then how my records would have sounded if I had worked with him. In fact, I suffered for a long time from the mediocrity of the arrangements and orchestrations at Vogue. I have had reason to believe that it would have been less difficult elsewhere!"

Her desire to work in a more sympathetic environment led her to cut much of her '60s recordings, in fact, in London, with arrangers such as Charles Blackwell, ex-Manfred Mann guitarist Mike Vickers, and, strangely enough, future Led Zeppelin bassist John-Paul Jones. She even did some tracks under the direction of the great American R&B guitarist Mickey Baker, who had played the classic calypso-blues-rock licks on the Mickey & Sylvia smash "Love is Strange" in the 1950s; by the '60s, he was a Europe-based expatriate that also worked with other French acts (including Ronnie Bird, the only truly credible male French rock singer of the mid-'60s). And she was beginning to make a dent in the highly competitive British market, where "Tous Les Garçons" made a belated appearance in the Top 40 in 1964; "Et Même," a stomping girl-group derivation, did likewise in early 1965.

By this time Hardy was making some attempts to crack the international audience by recording in English, and the hauntingly sad "All Over the World" became her sole British Top 20 entry in 1965. (She has also attempted to expand beyond the Francophone market by recording extensively in Italian and German, as well as a bit in Spanish.) Françoise wasn't bad at English, though the French originals were invariably better; it didn't mean much anyway in the United States, where her early records were issued by the small 4 Corners label, with one LP memorably (and somewhat misleadingly) titled *The Yeh Yeh Girl From Paris*.

"I would have thought that because of the way she looked and the way she presented herself, it would be certainly a lot more accessible to the American and British taste than her French counterparts," notes guitarist Jerry Donahue, a one-time member of Fairport Convention who would play on one of Hardy's early-'70s albums. "Johnny Hallyday and [French star] Sylvie Vartan"—both of whom Donahue also worked with—"wouldn't have had that appeal in English-speaking countries. If she wasn't bigger here, it was probably due to the fact that she didn't have enough of a workforce behind her to do something for her in England or America."

Her phenomenal French (and modest British) success was no doubt aided by her stunning visual image, crafted to a large degree by photographer Jean-Marie Périer, who also aided in the management of her early career (and was also romantically linked with the singer). Périer has recalled that Hardy was interested in little except writing songs and listening to the radio when he met her. He would transform Hardy—who, judging from her stick-like figure, subsisted on a diet of carrots and celery throughout the decade—into a mod icon of sorts. The array of French EP and LP sleeves from the mid-'60s, to take the most obvious examples, showcases her photogenic beauty in a deadly array of hairstyles, mini-skirts, and swinging '60s gear that will impress even the least fashion-conscious. Her film career was less successful. Aside from her cameo in *What's New Pussycat?* and a few other little-seen films, her most famous role was an exceedingly brief appearance in Jean-Luc Godard's experimental 1965 masterpiece *Masculin Feminin*. (When Hardy saw the film at a public showing, she reported in her bio, "All I remember is that my appearance provoked a general burst of laughing.")

Hardy began hobnobbing with rock royalty such as Brian Jones and Mick Jagger of the Rolling Stones. Plans by Périer to have Jagger and Hardy star side-by-side on screen in a remake of Jean Cocteau's *Les Enfants Terribles* came to naught; they had to content themselves with staging a great photo in which a scowling Hardy, the equally dour Jagger's arm resting on her shoulder, looks like Bianca Jagger's evil, cooler younger sister. It was all a welcome change for Hardy, who thought that in France she had an image of being, as stated in her biography, "sad and ungrateful" (although certainly the "sad" part was justified by the forlorn tenor of much of her music). Périer also went to lengths to arrange the aforementioned meeting between Hardy and the Beatles in Paris, although after all that trouble the parties evidently had nothing to say to each other.

Things went somewhat better when Bob Dylan swung through town in 1966. This was the famous tour in which Dylan, backed by the soon-to-be-named Band, debuted his recently electrified sound to mixed and occasionally hostile response. When Hardy went to see his performance at the Paris Olympia, the stage remained empty for a long time after intermission; Hardy was informed that Dylan would not resume his performance if she didn't pay a personal visit. She found his sickly appearance so alarming, she recounts in her biography, that she feared he was going to die. That didn't prevent her from going back with his entourage to the George V hotel, where, alone in his room, the singer played her his hot-off-the-presses recordings of "Just Like a Woman" and "I Want You."

As interesting as this celebrity gossip is to '60s aficionados, it's tended to obscure the generally excellent standards of her own recordings in the mid-'60s. There are a few dozen genuinely superb tracks, making it hard to single out highlights for the uninitiated, although a short list would certainly include the nasty "Je N'Attends Plus Personne," with a fuzz guitar line that sounds like the work of a young Jimmy Page; "Pourtant Tu M'Aimes," surely the best imitation Phil Spector production recorded in a foreign language; "Mon Amie La Rose," a gothic ballad that is Françoise at her most European; "Non Ce N'Est Pas Un Rève," a dead ringer for a female counterpart to the Righteous Brothers' Wall-of-Sound epics; "Tu Peux Bien," its thunder-of-doom drums emphasizing one of her most attractively sullen vocals (one of the very few times where it sounds like she's genuinely threatening to simmer into anger); "Il Se Fait Tard," one of the ultimate expectant Europop seduction ballads; "Le Temps Des Souvenirs," with its Gene Pitneyan sense of drama; and the glorious "Voila," boasting a thrilling orchestral climax that would do Dusty Springfield proud.

Through 1967 Hardy kept the tension between French sentiment and Anglo rock influences in admirable check. Yet in the latter part of the '60s, her music started to take on a more determinedly MOR direction. That's not to say these records are without their highlights. Yet in general Hardy does not only sound less inspired, but more the conventionally demure, even sappy female, continually pining away for her princes on eternally raining days. Isolated tracks like "Fleur de Lune," with its classic descending guitar line, are great, and unexpected French covers of Leonard Cohen's "Suzanne" and Phil Ochs' "There but for Fortune" are interesting, but the records are far spottier than her previous work. Hardy also decided to stop touring, a radical step in the late '60s. But as she explained in 1985 to *France-Culture*, "In the '60s, it was enough to sing 'Tous Les Garçons et Les Filles,' which is a completely linear song, it's the same note from beginning to end . . . but as soon as you put yourself to doing things a little more ambitious, a little more difficult, to sing on tour, it's another pair of sleeves!"

In accordance with those ambitions, by the end of the 1960s Hardy had ended her association with Vogue and moved to Sonopresse, where she was granted greater autonomy and artistic freedom. Somewhat surprisingly, the clear favorite of her albums is 1971's *La Question*, recorded with Brazilian guitarist Tuca (who also helped write much of the material). The spare, acoustic-flavored arrangements anchor some of Hardy's most frankly sexual deliveries, making this something of an alternate-universe (and much better) version of Jose Feliciano's fireside make-out music. "It's the only album that I re-listen to regularly, and I find that it still holds a punch," she remarks in her biography. "I touched a narrower but different public that I truly desired to seduce."

Hardy did make another effort to record in London, with British musicians, in 1972. This resulted in an unmemorable album, and a rather more memorable encounter with another cult figure, singer-songwriter Nick Drake, who was interested in writing songs for her. Drake was a musical kindred spirit of sorts with his brooding, textured folk-rock sound, though much less capable of dealing with the real world, and no collaborations actually occurred. Observed Hardy in *MOJO*, "Nick seemed—and was no doubt—so shy, so wrapped up in himself, that in retrospect I'm astonished that he managed to come and see me two or three times, even knowing that I appreciated his enormous talent."

The rest of the records Hardy made in the '70s and '80s are mostly notable for disappointing Anglo collectors who happened to chance upon these as their first Françoise finds. Several of these were produced by Gabriel Yared, now famous as the composer of the soundtrack to *The English Patient*; nonetheless, collectors felt burned after hearing MOR pop when they were, by virtue of her reputation, expecting a classically French '60s chanteuse. By the 1980s, in any case, Hardy seemed more interested in astrology than music, co-writing a 1986 book that analyzed the star signs and handwriting of French celebrities like Serge Gainsbourg, Sylvie Vartan, and Jane Birkin.

Still, she remained a hip fave in some surprising circles. Stinky Toys, perhaps the first French punk band to make an international impression, praised her early work passionately. Malcolm McLaren featured her voice on "Revenge of the Flowers" from his frostily received *Paris* album in 1995. A much greater boost to her visibility was a guest vocal on "To the End" with Blur, one of the most successful U.K. Britpop bands of the mid-'90s. In 1996, at the age of 52, she finally returned to full-scale recording with *Le Danger*, her first album since 1988.

Middle-aged pop-rock singers—in France more than anywhere, perhaps— tend to settle into meaningless adult contemporary music by this time of their lives, if they're still recording at all. It thus came as somewhat of a shock that *Le Danger*, in the exception that proves the rule, turned out to be Hardy's hardest-rocking effort ever. Not that it made much difference to the English-speaking market, where it's only available as an import; Virgin's New York and London offices, when contacted in late 1996, were unaware that Hardy was even part of the label's French roster. But with its appealing layers of distorted guitars—complete with hints of Britpop and grunge, even—it also found Hardy's voice virtually undimmed, if a bit thinner, with as much sensuality in her delivery as there was in any of her '60s recordings. It could be that Hardy has finally become the attitude-heavy rocker she seemed to be when she posed with Mick Jagger over 30 years ago.

Recommended Recordings:

Story (1962-64, 1964-65, 1965-67) (Vogue, France). Citing one particular introductory Hardy compilation is a vexing proposition, not just because of her wealth of good '60s material, but because no one has seemed up to the task of compiling a knockout one- or two-disc set. There *are* well over a dozen import '60s Hardy anthologies clogging the market, most haphazardly chosen and annotated. These three 20-track collections are about the best, though they're hard to find and leave off some fine items; otherwise, just make sure your first Françoise purchase bears songs from the years 1962-67.

L'Integrale Disques Vogue 1962/1967 (1995, Vogue). Comprehensive four-CD, 83-song box set includes all of her early French recordings (as well as the English-sung "All Over the World," a hit in the U.K.). It's expensive and hard to find in the U.S., but nonetheless a wonderful thing, with few clinkers. And if you're hooked enough on Hardy to start collecting her work, this will ultimately save you a lot of bread, gathering everything in one place (save her foreign language recordings) from her early career—material that is otherwise dispersed on countless half-hearted compilations.

La Question (1971, Virgin). Hardy's best '70s album by far, and her all-time personal favorite. It's romantic mood music at its most seductive, and one of the few efforts of this sort (by Hardy or anyone else) to achieve its goals via understated, even stark, acoustic arrangements rather than lush over-production.

Le Danger (1996, Virgin). One initially greeted the prospect of a 1996 comeback album by Hardy with dread. It's a surprise to instead find a very listenable, guitar-heavy, quite alternative-minded disc that's better (and more up-to-date) than almost any other '90s effort by a '60s icon you could name. It's not up to the level of her '60s classics, but the best tracks—particularly "Dix Heures En Été" and "Contre-Jour"—sound better than almost anything else on commercial radio in the late '90s, language barrier be damned.

The Outsiders

Holland, a tiny country of 15 million people, is stereotyped as the land of tulips, windmills, and fine cheeses, not as a crucible of rebellious rockers. Those who are familiar with the *Nederbiet* scene of the 1960s know better. Of the scores of scruffy R&B/beat groups who emerged from the lowlands in the mid-'60s, none were more magnificent than the Outsiders. They rang up hit after hit in their native land with both storming punk-blues numbers and wisp-o'-the-willow, melodic folk-rock; sometimes they would combine the incongruous forms into the same song. They were not just the finest Dutch group of the '60s, but the Finest '60s Rock Group from a Non-English-Speaking Country, period.

That may be a category too obscure ever to find its way onto *Jeopardy* or *Trivial Pursuit*, but the award is not meant to damn with faint praise. The Outsiders may not have ever gotten their records released in the U.S., but they were as good as all but the very best American and British groups of their era. Their music certainly is fraught with more tension than all but a few bands have generated. The punk rhythms play against the pretty melodies; the R&B grinds against the pop hooks; lust and desire merge with frustration and angst. One always feels that the Outsiders play with such intensity because doom is always lurking just around the corner, or, as leader Wally Tax sang in one of their very first songs, they can always sense that the "Sun's Going Down." Even when they blasted into psychedelic overdrive with their final album, menace and dread were far more consuming concerns than love and flowers.

In his liner notes for *Pebbles Vol. 15*, a compilation of Dutch '60s rock, Roeland Bajema deadpans, "The Dutch were masters of the blues, as befits a country with no black people and the highest standard of living in Europe." It's a funny line, but Outsiders singer and principal songwriter Wally Tax came by his blues roots way before the Rolling Stones had made them fashionable. Born to a Dutch father and Russian gypsy mother who had met in a World War II concentration camp, Tax lived near a seaman's hostel in Amsterdam that hosted many American sailors. As they did in Liverpool, the Yankees brought in R&B records for fans abroad, like Tax's father.

Tax began performing at the age of eight, and had already formed the Outsiders by the age of eleven, singing in English. Amsterdam had a way of growing up youngsters quickly with regards to foreign linguistic fluency. Tax learned English at a young age, he reveals, partially "to communicate with the American sailors. I also made a lot of money showing the guys around Amsterdam to good places to get laid. They paid me a dollar or things like that when I got them to a clean, good whore. So no," he concludes matter-of-factly, "it came quite naturally, the English language."

By the time Tax was 17, the Outsiders were ready to make their recording debut with a ferocious R&B-punk hybrid. "You Mistreat Me" betrays the overwhelming influence of the Pretty Things, the British group that scored a few British hits with rawer, even raunchier variations of the early Rolling Stones' approach, although they never made it in America. If the Pretty Things were the Rolling Stones taken to even more shocking extremes, the Outsiders upped the Pretty Things' outrage yet another notch, with dive-bombing bee-sting guitars, roller coaster tempos, and Tax's fetchingly rasping vocals. The equally impressive B-side, "Sun's Going Down," was a mournful, folky ballad with crashing drums and Aeolian harmonies that showed there was more to the band than R&B rave-ups.

Those two songs established the poles that would define the band's career from 1965 to 1969: raw, verging-on-sloppy blues-rock on the one hand, tender

The Outsiders (from Holland), mid-1960s. Singer Wally Tax on far right. Credit: Courtesy Wally Tax

melancholic folk-rock on the other. In the beginning, however, the band definitely favored the former approach. If ever a '60s group earned the term "amphetamined," it was the Outsiders. Their uptempo songs—already ridiculously fast to begin with—would accelerate in tempo like an Olympic sprinter closing in on the finish line. The band would lay down a nervous, stuttering groove, with cool staccato fuzz guitar, manic pumping bass, splashing percussion, and occasional furious harmonica bleats from Tax.

The most outlandish of such cuts—"If You Don't Treat Me Right," "Ain't Gonna Miss You," or the amazing "Won't You Listen," with one of the great extended squeaky fuzz guitar solos of all time—threaten to corkscrew themselves into unplayability. Drummer Buzz Busch in particular drives the rhythm with all the patience and finesse of outlaws fleeing the California Highway Patrol. That's part of the appeal, of course; it's like listening to hardcore punk with a heckuva greater sense of melody and *joie de vivre*. Check out their rare half-live, half-studio debut LP (on the most inappropriately titled Relax label) for the prime freeze-frame of the Outsiders in this phase. Its live cuts are especially out of control, with an audience that screams at their heroes as if they're cheering on matadors in the bull ring. It's far rawer than anything an American major label would have thought of unleashing at the time.

"We recorded rather fast, and of course there are mistakes," says Tax about their early sides, adding that the first album was recorded in the one-take mode. "But the drive—going faster and faster—yes, that was intentional. It was rough, but it was truthful and energetic. And that's what we liked about it. It wasn't phony. It was us." Did they play the songs faster in the studio than they did on-stage? "Oh no!" he replies. "Live we were *really* explosive. Even more so."

That would lend credence to Tax's assertion that "our lucky break was [in 1966] when the Rolling Stones did their second concert in Holland in a place where they auctioned cattle; that's the type of hall it actually was. At least ten groups were on the program, and we were right before the Rolling Stones. And we had a lot more success than the Rolling Stones. That broke us nationally."

Also in 1966, the Outsiders moved from the small Muziek Express Op-Art label (run by a music magazine) to the French Relax imprint, a classical (!) outfit whose financial losses forced the company to capitulate to the pop-rock boom. According to Tax, "Our manager at the time forced them into signing the Outsiders because they wanted one of his other groups, who were like the Hollies. The musical director of that company didn't want the Outsiders at all. We were much too rough and unpolished for his taste. But in order to get them, he had to sign us as well. A piece of blackmail, really."

"Lying All the Time" in 1966 inaugurated a long run of big Dutch hits for the band, although they would never become big outside of Holland, despite pockets of enthusiasts in Germany, Paris, and Rome. All of the four dozen or so songs that the Outsiders would release between 1965 and 1969 were group originals, usually written by Tax with help from guitarist Ronnie Splinter. If you think that's no big deal, try to think of other decent groups that also recorded a similar wealth of material from approximately 1965–69 without ever doing a cover (I can only think of the Velvet Underground and Buffalo Springfield myself).

Within a couple of years, the wall-of-speed rave-ups were tempered by folk-rock numbers employing haunting minor-keyed, occasionally doomy melodies and unpredictable tempo shifts between dreamy balladry and hard rock. Tax had never been an R&B purist, admitting a love for the folk-pop of Peter, Paul & Mary, as well as the emerging Californian psychedelic folk-rock of the Byrds and Love (the latter of which were barely known outside of California, let alone throughout the Continent). The Pretty Things influence was getting toned down as well, as Tax favored a hurt tone that could be both tender and sullen, though still powerful. The lyrics—sometimes romantic, but often bitter, frustrated, sarcastic, or accusatory, at times actually paranoid—complement Tax's delivery well. The hit single "Touch"—extremely suggestive by '60s standards—epitomizes the push-and-pull of the Outsiders, with jerkily paced, raw, bluesy verses alternating with a weepy, delicate bridge.

As to what made the Outsiders' records different from anything happening in either America or England, Tax muses, "I think there's a very Continental European touch to the thing. A song like 'Touch,' with that romantic interlude, is a rather European concept I haven't found in American groups. Also, the way we played the blues is not really an American way to play the blues. It also has a Continental flavor. I was tremendously into Robert Johnson, Elmore James, Sonny Terry, Brownie McGhee, Little Walter. But also you might have heard that we dug Jacques Brel a lot. You know 'Sun's Going Down'? That's more or less like a Russian folk melody with a bluesy lyric.

"The British were very much into copying the rhythm and blues thing a lot. Like the Rolling Stones—they started their recording career using American rhythm and blues material. We started our recording career with our *own* stuff. I think Mick Jagger, in the old days, tried to sound like a black R&B singer; I never tried to sound like anybody else but me. Keith Richard is somebody who started out trying to be Chuck Berry. But Ron Splinter never tried to be anybody else but Ron Splinter."

There was no shortage of fine Outsiders singles in mid-career, like "I've Been Loving You So Long," where the delicate windblown melody is stopped in its tracks by a bit of avant-garde sped-up tape that jolts with all the force of a plug getting pulled out of its socket. The ambitiously titled "I'm Only Trying to Prove to Myself That I'm Not Like Everybody Else" was yet another minor-key folkish rocker with militantly individualistic lyrics, get-it-over-with tempos, and a wild instrumental break embellished with electronic swoops and static, like a Saturday morning cartoon run haywire. Another indicator of Tax's increasingly romantic predilections was "Summer Is Here," a beautiful, almost entirely acoustic slice of baroque folk-rock with tasty balalaika and zither. "It's a rather European kind of melody, don't you think?" Tax offers. "And also the instrumentation was a giant step away from rock and roll."

Tax even took the opportunity to make a solo album, *Love-In*, with a symphony orchestra in '67. "But those idiots at Philips added bird noises in between tracks. I hated that title, too! I am a romantic, and I love the orchestra; I loved recording those romantic songs. But I wasn't into that commercialized hippie thing at all." It's appropriate, then, that when the Outsiders made their try at the concept album with the 1968 LP *CQ*, it would boast a far harder edge than most psychedelic efforts.

CQ was released at a time of commercial uncertainty for the band, on the heels of a couple of singles that had failed to become big hits. Rather than heed commercial considerations, the group pulled out all the stops for one of the finest unsung psychedelic records of the late '60s. Like some crazy distorted echo of Hendrix, early Pink Floyd, and psychedelic-era Pretty Things, *CQ* has plenty of sonic experimentation—elephant roar guitars on "Doctor," Bo Diddley-from-hell bass runs on "Misfit," eerie lost-in-space vocals on the title track. The lyrical tone is far earthier and sardonic than the typical flower-power outing, however, sounding more like a spaceship descending into anarchy than a smooth astral voyage. Periodically the album engages in spiraling accelerating tempos reminiscent of their early singles, but the ambience is far more unsettling now that they're wedded to more complex arrangements and words. With its funhouse shifts from punkadelic rock and jungle beats to soft, almost serene passages and eerie lunar sound effects, it's a heck of a ride—though even Tax seems at a loss to articulate whatever concept might be driving the journey.

"Most groups all over the world were into making concept albums," he remembers. "We got the same type of fever to really compose and create an album that was not only a collection of songs, but with sort of a coherence to it, like *Sgt. Pepper* and [the Pretty Things'] *S.F. Sorrow*. I think we quite succeeded in doing that in *CQ*, soundwise. It was psychedelic, definitely, but it wasn't like a dolphin's kind of high. It was pretty rough."

And with song titles like "Misfit," "Daddy Died on Saturday," "It Seems Like Nothing's Gonna Come My Way Today," and "Prisonsong," it might be added, it was far darker than most psychedelic meisterworks. Equal parts personal turmoil and interstellar overdrive, "a large part of it was autobiographical. But it was also a fairy tale. It was also about space travel, [which] was a lot on my mind. *CQ* is also a radio term, like 'seek you,' trying to make contact with another party." Perhaps a clear explanation of any sort of storyline would detract from the album's considerable mystique. It's worth noting that Tax was serious enough about space travel to buy a certificate from NASA for a spot on tourist flights to the moon, whenever those become available.

Aside from one last single—"Do You Feel Allright," with its rather shockingly matter-of-fact description of violence against a rather cheery solid rock groove—CQ was the last release by the Outsiders. The album, in Tax's words, sold "not too well—at least, not what we were used to. It sold instead of 50,000, maybe 12,000. A lot of people weren't up to it yet; we were ahead of our time, definitely. And we had all kinds of trouble with our manager who was robbing us blind. Splinter left the group for the third time, and that did it for me. I was also very much into Tim Hardin and Richie Havens, and wanted to get into acoustic rock."

Tax went to the U.S. in the early '70s, where he stayed with Hardin for a while. He, Hardin, and Jimi Hendrix played and sang some acoustic material together at Hendrix's Electric Ladyland studio in New York, shortly before Jimi's death. Tax also recorded an LP in the U.S. as part of the band Tax Free, John Cale appearing as a session musician on viola. Returning to Holland, he did some solo albums in the mid-'70s, but soon abandoned performing for working as a producer and songwriter. Another solo disc appeared in the early '90s, and he's readying another one for release.

But it's the Outsiders that continue to be Tax's calling card, and Tax is comfortable enough with the band's legacy to be planning a reunion tour with the original four Outsiders in late 1997. At long last, the Outsiders cult fan base has expanded across the ocean, as '60s rock fiends from America, often too young to have been born when Tax started recording, discovered the band in the '80s and '90s. Tax says that Outsiders fans have included Soundgarden and the late Kurt Cobain. And now he's working on his autobiography, to be published on his 50th birthday in 1998 (so far planned to be issued in Dutch only).

In the United States, the name Outsiders has always meant "Time Won't Let Me," the poppy horn-rock hit recorded by a clean-cut Cleveland group of the same name in 1966. When I talked with friends about including the Outsiders in this book, I would always have to fend off quizzical stares by hastening to add that they were the Dutch Outsiders—the *real* Outsiders, if an Outsider is one who works on the edge. The Outsiders from Amsterdam, you see, knew no other place.

Recommended Recordings:
The Outsiders (1967, Pseudonym, Holland). Their super-raw debut album, with seven extra bonus tracks, show the band at their most Pretty Things-influenced.
CQ (1968, Pseudonym, Holland). One of the most satisfyingly weird psychedelic records of all time, again embroidered with bonus tracks on the CD reissue. If you're hooked, also look for the two-CD *CQ Sessions*, rehearsal tapes with loads of alternate takes that provide a fascinating look at the work in progress.
Best of the Outsiders (1979, MFP, Holland). A comprehensive CD best-of package for the Outsiders is sorely lacking on the contemporary marketplace. This 16-track LP, if you can find it, offers a good selection of their 1966–68 hits.

"I can't seriously imagine the music I love being really dangerous to anyone. And when you stop and think about it, asking rock and roll to save us from political repression or social oppression is asking too much of it. We have to undertake those tasks for ourselves.

—rock critic Robert Palmer, in *Rock & Roll: An Unruly History*

The Plastic People of the Universe

In North America and Europe, Palmer's thesis may be true to a great extent. But in today's Czech Republic, the government is well aware of how much it owes to the galvanizing influence of rock music. When President Vaclav Havel—playwright, Frank Zappa fan, and politician, not necessarily in that order—took office after the demise of communism, it marked the culmination of 20 years of struggle for human rights in a system that denied personal and creative expression. Havel was also a fan and associate of the Plastic People of the Universe, the rock group that helped spur the formation of Charter 77, the human rights organization that was instrumental in fomenting dissidence in the former Czechoslovakia. If for that achievement only, the Plastic People did more than almost any other rock band to change the course of world history.

The PPU (as the band often abbreviate themselves) were not formed with the intent of creating political change. Merely daring to play creative rock music in Czechoslovakia in the 1970s and 1980s, however, was a political act in a state where music generated without an official seal of approval was tantamount to rebellion. For their artistic ambitions, the Plastics may have endured more harassment than almost any other rock band in history. Banned from public performance, they had to resort to giving their concerts in secret, or using weddings as excuses to air their songs in public. When they refused to cease playing their music, some of the members were beaten and jailed for their trouble.

An entire community of Czech dissidents sprung up around the band; the PPU and their fans were instrumental in keeping the flame of Czech artistic culture and political activism alive. All of which has tended to obscure their actual music, a spooky adaptation of the experiments of the Velvet Underground, Captain Beefheart, and Frank Zappa, imbued with classical and Central European influences. The band fractured in the late 1980s over business and artistic differences. A reunification in January 1997 was right out of a script that even Hollywood would have rejected as too unbelievable, with Havel inviting the band to play at a party commemorating the 20th anniversary of Charter 77 in the Spanish Hall of the Prague Castle—the very location where the conferences of the Communist Party took place.

The Plastic People of the Universe evolved from the Primitives, Prague's first psychedelic group, just around the time that Soviet tanks invaded the city to crush the "Prague Spring." But according to bassist and founding member Milan Hlavsa, who would write much of the band's material, "The Plastic People emerged just as dozens and hundreds of other bands—we just loved rock 'n' roll and wanted to be famous. We were too young to have a clear artistic ambition. All we did was pure intuition: no political notions or ambitions at all.

"Although the band was founded at the time of the Warsaw Pact invasion of Czechoslovakia, it had no influence on the origination of the band. We did not reflect the causes or effects of the invasion, we just took it as a harsh reality. Moreover, our friend Ivan Jirous and others, who were a little more familiar with politics, kept assuring us that things could not be the same for more than five years, and that we could outlast them even underwater. Well, they happened to miss out a couple of decades, but I think we did quite well underwater just the same."

Jirous was an art historian who had been the "art director" of the Primitives, and did the same for the Plastics. He was instrumental in exposing the group to the jagged, satirical, and outrageously experimental rock of Captain Beefheart, the Fugs, and Frank Zappa—artists that enjoyed relatively little media exposure even in the West. "Zappa was quite well known in Czechoslovakia at that time," points out Hlavsa, "perhaps thanks to his pervasive irony, which is the cornerstone of the Czech mentality." But Hlavsa had his personal

The Plastic People of the Universe bring psychedelic sounds to Czechoslovakia at the Music F Club in 1969.
Credit: Petr Prokes

epiphany upon discovering the debut album by yet another obscure, confrontational late-'60s band that wouldn't achieve international prominence until over ten years after their breakup: the Velvet Underground.

"The vogues of the days were Jimi Hendrix, the Rolling Stones, the Beatles," explains Hlavsa, who came across the Velvets' "banana album" in 1967 while visiting a friend who was getting records from relatives abroad. "My friend Stevich and I were a little frustrated because it increasingly dawned on us that we were unlikely ever to attain those qualities and somehow we didn't care. We were almost decided to finish with the band we had at the time.

"Fortunately I visited that friend of mine then, and I played that record in his home. I was totally, absolutely in trance. It was exactly what I could not find in other groups, and nothing else. It was raw, clear, transparent. Thanks to this encounter I did not throw my guitar in the dustbin . . . I really trusted [the Velvets] and I still do. I know what they did, they did from their heart without any calculations; I could immediately identify with their music.

"When Lou Reed was in Prague as a *Rolling Stone* reporter [in the 1990s], we threw a party for him, where Pulnoc [Hlavsa's post-PPU band] played. We recounted our story to him, which he had known in an outline. When we told him that had it not been for them in the 1960s, our band would never exist, he was very impressed and said that in all likelihood Velvet Underground had been much better known in Prague then than in the U.S.A."

The Velvets' influence extended to the PPU's live shows, in which they would employ psychedelic light shows, makeup, and outrageous costumes to create a multi-media happening not unlike the Velvets' early concerts as part of Andy Warhol's Plastic Inevitable. Like the Velvets, they also employed the unusual (for rock) feature of a viola player to give their music a shrill edge. It was too much for the Czech government, who revoked the band's professional license in early 1970. This was much more than an annoying technicality; the PPU could not earn money with their gigs or use state-owned instruments or rehearsal space.

"We faced the choice of either meeting the conditions of the 'sociopolitical consolidation' set by the then-establishment, which also applied to rock 'n' roll bands, or sinking among amateur groups," says Hlavsa. "We never saw ourselves as musicians in the proper sense, so we had no problem to say farewell to full-time playing, although it had some somber consequences." For a time the group got around government regulations by providing the soundtrack to lectures by Jirous, who was still a member of the Union of Artists. Jirous would show slides of Andy Warhol; the Plastic People would "demonstrate" Velvet Underground songs as accompaniment. Actually these were PPU concerts, not lectures, with the slide show lasting ten minutes, and the music a couple of hours. But the authorities soon realized what was up and prohibited these events as well. Canadian English teacher Paul Wilson, who sang with the PPU during this time (partially because he could translate the lyrics of the Velvet Underground and Frank Zappa), once estimated that between 1970 and 1972, the band only played live about 15 times.

"Some of us went to work in forestry to earn new gear, which we built ourselves," recalls Hlavsa. "But these things didn't affect our music at all. We never resorted to vent our frustration in our songs and decry the regime which used this indirect way to crush us underfoot. For several years we played not in the underground but as an amateur group under the franchise of various associations (soccer clubs, voluntary firemen), which sponsored a concert every now and then. We weren't forced underground until 1976, when the memorable trial was staged against the band and our friends."

The addition of saxophonist Vratislav Brabenec in the early '70s pushed the band more to the fringes of experimental art-rock, with avant-garde jazz and classical influences. By this time they began to sing only in Czech and play only original material. Some of this surfaced on *Egon Bondy's Happy Hearts Club Banned*, recorded in a chateau of a friend around 1973–74, although it wasn't released (and then only available in the West) until 1977. Although the primitive technological conditions made them sound like a garage avant-rock band, the originality of their vision comes through in the creepy cheap electric piano, ominous violin scrapes, gravel-textured vocals, and dissonant melodies that owed as much to the recesses of the Bohemian forest as Western pop. In some ways, it was a fusion of the sensibilities of the Velvet Underground and Frank Zappa—an ironic critical postulation, considering that the Velvets took mean-spirited swipes at Zappa on several occasions during interviews. Lyrics were supplied by Czech dissident poet Egon Bondy. PPU would record several more albums over the next dozen or so years, but *Egon Bondy* remains Hlavsa's personal favorite.

The PPU briefly regained their professional status around the time *Egon Bondy* was recorded. Two weeks later, it was just as suddenly revoked on the grounds that it was "morbid" and would have a "negative social impact." Over the next few years, the band would resort to playing announced shows in the Bohemian countryside. Often they found it easiest to play at weddings of friends, as these were considered private occasions rather than public functions; a divorced couple, according to a 1989 *Option* article, actually agreed to get remarried just to provide the group with that all-too-precious gig. Locations of shows remained secret until one day before the performance. Information about how to get there was then spread via word of mouth among friends, requiring the audience to walk miles from the nearest train or bus station to remote barns or farmhouses deep in the forest.

This didn't prevent the police from finding out about some of these events, beating fans with clubs at a March 1974 concert in Budovice at which the PPU never got to perform. This in turn instigated Music Festivals of the "Second Culture" (sometimes referred to as the "Other Culture") for the PPU and other underground bands. After the second of these festivals in 1976, police arrested numerous musicians and their friends, including all of the Plastic People. Over 100 fans were questioned by the authorities; the PPU's equipment, tapes, films, and notebooks were confiscated; Paul Wilson was expelled from the country. At their trial six months later, most of the arrested parties were released (partially in response to international protest), but four musicians earned prison sentences, including Brabanec and Jirous. The official indictment accused their lyrics of "extreme vulgarity with an anti-socialist and an anti-social impact, most of them extolling nihilism, decadence and clericalism." Brabanec, after some beatings and interrogations at the hands of the police, went into Canadian exile in the early 1980s.

In retrospect, the expulsion of Wilson may not have been the soundest strategic move the Czech government could have considered. Through diplomatic channels—mostly secured, says Hlavsa, by Vaclav Havel—recordings of the Plastic People were sent to Wilson in Canada, who arranged for the release of PPU material in North America and Europe. Havel, then a playwright, had met the PPU in 1976, when he and others launched a campaign in the group's support after their arrest.

That network of supporters soon evolved into the human rights organization Charter 77, Havel claiming that the PPU were defending "life's intrinsic desire to express itself freely, in its own authentic and sovereign way." Havel would also let the band use his country home to record. "When our saxophone player Vrata Brabenec was forced into exile," adds Hlavsa, "we lost our only songwriter, so we asked Vaclav Havel if he could produce lyrics for the next album, and he selected the material for *Midnight Mouse*. He himself didn't write anything, his contribution to the band was rather human than artistic."

Hlavsa is cautious not to attach undue significance to the Plastics' political influence. "Historians see the Plastics' arrest and sentence in direct relation to the origins of Charter 77. Of course I also see the relations, but only in that the trial brought together people concerned about the fate of our country. Vaclav Havel was the engine of the efforts. The band itself had no political ambition and we did not intend to destroy communism by our music, but if we helped we are only glad."

At the same time, Hlavsa states that "in the marasmus of 'consolidation' and 'normalization,' our community, which was, probably imprecisely, referred to as 'underground,' was a pocket of normal life, communication and joy of living (to be a little grandiloquent for a while). Had it not been for the PPU, there would have probably been no Festivals of the Other Culture. The Bolsheviks' heavy hand was felt in all walks of life in the 1970s and a certain community began to form around the band. People with feelings similar to ours were coming to our concerts, though their music preferences were not necessarily similar. But music wasn't as important there as meeting people and being together in a normal environment for a while. I don't know if anything like that would be possible had the PPU not existed then."

Does it bother him that the Plastics are probably more renowned in the West for their political/cultural effects than their actual music? "I believe it is totally alright, because the band became known, especially abroad, only after our arrest and trial. If anyone in this context wanted moreover to know what kind of music we did, all the better; if not, also good, why bother. But people should know that our ambition was in no way political."

In the meantime, the PPU continued to make music, recording in private homes "in the kitchen tradition" with progressively better equipment. According to Hlavsa, "We didn't make most of the recordings, in the early years, with the prospect of a later album, but just for the pleasure of ourselves and a few friends, and that explains their technical quality." *Passion Play*, one of the albums recorded at Havel's abode, was about Christ's crucifixion, a source of possible controversy anywhere in the world. Subsequent records found them getting—well, not exactly slick, but certainly approaching a more standard sort of Western art-jazz-rock fusion. The band grew to eight people, with more winds and a second violin; the compositions, in Hlavsa's words, "were more sophisticated, with fewer improvisations." The albums, it should be noted, did not have huge followings even in the Western underground; they sold to small, extremely specialized audiences, the music (apart from the fact that it was sung in an unfamiliar language) being too difficult and challenging even for many adventurous rock listeners.

Hlavsa describes the scenario leading to the PPU's split: "PPU applied to take part in a rock festival in 1987. It looked quite promising and there was good hope that the Plastics could be back on the stage. But the secret police exerted maximum efforts a week before the festival concert and twisted the organizers' hands, and the band was not admitted to the hall at all. A few weeks later we got a proposal from a club in Brno on condition that the name of the band would not appear on posters, and only 'a group from Prague' would be advertised. Some Plastics opposed it and would not appear on such conditions.

"I was frustrated. I felt the situation was getting ripe to start pushing more and more, and in the face of my fellows' reluctance I decided to found a new band. I made it clear that the other band members could keep the name PPU. I also said some bad words in those agitated days, which I regretted later, and I hate to remember them."

Pulnoc was formed with a lineup including Hlavsa, violist Jiri Kabes, and keyboardist Josef Janicek, all of whom had played with PPU since the late '60s. Comments Hlavsa, "I felt it somewhat interesting for a rock 'n' roll band to use a female voice to some extent. I like Nico, Laurie Anderson, or Marianne Faithfull, and I simply felt the urge to let the feeling come true. The guitar was also back after some time, and all told, the Pulnoc stuff was more aggressive, more rock than the Plastics' last creations."

However, "not only some PPU members were upset by the emergence of Pulnoc, but also many PPU fans. I understand their feelings to some extent, or, to be more accurate, I sympathize but fail to understand it. The greatest indignation and bitterness came from exiles, to whom the PPU were a symbol of resistance, and they saw Pulnoc as a betrayal of the ideal. But as I said, I didn't want to destroy the Plastics and I hoped someone else could take the relay, which simply didn't happen."

In 1989 Pulnoc actually toured the United States; famed rock critic Robert Christgau was so impressed with a tape of a New York show that he made the cassette his #1 pick in a year-end *Village Voice* poll. "The audiences reacted spontaneously and enjoyed themselves," remembers Hlavsa with pleasure. "Back home it often seems that 80% of the audience are music critics who only look for flaws. We brought back some fine stories: a man came to us in Seattle and said he only knew Pulnoc and Dvorak of Czech music, and both are excellent! Another fine moment was our playing at the post-mortem opening of Andy Warhol's exhibition in Paris. Lou Reed with John Cale did the *Songs for Drella* there, and because Sterling Morrison and Maureen Tucker were also there, they agreed to play 'Heroin.' That was one of the moments when one knows life's worth living."

Pulnoc recorded an album for Arista in the States, which although glossier than their live shows, drew some critical attention as a sort of modern-day take on the Velvet Underground's vision, particularly when Michaela Nemcova sang in a Nico-like drone. "The singer and the drummer announced they were leaving the band just after the release, which was a total shock both for Arista and our New York manager. Because the reviews were favorable and it all looked like a good start, another tour was contemplated. But the two also had personal reasons. We recruited a new drummer and singer, they were not bad at all, but Pulnoc had lost its drive and charge. We still played in Bohemia for a year or two until we realized at one point that it was high time to split."

In March 1997, Hlavsa was busy with a new band, Fiction; he is also working on a collection of cover versions of old PPU songs with a fellow Fiction member "with machines with no live instruments." And then there's a planned PPU tour that might, at long last, bring the group to the U.S., five longtime members intact. "Probably were it not for Vaclav Havel, it would never be possible to bring this band together again," admits Hlavsa. "I had fantastic feelings of the meeting in January and the brief [reunion at the Prague Castle]. The problems we all carried inside, which had mounted in a few years because we didn't communicate with each other (at least I occasionally talked various rubbish about the band and in fact tried to burn all bridges behind me), were forgotten. I believe if the PPU make it to the U.S.A., it would be of great satisfaction to me, and the U.S. public would take them without prejudice.

Thanks to Michal Stasa for translating the Milan Hlavsa interview.

Recommended Recordings:
By the Plastic People of the Universe:
Egon Bondy's Happy Hearts Club Banned (1977, Bozi Mlyn). The first and most primitively recorded album by the group is still the fans' favorite, and a likely hit with those who want a grungier variation on the early Mothers of Invention. The PPU's entire output, constituting all of their albums and some unreleased material, is available on the 1992 *Plastic People of the Universe* box set (on Globus International). Only 1000 boxes were produced, and due to the experimental nature of much of the material, it can only be recommended to the heavily committed, but it's theoretically obtainable for those who want to immerse themselves in the Plastic People of the Universe's universe.

By Pulnoc:
City of Hysteria (1991, Arista). Though it's not the Plastic People, this has the virtue of being more accessible to most rock fans' ears and, as it was released on a major label, much more easily available for purchase. Some hardcore collectors prefer the earthier *Live at P.S. 122* tape that Robert Christgau championed, though connections in the rock collector network are necessary to find a copy.

Rock Behind the Iron Curtain

For all their obscurity, the Plastic People of the Universe may actually be the most famous of the bands to emerge from the Eastern bloc before the fall of the Berlin Wall. Any "survey" of rock from Eastern Europe is necessarily limited in scope by the fact that hardly any of the records made by bands in Czechoslovakia, East Germany, Poland, et al. were available in the West. Many of the groups never got the opportunity to record at all; if they did, it was often in state-controlled circumstances, or primitive studios, which inhibited the musicians' artistic expression.

At the 1990 South By Southwest music conference in Austin, Texas, I heard an acclaimed record producer credit rock 'n' roll as the force that brought down the Berlin Wall. Those that view this as an outrageous assertion should consider that rock music was viewed as a threat to the interests of the communist state almost from the time Bill Haley recorded "Rock Around the Clock" in the mid-1950s. Rock 'n' roll could not be licensed for official distribution in Eastern Europe, leading to busy trade in an underground black market for these precious recordings. Lacking the pressing plants and free enterprise to mass-produce illegal recordings on a widespread basis, rock records were actually often pirated onto the emulsion of discarded X-ray plates.

The mere unavailability of records in official retail outlets didn't stop the influence of the music from spreading among the youth of East Germany, Bulgaria, Romania, Poland,

Hungary, Czechoslovakia, and the former Soviet Union. The government's response could be harsh; East German head of state Walter Ulbricht personally denounced "the endless monotony of this 'yeah, yeah, yeah'" in 1965. Several years prior to that, he had endorsed the non-starting "Lipsi" dance craze to combat the evil effects of the tango and twist.

As in North America and Western Europe, the Beatles were immediately embraced by the region's youth in the mid-'60s, despite the pronouncement by leading Soviet jazz musician Tsafsman in February 1966 that "the Beatles are already out of date." Sporadic appearances by big-name British Invasion acts—Manfred Mann in Prague in 1965, the Rolling Stones in Warsaw in 1967—were rapturously received, the Stones concert causing a genuine riot. And, as elsewhere around the world, scores of local combos formed in emulation of the Beatles and Stones.

Not many of these groups recorded; in the Soviet Union, in fact, the first homegrown rock album, David Tukhmanov's *How Beautiful Is This World*, would not appear until 1973. (The Beatles' *A Hard Day's Night* was not officially released there until 1986.) To say that the '60s reissue boom has passed this corner of the world by is an understatement. To my knowledge there are only two collections of '60s Eastern bloc rock that have been released in the West. The *Czechoslovakian Beat 65–68* compilation (on the Italian Reverendo Moon label),demonstrates that the country produced some relatively primitive British Invasion-derived sounds with cheesy organs, snarled vocals, and fuzz guitars, just as regions like Texas, Quebec, Amsterdam, and so forth produced their own variations of international heroes. Thirteen '60s instrumentals from East Germany, Czechoslovakia, Romania, and Poland show up on AIP's *Surfbeat from Behind the Iron Curtain*, and display surprisingly competent, at times wildly imaginative, variations on the guitar instrumentals of the Ventures and the Shadows. Intriguing-sounding releases like Illés' "white album," a Hungarian record that contained a "human rights oratorio dedicated to Angela Davis" (according to Timothy W. Ryback's *Rock Around the Bloc*), have to this day been heard by very few in the West.

You could put a spin on Cold War rhetoric by suggesting that the Iron Curtain worked both ways: the Eastern bloc did not have untroubled access to Western rock, yet those on the other side of the Wall had perhaps even less access to Eastern European bands. The meager existing evidence, however, does not suggest that a motherlode of unknown rock awaits discovery. Merseybeat, mod, psychedelia, progressive, metal, even punk: all these trends were aped by bloc bands, in uncertain English or languages that were far more impregnable to English-speaking listeners than German, French, or Spanish. Bands like the Plastic People were developing more original strains that incorporated classical, folk, and Eastern European musics, as well as poetic, socially conscious lyrics. But as we saw in their chapter, this kind of creativity tended to be discouraged by the authorities, some-times violently so.

When I was working at an alternative music magazine in the 1980s, five to ten al-bums a year from the Eastern bloc would arrive, unsolicited and unexpected, at our of-fices, *Option* being just about the only American publication that would even give the records a listen, let alone review them. While none of them struck me as overlooked bas-tions of brilliance, I always appreciated their relative oddness: the lack of adherence to blues-based melodies, the jerky, unpredictable compositions, even the homemade-looking covers. The art-rock of Frank Zappa seemed to be a particularly strong influence on many of the bands. Perhaps the sarcastic absurdities of Zappa's lyrics struck a particularly poignant chord with citizens of nations whose governments enacted such absurdities on a day-to-day basis (not that America itself had a shortage of such satirical targets). The most internationally renowned underground Eastern European band of the time was Laibach, from the former Yugoslavia, although that nation was not part of the Eastern bloc. If the Plastic People made dark music, Laibach's was exponentially bleaker, whether cri-tiquing capitalism and fascism, or devising a twisted cover of the Beatles' *Let It Be* album (in its entirety) that turned the Fab Four's music into Teutonic dirges.

When a few Eastern bloc bands actually gained somewhat wide Western exposure (and recording contracts) as East-West relations thawed, capitalism unsheathed its dou-ble-edged sword. While Aquarium and their leader, Boris Grebenshchikov, had long been hailed as the Soviet Union's most important band, when the singer had to compete on equal footing with Bruce Springsteen with his 1989 Columbia album, Western reviewers found it derivative and tame. Part of the problem was that what was radical in Eastern Eu-rope was taken for granted in the West. Another part of the problem was that such acts' rough/experimental edges were sanded off by the big beat of the Western commercial production machine.

In the late 1990s, Eastern European rock is thriving as never before, largely free of the government hassles of decades past, and with greater freedom than ever in terms of concert and recording opportunities. But very, very few of these bands make any Western impact, due to language barriers, limited distribution, and the overwhelming quantity of product inundating the media in both North America and the British Isles. The political/symbolic importance of groups like the Plastic People has been diluted now that the region's governments are more democratic and tolerant. One would have to think, though, that the trade-off's been worth it.

The Savage Rose

In 1967, Thomas Koppel was ensconced at the Royal Danish Academy of Music, "fighting those big black grand pianos, to make them play Beethoven and Chopin in the modern way." The youth on the streets in Copenhagen, however, weren't interested in interpreting the old classics. Revolution was in the air, with the Beatles, Rolling Stones, and Bob Dylan providing the soundtrack.

"I was trying all the limits," remembers Koppel, who had been composing music since he was a small child. "I did a lot of big strange symphonic pieces to the limit of what was acceptable, even at that time. Then I felt a little lonely, because on the streets, I saw all the youngsters on the move. They were occupying houses in the slums, and protesting the wars and weapons. It was obvious that the new thing happening was not to be alone with the big grand piano, but to be together with the other young people. I felt that I had to move down to the street."

Thomas and his brother Anders, sons of the well-known Danish composer and pianist Herman Koppel, had already achieved much considering they were only in their early twenties. Thomas had won several composer competitions; Anders, also a keyboardist, had published his first novel, and was working as a producer's assistant at the Royal Theatre. It would have been a comfortable road to remain in the echelons of highbrow culture. But the Koppels were determined to become a rock band, Thomas handling piano, Anders on organ. With jazz drummer Alex Riel—who had played with Bill Evans, Roland Kirk, Dexter Gordon, and Lee Konitz—they formed the Savage Rose, perhaps the most ambitious and eclectic band to ever emerge from Continental Europe.

For most of their 30-year career, Savage Rose have remained a primarily Scandinavian phenomenon, although at one time they were poised to become one of the few rock groups from a non-English country to gain wide international success. A rave review in *Rolling Stone* in the early '70s was not enough, however, to market a band that combined classical composition, gospel, psychedelic rock, jazz, soul, radical politics, and European folk music into a sound that eluded easy description. On top of all that were the woman-child vocals of lead singer Annisette. Her style—a bridge between Aretha Franklin and Kate Bush—was described by critics of the day as a "seven-year-old hung up on Edith Piaf and Janis Joplin," "a child-whore crooning in the streets of a liberated village," and "Minnie Mouse on belladonna." She inspired either devotion or distaste, but was never forgotten by those who heard her.

Annisette originally wasn't in the picture when Savage Rose began crafting material. Thomas Koppel knew, however, that "we didn't want to limit ourselves into a known style. We wanted to combine rock and roll with what we had learned from classical and folk music from all over the world. We were struggling, because we wanted to get to a place where we could stay in our own style, and still include everything. In the beginning we wanted to do it all, so we moved from one place to another restlessly all the time. But I think we [were] able to maybe really make a new kind of music that had it all—elements from classical and folk and jazz and rock and soul and all of it in one go, as *one* style, not as a mix of a lot of styles."

Savage Rose were distinguished from most other psychedelic rock bands at the very beginning by their keyboard-dominated sound. On top of the piano-organ blend that had been pioneered by Procol Harum was a harpsichord, played by Thomas' wife of the time, Ilse Maria (who would leave after the group's first few albums). On all of Savage Rose's records in the late '60s and early '70s, the most distinguishing instrumental feature would be Anders Koppel's ghostly, eerie organ sounds, which made the instrument sound as though it was being filtered through an aquarium tank. The most important missing piece of the puzzle was located when the Koppels became aware of the lead singer from a local beat/soul band, the Dandy Swingers.

Savage Rose in the 1977; Annisette on left, Thomas Koppel second from right.

Annisette Hansen (she has always remained known simply as "Annisette," even after becoming Thomas Koppel's wife) had been singing since the age of seven, when she sang with traveling amusement caravans and performed for children's records. By her teenage years she was moving from Italian serenades into rock and soul, falling under the spell of Aretha Franklin, James Brown, and Sam & Dave, as well as older gospel, jazz, and blues singers such as Bessie Smith and Billie Holiday. With the Dandy Swingers, she had just scored a big Danish hit with a cover version of Ike & Tina Turner's "River Deep, Mountain High." An invitation to rehearse with the embryonic Savage Rose broadened her horizons.

"I went to rehearsal with them, and it was such a great experience, because I had never sung a song which had not been sung before," she says today, with a sense of discovery that hasn't faded in the intervening 30 years. "For the first time, I had that experience of my own thing, my own soul, my own style. I always had to imitate someone else. But this time, I had only my own soul, my own style, my own voice — and that was such a fantastic feeling. From that day, I knew that's what I wanted. When they asked me to choose between Dandy Swingers and Savage Rose, I said, I have to go with this new thing. Because this is something to build on, to learn from the beginning what it is to create, with your own fantasy, what's inside you." For good measure, two of the other Dandy Swingers also joined Savage Rose, which released their self-titled debut in 1968.

The entire band were virgins in the art of writing and singing original rock music, but as Annisette's comments indicate, this may have ensured that the resulting record sounded like nothing else in 1968, in Denmark or elsewhere. While there are dim echoes of psychedelic bands such as the Jefferson Airplane and the Doors, the album has a charmingly wistful, subdued air that draws more upon classical keyboards, European folk melodies, and jazz rhythms than conventional rock and blues progressions. The words were infused with odd hints of longing, doom, and regret. Writing Danish lyrics was never considered as a serious option. English was the lingua franca of both the revolution and pop music, and English is what the words were written in, even if it gave rise to some awkward phrases. This is especially evident on several tracks from their early albums where Annisette sings from a male point of view, bemoaning the loss of "A Girl That I Knew" or calling herself "The Poorest Man on Earth." (The bizarre "My Family Was Gay," from their third record, was an especially controversial title.)

The album was a quick success in Denmark. It was followed by a couple of inconsistent affairs in which the band pursued a heavier rock sound, though light, flitting folk-classical-flavored numbers and gothic compositions were always present as well. Polydor, trying to break the group into the international market, arranged some sessions in London with Giorgio Gomelsky. The British impresario had worked with the Yardbirds, Soft Machine, and numerous other innovative U.K. bands. But the collaboration was not a success, resulting only in an obscure single. "In the studio, we just didn't get to the place where our kind of creativity started," says Koppel about the sessions. "We felt like the road was blocked somehow. It didn't work out. In situations like that, we became anarchists." It wasn't the last time they hooked up with a big-name producer—they recorded *Refugee* with Jimmy Miller, who was also handling the Rolling Stones at the time, in 1971. But as Thomas admits, "We were never really the typical kind of artists that wanted a producer at all."

By the summer of 1969, Savage Rose were playing the Newport Festival in the States, given a most unenviable slot between Sly & the Family Stone and James Brown. (Thomas: "We felt like a very small hot dog in a very big hamburger.") The band were nervously awaiting their spot when crowds broke through the fences during Sly Stone's performance, causing a big fight between the intruders and the police until, as Thomas remembers, a giant tropical shower cooled everyone's tempers off. Fortunately for the band, their own performance was postponed until the next day, when they opened for James Brown. Savage Rose's music, as well as Annisette's gypsy-like presence as frontwoman, went down well with the crowd; the next day, onstage photos of Annisette and James Brown ran side by side on the front page of the Newport daily paper.

Savage Rose undertook a more extensive tour of the United States shortly afterwards. In early 1971 the band received fulsome praise from *Rolling Stone*, which exclaimed breathlessly: "The range of Annisette's voice, both in terms of octaves and emotions, is incredible in every way, and the band's assimilation of seemingly all the major developments of R&B for the past ten years, combined with the classical element is astonishing, and the integration of all these elements is, quite simply, beyond belief." But RCA, which released the band's fourth LP (*Your Daily Gift*) in the States, wasn't prepared to give it a major push, especially with the emergence of the band's political consciousness.

Explains Thomas: "We were actually offered a very, very big contract from, I think, RCA at a certain time through American managers. They wanted us to go and play for the soldiers in Vietnam on the bases. We just couldn't do it. I mean, who could, at the time? All the bands were against the war, and wanted the war to stop. We felt like we would be supporting the war. The business people were very disappointed with us. They refused to give us a big contract, and they gave us a very small contract instead. After that, I don't think anyone really tried hard" to break Savage Rose in the U.S., he believes (in fact, to this day only three of the group's albums have been released here).

By this time the band's politics were extending into considerably more radical territories than anti-war opposition. They were inspired by the Black Panther movement to make a gospel rock album, *Babylon*, "because we felt that we could contribute and make a new kind of gospel with the life on earth, instead of the life in heaven." Jazz great Ben Webster, then living out his final years in Copenhagen, contributed some sax to the recording. An opening spoken dedication to

Malcolm X set the tone for a work that, in Thomas' estimation, "the record company absolutely didn't want to release internationally at all." Savage Rose were frequently playing at political rallies and benefits in Europe, and were even invited by the Black Panthers to play at a rally in support of Panther Bobby Seale's mayoral campaign in Oakland, although the event was canceled a week before it was scheduled to take place.

It wasn't all political R&B-progressive rock for the band in the early '70s. Their biggest success came with another record that Polydor initially didn't want to touch. In 1970, Thomas had been asked to compose the score for a ballet by Flemming Dindt, *Dodens Triumf* (Triumph of Death). This mostly instrumental record is not only the group's most impressive fusion of rock and classical sensibilities, but one of the rare rock albums in this vein that truly presents the best of

Annisette on stage.

both worlds, with a haunting delicacy reflecting both storm clouds and spiritual grace. An art-rock landmark of sorts, it's all but unknown outside of Scandinavia.

"We felt like it was a big chance to open all the gates and make a real true fusion," declares Thomas. "Not just a mix, but a fusion. The record company didn't believe in the record, because it [had] only one vocal track, and the music was different." They initially only pressed 500 copies; by 1997, it had sold, according to Thomas, about 200,000 copies in Denmark, which would translate to about ten million units in a country the size of the United States. The Royal Ballet performed the work "for, I think, seven years, and only [to] full houses all the time."

Conflicts about musical and political direction, however, had reduced Savage Rose to a trio by the time of *Babylon*. A quieter, folkier album, *Wild Child*, followed in 1973, with some of the group's loveliest pieces. Anders Koppel, who had written most of the band's material with Thomas, left in 1974. And at this point, Thomas and Annisette, though committed to continuing Savage Rose with other musicians, had tired of the politics of major label record companies, even as their enthusiasm for real-life leftist politics grew.

"It had something to do about our development as human beings," observes Koppel. "We could never separate the songs from the reality of our lives, and the reality of the world. We couldn't get there through this record company at the time. We had to free ourselves, move out of the business, out of everything—canceled our contract, canceled tours."

It was a most radical step for a band that still enjoyed a lot of popularity in Denmark, but more radical changes were to come. They spent much of the '70s living, out of choice, in the slums of Copenhagen. They contributed material to an album benefiting Christiania, the famous community in Copenhagen that promulgates alternative lifestyles, politics, and art. A fine, light album appeared on the Sonet label in 1978 that found the band, for the first time, singing most of their songs in their native Danish. Continuing disenchantment with record company politics, however, meant that by 1980 Savage Rose were again without a contract, and spending much of their time playing benefits and free concerts in Europe and the Middle East. In the spring of 1980 they even accepted an invitation from the P.L.O. to play at hospitals, schools, and refugee camps in Lebanon. Savage Rose are almost certainly the only big-name rock group to play at Palestinian refugee camps, singing in Danish rather than English, no less.

This period gave rise to somewhat misleading speculation that Savage Rose had basically ended their professional activities to become revolutionaries. In fact, Thomas points out, the group were still playing ordinary concert halls and festivals in Northern Europe. "We just had to take a step back, and get out of the business to get back to what it was really about in the first place, to make music and find new ways and be with people, and make stories into songs to tell people, and see all those youngsters filled with happiness or tears or whatever when you were singing a song. We couldn't get there, as long as we had all those business ties on us."

Elaborates Annisette, "Many other bands followed the trends and were happy to do that. Some of them were satisfied just to be on the road and do rock and roll and make people happy. But we wanted something more. We wanted to combine it with the life and the style of the life we were living. That was much more difficult. You meet so many stories, so many people, and if you combine that with the music...maybe the business people were a little afraid. When you're telling the truth, you are suddenly political.

"They tried to tell us that people don't want that. We found the opposite. We found out that if you told a story which had something to do with the lives of most people, then most people would want to hear your music, and give you back what they got from you. Even when we were traveling in Lebanon in the Palestinian camps, even when you're telling a story in your own language—they can feel what you are doing. They are giving you back so much happiness, and so much will to live and positive feelings. That energy, you can't buy."

When Savage Rose returned to recording in the early 1980s, they initially released their work on tiny independent labels. "We wanted to make records all the time," emphasizes Thomas. "But the business had to get accustomed to what was happening to *us*." Adds Annisette, "They wanted to tell us which kind of rhythm we should play, and how you should look. We told the business people, *you* have to find out how you want to sell this. We are doing our music and we are playing for the people. If you can't find out how to sell it as a chicken from the supermarket, it's your fault."

Eventually the band finally re-entered the world of large commercial distribution on their own terms. Signed to Mega Scandinavia, Savage Rose are again a big act in Denmark, singing in English after over ten years of Danish-only recordings. When I call Thomas and Annisette at their Copenhagen home in early 1997, the English-language *Black Angel*, according to Thomas, is closing in on *Dodens Triumf* as the band's all-time best seller. Recorded in Los Angeles in 1995, with guest appearances by ex-Rolling Stone Mick Taylor on guitar, it contains some remakes of old Savage Rose songs, which the Koppels revisit and update for new audiences, along with presenting new material. Thomas also keeps busy with composing projects in a more classical-oriented vein (he recently released his soundtrack to a theatrical production based on Franz Kafka's classic short story, "Metamorphosis"). Annisette is preparing for the lead role in a musical drama that she wrote.

The Koppels are pleased that, after years of waiting for the music business to meet them on their own playing field, they're able to do what they please, even if, just as when Savage Rose started, their work is little known outside of Denmark. "It's a little bit like a fairy tale, because it shouldn't be able to happen, things like that," Thomas admits. "But it actually happened."

Recommended Recordings:
The Savage Rose (1968, Polydor). The band's most innocent album is in some ways their most consistent, the engaging psychedelic lightness balanced by glimpses of darker visions underneath.

Dodens Triumf (1972, Polydor). Although a rather atypical effort in that only one song has vocals, this is one of the rare successful matings of classical composition with rock instrumentation and spirit, palatable to both rock and open-minded "serious" music fans.

25 (1993, Mega, Denmark). The only survey of the band's career, one disc of this double CD covers their early albums; the other focuses solely on post-1980s recordings. The band's output is so diverse, however, that they're better served by individual albums, all of which have something to recommend them. All of their first eight albums from 1968-1973 have been reissued on Polydor in Europe, and thus are technically in print, though you'll be lucky to find them in North America or the U.K.

Eurobeat

The Outsiders, Savage Rose, and Françoise Hardy are but the tip of the iceberg of a '60s European rock scene that remains virtually all but unknown outside the world of geek collectors. The British Invasion's effect on the U.S. is well-documented; thousands of bands sprang into action overnight, determined to rock hard and write their own material. What's less well known is that precisely the same phenomenon was taking place all over Continental Europe, even though English was not the official language of any of these countries. English *was*, however, the unofficial language of pop music, and these bands weren't going to let piddling matters like awkward accents and goofball sentence construction stand in their way.

Occasionally such bands were lucky enough to score an international hit, as Los Bravos (from Spain) did with their Gene Pitney imitation "Black Is Black," and Shocking Blue (from Holland) did with "Venus." Commercial success for these groups, however, was usually confined exclusively within their national borders. While this must have been quite frustrating in terms of obtaining worldwide success, it also meant that a lot of bands got the opportunity to be big fish in small ponds, although the likes of the Beatles and the Byrds would have wiped the floor with them. But occasionally, a band that was truly of world-class quality would emerge from these backwaters, only to be discovered by Anglo collectors decades after their existence.

English, to generalize, is spoken with far greater fluency in the North of Europe than in the South, so it comes as little surprise to find that the best Continental '60s bands came from Northern territories. The Outsiders were just the best of an incredibly active Dutch scene, which from the sounds of things was more influenced by the manic R&B of the Rolling Stones and Pretty Things than the more tuneful strains of the Beatles. Many groups stripped down the Pretty Things' frenetic R&B/rock hybrids into even more elemental, primitive, and downright uglier forms. The result wasn't just imitation British R&B. The Dutch bands added a peculiarly morose, sullen stance that seemed to carry around a perpetual cloud of gloom, even as it was pinned to standard blues guitar and harmonica riffs.

Aside from the Outsiders, Les Baroques were the most interesting Dutch band, paced by the vocals of Gary O'Shannon, who sounded a bit like Van Morrison in the early Them days. That's also true of the rest of the band, which offered a spooky R&B/pop recipe, dominated by lean organ riffs and spidery guitar riffs. They were life's eternal pessimists, grinding out a lengthy succession of minor, bluesy melodies with lyrics about romantic rejection, lost/doomed love, and frustration that allowed no possibility of sunny times around the corner. Upping the pure strangeness factor were almost comical, polka-ish horns that would occasionally (and incongruously) bleat through the foggy doom. The group were dealt a death knell when O'Shannon left, although a couple of subsequent singles were worthy.

Swedish bands generally struck a much lighter mood than their Dutch neighbors to the south. Many of the bands were struck mad by mod; the crunching guitar and power-pop melodies of the Who were influencing Swedish rock records as early as 1965, long before most Americans could tell a mod from a rocker. *Searchin' for Shakes, Swedish Beat 1965–1968* (on Amigo, Sweden) is a superb compilation of mid-'60s Swedish rock, with fine Whoish cuts by the Lee Kings, Namelosers, and Bootjacks; the purer pop instincts of the Beatles and Merseybeat also make their presence felt on tracks by groups like the Mascots. The Lea Riders' "Dom Kellar Dos Mods" is one of the most inspired slabs of psychedelic madness issued in any country, with a grinding guitar riff anchoring demented lyrics and astonishing pop-art freakout sound effects.

The best of the Swedish groups were the Tages, who could have passed for a bona fide British beat group with their hooky, hard guitar pop tunes, which appropriated some of the best features of the Who, Small Faces, Kinks, and Beatles. They weren't nearly as long on distinctive personality as the Outsiders. They just offered a bunch of excellent songs, like the shotgun marriage of Mersey and mod on "The One for You," the weird mix of Bo Diddley beats and flamenco guitar on "Crazy 'Bout My Baby," and the Kinky balladry of "Miss McBaren." Swedish EMI issued a fine double LP of the Tages' best material, which like most great Eurobeat can only be found by haunting specialist mail-order record outlets.

Germany, to generalize, was much better at honing British bands in Hamburg than developing homegrown talent. Most German groups (predating the advent of electronic/progressive "Krautrock," detailed in a separate sidebar) played in a stiff, unimaginative manner that was too close to marching bands for comfort. The Rattles had a bit of international success, but better were the Lords, whose repertoire consisted largely of zanily rearranged tunes drawn from the skiffle, R&B, and pre-Beatle rock eras. Their goose-stepping rhythms approached self-parody in their sheer speed; they laid on the whammy bar guitar reverb with as much restraint as a sailor on shore leave. They were also among the first groups to use Lesley guitar amplification, which gave their guitars an organ-like texture (used, much later, by the Beatles on their *Let It Be* sessions). A comprehensive retrospective of their best work—there's enough to fill up a double CD—is again long overdue.

France, true to its stereotype, preferred to sing in French rather than conform to the English-language norm. Françoise Hardy had enough magnetism to succeed in any language, but much '60s French pop was way too sentimental to gain an audience abroad. The most notable exception was Ronnie Bird, who recorded some quite respectable (if rather derivative) mod guitar rockers in the mid-'60s. One of his backing musicians was the legendary Mickey Baker (of Mickey & Sylvia "Love Is Strange" fame). That certainly looks like Mickey playing guitar behind his back on the back cover of Bird's *En Public* reissue, a year or two before Hendrix rose to fame with a similar gimmick.

Spain in the 1960s was still under the rule of Franco, and rowdy rock 'n' roll did not thrive. Yet some raunchy groups did manage to sneak into the studio nonetheless, and as is often the case when music is made under the yoke of oppression, the results sometimes had a ferocious punkish energy. Numero uno among these acts would have to be Los Cheyenes, who made a bunch of EPs and singles between 1965 and 1967 that presented even rawer variations of the early Kinks' sound, sung in Spanish. By contrast, Los Bravos were far tamer, despite their international success; most of their music sounded like it could have been recorded in New York, such was its mainstream pop-rock flavor.

Every European country had an active rock scene, even if these might not have been as interesting as the scenes detailed above; Switzerland, Denmark, Italy, Greece, Belgium, and other nations produced plenty of regional rock, much not worth bothering about, some quite good. There were also hotbeds of beat music and garage rock in non-English speaking countries in other continents. Uruguay produced both the Shakers, one of the most accurate and best early Beatles imitators anywhere on the globe, *and* the Mockers, who were just as successful in emulating the *Aftermath*-era Rolling Stones. The best source by far to learn about Eurobeat and its offshoots (as well as many other cult '60s bands from America and Britain) is *Ugly Things*, available from Mike Stax at 3707 Fifth Avenue #145, San Diego, CA 92103 (some back issues remain available).

The Outsiders, late 1960s.

Folk Music; Rock Attitude

Some of the most interesting non-stars of rock history may not have thought of themselves as rock musicians at all. When it comes to non-rockers that have influenced rock, I've been most intrigued by folkies who profoundly affected the course of rock. In the process, they seemed to become rockers themselves, almost unconsciously, as if the intermingling between folk and rock had taken on a life of its own.

Genre-benders looking for folkies with rock appeal could start with Bert Jansch (a big influence upon Neil Young and Jimmy Page), Fred Neil (a recluse since the end of the '60s with a lo-o-o-w, bluesy voice, whose songs were covered by the likes of the Jefferson Airplane), Sandy Bull (whose use of ragas and Middle Eastern music preceded a similar East-West blend in early psychedelia), and John Fahey (whose relentless mutations of blues, folk, and experimental weirdness also bore an affinity with psychedelic rockers). Were these rockers who happened to use acoustic guitars, as some have charged? No. What made them appeal to cult followings composed of rock listeners was their attitude—a simultaneous mastery of folk conventions, and a desire to reshape them in a contemporary, even avant-garde fashion.

The careers detailed in this section are not at all similar to each other, except for the crucial—and largely overlooked—roles they played in the assimilation of folk forms into rock music. Davey Graham would probably never identify himself as a rock musician, but any rock guitarist who draws from a wide assortment of genres—Richard Thompson, Ry Cooder, or Paul Simon, for starters—owes him (in Simon's case, substantially). Sandy Denny may have done more than any other figure to bring British traditional folk music and electric rock to-

Davey Graham emulates the pose of one of his heroes, Django Reinhardt. Credit: Courtesy Davey Graham

gether—a fusion that has shaped the British roots scene for the last several decades. The Holy Modal Rounders first brought a rock 'n' roll attitude to old-time music, and then an old-time hootenanny attitude to rock 'n' roll. It wasn't always easy to tell where one left off and the other began; the common ingredient was the sense of fun, not to mention lunacy, the group brought to their work.

Sandy Denny

If Nick Drake was British folk-rock's dark prince, Sandy Denny was its haunted queen, her music sharing an equally eerie sense of timelessness. The similarities between the two can be taken further. Both were singer-songwriters that were nurtured by producer Joe Boyd in the late '60s. Both were artists who cultivated a specialized—and wildly devoted—audience that was attracted to the artists' uneasy mix of romance and impending doom. And the mythic status of both singers was ensured by a premature, unexpected death.

The similarities only stretch so far, however. Nick Drake only released three albums during his lifetime; Denny's discography is a dense jungle in comparison, encompassing a steady stream of solo albums and recordings as a key member of Fairport Convention, Fotheringay, and the Strawbs, spanning almost a dozen years. Drake was known only to a few thousand during his career, and played barely any concerts; Denny topped *Melody Maker* polls for best female vocalist, periodically dented the charts in England, and toured internationally. Drake could be withdrawn to the point of catatonia; Denny may have had her moods, but was by almost all accounts a warm and outgoing personality.

Denny was not especially noted for high drama or sensationalized rumors of odd behavior. What's keeping her memory alive is that voice, with its chill that cuts through the speakers like wind on the English moors. As distinctive as any of her time, it brought the mystery of centuries-old British folk traditions to life, with as much immediate shock as finding a ghost at the dinner table. It was that peculiarly British quality, perhaps, that prevented her from finding stardom in the U.S., but has kept her own ghost alive at a time when many of her more famed contemporaries are nothing more than names in rock encyclopedias.

The lion's share of Denny's renown was generated by her stint in the late 1960s with the most acclaimed British folk-rock band of all time, Fairport Convention. Yet Denny was only a member of Fairport for about 18 months, sang lead only on a portion of their songs (albeit a significant portion), only wrote a few songs for the band, and was already an accomplished folk singer with several recordings to her credit when she joined the group in May 1968. In the mid-'60s she had been romantically involved with an expatriate American folk singer, Jackson C. Frank, putting several of his songs into her repertoire. Soon afterwards she made her recording debut on obscure acoustic folk releases by Alex Campbell and Johnny Silvo. The songs on which she sang lead have been repackaged as *The Original Sandy Denny*; while much of the material was plainly arranged (acoustic guitar only), standard '60s folk, the magnificent high, slightly smoky voice was already striking.

Denny made her entrée into the world of folk-rock (albeit of a mildly electrified sort) when Dave Cousins asked her to join the Strawbs. Sandy recorded one album with the group in Denmark in 1967, singing strong leads on most of the tracks, tuneful pop-folk pieces that were largely written by Cousins. Denny offered a wistful original of her own, "Who Knows Where the Time Goes"; her writing debut would end up being one of her most popular compositions, and was quickly covered by Judy Collins as the title track of a 1968 LP. The Strawbs couldn't find a British deal for the record (it's now available on a Hannibal CD), and by May 1968 Denny had joined Fairport Convention, replacing Judy Dyble.

Fairport had already released one fairly solid folk-rock album in a sort of imitation West Coast rock style, but Sandy's arrival would truly spark the band's golden age. "Sandy was a completely different person than Judy, a much more powerful singer," says Joe Boyd, Fairport Convention's producer at the time. "The band became less tentative with Sandy, because Judy was a delicate singer. There might have been a little bit of a feeling of holding back, or hesitancy about being too aggressive in the band, because the vocalist was so tentative, frail.

"But with Sandy, you had a powerhouse. The fact that she chose to join Fairport boosted the band's confidence because she was quite well known as a solo artist. She brought her own songwriting, and ultimately she was really the key person responsible for introducing them to folk music, because she had a large repertoire of songs that she used to sing with the band on the road or in hotel rooms after concerts."

When Denny first joined Fairport, the band continued to concentrate on a mix of group originals and covers of obscure compositions by American folk-

Sandy Denny, angel of British folk-rock. Credit: Courtesy Hannibal Records

rock giants such as Bob Dylan, Joni Mitchell, and Leonard Cohen. Her first two albums with Fairport, *What We Did on Our Holidays* and *Unhalfbricking*, were instrumental in establishing an identity for British folk-rock as a separate entity from American bands like the Byrds. This was particularly evident on their electric updates of traditional British folk material like "Nottamun Town" and "She Moves Through the Fair"; Denny also proved skilled at writing extremely haunting originals in the same style, such as "Fotheringay."

The band, still unknown in the U.S., were gaining momentum on their home ground, where their albums were cracking the Top 20. But the very existence of Fairport was threatened by a serious road accident in mid-1969. Drummer Martin Lamble, and guitarist Richard Thompson's girlfriend Jeannie Franklyn, both died in the mishap. When the musicians regrouped, they had decided to plunge full force into electrified traditional British folk, a decision that to a large extent has shaped the British folk-rock scene to this day.

Explains Boyd: "The defining event which led to the *Liege and Lief* period—which made Fairport what it has come to be ever since—was the accident. The group at first was very unsure that they would play together again. When they began to consider the possibility of reforming, they were very, very clear that they would never perform the old songs that Martin had played on. They would have to start from scratch with repertoire.

"That led to the question: What *will* we do? That all happened around the time [the Band's] *Music from Big Pink* came out. That was a big influence—they were stunned by that record. It was so rooted in American traditions that they felt that if they could come up with a kind of music which was as English as that record was American, it would justify re-forming as a group. It had already begun to be interesting during *Unhalfbricking* with 'A Sailor's Life' [an 11-minute electric update of a traditional folk tune that featured future member Dave Swarbrick on fiddle]. But it hadn't really occurred to them to just go completely over to that other direction. That was the thing that triggered the change."

Swarbrick was in the Fairport lineup that made *Liege and Lief*, which shifted the band's focus from original/contemporary material to rocked-up traditional British Isles folk. Denny in particular shone on the murder ballad "Matty Groves" and the Halloween doom anthem "Tam Lin," the latter of which may be Fairport's most famous performance of all. (In 1977, shortly before her death, Denny carped to writer Colin Irwin, "If I have to sing 'Matty Groves' one more time, I'll throw myself out of a window.')

Bassist Dave Pegg, who played alongside Denny in Fairport Convention in the mid-'70s, thinks that "obviously her forte was singing traditional music. She had such a good feel for it, and was not restricted in the way she would attack songs. Sandy had spent most of her singing career up to that time just going round with a guitar and singing traditional songs, which is all people used to do at folk clubs. There was never any drums and bass or electric guitars, and never anybody singing the way that she did. It was pretty shocking stuff for the folkies in England. Not all of them enjoyed it. A lot of them used to whinge about it. But that is the influence, really, that she had." It's an influence that has also been felt in the work of top post-1970 British female folk singers such as Maddy Prior (of Steeleye Span) and June Tabor; Pegg detects a bit of Sandy in a more unlikely artist, Kate Bush.

For most of the past three or so decades, the sort of approach found on *Liege and Lief* has been Fairport's bread and butter. But Denny, for the most part, wouldn't be around for it, leaving the group near the end of 1969 to found a band with her future husband, guitarist Trevor Lucas.

American Jerry Donahue would be the guitarist in Fotheringay, after noted British country guitarist Albert Lee (who was recommended by Richard Thompson) decided to bow out of the new group after some rehearsals. Denny had just won *Melody Maker*'s poll for top British female vocalist, and Joe Boyd, according to Donahue, "could see that it was clearly a good opportunity for her to capitalize on that by going solo. And he did his best to persuade her to do so. But she was adamant that she was going to start a band with Trevor. They'd be able to write together, and probably have more control over what gets used and what gets thrown out than she would have had in Fairport, where there were a lot of other voices."

Fotheringay's sole album (from 1970) was for Denny a move back to the mix of originals, contemporary covers, and British traditional songs that Fairport were playing before their gear-shift into plugged-in olde British folk. While it was not as impressive as Fairport's late '60s records, it was a promising beginning, particularly "Banks of the Nile," another traditional epic along the lines of "Tam Lin" and "Matty Groves." Fotheringay were in the midst of recording a second album when Denny suddenly announced her departure for a solo career.

"Sandy was in the control room in tears," remembers Donahue. "She loved what we were doing; she was so enthused about the tracks that we'd done so far." Jerry adds that he never felt Boyd had his heart in Fotheringay anyway—"he was usually reading a newspaper with feet on the desk." According to Donahue, Denny informed the band that Boyd had turned down an offer to head Warner Brothers' film music department in Los Angeles—on the condition that Denny become a solo artist.

Donahue: "She was just so bowled over by his willingness to do that, and the apparent confidence that he had in her career. She felt like it would be kind of a slap in the face to turn something like that down, when he was willing to give up so much in order to further her career. The pressure was put on to the extent that she felt there was just no way to say no to that. Her heart was telling her to stay with Fotheringay. But logic, reasoning, and Joe's demonstration of loyalty and confidence in her persuaded her to basically do what he wanted this time, having resisted him so adamantly a year prior. I certainly supported her decision once I realized the importance of the situation, the way it was presented to her by Joe."

Pegg offers a different perspective. "Sandy had a lot of output. Some things that Sandy was writing at the time, and her whole approach to music—there was lots of elements which couldn't be catered for with a band. I'm sure that she was aware of the fact that she would have to do some stuff on her own as well. A group would have been a fairly inhibiting and restricting way for her to carry on, really, the way she started writing. I think it was inevitable that she would start doing stuff on her own."

Fotheringay's second album was never completed, although some tracks show up on the Sandy Denny box set, *Who Knows Where the Time Goes*. Boyd would actually end up moving to California to work at Warner Brothers anyway in the early '70s. Denny, for better or worse, was now establishing a solo career that would find her releasing four albums over the next few years. Opinions vary greatly on the issue—Fairport Fanatics are a particularly fierce and loyal lot when it comes to championing their heroes—but for many listeners, none of her solo records were as consistent as the ones she had made with her previous bands, especially Fairport Convention. The arrangements sometimes had a too-smooth, '70s session musician feel.

Denny's songs tended to work best when the settings were intimate and sparse enough to amplify the magical qualities of her voice. There are such recordings from the 1970s, yet these tend not to be found on her solo albums, but on BBC broadcasts, on which she often performed accompanied only by her own guitar or piano. "Bruton Town," a stark traditional BBC number found on her box set, is certainly one of her most broodingly effective performances; others have shown up on bootleg (most notably *Dark the Night*), and an official CD release of BBC material surfaced briefly in 1997 before being withdrawn immediately for legal reasons.

The most positive notes sounded by her solo albums were her increased opportunities to present her own songs and develop as a composer. Her frequent references to rivers and other natural elements—as on what's probably her most FM radio-friendly track, "Blackwaterside"—amplified her image as a sort of spectral earth mother of folk-rock. On a BBC world service interview in 1972, Denny's comments did nothing to tarnish that perception, whether accurate or not: "They're usually written from . . . my experiences of people. Like sometimes those kinds of metaphorical things about rivers and streams might be referring to a particular person. Which is an unusual thing to say, perhaps, but . . . some people are very easily described in natural terms . . . the way I feel always comes out in some kind of description of some kind of natural force. I don't know quite how to explain, I mean, I can't explain much more than the song itself."

Comments Pegg, "Having the opportunity to do token kind of pseudo-jazz things, and do things with whole string sections with the benefit of a great arranger—obviously, that's how her songwriting developed. That was a difference between her solo work and stuff that she did with the Fairports, really. A band's a very restricting thing, 'cause you have to take into account everybody else's opinion. And if you're someone with as much of a personality as Sandy had, everybody else kind of has to fit in the background." Did she enjoy the chance to record with orchestras and such? "I think she took great pleasure and satisfaction from being able to do all that stuff," states Pegg, who fondly remembers when Denny, fortified by wine, spontaneously led a jazz band in the middle of a revolving restaurant through a version of "Foggy Day in London Town." "She liked nothing better than to get up and sing something different."

To most American listeners, Denny remained not so much an enigma as a nonentity. The only time most mainstream rock fans heard her in the 1970s was when she added backup vocals to Led Zeppelin's "The Battle of Evermore," or when she sang two lines as a nurse in the London Symphony's production of the Who's *Tommy*. She rejoined Fairport for a couple of years in the mid-'70s, while continuing her solo recording career. Although fans and bandmates alike welcomed her presence, this lineup lacked the magic of earlier times, particularly as guitarist Richard Thompson was long gone. Jerry Donahue says that Denny and Lucas wanted to reform Fotheringay in the mid-'70s, but Donahue, by then in Fairport Convention himself (as was Lucas), regretfully declined the offer (though he, Lucas, and Denny would all play together in Fairport for a couple of years).

Some opinion holds that Denny was declining in her final years. But though her material and arrangements may have been erratic, a good-sounding bootleg of her final show from November 27, 1977 (*One Last Sad Refrain—The Final Concert*), demonstrates pretty conclusively that her vocals retained their characteristic power and mystery. By this time British folk-rock was in serious commercial trouble, as punk and new wave were hogging the media spotlight and beginning to crowd many older acts off the charts. It would have been interesting to see how Denny would have weathered the changing music trends, but tragedy struck unexpectedly when she fell down a flight of stairs at a friend's house in April 1978. Suffering a brain hemorrhage and lapsing into a coma, she died a few days later, at the age of 31.

Recommended Recordings:
Who Knows Where the Time Goes? (1985, Hannibal). Denny recorded in such a variety of contexts—solo, and with three different bands, all of which sometimes featured different singers—that it's difficult to recommend any one or two albums as a starting point. This box set is an expensive introduction, but it does tie together many of her highlights from her solo LPs and some of the best songs she sang with Fairport Convention and Fotheringay (one number from the

Strawbs album is also included). There's also a good deal of unreleased and rare material, some of which is actually among her very best stuff. It does lack some of her best early Fairport Convention performances, such as "Fotheringay" and "She Moves Through the Fair," which can found on the Fairport albums *What We Did On Our Holidays* and *Unhalfbricking*.

The Original Sandy Denny (1967, Mooncrest, UK). Her early solo folk tracks, still known almost solely to fanatical collectors, but worth hearing for anyone who appreciates wonderful singing.

Sandy & the Strawbs (1967, Hannibal). Denny sings most of the tracks on this engaging set of perky, light folk-rock, including her original version of "Who Knows Where the Time Goes?"

Dark the Night (1990s, Nixed). Exceptionally well-produced for a bootleg, this CD has 73 minutes of otherwise unreleased, sparsely produced BBC tracks from the early '70s; a couple solo acoustic BBC performances from 1966; excellent solo acoustic home demos from 1966; and a couple of rare, beguiling items from an obscure 1972 soundtrack. Some excellent Denny-sung BBC tunes with Fairport Convention can be found on the official Hannibal release, *Heyday*.

The BBC Sessions 1971–73 (1997, Strange Fruit, UK). Although eight of these twenty tracks appeared on the *Dark the Night* bootleg, twelve did not, making this release—consisting largely of "unplugged" versions of songs from her first three solo albums—essential for fans. Unfortunately, it was available only briefly in the spring of 1997 before being pulled from distribution for legal reasons, although the material will most likely see the light of day again in the future.

Davey Graham

You could not, by most stretches of the imagination, call Davey Graham a *rock* guitarist. But the fact is, you couldn't really call him a blues, folk, or jazz guitarist either. He's all of those things—or none of them.

What Graham did in the '60s was bring an unsurpassed eclecticism to the craft of guitar virtuosity. He both anticipated and influenced the British psychedelic rock, blues-rock, and folk-rock scenes to an extent that is woefully underappreciated to this day. Like American cult guitarists John Fahey and Sandy Bull, his influence was not so much felt in actual sound as in open-minded approach. As the title of his best album proclaimed, Graham played "Folk Blues and All Points in Between." Like Fahey and Bull, Graham was one of the first Western guitarists of any sort to incorporate middle eastern modes and Indian ragas into

Davey Graham in concert. Credit: Courtesy Davey Graham

his music. Unlike Fahey and Bull, however, Graham is mostly unknown in the U.S. even on a cult level, as most of his records were never released stateside.

It hasn't helped, of course, that Graham has barely recorded since 1970. By that time, however, his influence had already been felt in the guitar playing of Bert Jansch and John Renbourn, the twin guitar leads of Britain's most ambitious folk-rock-jazz hybrid, Pentangle. Paul Simon, who met Graham in the mid-'60s during a residency in England, even asked Davey to join him as an accompanist at one point. When you hear Jimmy Page play intricate acoustic guitar leads in Led Zeppelin's quieter moments, or Richard Thompson genre-hopping between folk, blues, and more, you're also hearing Graham's legacy. British songwriter Pete Brown, who co-wrote several Cream classics with Jack Bruce, calls Graham "one of the first world musicians," and sees him as the start of "a whole kind of genre of people" extending through Renbourn, Jansch, and Thompson in particular.

Another veteran of the British blues/folk music scene warns me that Graham can be a difficult interview subject. Years of drugs and psychological problems mean that he can have his good and bad days, depending upon when you catch him. "And whatever you do," he adds cryptically, "don't mention Bert Jansch."

When I phone Graham at his London home in early 1997, it seems to be a good day at first, although he seems more concerned with reciting a prepared biography than answering my questions. Then his mind starts to drift. Queries about his influence on other guitarists, about his relationship with Paul Simon, about those fine rare '60s Decca LPs, go unanswered as he mumbles about a painting on his wall and the Clinton–Gore inauguration. He attempts an inscrutable joke about two cannibals locked in an elevator, and offers to teach me the Arabian lute. Graham is still alive and performing, but remains just as much an enigma when I hang up as he did when I first came across his "Blue Raga" on an obscure import compilation LP 15 years ago.

We do know this: Davey Graham (his name is sometimes spelled "Davy Graham" on record) was born in England in 1940 to a Scottish father and a mother from Georgetown, Guyana. He played a minor role in the early British blues scene in the early '60s, holding a guitar seat in Alexis Korner's seminal outfit Blues Incorporated, which spun off personnel to the Rolling Stones, Cream, Manfred Mann, and many others. He also briefly played guitar with another British blues godfather, John Mayall, a couple of years or so before Eric Clapton would join Mayall's Bluesbreakers.

Graham even recorded an EP with Korner in 1962, 3/4 AD, but their association was to be short-lived. "Alexis and I were great friends," explained Davey to Spencer Leigh on the sleeve notes of the Folk Blues and All Points in Between reissue, "but there was a tension about everything we did. When we were together in Blues Inc., Alexis wanted to be both the vocalist and lead guitarist, and I also wanted to be the lead guitarist."

In any case, it seems doubtful that Graham would have been content to limit himself to the blues, or the blues-rock that Mayall and others were moving towards. He had an extraordinarily long and diverse list of heroes and influences including Leadbelly, Big Bill Broonzy, classical guitarist Andres Segovia, Sonny Rollins, Ali Akhbar Khan, Ravi Shankar, Charles Mingus, Ornette Coleman, and British folk giant Martin Carthy (whom Graham met in the late '50s). Graham wasn't thinking purely in terms of guitar sounds, noting, "I picked a lot of my riffs from flautists and horn players, trumpet players and sax players alike."

Although Graham's 1963 debut, *The Guitar Player*, was a tamer and more conventional effort than his later output, he was already determined to blend acoustic folk styles with a blues sensibility and a jazz swing. "When people ask me what kind of guitar I play," he wrote in the sleeve note, "I usually say 'blues, bits and pieces.' The numbers on this album are a mixture of jazz and folk influences. I think that every number has its own particular mood. Before I play I don't know exactly what notes will come out, but I know the *mood* the number conjures up in me, so that on the framework of, say, a 12-bar blues with a slow tempo and in a minor key, I can make the guitar cry by whining the strings.

"On the other hand, for a calypso or fast rocking blues, I can use running single-line phrases with clipped notes to convey movement and excitement, filling in with block chords to keep the pulse of the number. For me, the richness of the guitar as a solo instrument, or accompaniment to a singer lies in its many voices and moods." More than anything on *Guitar Player*, this sort of pre-world fusion was achieved by the instrumental "Anji" from the EP with Alexis Korner. Influenced by the Middle Eastern music he'd been exposed to while traveling in Morocco and other places, the piece was popularized several years later by both Bert Jansch and Simon & Garfunkel, who included it on their *Sounds of Silence* album. (The 3/4 AD EP has been reissued as bonus tracks to the CD reissue of *The Guitar Player* on See For Miles in the U.K.)

Before taking a bolder step to fuse various styles, Graham collaborated with British folk singer Shirley Collins in the 1964 album *Folk Routes, New Routes*. It's been hailed in some quarters as a foundation of British folk-rock, particularly in regards to Collins' vocals, which most likely influenced such singers as Sandy Denny (Fairport Convention) and Jacqui McShee (Pentangle). Also influential was Graham's guitar accompaniment, on which he played acoustic guitar in a manner that owed as much to blues and jazz stylings and rhythms as folk ones.

"The challenge of Shirley's very pure singing, not sensual in the normal sense of the term, meant that I had to try and fit a complete arrangement behind her that would leave her free to sing and phrase in her normal manner," explained Graham in *Melody Maker* in 1980. "I had to try and make the guitar sound like an orchestra when I didn't really know how to orchestrate, also to make every song sound different with what was still a very limited right-hand technique."

Graham truly hit his stride with 1965's *Folk Blues and All Points in Between*, on which he also began to sing as well as present instrumentals. Davey's vocals would always be his chief handicap, with a limited range and expressiveness that was adequate at best. The guitar playing was breathtaking, however—dextrous and fluid, with a fiery imagination. Graham was showing it was possible to play acoustic guitar that swung and rocked on material from Big Bill Broonzy, Lead-belly, Charles Mingus, and others. Blues was the dominant style, but the most exhilarating cut, "Maajun (A Taste of Tangier)," was his first piece to fully explore Middle Eastern/Indian modes, months before anyone had thought of doing the same in rock or pop.

Folk Blues and All Points in Between was the prototype for Graham's series of Decca albums in the 1960s, in which he started to lean less on blues and more on the Eastern influences. Not that blues, folk, or jazz would ever be abandoned. Only a sporadic composer, Graham's particular genius was his ability to rearrange blues and jazz standards in a way that made them sound exotic and fresh. An especially striking example is his 1968 overhaul of Joni Mitchell's "Both Sides Now," which moves from a more or less straight Indian raga into explosive folk-jazz verses. The instrumental "Blue Raga," also from 1968, was probably his most definitive statement in terms of his ambitions to, as the song title indicates, fuse blues with raga, in a more or less folk context.

On *Midnight Man* (1966), Graham moved into a harder, fuller sound, sometimes with bongos, and also inaugurated his series of Lennon-McCartney and Paul Simon covers (still a somewhat unusual move those days in folk circles). On cuts like his cover of Lalo Schifrin's "The Fakir," he could even approach the avant-garde, wedding a hypnotic raga riff to Mingus-like bass parts. Those Beatles and Paul Simon covers made it clear he listened to rock, but the closest he came to actually making rock music itself was 1968's *Large as Life and Twice as Natural*, which featured backup from bassist Danny Thompson (Pentangle) and drummer Jon Hiseman and saxophonist Dick Heckstall-Smith, both of whom had played with British blues-rockers Graham Bond and Colosseum.

Though Graham's Decca LPs—most out-of-print and extremely hard to find in the U.S.—could not be termed rock, they have a great deal of appeal to '60s rock aficionados with their almost psychedelic sense of unpredictable eclecticism and exploration. Graham never stuck to one style; folk ballads would follow ragas, blues would follow Beatles tunes, and lengthy quasi-Indian workouts would stretch the limits of instrumental acoustic guitar pieces. Graham admits that he was a prolific quoter of ideas that caught his fancy, "though wasn't everybody? I'm a quoter of a two-bar phrase and the great Sonny Rollins if I thought it would enhance my blues." In musical terms, "I suppose I saw myself as some kind of a Marco Polo. Because I wanted to be able to get on with the Pope *and* Genghis Khan, you know?"

Such versatility, however, probably did him little good in commercial terms. If only his vocals were better, there would be no doubt that he could have at least attained a folk stardom on the level of, say, Bert Jansch. As it was, he was too adventurous for the traditional folk circuit, and not electric enough for the pop world. He attained his peak with 1968's *Large as Life and Twice as Natural*, though three albums that followed in 1969 and 1970 were nearly as solid. His two 1970 albums were co-billed to his American wife of the time, Holly Gwyn, who was a better singer than Graham, but not all that interesting. 1970's *Godington Boundary*, however, would prove to be his last top-notch recordings, as Graham found himself without a contract for most of the '70s. At one point, he told Spencer Leigh, "Paul Simon asked me to join him . . . but I turned it down. I don't know why, but it was one of the biggest mistakes of my life."

Graham devoted much of the '70s to studying classical guitar, and made two low-key albums for the American Kicking Mule label at the end of the decade, as well as performing with American folk guitarists Stefan Grossman and Duck Baker. Never particularly well-suited for the pop world, by the '80s he was making his living as a guitar teacher rather than a recording/performing artist. "I was studying classics like Bach fugue, and I played a few Bach pieces in my repertoire in clubs," he says. "People didn't altogether like it. They wanted to see a blues artist, particularly if he was destroying himself. This is human nature."

Along with Bert Jansch and Martin Carthy, Graham contributed to a recent CD called *Acoustic Roots*, as well as returning to recording as a solo artist with *Playing in Traffic* on a small label. Much of his time these days, he says, is spent playing Balkan music with a band called Doppelganger. It's hard to judge whether he feels overlooked by history, or, for that matter, whether he even remembers those great '60s records clearly. It seems equally likely that those are just part of a lifelong quest to explore all kinds of new sounds on guitar — whether he happens to be in the studio or not.

Recommended Recordings:
Folk Blues and All Points in Between (1965, See For Miles, UK). Graham's first fully formed statement as a solo artist. The CD reissue effectively functions as a best-of by adding a handful of the better cuts from his late '60s albums.

Midnight Man (1966, Decca, UK). A more forceful approach, with a couple of stone-cold gems in the jazz-raga instrumental "The Fakir" and the lovely, beguiling jazz-folk-samba of "Hummingbird."

Large as Life and Twice as Natural (1968, Decca, UK). Probably the most approachable Graham effort for rock-oriented listeners, with backing by members of Pentangle and Colosseum, and several sparkling raga-folk fusions, particularly "Blue Raga" and the daring cover of Joni Mitchell's "Both Sides Now." Like *Midnight Man*, it's only available as a rare, out-of-print UK import, and crying for CD reissue.

The Holy Modal Rounders

One of the most memorable scenes of the 1969 film *Easy Rider* shows a young Jack Nicholson, proudly decked out in his high school football helmet. With drug-dealing hippies Dennis Hopper and Peter Fonda, he sets off across the American heartland on motorcycle, accompanied by the strange whine of an out-of-key acid-folk group. "If you want to be a bird," squalls the half-cracked voice on the soundtrack, finishing the sentence with a kaleidoscope of reverb-flecked, cacophonous barroom piano and wordless moans. It was the only time most Americans would hear the Holy Modal Rounders, the cracked acid folkies that made a career out of being unable to play it straight.

The Holy Modal Rounders, August 1967; Peter Stampfel on left, Steve Weber on right.
Credit: Courtesy Peter Stampfel

The unit that called themselves the Holy Modal Rounders was as unstable as their music, with an ongoing series of personnel shifts and side projects that can befuddle all but the most committed of trainspotting record collectors. The core axis of the Rounders, however, was the unlikely partnership of Peter Stampfel and Steve Weber, brought together by their mutual love—and desire to dismantle—traditional folk music. Stampfel, claimed the first edition of *The Rolling Stone Record Guide*, "has a working knowledge of almost every song ever written, and Weber . . . only sometimes has a working knowledge of his own compositions."

Saturday morning Chez Stampfel is a bit like falling into one of his songs. A small platoon of tropical birds squawks in the background as Stampfel excitedly recounts the high and low points of a multi-decade career. Even at the age of 58, his high voice constantly sounds on the verge of breaking. "Lily!" he barks at his five-year-old daughter at one point. "Put clothes on! Right now! You're in front of a window naked!"

A child dressed in her morning suit probably isn't apt to cause much comment in lower Manhattan, and Stampfel is far more grounded than his songs or his comic patter might suggest. The only man to play with Bob Dylan, Mississippi John Hurt, playwright Sam Shepard, They Might Be Giants, *and* Buckminster Fuller is now an associate editor at a Penguin-distributed publishing house specializing in science fiction, horror, and fantasy. The father of two young daughters has also reformed considerably since his self-described amphetamine-crazed days, and has been stone cold sober for nearly a decade. A recent Holy Modal Rounders reunion garnered high praise in the *New York Times*, which described the group as having "a following too small to even be called a cult."

Stampfel's been marching to his own drummer since at least 1960, when the fiddler played a gig at a Brooklyn halfway house for troubled Jewish girls. The inmates loved it. The parents and the supervisors were not at all pleased, especially when a pipe that was used as a prop in one of his group's skits hit the head matron in the forehead. Stampfel was not invited back, but he found some work with several folk bands in the exploding early '60s New York scene. Then, around 1963, he found his musical soulmate.

When he first met Steve Weber, Peter remembers, "I'd heard all these terrible things about him. He was this evil speed freak who wore nothing but black clothes that he got from garbage cans that were too small. I didn't realize he played funky blues guitar brilliantly. My first thought was, my God, it's my long-lost kid brother that I never even thought I had. The very first time we played together, it worked perfectly, like we'd been doing it all our lives. There's this very strange way in which we fit together, which was a gift from fate."

Stampfel and Weber were united by their simultaneous devotion to, and irreverence for, traditional folk forms. "When we started out, we found that we actually knew many of the same traditional songs, because we listened to the same handful of reissues of old 78 albums that were around in the early '60s. In fact, all the reissued 78 rpm stuff would probably fit in the backseat of a Volkswagen. It wasn't hard to be exposed to just about everything that was available, 'cause not much was."

Stampfel has commented that his idea was to play traditional folk music not with an eye for duplication, but for a sense of how the musicians of the 1920s and 1930s might have played had they been exposed to modern styles. "The purist attitude at the time was that this golden age was gone, and the right way to do it was to try to recreate it down to the pop and scratch on the old 78 rpm record. That's certainly a valid viewpoint, but it wasn't mine."

The Rounders didn't endear themselves to the guardians of tradition when they changed the words and melodies of old standards to suit their tastes. Stampfel even once wrote in the liner notes that "I made up new words to it because it was easier than listening to the tape and writing words down." Their first two albums (recorded in the mid-'60s for Prestige) are their most folk-oriented. But there's no getting around the fact that the off-kilter execution, wobbly vocals, and downright spaced-out lyrical preoccupations were not going to be embraced by anyone but a cult audience (which may have included the Lovin' Spoonful, who recorded a couple of songs that the Rounders had retooled). Authenticity didn't matter as much as idiosyncrasy, although Stampfel admits today, "When I started writing songs, I wasn't very good. I mostly did it in the way Bob Dylan started writing songs in 1961, which is putting new words to old songs. Which, of course, is what Woody Guthrie did a lot before Dylan."

Stampfel does hold a good deal of affection for the Prestige albums, but goes on to remark that "the second one is kind of crappy, because we didn't want to record any of our original songs which we were writing at the time. Because when Paul Rothschild [later to become famous for producing the Doors, Janis Joplin, and others] signed us to Prestige, about three weeks later he quit the label and went to Elektra. We wanted to get out of the contract, which was for two records. On the second album, we basically didn't want to do any of our original or fresher stuff. So the album isn't as stunning as the first. Also, the *asshole* that did the sequencing put all the songs in the key of A in a row." In his opinion, it couldn't have been ordered any worse "if someone would have made a list of exactly the wrong way to put songs together because they would be the most similar and stupid."

Stampfel had been rediscovering his love for rock 'n' roll even before the Beatles hit. By 1964, he was learning electric bass and doing his bit for founding underground rock by playing on the Fugs' first records. Peter already knew about Fugs leader/writer/activist Ed Sanders from Ed's magazine, *Fuck You—A Magazine of the Arts.* Weber had contributed poetry to the 'zine, and Stampfel's eye was caught by a capsule sketch of his partner in the credits—"the one about Weber was that he had this all-night sexual romp with a gazelle in the Central

Park Zoo. And I thought, wow, cool, not knowing Sanders at the time, not under-standing his tendency to make up fantastic stories just for the sake of amusement.

"In late '64, Weber said Sanders was putting together this dirty rock 'n' roll group, and they'd written 60 songs with titles like 'Coca Cola Douche.' Sanders, Tuli Kupferberg, and Ken Weaver decided to have a dirty rock 'n' roll group, knowing nothing about music whatsoever at all. They couldn't play, they couldn't sing, or anything, but they just wanted to do it. And they wrote about 60 salacious sex and drugs songs. It was just like the punk thing that happened ten years after—the idea that you have an attitude and rebellious viewpoint, and despite the fact that you have no skills, chops, or talent, you just go ahead and do it anyway. I felt that they were doing something that was so neat, cool, and right on that I volunteered me and Weber to be their backup band."

Stampfel and Weber played on the Fugs' first album in 1965, a jugband-cum-folk-rock hunk of sloppiness that did its best to explode lyrical taboos against drugs, sex, and leftist politics. Weber contributed "Boobs a Lot," which would become one of the most beloved/notorious items in both the Fugs *and* the Rounders' repertoire. Yet by mid-'65, the Stampfel-Weber partnership had ruptured, because of Weber's obstinate refusal to rehearse new songs. The Rounders were put on hold, and Stampfel left the Fugs, which he regrets to this day—"by '66, they were really a good band."

ESP Records, however, helped rebuild the Stampfel-Weber team by getting them back with the studio in 1967. Sam Shepard, now one of America's most re-spected playwrights, was in tow as drummer, having met Stampfel in late 1966 when Peter was getting his fiddle out of the pawnshop. The Rounders were now more of a rock band, but the result was, even by Rounders standards, unholy drug-crazed chaos. "We went into the studio, and basically hadn't played to-gether for a couple of years," explains Stampfel, without trying to make excuses. "The reason the record sounds so crappy is that Weber wouldn't rehearse."

What Stampfel diplomatically terms as Weber's "obstreperous" qualities would also hinder the sessions for their next recording, on the larger Elektra label. Peter went to producer Frazier Mohawk and said, "'The reasons this sounds so crappy is because Weber wouldn't practice, blah blah blah. You want a record to sound good, ya gotta stand there with a gun pointed at his crotch, cock the trigger, and say practice, motherfucker!' He said he would. Then when it was time to actually rehearse, when we all got to California, he said, 'Okay, everything's fine, I talked to Weber, he'll be great. I'm gonna get some coffee—go practice.' Of course, Weber didn't want to do that. So again, we went into the studio absolutely cold."

Stampfel makes it clear that he holds no love for the record, but *The Moray Eels Eat the Holy Modal Rounders* is a pretty cool artifact in its own right. By far their most psychedelic outing, its deranged segue of incomprehensible folk-rock, with prominent elements of jugband, country, blues, ragtime, and druggy madness, is like a rawer, even more crazed counterpoint to the Mothers of Invention's *We're Only in It for the Money*. "My Mind Is Capsized" and "Half a Mind"—the latter a psychedelic blues-rock stomp sung with all the finesse of Rodney Dangerfield on mescaline—are typical of the lyrical focus on a record that ends with a mangling of the Pledge of Allegiance. As it turns out, it wasn't even the Rounders' idea to make the songs run together as an uninterrupted suite. "Both of the engineers decided it would be a cool thing to make the records without any grooves between the songs, 'cause it would be more psychedelic or something. And also, I stupidly didn't go to the mixing session. I didn't realize, at the time, going to mixing sessions was key when you're making an album. I'm a very slow learner, and often have to do things the wrong way many times before I get the hint."

"Bird Song" would give the Rounders whatever slim national attention they received when it was used in the *Easy Rider* soundtrack, but Stampfel, again, doesn't exactly harbor glowing memories of the music. "God, what an awful cut!" he exclaims. "I just heard it about a year ago, and I was incredibly embarrassed. Peter Fonda heard it on the radio—one of the few times the record was played on the radio—and thought that would be perfect for the movie. It was good luck that it got used."

The group were clearly having trouble finding the right balance in the studio, and the pendulum swung in the opposite direction with *Good Taste Is Timeless*. Recorded in Nashville with ex-Elvis Presley guitarist Scotty Moore as engineer, some of the musicians had trouble letting loose in the studio, leading to a record that, in Peter's words, "is kind of stiff, although it has its moments." Shepard had left to write a movie for the Rolling Stones, *Maxigasm*, which was never filmed. New members were recruited, and "suddenly we had a really good rhythm section, which we really hadn't had before that, as well as a saxophone player. At that point, the band began to become really interesting."

But the group—never too stable a unit to begin with—began disintegrating after first moving to Boston (Peter continued to live in New York), and then to Oregon, at which point Stampfel left for good. With the exception, that is, of periodic reunions, a couple of which were captured on record. In the eyes of most critics, however, Stampfel's finest work was reserved for the *Have Moicy!* album, a collaboration with Michael Hurley and Jeffrey Fredericks that became one of the most critically acclaimed folk records of the last 25 years. "Everyone just happened to have a bunch of really great songs," says Stampfel. "The stars were right, the moon was in Cleveland."

Despite, as he puts it, being "spleenful, bileful, moaning, groaning, complaining and whining about the misfortunes of the past," Stampfel retains a good deal of pride in the relatively few Rounders albums that came out, in his eyes, halfway right. He's prouder, it seems, of his several post-Rounders projects in the 1980s and 1990s, including albums with the Bottlecaps, and a 1995 record (*You Must Remember This*) with warped, affectionate interpretations of "obscure pre-rock pop songs" (although the James Bond theme "Goldfinger" sneaks on as well). It's his favorite among all the records he's done to date, and he has several more in the pipeline, including a completed album with guitarist Gary Lucas (who has also worked with Captain Beefheart, Jeff Buckley, Kevin Coyne, Joan Osborne, and many others in addition to playing with his own groups). His most distinguishing characteristic remains that one-of-a-kind voice, a wavering, gleeful, careening yelp that inspires either warm-hearted smiles or sincere loathing.

The Rounders, he notes, "were too screwed up to capitalize on our positive aspects. There was just too much drugs, alcohol, and bad attitude in the band, and too many fucked-up characteristics, combined with a lot of bad luck, to have anything happen." Yet when he reunited with Weber for a series of Holy Modal Rounders shows in 1996, "it was a delight and a joy. Performing with him was really fun. I didn't expect to have such an enjoyable time." This despite the fact that Weber, who's been "multi-abusing since the '50s," is now nearly toothless. He's also prone to interrupt the sets mid-song with non sequiturs, and verbal expressions of displeasure and disinterest. At the gig reviewed by the *New York Times*, he spotted his fiancée in the audience and began, in critic Neil Strauss' account, "improvising a song that detailed their problems in the bedroom." On top of all that, reiterates Stampfel, "He still doesn't like to rehearse. Getting him to work on a new song that has more than three chords is like pulling teeth."

So what keeps the collaboration going after over 30 years? "I've been focusing on all the good parts of what we do together. Accentuate the positive and eliminate the negative. Sometimes when he is bad and fucks up, it's actually kind of interesting and funny. So it isn't a case of whenever he does something bad or wrong, it's a disaster or tragedy. On the other hand, it's a real pain in the ass!" he whispers. "For years I just didn't want to have anything to do with him, because of all the disappointments and betrayals. But we do fit each other in this really unique, bizarre, really strange way. People mellow out when they get older, and are more aware of how precious the positive aspects of anything that you happen to be involved with are. That's why I'm trying to go in the direction of doing as much recording with Weber as I can, as long as he's still around."

Recommended Recordings:
The Holy Modal Rounders (1964, Prestige). The group at their most traditional, although by most standards this is still fairly twisted. *Vol. 2*, also done in 1964, is similar, although as Stampfel has said, the material isn't in the same league as the debut.

The Moray Eels Eat the Holy Modal Rounders (1968, Elektra). One of the very oddest records from a very strange era. This montage of acid folk is highlighted by the deranged "Half a Mind" and "Bird Song," the latter of which was tapped for the *Easy Rider* soundtrack.

ESP Records

The Holy Modal Rounders' *Indian War Whoop* and the Fugs' first album were but two of the more high-profile releases on ESP, arguably the first label dedicated to "underground" music. Its radical intentions were apparent from its very first release, an album of songs and poetry in Esperanto, the international language. The record was about as much as a commercial success as the language itself. When Esperanto Disk, as the label was then called, shortened its name to ESP, the product would become only slightly more mainstream, whether ESP was issuing avant-garde jazz, bohemian folk-rock, or experimental audio collages.

ESP was founded by attorney Bernard Stollman in 1963. As a music lawyer, he had "attracted a clientele of pretty desperate musicians who were composers in a new idiom." This was the outside jazz of New York-based performers who were taking the innovations of John Coltrane to even more extreme levels—in Stollman's words, "the spiritual descendants of Ornette Coleman and Cecil Taylor. They were totally ignored by the established industry. The record companies *could* not bear them, *could* not stand to listen to them. I quickly concluded that the thing to do was record them."

In its early days, ESP issued groundbreaking free jazz by Albert Ayler, Pharoah Sanders, Sun Ra, Ran Blake, and Paul Bley. Long before he was cranking out wallflower fusion, pianist Bob James went way outside on his 1965 ESP release, *Explosions*. But Stollman wasn't interested in achieving commercial success, as demonstrated by his method of operations, which were, um, unconventional, to say the least.

"ESP never had a staff producer," he remarks. "There *were* no producers. I never asked an artist whom he was going to use in his group, or the size of the group. They picked the time they wanted to go into the studio. They picked their own repertoire. There was no post-mixing of any kind. What you heard was what you got. I would call it an ideal environment for a serious musician."

Most record industry officials would rather give up their mistresses than play by such nonexistent rules, but in Stollman's eyes, "these were highly disciplined people who were ready to be heard and ready to be recorded. A typical session would last 45 minutes. Within two hours they'd be out of the studio. They had already spliced the tapes. The engineer would sequence the tape and splice them. One could say that economy and brevity were the order of the day. There were no second takes—ever. So there was no question about what to do with an outtake. There simply weren't any. They laid down the music they wanted to be heard. There was no rehearsal necessary. That was a very, very good environment in which to do a very, very ambitious program with very modest cost."

Stollman's just getting warmed up. "You must understand that ESP did not audition artists. The vast majority of the artists neither brought me demo tapes, nor did they audition. I happily did not have to make decisions. The artists themselves made the decisions for ESP. They nominated each other. They nominated the people they had played with before, and would choose to play with again. It was a community of equals. I think that's why the label has a certain cohesiveness, or a certain level of expression. Because these people were a community." The artists would often supply the artwork for their records themselves—which, along with the fact there were usually not allotments in the budget for color separations, gave most of the releases a stark black-and-white, newspaper-graphics feel.

By the mid-'60s, this community had begun to extend beyond the jazz into the burgeoning underground rock movement. In New York City, the poet laureates of that scene were the Fugs, who—after making their first album on Folkways (soon reissued on ESP) with Holy Modal Rounders Peter Stampfel and Steve Weber—became a natural fit for the ESP label. "When they actually came to us and asked to be recorded, I was ecstatic," says Stollman. "Because I knew I had a group that, culturally at least, had its own statement to make. Sure, they weren't musicians, really, at all. But they were poets, and I was very much taken with their statements; I consider their work very important. They were also, of course, vehemently anti-war, anti-Vietnam. This was our first project as a record company to confront the war, and try to deal with it in the media. It had its consequences, some of which were not exactly highly favorable to our survival."

In particular, Stollman is referring to the Fugs' second album (*The Fugs*, 1966), a landmark effort that smashed many popular musical taboos against lyrical references to raw and enthusiastic sex, anti-war protest, drugs, government hypocrisy, and profane language—all to a catchy, hard folk-rock beat. The LP actually made it into the *Billboard* Top 100—an amazing feat for a tiny, avowedly uncommercial label. But, according to Stollman, ESP wasn't seeing much in the way of dividends.

"With respect to chart activity, it was interesting, because our sales did not reflect that. At that time, there were no federal anti-bootlegging statutes. Because of the very careless and slipshod operation that I ran, my pressing plants were able to go into business on our product. I'm fully convinced that the chart position was warranted by sales in the stores. But we didn't share in it because there was no way we could control what the plants were doing, and we were not even fully aware of it."

In his liner notes to the Fantasy reissue of the record, Fugs leader Ed Sanders remembers being told "that the Mafia was illegally manufacturing Fugs records and selling them." Stollman declines to cite the Mafia in particular, but emphasizes, "It should have been very profitable for us. It wasn't, because the plants were doing business through the back door with distributors. So our jazz product sat on their shelves, while they did brisk business in our pop product." Stollman also thinks the same thing may have happened with another ESP album that managed to scrape the pop charts (by Pearls Before Swine).

There was also some reluctance to handle a record with songs like "Kill for Peace" and "Dirty Old Man," no matter who was supplying the vinyl. "At one point, our distributor in

Indiana called me, or I called him. He was a very genteel, nice man. But he said, 'Bernard, I got a problem. I was playing golf the other day with the governor. He turned to me as were on the links and said, I don't want those dirty Fugs in my state.' There were no sales."

In any case the Fugs, after supplying just one record to ESP, moved to Reprise— Frank Sinatra's label—in search of a bigger audience. There was some bad feeling between Stollman and Sanders after ESP put out some Fugs outtakes. "It was the one instance in which I broke with the credo that I had established for the label, which was: the artists alone decide what you will hear on their ESP disc. In that instance, I violated that. It was very stupid on my part. I think Ed had every reason to be enraged that we had put out material that he had not previously determined that he wanted to have out. At that time, I guess they were a little bit nervous about songs like 'CIA Man' being issued."

Stollman continued to issue records of even less commercial rock groups. Pearls Before Swine landed on ESP as a result of a demo tape from a young Floridian named Tom Rapp; his group slept in Stollman's parents' living room when they came to New York to record. The Holy Modal Rounders unleashed their most crazed offering, *Indian War Whoop*, in 1967. The Godz stripped rock songs to repetitive, amateur minimalism with violin and plastic flute augmenting the standard guitars. The results, depending on your viewpoint, either anticipated the breakthrough of punk ten years later, or were marginally less pleasant to endure than the sounds of cats trapped inside concrete walls. "I was inordinately attached to the Godz," admits Stollman. "What they did was, in its own way, iconoclastic and liberating. I think they certainly did help to influence the punk movement."

All along the way, ESP continued to issue outside jazz comparable to little else from the period or since, such as pianist/singer Patty Waters, who would move in a heartbeat from whispery jazz ballads to hair-on-end, Yoko Onoesque vocal improvisations/contortions. There were also such defiantly uncommercial projects as an audio newspaper, *The East Village Other* (including a contribution by the Velvet Underground, "Noise," on which their rays of feedback fight it out with a broadcast of the marriage of President Lyndon Johnson's daughter). On *No Deposit, No Return*, Fug (and noted poet) Tuli Kupferberg read the ads.

The ESP operation came to an end in 1974. According to Stollman, whenever some cash was realized by the label's sales, "we turned the proceeds into making new jazz product, for the most part. Which is a wonderful opportunity to drive yourself into the ground, because jazz sold minuscule amounts. We effectively defeated ourselves. The rules of commerce are pretty rough. If you don't understand the rules and you can't deal with it, then you shouldn't be there. And we probably should not have been in business.

"In retrospect, I think it would have been much more intelligent for ESP to have been producing for other companies. There were certain indications that we could have done that. At one point, Warner Brothers called us through an intermediary and asked whether we were interested in being acquired." If that had been the case, however, it's unlikely that the German label ZYX would have licensed the ESP catalog for CD reissue in the early 1990s—every damn last one of them, numbering about 125 in all. Noted longtime underground rock critic Byron Coley is now co-writing a book on the label with Thurston Moore, guitarist of Sonic Youth.

Now the Smithsonian is trying to work out a relationship with ESP whereby ESP will be part of the Smithsonian archives, and Smithsonian Folkways Records will reissue ESP titles on CD. (The Smithsonian has also asked a reactivated ESP to document the current New York "new music" scene.) The label that was once banned by the governor of Indiana will now be archived by the nation's most prestigious scholarly institution. Sometimes life really is stranger than fiction.

The Holy Modal Rounders. Credit: Courtesy Peter Stampfel

Comic Relief

For many collectors and **trainspotting rock** enthusiasts, rock cultism is a deadly serious business. Records are not so much to be enjoyed as to be catalogued; the human stories behind the grooves are not as important as the dates, chart statistics, and family trees. We rock historians need occasional reminders of that mysterious outside world that relies not so much on obscure anecdotes and little-heard flop records as day-to-day jollies. Thank God, then, for that unexpected phone call from a cult legend man enough to bellow into the phone, "This is Swamp Dogg!"

Swamp Dogg, as you'll read, is a funny guy. He could have been a standup comedian. So could Screaming Lord Sutch, and Neil Innes of the Rutles. Yet all are extremely serious about their music. If they come off as clowns sometimes, there's a lot of thought and skill behind the jokes. Those who find them light-weight company in the midst of ultra-serious *artistes* such as Scott Walker and Nick Drake might consider how the role of comic rocker is perhaps more diffi-cult than that of any straight man. It's hard to be funny; it's hard to make good music. It's exponentially harder to be both at once. Frank Zappa managed it (much of the time, anyway), but few others have achieved anything like mass success with this approach, contemporary hardy-har-har jokers Ween aside. The Fugs and the Bonzo Dog Band (from which Neil Innes graduated) also had a brush with commercial success, to the extent that they could be considered just a little too renowned for a book such as this.

The ghettoization of these three particular artists into one corner of this book shouldn't be taken as a slight upon their purely musical abilities; each

The Rutles and their moptops, 1996. Credit: Courtesy Virgin Records; photo Timothy White

could have easily been placed under another category. It should also be noted that many, perhaps most, of the other figures throughout this volume made humor a vital component of their work. If you can wade your way through the repertoire of Syd Barrett, Skip Spence, the Holy Modal Rounders, or the Hampton Grease Band's "Maria" without breaking into smiles, you really have been holed up with those Smiths records for way too long.

The Rutles

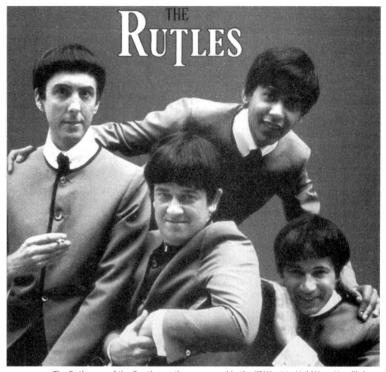

The Rutles spoof the Beatles as they appeared in the "I Want to Hold Your Hand" days. From left to right: Eric Idle, John Halsey, Rikki Fataar, Neil Innes.

"What are you, a pervert?" Neil Innes asks me. I've just told the head Rutle that, at the age of 16, I watched the original NBC broadcast of the Beatles satire *All You Need Is Cash*—which, according to Neil, has the distinction of being the lowest-rated prime time show ever. "Oh, you were gated or something?" he chides. "You could have watched *Charlie's Angels!*"

For a low-rated 1978 TV special, *All You Need Is Cash* has proven to be surprisingly durable, getting reissued on video (it's currently available on Rhino). The same could be said of the Rutles, the group that cleverly deflated the Beatles myth with humor and respect. The Rutles self-titled album was reissued on CD by Rhino in 1990, with six previously unreleased bonus tracks, no less. The 1990 compilation *Rutles Highway Revisited* (on Shimmy Disc) featured 20 alternative bands, such as Shonen Knife and Galaxie 500, covering the Rutles repertoire, in what is surely one of the few examples of a "tribute" album to a band that never existed.

And now, just as the Beatles' own *Anthology* project is coming to a close with the October 29, 1996, release of *Anthology Vol. 3*, the Rutles have coun-

The Rutles, reunited in 1996. From left to right: Rikki Fataar ("Stig O'Hara"), Neil Innes ("Ron Nasty"), and John Halsey ("Barry Wom"); original Rutle Eric Idle ("Dirk McQuickly") declined to participate in the reunion. Credit: Courtesy Virgin Records; photo Timothy White

tered with their own *Archeology*, which purports to be a similar exhumation of previously unreleased material (although in fact most of it was recorded in the mid-1990s). When I catch up with Innes in autumn 1996, he's just returned to England from a promotional jaunt to New York, where the Rutles mimed some material on the rooftop of The Hard Rock Cafe (in a spoof of the famous rooftop concert from the Beatles' *Let It Be* film).

Along with Spinal Tap, the Rutles are one of the very few successful rock parody bands, perhaps because of the very real affection the project holds for its satirical targets. One of the key ingredients to its acclaim among Beatlemaniacs and general viewers/listeners alike was the songwriting of Neil Innes, who played Ron Nasty, the counterpart of John Lennon, in the video itself. Peppered with musical and lyrical quotes from actual Beatle songs, Innes' Rutle tunes turned the Beatles into something recognizably Beatleish but quite silly, as if Lennon-McCartney had been filtered through Monty Python. "Help!" inspired "Ouch!"; "Penny Lane" became "Doubleback Alley"; "I Am the Walrus" mutated into "Piggy in the Middle." Other song titles were less explicit, but similarly mocked all phases of the Beatles' journey, from their Hamburg rocker days through bouncy British Invasion ditties and Indian-influenced psychedelia.

The Monty Python influence was unsurprising, considering that Innes had collaborated with Python member Eric Idle on a British comedy series in the mid-'70s. A friendship between Idle and Harrison resulted in a satirical film clip of the Rutles, performing what was obviously a spoof of the concert scene from *A Hard Day's Night*. After it was shown on *Saturday Night Live*, the show's producer, Lorne Michaels, convinced Idle to develop a full-length Rutles television movie for NBC. Idle ended up playing Paul McCartney's doppelganger, Dirk McQuickly, in the "documentary" (although, unlike the other original Rutles, he doesn't play on the soundtrack recording, to which the late Ollie Halsall heavily contributed). The lineup was filled out by drummer John Halsey, guitarist/bassist Rikki Fataar, and Innes, who was told to come up with some suitably comic Beatlesque tunes pronto.

Many viewers who watched the Rutles were unaware that Innes was a veteran of a fine British comedy rock outfit, the Bonzo Dog Band, which released several albums in the late '60s. Not only that, Innes had already met and worked with the Beatles themselves on more than one occasion. In September 1967, the Bonzos played "Death Cab Cutie" in a scene at a London strip club for the ill-fated *Magical Mystery Tour* film. A bit later, Paul McCartney himself produced the Bonzos' "I'm the Urban Spaceman," a Neil Innes tune that would become their only big British hit.

Yet when Innes was given the assignment of writing the Rutles soundtrack, he admits, he was hardly a Beatles expert. "I'd never been a *fan* fan, you know what I mean?," he says over the phone, after interrupting a fight between two of his cats. "I'd been aware of that music from what I'd heard, and I enjoyed it. At the time of the Bonzos, the Beatles were certainly everywhere—'Here, There and Everywhere.' But the thing that made me sit up was that 'Penny Lane' song. I thought that was really an excellent piece of songwriting and recording and routining. That's what made me think there was a lot more to them than these sort of happy-go-lucky tunes."

All You Need Is Cash was filmed with some degree of cooperation from the Beatles themselves. George Harrison played a small role in the film, and Idle got clearance to use actual Beatle documentary footage of audiences and concert backgrounds to add authenticity to the scenes in which the "pre-Fab Four" play Shea Stadium, receive greetings from the Queen, and so forth. Mick Jagger, Bianca Jagger, Paul Simon, and much of the *Saturday Night Live* cast also took cameo roles in the final production. And, of course, you couldn't go to all this trouble without a soundtrack album. That's where Innes' contributions became invaluable.

"I put as much as I could into the songs, because it would be all too easy to just knock off something," reflects Innes. "I wanted the songs to have something tangible in them, so that the rest of the jokes would stand up. It's not that rigorous a copy of anything. It's more or less something that's done in the spirit of something, and as a celebration of something, rather than a parody.

"There have been some sharp things said in reviews, assuming that I want to sort of take the piss out of the Beatles, or demean it in any way. Nothing could be further from the truth. I don't know how they hear that in there. I want to go on record as saying that I've always admired the Beatles' music, and it was fun to do the Rutles in the first place.

"It was useful to *them* that we did it in the first place," he adds. "The first time the Rutles came into existence, there was a reason for it, and that was to almost tell the story of the Beatles in the silliest possible way, with their approval. And it kind of got the pressure off them to get back together."

But how *did* the Beatles react to seeing their story retold "in the silliest possible way," whether it's Eric Idle pulling lemon-sucking faces as Paul McCartney's counterpart, or Neil Innes taking a fully clothed shower with his neo-Nazi bride, in an apparent caricature of Lennon and Yoko Ono's conceptual art pieces? "Paul was not too pleased," admits Neil, "although he'd given clearance, like the others, for us to use footage that Apple had. Paul had an album out called *London Town* when the Rutles came out. Everywhere he went, everybody was sort of asking what he thought of the Rutles. I don't think it went down at all well, because of all the people playing the characters, I think Eric was a bit hard on Paul, with his sort of funny faces and whatnot. But I saw Paul two years ago, and he said, 'No problem, it's all under the bridge, it was all a lot of fun.' Ringo, I gather, he sort of liked the first part, not the second part. And John was quite fascinated by it."

Without a proper Beatles reunion in the offing, the *All You Need Is Cash* soundtrack (initially released on Warner Bros.) may have been the next best thing. The resemblance was too close to comfort for ATV Music, which, according to Innes, "bullied my publishers into giving them half of the royalties without going to court. My publishers just abandoned it. They put it to me as if, 'Yes, but Neil, even if we do win, we might not get costs!' Effectively, that's why I didn't have much more to do with the music business. It's not a very pleasant business. It was always crooked when it began, and if there's anything good in it now it's the people further down the chain who actually enjoy music. But the rest of it is pretty corrupt, I'd say."

Which didn't stop the Rutles—sans Idle ("he could have been more involved if he'd wanted to be") and Halsall, who had died in 1992—from recording *Archeology* as a trio, with a little help from many friends. A few bona fide archive tracks that remained from the late 1970s were dusted off, but most of *Archeology* was written and recorded fresh. As the Rutles had never properly existed in the first place, they carried little baggage to the reunion in terms of impossibly high expectations or previous internal friction. Most rock reunions are doomed to failure for these reasons, and the relative absence of these factors may explain why the Rutles' long awaited "follow-up" is about as delightful as their first album. Innes' ability to mimic and quote classic Beatle cuts remains undiminished—indeed, his referencing of obscure cuts like "I Will" and "Savoy Truffle" is so subtle that many of his sources don't emerge until after several listenings. The musicians also achieve, ironically, a much more accurate approximation of the "classic" Beatle sound than other acts which deliberately set out to imitate and re-create the world's most famous rock band.

Given that Innes is not a confirmed Beatleologist, he's got an uncanny knack for emulating all eras of the Beatles' evolution, whether simple boy-girl songs, psychedelic mysticism, or nasty Lennonesque surrealism. "The earlier songs are harder to write," he allows. "I had to try to think about where I was, what age I was, when those songs first came out. Well, go back even younger maybe, remembering my first date or something like that, the first kiss or something, and the power of those relationships. They're basically simpler songs. So you've got to come up with a reasonable, simple tune that's different.

"Even though you've got the chords, it's how you play the riffs. That's where it starts to sound similar. A lot of people are just completely taken in by that. They think that's a deliberate lift. But in fact if you were to do a real study, you can probably say, well, that was in some other band in the '60s that did that riff, or that one came from Bo Diddley.

"I like the idea of the Rutles actually becoming a verb," he concludes. "To Rutle, to sort of copy somebody you admire. In that sense, the Beatles were Rutles too. Because when they started, they were copying Elvis Presley and the Everly Brothers and Little Richard—all the best of rock and roll of *that* era. I think that's the way music goes around."

Recommended Recordings:
The Rutles (1978, Rhino). The soundtrack to *All You Need Is Cash,* reverently mutating everything from "I Want to Hold Your Hand" and "If I Fell" to "Get Back" (on "Get Up and Go") and Lennon's surreal wordplay ("Cheese and Onions"). Originally released with 14 songs, the Rhino CD reissue adds six more tunes that were recorded for the film in the late '70s, but not included on the LP.

Archeology (1996, Virgin). The successful "comeback" finds their talent undimmed, though this is somewhat less wide-ranging in its scope than the original Rutles record, concentrating more on facsimiles of the Beatles' late period.

Recommended Video:
All You Need Is Cash (1978, Rhino). Still the best mock "rockumentary" this side of *Spinal Tap,* and the perfect footnote to deflate any sadness you may feel after getting through all ten hours or so of the Beatles' own *Anthology* videos.

The various guises of Screaming Lord Sutch: rock 'n' roll politician (top), knife-wielding ghoul (bottom right), and inventor of the Flock of Seagulls hairstyle (bottom left). Credit: Courtesy Screaming Lord Sutch

Screaming Lord Sutch

Wind howls, rain swirls and a coffin slowly creaks open. An agonizingly elongated, *Phantom of the Opera* scream shakes the stylus for a good 15 seconds. Screaming Lord Sutch, the prince of horror-rock, is most definitely in town. It's hardly the stuff that hit singles are made of. Especially a debut effort in late 1961, in the dark days of British rock, well before the Beatles and the Stones have steered the country away from wimpy teen idols.

No one could have predicted Sutch would be something of a national institution 35 years later, known more for his satirical political campaigns than his music. And if the man himself approached you in the pub and claimed to have been at the helm of a band that counted Jimmy Page, Jeff Beck, Nicky Hopkins, Ritchie Blackmore, and other luminaries of British rock among its ranks before any of those musicians became famous, you'd most likely dismiss him as a Loony. Which might have been wholly appropriate, given that the Lord has been long-standing ringmaster of the Monster Raving Loony Party.

The thing is, it all happens to be true. There have been no hit singles for Screaming Lord Sutch in his 35-plus-year career. In the United States, his name evokes only blank stares, although he continues to visit the British papers with regularity. But it's no exaggeration to state that few rock musicians have been there and done that as much as Screaming Lord Sutch—Dave to his friends—has in his 55 years. You could write a book. And Dave has, as a matter of fact (*Life As Sutch*, Fontana, UK).

In the late summer of 1996, Sutch is gearing up for the next British general election, providing the real-life equivalent of Monty Python's "Silly Party" to inject some humor—and some valid concerns—into a debate that's often riddled with clichés. His onstage graveyard image is no joke: Sutch politely warns the unwary not to call his home before 1:30 in the afternoon. When I ring the bell at his London home at 1:30 on the dot, it takes him a while to rouse himself as he putters around in the kitchen and brews some tea. David Sutch is clearly not a morning person.

When Sutch emerged in the early '60s, there were hardly any musicians in the entire country who could play guitars and saxophone with anything approaching a genuine rock or R&B feel. There were rare exceptions, such as Johnny Kidd & the Pirates (who did the original version of "Shakin' All Over") and Vince Taylor (best known for "Brand New Cadillac"). But there was really no precedent for this wildman, running through '50s rock 'n' roll tunes at 100 miles per hour, dressing up in Jack the Ripper costumes, leopard skins, and buffalo horns onstage. Sutch was also the original long-hair, with a coiffure that fell below his shoulders before the Beatles had even introduced their bangs.

"I literally put musical vaudeville to rock and roll," Sutch notes proudly. He also most likely stole a few pages from the book of American wildman Screamin' Jay Hawkins, who would also shriek and snort his way through R&B songs with ghoulish themes, most notably the demented classic "I Put a Spell You." Like Sutch, Hawkins also used coffins in his stage act, though Sutch went one further with his use of severed heads, knives, swords, razors, and onstage impersonations of Jack the Ripper.

Sutch's fascination with Halloween-type imagery made him a natural match for Joe Meek, the mad genius of early '60s British rock production. Their first single, "Til the Following Night"/"Good Golly Miss Molly," established the formula they'd stick to for all of the half-dozen or so singles they made together between 1961 and 1965: a horror-rock novelty on one side, a revved-up R&B/rock chestnut on the other. Nothing else in Britain sounded like that debut 45. The blood-curdling screams of the A-side would have put Alice Cooper to shame, backing a full-throttle attack by the Savages that was highlighted by a futuristic bombs-falling-from-the-sky descending guitar riff on the instrumental break. No less of a thrill was "Good Golly Miss Golly," executed at the tempo of a Japanese bullet train about to fly off the tracks.

It wouldn't have translated to record, though, without the help of ace musicians in his backing band. The Savages employed the cream of the first generation of British rock musicians who had actually grown up with the music. This was especially crucial considering that Sutch's vocals were much longer on enthusiasm and goonish humor than pure talent. Who played what on what session seems to vary according to whom you talk to, but it's certain that Jimmy Page, Jeff Beck, and Ritchie Blackmore can all be heard at various points, way before the Yardbirds and Deep Purple. Nicky Hopkins was a full-time Savage as well, before becoming Britain's top rock session pianist. Matthew Fisher also played with the band, warming up the crowds with the "Whiter Shade of Pale" riff just prior to throwing his lot in with Procol Harum.

Fisher, according to Sutch, "used to start off with a lot of classical music, 'cause he had a Hammond organ. And [drummer Carlo Little] used to throw a bit of chalk at him or cigarette packet and say, 'Shut up, Ethel. That's bloody rubbish, we're a rock and roll band. Our audience see you playing classical music, they'll drop us. So stop with that shit.' Carlo had another gig about a month later, and he was tuning up the organ again with this classical stuff. So Carlo threw a cigarette packet at him and said, 'Stop it. They're coming in now. Play one of the rock and roll.' He said, 'Well, I just did that a couple of weeks ago on the start of a session. The producer went mad on it. He really appreciated it.' [Carlo] said, "We're not making records.'

"The next thing we knew, this guy said, 'That record I made, it's #18 in the charts.' And we said, 'What? 18 in the charts? What are you talking about?' It was 'A Whiter Shade of Pale,' Matthew Fisher on the organ. The same thing he was playing that Carlo threw the thing at him."

Early Savages drummer Carlo Little gave lessons to a young, pre-Who Keith Moon, and also played some gigs with the earliest Rolling Stones lineups (other Savages, pianist Andy Wren and Ricky Brown, also did pickup gigs with the Stones in their early days). "They were just doing Chuck Berry and Bo Diddley numbers in the early days, and they literally got booed off," remembers Sutch about the Stones. "The Gunnell Brothers [who ran the Flamingo Club in London] said to Carlo, 'What're you doing with these idiots? Because you're gonna get nowhere with these. You oughta stick with Sutch and Long John Baldry and people like that you've been with, 'cause they at least headline and go over alright.'

"With that, Carlo was so embarrassed he was in there that he lent over and picked up a cigarette packet and tore it up and wrote on it 'Charlie Watts,' and gave it to Mick Jagger and said, 'Look I can't do any more gigs. Give my mate it. Good friend of mine, covers for me. We cover for each other. Give Charlie Watts a ring. He'll be ideal for you.'" Carlo says now, 'If only I didn't have bent over and picked up that cigarette packet, not only could I own [my] house, but I could own the whole street and probably streets beyond.' But that's life, innit?"

It's ironic that Little was advised to stick with the Savages, as they were really anything but commercial, with follow-ups like "Monster in Black Tights," "Dracula's Daughter," "Jack the Ripper," and the deliriously silly "She's Fallen in Love with the Monsterman." "We couldn't get hit singles," admits bassist Tony Dangerfield, who's played with the Savages off and on since the mid-'60s. "But I don't know where we could have found one from! We were too cult. 'The Ripper' is about as commercial as we could have gotten! We once or twice went in and did things with Joe [Meek] that were sort of bordering on commercial, but it didn't work. Nobody had the heart. It could have blown the whole thing if we had a hit record, you know? The mystique would have gone."

But, as Dangerfield is quick to add, "You could get Liverpool bands—the Searchers, the Big Three—if they were on with us, we blew 'em completely away, even with their hit records. Pretty boys in suits couldn't follow that, in spite of their hit records. We got banned from a lot of places, as the Pistols did when they came, we had all that shit. We were banned from a lot of big chains of ballrooms, due to the act. But we never ran out of work."

Combined with the continuing defection of the Savages to more celebrated bands, that could have meant the relegation of Lord Sutch to a trivia question, except for an inspired brainwave that started as a publicity stunt. "That's why he brought in the political thing," insists Dangerfield, who recalls that manager Reg Calvert urged Sutch to run for Parliament as a representative of the National Teenage Party. "Reg said [to run for office] to keep the gigs coming in, and keep your price up." So it was that Sutch stood for election in August of 1963, receiving the grand total of 209 votes, on a platform that advocated lowering the voting age to 18, the introduction of commercial radio, and the abolition of the 11-plus (a British school examination that separated pupils into certain courses of study at an early age).

Since then, Sutch has run for Parliament about 40 times, usually on the Monster Raving Loony Party ticket, never garnering more than 1,114 votes. Scoff at him all you want, but his platform isn't total nonsense. Many voters lampooned his 1963 platform, yet years later, the voting age had been lowered, and the 11-plus had been abolished. Sutch's attempt at launching a pirate radio station (Radio Sutch) in the mid-'60s foundered, but by the 1990s, there was far more diverse and regionally oriented programming on the radio airwaves. While policies like giving votes to all family pets, "demoting John Major to Private," and "attaching all sitting MPs to a lie detector light bulb, thereby lighting up all of Westminster" are clearly nothing more than comic relief, others are quite workable. It may seem unlikely that all utility charges will be waived for senior citizens to lighten the burden for pensioners, as he has advocated—but they said the same thing about letting teenagers vote, too.

Sutch would like to be remembered as the "first rock and roll politician. The two can be mixed." His political career has been a lifesaver of sorts for his career as well, considering he hasn't recorded much over the last couple of decades. A brief sojourn in California produced a shambling supersession album of sorts also featuring Jimmy Page, John Bonham, Jeff Beck, Nicky Hopkins, and Noel Redding. With his over-the-top live show, he's rarely lacked for live work. In the late '70s, he was acknowledged as a godfather of sorts for the punk/new wave movement, touring with the Cramps and the Damned (both of whom also found horror and rock to be birds of the same feather), as well as the Stray Cats.

And for all his clowning, Sutch is cognizant of his political influence. He draws a comparison between the Monster Raving Loonies and the Green Party, noting, "If they see you get a few votes, they actually are shocked by this, and they look into your policies then. [When the Greens] suddenly picked up a lot of votes, then all the other parties—Conservative, Labor, and Liberal—all picked up on the Green Party's policies. They nicked all their ideas. And now the Green Party's got nothing to say, 'cause all the other parties picked up their policies. But that's the way. They adapted it, and a lot of things have become law."

Or, Sutch declares on the fake million pound note that he prints for his campaign, "Vote for insanity! You know it makes sense."

Recommended Recording:
Story (EMI, UK). Not very easy to find these days (and never easy to find in the U.S.), this has the 1960s Joe Meek sides upon which Sutch's recorded legacy rests. In a sense, Sutch played his aces with the "'Til the Following Night"/"Good Golly Miss Molly" single. But although nothing else makes the adrenaline run as fast, this is good over-the-top fun, with some hot licks by British guitar legends to boot.

Recommended Reading:
Life as Sutch, by Lord David Sutch (1991, Fontana, UK). "The Official Autobiography of a Monster Raving Loony" focuses more on his political career than his musical one, and is given to fancifully mischievous (if droll) recollections of his meetings with the powerful and famous. Could have been better, but it's certainly ticklish in spots.

"If you know the extension of the party with whom you wish to speak, dial it and stop wasting our time! If you have money due us, owed us, or just for us, please wait until this message is over and SCREAM your name! We may be listening!"
—Swamp Dogg's answering machine, February 1997

Swamp Dogg

Twenty minutes after I call his record company, Swamp Dogg's on the phone, ready to schedule an interview. I ask him if the publicist has told him what my book's about. "Sure," he fires back cheerfully. "It's about all the motherfuckers who didn't make it!"

It's already clear that Swamp Dogg the conversationalist is very much like Swamp Dogg the singer: wittily profane, happily bemused by the cruel twists and turns of the music business, and totally fearless when it comes to cutting to the heart of the matter. He's no mere Redd Foxx-as-soul-singer, though. For decades he's bent R&B/soul traditions as far as they can stretch. Funk grooves are wedded to old Fats Domino licks. Raunchy tales of sexual (in)fidelity butt up against lyrics probing social injustice, racism, and the waste of war. His keening voice is a blend of Jackie Wilson, Van Morrison, Percy Sledge, and pure Swamp Dogg, drawing from soul, rock, and even country. He's made about 20 albums since 1970, without getting anything close to what you could call an across-the-board hit. It's black popular music that's too eclectic to pigeonhole—and, for some tastes, too hot to handle in its frank examination/reflection of American society. Even if it *is* funny.

Anyone keeping tabs on Swamp Dogg's early career would have been shocked by the Sly Stone-meets-Frank Zappa tone of his 1970 debut, *Total Destruction of Your Mind*. Born Jerry Williams in Portsmouth, Virginia, he'd spent the entire 1960s, for the most part, as one of dozens of soul journeymen on the underside of the record business. He produced sessions on minor hitmakers like the Exciters, Tommy Hunt, the Toys, Patti LaBelle & the Bluebells, and Charlie & Inez Foxx. He wrote songs with Gary U.S. Bonds, and toured with about half the R&B/soul singers ever to make the hit parade. And he recorded as a solo act for about a dozen labels, sometimes as "Little" Jerry Williams. The lattice of records that he contributed to during this period—as featured act, session man, producer, and songwriter—is so criss-crossed that it's doubtful anyone could assemble a comprehensive list.

Occasionally one of his singles would stir up some minor national action, or become a regional hit: "I'm the Lover Man" (1964) and "Baby You're My Everything" (1965) were the biggest. "At that time, I was in with the norm," says Swamp Dogg. "I was being what everybody wanted, felt they needed. I was just trying to help supply the demand.

"But while I was out there watching what was going on, it hit me that I wasn't nearly as good as those people at the top of the ladder who were *supplying* the demand. My songs were just as good, but I didn't feel that I had as much heart in my songs as they had in theirs. When I sang about being wonderful, I didn't really believe it. 'Cause I've never been caught up in a 'I'm a great lookin' guy, and when I walk onstage, the bitches fall out.' I never believed no shit like that. And I had good reason not to believe it, because it never fucking happened!"

Exit Jerry Williams, average soul singer; enter alter ego Swamp Dogg. "I took a chance and bet on myself. I said, I've got to change everything, and I've got to be drastic in this change. It took a lot for me to make up my mind, because I've always been crazy about my name, Jerry Williams, Jr.—I love my father, I loved carrying my father's name. To have to change it to something just to catch your ear was a heavy decision for me. But that enabled me to jump into some music that I wanted to do, some lyrics that I wanted to do."

With Gary U.S. Bonds, the early soul pioneer noted for dance-party smashes like "Quarter to Three" and "New Orleans," Williams was already starting to write songs that couldn't find a marketing niche on soul or rock radio. "We would do tributes to people who were alive, but we did 'em like they were dead. We thought this was funny. I know that it's sick, but we were doing a lot of sick shit,

Swamp Dogg in an unusually solemn mood. Credit: Courtesy Pointblank Records; photo John Wooler

just for our own enjoyment. Later in the '60s, we started writing some acid-type lyrics. [One song from this period, "Dust Your Head Color Red," would appear on his first LP.] But there was no call for it. People'd say, we don't want this shit.

"I had started writing some songs that nobody—*nobody*—wanted to record. Including Jerry Williams or Gary Bonds or anybody else in our little circle, or outside our circle. That was another reason Swamp Dogg was right on time when he arrived. 'Cause he would sing any fucking thing!"

In his liner notes to the *Best of 25 Years of Swamp Dogg* anthology, Williams writes, "I came up with the name Dogg because a dog can do any-thing, and anything a dog does never comes as a real surprise; if he sleeps on the sofa, shits on the rug, pisses on the drapes, chews up your slippers, humps your mother-in-law's leg, jumps on your new clothes and licks your face, he's never gotten out of character." The unexpected was commonplace on *Total Destruc-tion of Your Mind*, where hillbilly piano licks were jumbled with wah-wah funk guitar, and hard rock riffs with swamp soul. With the exception of Sly Stone, no one else was merging soul and rock styles as effectively, though Swamp Dogg was an even slippier man to get a grip on than Sly.

"My music really didn't change too much," he maintains. "You could hear the same basic chord structure, the same basic grooves, just dressed a little. Put some ragged jeans on the song, and some sneakers instead of Florsheim shoes. I had a hell of a lot of influences that I've wanted to fuse, like Sly Stone and Amos Milburn [the barrelhouse R&B pianist of the late '40s and early '50s]. I wanted to see what the two would sound like together, have a boogie thing running under kind of a funk-rock."

Amos Milburn, however, would probably not have touched the acid-tinged lyrics of "Dust Your Head Color Red" or "Synthetic World." On "Mama's Baby, Daddy's Maybe," Swamp Dogg sang bluntly about uncertain paternity. Even his cover choices were off-the-wall; he tackled racism via Joe South's "Redneck," and opted for a tune by MOR superstar Bobby Goldsboro, "The World Beyond." In 1970, it must be remembered, not many soul performers were writing controver-sial message songs, beyond Sly Stone, Curtis Mayfield, and Motown producer Norman Whitfield. George Clinton and the Parliament/Funkadelic brigade were still feeling their way into progressive funk. Marvin Gaye and Stevie Wonder had yet to establish their identities as socially conscious singer-songwriters. In the world of black pop, Swamp Dogg was an unheralded pioneer in this regard.

His straight dope approach to both sex and radical politics is also a subtle, unacknowledged forerunner of rap lyrics. Does he have a preference when it comes writing about the bedroom or the Pentagon? "Like, do you like chicken better than steak?" he asks rhetorically. (I haven't the heart to tell him I'm a veg-etarian.) "Depends on what's happening. I like one 'bout as well as the other."

Swamp Dogg views his songwriting less as an act of genius than as a reflec-tion of American social and racial turmoil in the late '60s and early '70s. "My thoughts weren't that heavy—what was *happening* was heavy. What I was thinking was right before my eyes. I really didn't have to give it that much thought. I'd just write about it, because it bothered me one way or the other."

The social commentary became more pointed when he signed to Elektra for 1971's *Rat On*. "Remember I Said Tomorrow" projected a sad, dignified anger at the eternal delay of justice for African-Americans. Faced with the prospect of issuing a song called "God Bless America, For What," Elektra got cold feet and simply titled the song "God Bless America." The Irving Berlin Foundation was neither fooled nor amused, and sued Swamp Dogg. Yet in the midst of this was a cover of the Bee Gees' "Got to Get a Message to You," and more oddball expositions of sexual immorality such as "That Ain't My Wife," sometimes written in association with old buddy Gary Bonds.

The cover showed Williams/Swamp Dogg with arms raised in triumph, riding atop a huge white rat—a symbol, perhaps, of the black American getting a ride on the white man's back for a change. Sharing an attorney with Jane Fonda led to involvement with a group called Free The Army, a mixed-media entourage (also including Fonda, Dick Gregory, and Donald Sutherland) formed in opposition to the Vietnam War. They gave a concert at a massive anti-war rally at the Washington Monument, which Swamp Dogg's wife, Yvonne Williams, helped organize. The event yielded a documentary film, which never came out, according to Swamp Dogg, because "everybody started showcasing. It wasn't a Free The Army thing, it was like, watch me and give me a fucking deal. I wasn't a part of that. 'Cause I already *had* a fucking deal."

A deal which would soon fall apart, Swamp Dogg thinks, because Elektra didn't cotton to the idea of such a radical black performer on their roster. "I was with Jane Fonda, we were out protesting the war, and they said, 'We don't need this,' [though] it was alright for MC5 to come onstage and pull their pants down and shit. It was a very strange company.

"When they signed me, they had one black act on the label, the Voices of East Harlem. And when they signed me, they let them go. It was like one to a customer. They didn't want no more black acts. They told me that."

The FBI, he adds, viewed Swamp Dogg as enough of a menace to American society to tap his phone for a while. In addition, association with Jane Fonda was enough to land him a spot on President Nixon's coveted enemies list, an honor he still can't take seriously today. "I wasn't trying to help overthrow the government. I was just trying to enlighten people and say what I thought I had the right to say in a free society. I guess after a while they said, 'This son of a bitch ain't about too much of nothing. He's silly.'"

Those two early '70s albums may count as Swamp Dogg's most consistent works, but there's usually more of the same to be found on the labyrinth of records he's released since then. Trying to keep pace with his career is made all the more difficult by his endless succession of one-off deals. One record to a label seems to be Swamp Dogg's motto, an easy proposition to pull off since his method is to deliver finished product to companies for release before signing deals.

Pointblank's *Best of 25 Years of Swamp Dogg . . . Or F*** the Bomb, Stop the Drugs* is the best sampler of his eternally confusing discography, including such nuggets as "Call Me Nigger." Bedroom politics take another weird turn in "Or Forever Hold Your Peace," in which the singer finds his son about to be married with an all too familiar female acquaintance. Those whose interest is piqued may find the individual albums worth tracking down, if for nothing else than Swamp Dogg's unsurpassed taste in song titles and liner notes (nobody writes a meaner and funnier liner note than Jerry Williams). There's also the oxymoronic cover art—1981's *I'm Not Selling Out/I'm Buying In* shows him standing on a boardroom table in white tails and white hat, surrounded by executive types. 1991's *Surfing in Harlem* shows him doing just that, capped by a contender for song title of the year, "I've Never Been to Africa (And It's Your Fault)"—which, in the words of *Village Voice* rock critic Robert Christgau, "sums up his worldview if anything does."

Snazzy sleeve graphics haven't helped him or his labels shift huge numbers of records that don't conveniently fit into any radio format. Swamp Dogg has described his audience as 99.9% white—a supreme irony, I observe, considering the strong R&B foundations of the music. "I know it!" he responds. "And my messages are black—most of 'em. Black radio never played me that much. The areas I would take off in, it was secondary pop radio. Like [*I'm Not Selling Out/I'm Buying In*] went to #1 the first week out in Montpelier, Vermont. There ain't no niggers in Montpelier, Vermont, man! We don't be fucking around no ski resorts and shit!"

They might love Swamp Dogg in Vermont, but he couldn't make any headway in Nashville when he was signed to a country contract by Mercury in 1988. "Mercury got cold feet," he explains.

"Was it because of the songs, or . . ." I ask.

Swamp Dogg knows what I'm about to say. "It was because of the *color*. And I understood it. My friend [who got me on Mercury] called me after we'd been through months and said, 'This shit ain't gonna fly upstairs.' I said, I understand. Which I did. I didn't want him losing a fucking job trying to drag another black into country music. They had Charley Pride," he states ironically, "and I guess that was enough." He may be getting the last laugh on Nashville; in February 1997, a song he wrote with Gary Bonds, "Don't Take Her She's All I Got," was climbing the country chart as a single by Tracy Byrd. (Swamp Dogg is also certain that Eddie Rabbitt reworked one of his songs into a hit.)

Always a prolific songwriter and producer, Swamp Dogg is juggling several projects when I call him at his Los Angeles base of operations. He's just done an album with soul vet Tommy Hunt, and is getting ready for a blues album with Little Johnny Taylor, as well as an urban-type recording with his daughter. When I mention that he was rumored to have been driving taxis for a living a few years ago, he explodes in laughter. "Ain't no fucking taxis out here! My wife is always telling me, 'you could never drive a fucking taxi,' 'cause I get lost all the time."

He certainly sounds far from a man down on his luck. "When I was in the '70s, I was very wealthy. But I was a fucking basket case. I had a nervous breakdown, I had an identity crisis, and I wasn't happy with the money. I have become everything that I really wanted to be, found myself, got my shit together. Now if I could just reach back and get my fucking money that I had, I'd be cool. Other than that, I consider myself one of the three happiest motherfuckers on earth. And once I get my money . . ."

"You'll be one of the *two* happiest motherfuckers on earth," I suggest.

"My bank'll be the first," he retorts. There's no one-upping the Swamp Dogg.

Recommended Recordings:

Total Destruction of Your Mind/Rat On (1991, Charly, UK). A handy transfer of the first two albums onto a single compact disc. Landmark soul for the thinking person.

Best of 25 Years of Swamp Dogg . . . or F*** the Bomb (1995, Pointblank). It's pretty difficult to adequately represent the scope of an artist with approximately 20 albums to his credit on one 18-song compilation. Yet as of this writing it's the most comprehensive anthology of career highlights, including "Redneck," "Call Me Nigger," and "Or Forever Hold Your Peace."

Swamp Dogg, still the industry outsider, mid-1990s. Credit: Courtesy Pointblank Records; photo John Wooler

Punk
Pioneers

9

It's been written so often that it's become a cliche: Punk music had the liberating effect of smashing the entrenched star machinery of the record business. Anybody could now make a record; almost everybody, it seemed, did. Whether or not you believe this critical orthodoxy (and there's plenty of room for argument), it's undeniable that the punk revolution spawned an unholy mass of vinyl product, on par with the rockabilly and garage rock explosions of decades past. If the goal was anti-stardom, however, many of these acts succeeded all too well. The sheer quantity of releases ensured that many punk groups would go relatively unnoticed, their influence barely acknowledged. As with other kinds of cult artists, it would take a good couple of decades before many of them were truly discovered by a wide audience of informed rock listeners.

Like any other genre, punk spawned a multitude of hopelessly derivative groups that made it difficult to detect the truly unique ones. Even those who dislike punk (and there are still many who do, even among cult rock collectors) would have to admit that there was more diversity in the form than was apparent on first glance. There are dozens of groups that would qualify for inclusion in this book on those grounds: just look through the *Trouser Press Record Guide*. I can hear the howls of protest already: where are Eater, the Electric Eels, the Sleepers, Crime, the Nuns, Wreckless Eric, or the Adverts? Not to mention the no-wave acts like James Chance, confrontational Brits like the erroneously named Pop Group, or art-damaged indie bands like the Swell Maps?

What we have here, at any rate, is a cross-section of punks from both sides of the Atlantic. If there's any common denominator, it's that ultimately, with the

The Raincoats, in a less frivolous state of mind. Credit: Courtesy DGC Records; photo Eric Watson

possible exception of Crass, none of them were committed to punk as the end-all of artistic expression. Punk happened to be the medium through which they found their initial impetus; all of them evolved into something quite different and unexpected, expanding the boundaries of punk until it had become something rather different, and more interesting. Except maybe, again, for Crass, which came to a conscious stop in 1984 rather than become an institution; in the meantime, they had put their mottoes into action as few punks (or rock bands) before or since.

The Avengers
Penelope Houston

Penelope Houston, then: punk singer in the Avengers, late 1970s. Credit: Marcus Leatherdale

Penelope Houston–punk siren,, screaming "We Are the One" with the Avengers as the opening act for the last show of the Sex Pistols' legendary American tour in January 1978? Or—Penelope Houston, a singer-songwriter, performing maverick alternative folk-rock with a voice more given to soft, wistful sweetness than harsh wailing?

As Houston, now nearing 40, serves me herbal tea in her Berkeley home and snaps sunflower seeds over the kitchen table, it's hard to imagine her as the teenager with a shocking blond brush cut, imploring her audience to ask not what you can do for your country, but what your country's been doing to you. She's still known to many punk fans only for her short stint in the Avengers, one of the first California punk bands, in the late 1970s. In Germany, she enjoys a large following and has been fêted by the press, which has dubbed her "the Queen of Neo-Folk." In her native U.S., despite landing a major label deal after nearly 20 years in the music business, she remains virtually unknown outside of the San Francisco Bay area. Maybe that's due to change—for one thing, this week she's started writing songs with fellow Berkeley resident Billy Joe Armstrong, of punk rock superstars Green Day.

Penelope Houston, now: 1990s alternative folk-rocker.
Credit: Stefano Massei

It's been a strange and fitful odyssey since Houston formed the Avengers about 20 years ago with fellow San Francisco Art Institute students Danny Furious (drums) and Greg Ingraham (guitar). Houston appointed herself singer at her bandmates' warehouse after singing along to records on their PA. There were other punk bands in California at the time—the Nuns and Crime in San Francisco, the Dils, Weirdos, and Germs in L.A.—and the Avengers would play with many of them during their brief existence. What distinguished the Avengers from the pack was their anthemic punk sensibility, as well as a keen sense of political/social critique in tracks like "The American in Me" and "White Nigger."

"At the beginning of the whole punk rock thing, all the bands were really distinct," Houston points out. "You wouldn't confuse Devo with Crime or the Nuns. It was like everybody had their own thing. We were sort of straightahead classic punk before punk turned into its really boring 1980 version, which it continued to be forever and forever."

But punk was much less of a clichéd genre in 1977, when the Avengers attracted the attention of the Sex Pistols' American tour manager, Rory Johnston, who got them an opening slot for the Pistols' notorious show at Winterland in San Francisco on January 14, 1978. Sex Pistols guitarist Steve Jones ended up producing a four-song EP by the group, although Houston clearly wasn't too sold on his skills, re-recording her vocals without him before the record was finished. "He did some piano playing on it—that was funny," she observes dryly. "You won't really know it from listening to it. It's more the thumb going down the keyboard."

Some of the Avengers' mystique is no doubt due to the limited quantity of material that they actually managed to record. There were only two EPs issued while the group were together; embellished by a few previously unreleased cuts, these formed the basis of their only album release, *Avengers*, which didn't come out until 1983. That release itself is now out of print, meaning that the Avengers' legacy is basically unavailable to the current market. With the now-inactive CD Presents label retaining the rights, that situation isn't likely to change anytime soon.

The Avengers' slim recorded output, claims Houston, is due to the limited options for underground indie bands in the late '70s. "Now it's hard to imagine there not being somebody who lives right down the street who's got a record company. Or me, I've got a record company, I put out my own tapes. But back then, there wasn't that whole sense of 'we'll just go in and record something ourselves and do it.' It was kind of like waiting for somebody to recognize that we're this hot little punk band, and that somebody should pay to have us record it."

By 1980, the Avengers had dissolved, and in the eyes of the alternative music community, Houston would all but vanish for most of the 1980s, though in fact she rarely gave up on her musical projects. She moved to Los Angeles briefly to work in film and video. There she also recorded some material in more of a pop-new wave vein; one of the tracks featured string arrangements by one David Campbell, father of '90s lo-fi folk-rap star Beck. In the early '80s, she left L.A. to live in England for a while, where work with ex-Buzzcocks/Magazine songwriter Howard DeVoto resulted in virtually nothing in the way of actual recorded product.

By the time she returned to the States in 1984, Houston in any case had lost interest in punk and new wave sounds. "I was sick of electric guitar," she emphasizes. "I thought, if I have a band without an electric guitar in it, that would be great! I started getting interested in different instruments, from listening to Tom Waits, the Violent Femmes, [and] a bunch of people that were coming up at the beginning of the 1980s with weird sounds."

Arriving in San Francisco to try and collect compensation for the Avengers' album from CD Presents, Houston reconnected with Avengers guitarist Greg Ingraham. The two began writing songs together, but the resulting music owed far more to Houston's early British folk-rock heroes, like Fairport Convention, the Incredible String Band, and Pentangle, than the Sex Pistols. "For a long time, there was no attempt at having anything related to rock in our music," she notes with some pride. "It was all these other influences, like jazz and country and folk, and a little punk. But more of a punk *attitude*.

"I guess it was 1984 that I did my first show that was acoustic. The idea of having these big holes in the music, where there was no sound and then my voice would come out, was the most terrifying thing to me. I thought it was much more frightening than getting up in front of a Marshall stack three-piece band and screaming your lungs out. It was like stepping on a tightrope over this huge hole that was left in the music."

San Francisco alternative audiences remembered Houston as a punk diva, and were not a little unsure what to make of her new sound. "There's a big [traditional] folk scene in Berkeley, and we weren't really accepted by them. And we weren't accepted by the alternative clubs because we were quiet, so we were kind of in a hard place. In fact, I did an interview with (international punk magazine) *Maximum Rock'n'Roll*, and on the air they accused me of selling out. I just thought that was outrageous, because obviously if I wanted to sell out, I'd reform the Avengers and go touring around."

Playing with a rotating group of musicians (including her husband of the time, mandolinist Mel Peppas) as Treehouse, -30- (who issued one single), and finally just as Penelope Houston, it took a few years for her first non-punk album to come out. *Birdboys*, which finally saw the light of day near the end of 1988, was a shock for those who hadn't heard Houston since the Avengers days. Produced by the late San Francisco underground guitarist Snakefinger, the scabrous anthemic rants had been replaced by gentle, haunting folk-rock that relied primarily upon acoustic instruments, including accordion, bells, mandolin, and string bass. Although no longer as explicitly rebellious, Houston's lyrical attitudes were as uncompromising as ever, examining relationships and the struggles of growing into adulthood with a searching melancholy that marked her as a soul sister to such British folkies as Nick Drake and Sandy Denny.

"A lot of people would hear the music I was doing and say, 'Oh, this music sounded really nice and pretty and lovely and stuff. And then I started listening to your lyrics and I just thought, these lyrics are twisted and warped and weird!'" she comments with some amusement. "Some people feel like the music isn't representing the lyric. Other people feel like, the lyric is ruining the music for them. For me, the lyrics have to be there. If I don't like the lyrics, I can't stand listening to the song."

Houston's brand of acoustic rock anticipated some aspects of the alternative-minded pop-rock of Liz Phair and Aimee Mann, two other woman songwriters who addressed tough topics with a direct honesty and feminine perspective, and who would receive considerable commercial and critical acclaim in the 1990s. Houston failed to find a big audience in an underground that was moving from post-punk to grunge. Too dark for the Suzanne Vega crowd, and not noisy enough for your average college radio station, she found herself without a label for several years, resorting to putting out albums as self-released cassettes. In the early '90s, she finally took the chance of going into debt to finance a studio album herself, eventually placing the record with San Francisco-based indie Heyday. The album in turn was licensed to the German Normal label, setting up an unexpected chain of successful events that generated a far bigger audience for Houston in Germany, Austria, and Switzerland than she had ever enjoyed at home. This culminated in her signing to a major label (WEA) in Germany, which in turned licensed her work to Reprise in the States.

It's a roundabout way to get on a major label in the U.S., to say the least. Perhaps realizing that there was a lot of lost time to make up for— Houston, after all, had released about five albums' worth of material, some available only in Europe—Reprise decided to make their first Houston album a sampler of sorts, combining new material with re-recorded versions of some of the most notable songs from her back catalog. When I speak to her on Halloween in 1996, Houston has just gone through the ordeal of firing her band as part of her move from acoustic-oriented music to a harder-rocking sound.

It's time to end the interview with the question she's been asked dozens of times by now: What is the connection between the Penelope Houston that sang punk rock with the Avengers, and the Penelope Houston that sings acoustic-based folk rock with an alternative slant?

"I remember I used to tell people that we were a folk band when I was in the Avengers," offers Houston. "What I meant was that we were just playing music that we made up for our friends. Folk is music that's played by regular people. It's not played by a the court entertainers for the king. It's just the music that people go out on their porch and start strumming, and the neighbors come around. When I said the Avengers were a folk band, I just meant that we were making it up ourselves, that we'd taken it out of the realm of arena rock and the gigantic showplaces, and taken it back to the garage.

"Take a song like 'Glad I'm a Girl,' which is on the last album but was written maybe five, six years ago, when I was in the throes of the acoustic thing. 'Glad I'm a Girl' could be done by a punk band, and it would sound exactly like punk rock. There's nothing about it that would be in any way indicative of being a folk song, or anything like that. If you take the trappings of the music and change it, people think that somehow there's a big change. But actually, good songwriting will lend itself to different interpretations. I think that myself and my attitude towards life and my willingness to express it is the same as it was then."

There's a satisfying irony, then, in the prospect of Houston the former punk rocker teaming up with one of the most successful punk songwriters of all time. "I was just over at Billy Joe from Green Day's house yesterday, and we're going to write some songs together, amazingly enough, for my next album. We sat around talking about how all these people had accused both of us of selling out. I said, at least you have a ten million-selling album to prove that you did!," she laughs. "I sold out, I got nothing." Then she gets more serious. "No, I never sold out. I'm true to my punk attitude."

Recommended Recordings:
By the Avengers:
Avengers (1983, CD Presents). The definitive (and, actually, only) full-length document of the group, including both of their EPs and various other tracks from the 1977–78 era.

By Penelope Houston:

Birdboys (1988, Subterranean). Houston's first folk-rock album maps out the territory she has explored ever since. For eclecticism and purity of vision, she's never exceeded it, either, though subsequent albums have often found her pushing the arrangements from folk to rock.

Cut You (1996, Reprise). A Houston greatest hits of sorts, combining rearrangements of old material (some of which had only been available in Europe) and newly recorded songs.

Never interested in conventional promo tactics, Crass' album sleeves featured montages such as these, rather than straightforward pictures of the band. Credit: G Sus

Crass

"We never were a band. I don't think we even saw ourselves as a band. I mean, we weren't interested in making records. We were interested in making statements, and records happened to be a way of making statements."

Penny Rimbaud, drummer for Crass, is patiently outlining some of the differences between his former, for lack of a better word, *band* and other early British punk groups such as the Sex Pistols and the Clash. "The Pistols and that group, those commercial people, lasted for about two years. They were just an extension of the usual music business tactics. They had no sort of political overview whatsoever. It was us, and bands similar to us, that introduced a meaningful overview into what was then called punk."

It's the end of 1996, and the Sex Pistols, presumably, are counting the millions they've earned from their international reunion tour. Rimbaud, in contrast, is still living in the farmhouse 15 miles outside of London where he and others founded an anarchist commune of sorts in the late '60s. Two other Crass people—singer Steve Ignorant and artist/sleeve illustrator/tape collagist G Sus—continue to reside there as well. Penny and G are in their fifties now, and still trying to live their lives in accordance with the anarchist ideals that many early punk acts gave mere lip service to during their charge up the hit parade.

Crass, however, were never one to compromise their values for something as trifling as hit records. More than almost any band before or since—even militantly "underground" ones—they attempted to put their beliefs into action. Avoiding major labels with a passion, they set up their own company to unleash a blitz of albums with direct attacks upon social injustice, sexism, the Falklands War, and organized religion (not to mention sell-out punk bands). They supported a wide range of anarcho-pacific causes, helped fund an anarchist center, debated the Falklands War with a conservative MP on the BBC, and released vinyl by other hard-hitting punk bands on their label. Crass records were packaged in fold-out posters with striking black and white graphics depicting institutional violence, social horrors, and the odd ray of hope. These were designed by G Sus, who, although her contributions were primarily artistic, was considered as much of a band member as anyone who played an instrument.

With all the colorful controversy and packaging, it might have been easy to overlook the music. Today these releases are recognized as building blocks for the extreme style of punk known as hardcore. Back then, when punk had barely become a widely used term, it was unimaginably difficult and shocking. The songs tended toward impossibly noisy, fast blurs of guitar and drums, with ranting lyrics delivered in thick British accents that were often impenetrable (and literally indecipherable) to American ears.

That made the insertion of lyric sheets doubly important. Accompanying texts could deliver sociopolitical commentary or (in *Christ—The Album*) the fascinating tragedy of a friend who had his soul and mind destroyed at the hands of state mental institutions. Indeed, for those whose taste ran to more melodic punk—like the Sex Pistols and Clash—the words held far more interest than the grooves. As the *Spin Alternative Record Guide* so pithily notes, Crass were "probably the first rock band whose liner notes are not only indispensable, but often better reading than the records are listening."

Crass puzzled, angered, and inspired listeners, some of whom couldn't for the life of them comprehend why any band would display both peace and anarchy symbols at their concerts (as Crass did, with pride). These symbols, however, weren't mere fashion plates. Penny Rimbaud and G Sus, who had known each other since they were teenagers in art school, had been pursuing the anarcho-pacifist lifestyle since the late '60s, when Penny found a house in the Essex countryside that became Crass' base of operations. Crass, it turns out, were hippies. Hippies playing hardcore punk?

For Crass, that wasn't as much of a contradiction as it might seem. "Pen and I both took the whole sort of '60s hippie thing for real," G laughs. "We wanted to have a house that was very open, a safe house, somewhere people could rest and think and share ideas." She goes on to reveal that this most underground of bands counted the most commercially successful rock group in the world as a big influence. "Musically, we were affected by the Beatles a hell of a lot, especially [by] John Lennon and Yoko Ono's stuff. They were a big driving force for us because the sentiments were very similar to our own. We were outright hippies, but hard-edged. I suppose that's why Crass happened."

When they teamed up with other musicians to form Crass, however, they knew that punk was the vocabulary of the moment, even if some of the members had already passed their thirtieth birthdays. "I think we all felt that it wasn't enough to stand up and write a poem or write a book," says G. "It had to be up there on stage. I personally felt very strongly about what was happening to this country, and that youth needed a voice again. Obviously, if you wanted to share what you'd understood up to then, you had to find the right language. And the right language at the time was how we did it with Crass."

Signing with CBS, as the Clash did, was never an option, she adds. "None of us ever believed that you could sing with a big company and think you could play it your way. We always felt that we'd never, ever allow anyone else to dictate how we were going to do it, when we were going to do it, and for how long. For us, it was to share with people, to say, well, just don't hang around waiting for someone else to hand it to you. Just do it." That meant that Crass records sales were chiefly limited to underground punk devotees; it also ensured that the message would be undiluted.

With their debut 12-inch, *The Feeding of the 5000*, it quickly became apparent that not everybody appreciated what Crass had to say. Workers at an Irish pressing plant refused to manufacture the record. The problem was "Asylum," a poem (spoken by Eve Libertine) which described Jesus Christ as pornography, offering (quite literally) vomit rather than prayer to the deity. Initially it was issued with a three-minute silence where the track would have been. When the band pressed it themselves as a single, Small Wonder Records in London was raided by Scotland Yard's Vice Squad, which then paid a visit to Crass themselves.

Rimbaud chuckles at the absurdity of it all. "They couldn't really understand quite why they'd been sent out to a cottage in the Essex countryside to investigate the record. They were completely out of their depth, basically. About six months later, we actually heard that they had decided to drop the case. But we were given a very stern warning not to release any similar material, which naturally encouraged us to release more." As for courting controversy with religious imagery, Crass upped the ante again by naming a 1982 release *Christ—The Album*.

"Asylum" itself was an indication that the band were not content to deliver a steady diet of proto-hardcore, though it could sometimes seem that way after listening to several of their faster numbers (often sung by Steve Ignorant) at once. The third album, *Penis Envy* (Crass never missed an opportunity to make people nervous with their titles), took some listeners aback by switching the focus of the vocals from Ignorant to Eve Libertine and Joy de Vivre (Ignorant, in fact, does not even appear on the record, although he remained a full member of the band). *Penis Envy* actually entered the British charts at #15. The next week, it had vanished from the listings; in the liner notes to the *Best Before* compilation, the band speculate that "it seemed obvious to us that if the major labels paid to get their records 'in' the charts, they'd pay to get ours 'out'."

"Every time we went into the studio, there was the sense that we weren't prepared to give them another one of the same," claims G. "People got comfortable with *Feeding the 5000*, and *Penis Envy* was totally opposite to what people expected. I think it's too easy to record comfortably and know it's going to sell. We tried to push it and take chances each time, and keep to what we wanted to do." There were flashes of sonic diversity as the band's output mounted, with occasional use of tape collages, harmonium, spoken poetry, and even a bit of strings, although noisy, amelodic punk was always more or less at the forefront.

Rimbaud questions the very notion of discussing the band's career in terms of "progress." "I don't think we were in the least bit involved in developing as a band. Our political analysis broadened, then narrowed, and broadened, or whatever it did. And what we produced as a band was a reflection of where we stood politically. It would have been nice to have had that time to think, 'it would be nice to use a C sharp there.' But it wasn't like that.

"I don't think we were involved in any evolutionary process, in the sense that we weren't a band for musical or lyrical reasons. We were a band for political reasons, and therefore increasingly, as the years wore on, we were producing stuff out of response to social situations. Therefore, artistic or aesthetic considerations didn't really come into it. I think we became increasingly angry, increasingly aware of our impotence, which makes our work increasingly more desperate. But it was desperate in response to what was happening in the country, or globally, at the time."

Crass' music reached a height of desperation during the Falklands War, when to come out against Thatcher's military policies was an unpopular proposition indeed. After the release of the "How Does It Feel to Be the Mother of a Thousand Dead" single, a sympathetic MP posed that very question, in exactly those words, to Margaret Thatcher during the prime minister's question time in Parliament. "We were quite hot news at the time, because we'd actually divulged quite a bit of official secrets about the Falklands War," remembers Rimbaud. "We had a contact who was actually serving in the Falklands, so we actually got a lot of classified information sent to us by him, which we were able, one way or another, to sort of get out."

Tory MP Tim Eggar was assigned the task of opening prosecution against Crass on grounds of obscenity. According to Rimbaud, "We ended up on the [BBC] radio being confronted by Tim Eggar. Basically, he was completely flattened by our arguments. At that point, the Tories withdrew. He withdrew proceedings, which hadn't gotten any further than the Director of Public Prosecutions looking at the case."

By this time, Crass were becoming more notorious for their political activism than their actual music. This was especially true in the U.S., where they didn't have a record deal, and their releases were only available as imports in a few specialist shops. They scored one of the most memorable political pranks of recent times when they circulated the so-called "Thatchergate Tapes" among the international press. This finely edited tape collage purported to be a telephone conversation with Thatcher and Ronald Reagan; at one point, the sound bites were manipulated to produce a threat by Reagan to "nuke" Europe in defense of American interests.

"We just really didn't think people would be taken in by it," G laughs heartily. "It just goes to show what you can do." The fun almost went further. "We were very close to getting compromising photos of Dennis Thatcher. The person who had them backed out at the last minute. That would have been *such* a wonderful thing as far as I'm concerned. I would have been *extremely* pleased with that!" Previous to the Thatchergate Tapes, the band had pulled another fast one on the British romance magazine *Brides*, submitting a bathetic number entitled "Our Wedding" under the pseudonym of Creative Recording and Sound Services. The song was given away as a flexi with the publication before the hoax was exposed.

"We were sort of relatively fearless in our attacks and our attempts to confront the authorities," says Rimbaud. "We were constantly testing the boundaries. It seemed that we could do anything that we wanted to do. The only limitation was our imagination."

Not everyone was amused, and Crass were prosecuted for real in connection with a raid on a record shop in Manchester. Crass fought the obscenity charges, winning their appeal, except on one count: one track was still classified as obscene, even though, as Rimbaud recalls, it "actually was a sort of feminist statement about Chinese foot binding." Without missing a beat, he continues, "We were fined peanuts for it. But the case actually had cost us a phenomenal amount of money. We'd been promised money and support from quite a few of the underground distributors and the alternative music biz. But when it actually came to it, we got very little support, and certainly very, very little finance."

Under similar circumstances, the Dead Kennedys would suffer a similar attack in the U.S. a few years later; the breakup of that band can at least be partially attributed to the strain. The obscenity charge, however, wasn't a factor in Crass' dissolution in 1984. The group had always intended to end on that date, even numbering their album releases as a countdown to the Orwellian year. According to G, any question of continuing regardless was squelched by the departure of rhythm guitarist Andy Palmer for art college.

She does admit that by the time of 1983's *Yes Sir I Will*, the climate of Thatcher's reign had dampened spirits. "I think the most significant change you can hear, really, is the total desperation about the Tory government. There's this enormous weight. The fun has gone out of it, really. The jokes are there, but they're very black. I personally didn't want to paint another corpse. A lot of young punks here were immersed in death and disaster. And they were forgetting *why* they were angry. I thought that was very negative."

Adds Rimbaud, "Certain situations were just so appalling, it starts to become sort of absurd to try and deal with it through that medium. Protest rock 'n' roll can just be a joke against the real situation. That was a big question for us over the last few years. Obviously, no musical consideration comes in. The considerations were, should we be doing this at all?"

Crass members didn't retreat from the struggle into their country cottage. Some still live there, true, but they remain extremely busy with other artistic and musical endeavors. Ignorant formed Conflict, and is now playing with a soul-punk band. Rimbaud has published several novels. G concentrated on her own artwork, though she took stock of the past in a collection of Crass-related pieces that was scheduled to be published by AK Press in 1997. A few months before our conversation, both participated in a ten-day anarchist festival in London; Penny did a play, and G presented an art show that also served as a meeting point for a lot of punks that had come to the event from around the world.

The influence of Crass, they maintain, is felt in alternative culture worldwide. The American hardcore punk scene (which certainly borrowed a lot from G's graphics), for instance. But their strategy also lingers in the tactics of British citizens who engage in "road protest" to prevent overdevelopment, or "new age travelers" in England who are determined to pursue an itinerant lifestyle that owes much to anarchist ideals. It's evidence that Crass were doing more than preaching to the converted, or generating stacks of hate mail from irate parents who found *Penis Envy* in the living room. In any case, says G, "I much, much prefer to be a little worm burrowing underground somewhere and coming up in unexpected places. I'm not interested in being a big media personality. I don't think you can get half the stuff done that way. I think Crass is still niggling away down there, and that's great."

Recommended Recording:
Best Before (1986, Crass, UK). With Crass, a little goes a long way. A "best-of," as this is, is a more manageable way to investigate a band that will likely appeal to pretty specialized tastes, no matter what your political sympathies. It has key tracks like "Do They Owe Us a Living" (answer: "Of course they do!"), "Nagasaki Nightmare," "Reality Asylum," and the Falklands War protests "Sheep-farming in the Falklands" and "How Does It Feel to Be Mother of a Thousand Dead." Those with a yen for individual albums might want to start with *The Feeding of the 5000*, which is the band at their most straightahead punkish, or *Penis Envy*, which gives more prominence to female vocalists Eve Libertine and Joy de Vivre than any of their other efforts.

The Dils

As the history of punk rock starts to get etched into stone, London and New York dominate the coverage to an ungodly extent. The unwary might easily believe that nothing was going on outside of those massive metropolises. California punk—an even more brutal variation on the form—is sometimes deemed to have started only after Sex Pistols and Clash imports had made their way into the U.S.

The truth is somewhat more complicated than that. Even before the Sex Pistols and Clash had records out, there were Californian groups blasting out short, sharp shocks of guitar-based, anthemic punk. The problem was that there was no independent label network to ensure adequate representation for such bands on record. The major companies certainly weren't interested—they weren't even releasing Clash and X-Ray Spex records domestically in 1978. Names like the Nuns, Crime, the Weirdos, the Zeros, and the Screamers are now remembered mostly as names on crude posters, or for the smattering of lo-fi indie singles that some were lucky enough to record.

The Dils, left to right: John Silvers, Chip Kinman, Tony Kinman. Credit: Courtesy Chip Kinman, photo Richard Peterson

The Dils were not as lucky as some in this regard, but still luckier than most. In 1977, they managed to scrape together two 45s—"I Hate the Rich" and "Class War"—that matched the energy of anything being generated by the Ramones or the Clash, though their uncompromisingly anti-bourgeois attitude may have borne more similarities to the latter group. They continued to play constantly for the next few years—they even opened for the Clash once. But no more records were forthcoming, until a three-song EP in 1980 that found them already starting to move beyond punk rock.

These three singles would be the sum total of official releases during the Dils' lifetime. An album? Forget it, although a couple of full-length posthumous releases were assembled with the addition of crude, bootleg-fidelity live tapes. "Which is a shame," agrees singer and guitarist Chip Kinman, who along with brother/bassist Tony Kinman, formed the core of the Dils. "I listen to those bootlegs and live records, and those are really great songs. I think it would be a classic, as much as [our] singles are in the micro-world of punk rock classics."

Even before the advent of punk rock, the Dils were not content to be just another band. As teenagers in Carlsbad, California, near San Diego, most of the groups from their high school were hard rock/metal cover bands. Chip and Tony preferred to write their own material ("plus, we weren't good enough to be in a cover band"). The Kinmans moved up to San Francisco in 1976, saw a poster for a gig by the Nuns, and turned up at the venue, only to be told by the owner that the show had been canceled, though the Nuns were receiving visitors at their rehearsal space. The Kinmans were the only ones to take up the Nuns' invitation, which gives you an indication of just how small the punk rock world was in those days.

Chip admits that at the time, he thought that bands like the Nuns and the Weirdos "were better than us. They were more solid-sounding, they were more in a good late-'70s punk rock style. Whereas the Dils were, like, quicker. If this makes any sense, we were at the same time more melodic, and at the same time a bit more dissonant. Tony and I, as much as we tried to not get away from a basic pop structure in all of our bands, just had that basic pop song structure in our mind.

"I think that tended to separate our music from the others, because we actually had bridges and all those kind of riffs and refrains and all that kind of stuff in our music. And it didn't sound forced. Whereas a lot of bands, when they decided that they wanted to get a bit more musical with punk rock, it sounded [like] an excuse for melody. They'd go 'Wo-oh-oh'"—Kinman does a dead-on impersonation of a clichéd punk rock chorus—"and that would be a melody. A three-note descending thing, and they'd go wow, we just wrote a pop song. It's like, well, not exactly, guys.

"We were just as fierce and fast and loud as any of these bands, but we were a bit more musical, which I think helped our music stand up a bit more over time. Because it's not all rage. Rage doesn't wear real well, unless there's something backing it up."

Nevertheless, there was plenty of rage in their debut single, "I Hate the Rich"/"You're Not Blank," recorded in 1977 for the princely sum of $60 (borrowed from Mom Kinman). "I hate the rich, I hate the poor," the Kinmans wailed throughout the minute-and-a-half blast of power chords. Sentiments that would seem to cover most of the rebellious bases, though there was a pop sensibility present even in this fiercest and most basic of Dils songs. Issued on Chris Ashford's tiny What label in 1977, it was one of the earliest California punk 45s, and one of the most highly regarded in the entire genre by collectors.

The session was not your run-of-the-mill debut recording situation. "It was funny, 'cause we played the song, put up the mikes. The guy who engineered it was a hippie, right? He was just like, oh God, what's going on? He probably never even heard of punk rock. We ran in there and played it, and he went, okay, here's your record"—at this point Chip bursts into giggles at the memory. "When he played it back on the monitors, he played it back really loud. Of course in a recording studio, anything you play really loud sounds fucking great. So we were just thrilled. And then of course when I got home and listened to it, it was like oh no! Oh *no!*"

When the song was submitted for mastering, its length—all of 100 seconds—was almost chopped even further by overzealous technicians. "It was so early in the punk rock game that the people who mastered the records had no idea what was going on. They faded it out after the first chorus, and the song doesn't fade out, it has a very definite ending. Tony and I are like, what, is that an editorial statement? Do we suck so hard? Then of course we told them, 'Hey, let the record go to the end.'"

To the first-time listener, "I Hate the Rich" seems to contain definite echoes of the Clash and the Ramones. Chip, however, is careful to mention that the Dils hadn't heard *any* British punk groups at this point, with the possible exception of the Buzzcocks and the Damned. "If there was any influence, it's probably just because we went back to the same sources as the Clash and all those bands did. We listened to reggae music and early rock music, rockabilly, and that sort of thing. We didn't need to rip off the Clash when we could rip off Buddy Holly," he laughs.

A second, similarly no-nonsense punk/pop single, "Class War"/"Mr. Big," appeared on the Dangerhouse label in 1977. From the titles alone, it was apparent that the Dils took punkoid revolutionary rhetoric seriously. Tony called himself a socialist in an interview in the early punkzine *Slash*; Chip wore a hammer and sickle T-shirt onstage. Maybe that's why Greg Shaw of Bomp Records, which released several of the first California punk singles, told the band they were too serious, although an examination of the Dils' entire repertoire reveals that they sang about class war and politics only part of the time.

"At the time, it was something we believed in," says Chip. "We thought, well, this sounds good, that sounds right, this looks wrong, this is what we'll have to do to go about to change this, and we'd thought we'd sing about it through our music. Which we did, but not to the exclusion of singing about girlfriends, cars, sex, what have you. After a couple of years went by and we started reading more and more about this whole communist and left-wing strata, we realized how awful communists really were, what a terrible system it is, how many millions have died under that system. And we decided, well, perhaps that's not such a good idea after all.

"It wasn't an accident. We were out there on the front lines. But we never affiliated ourselves with any of the local or national communist parties and stuff. They always tried to glom on to what we were doing, and we would never let them do it. We said look, all these kids are coming here to see us because we play this music, not because of your stupid little newspaper. So no, you can't come to our show and set up a booth or something. So they all hated us."

Posthumous compilation albums of live material reveal that the Dils had a lot of songs that they never recorded in the studio. Had they been recorded in even a semblance of professional studio conditions, there's no doubt they would have been remembered as among the sturdiest early American punk releases, combining furious energies with a talent for pop hooks and brotherly harmonies. It's difficult to judge their lyrical worth in some cases, however, given that the vocals on these live tapes were so faintly recorded. But if Chip Kinman is to be believed, that's what you might have heard at a live gig anyway.

"In those days—I don't know why we got away with this," he confesses. "But we played our amps on 10. Everything was full up, full blast. Even in Blackbird, which was our massive wall of sound noise band [in the 1980s], I couldn't get my amp over 3 without soundmen pulling their hair out. [We were] just like screaming into the mike. I think a lot of it had to do with the sheer presentation of the whole thing, and that's why some of those tapes, you won't be able to hear the vocals, 'cause probably hardly anyone could either! But it is kind of a shame in a lot of the songs, 'cause we did have some cool harmonies and neat vocal bits worked out."

Running through a succession of drummers over the next few years, the Dils never did manage to record most of their material properly (though to this day, the Kinmans are fielding offers to finally get the tunes cut in the studio). In the 1990s, with dozens of indie releases coming out every week, it's difficult to remember just how little record company interest there was in alternative rock in the late '70s. "No one threw money at the Dils and wanted to record a record," Chip points out. "We certainly didn't have the wherewithal. Jesus, we were poor! I had to go get emergency food stamps at one point in time. We didn't have *any* money. So we couldn't just go out and record ourselves."

The Dils sometimes showed a rootsy bent onstage, covering tunes by Buddy Holly and Roy Orbison. A bit of pop/folk sensibility began to make itself apparent on the final single in 1980, the melodic "Sound of the Rain" especially acting as a signpost to the country/folk sounds of the Kinmans' subsequent band, Rank & File. "The Dils were one of the few punk rock bands that would play ballads," says Chip Kinman. "Most bands wouldn't do it, but we thought it was one of our strengths, to pull something like that off. We thought slowing down was as radical as playing fast. At that point, everybody was getting faster and faster. So we just kind of opened up the sound a bit, added an acoustic guitar, and slowed down. 'It's Not Worth It' [from the final single] was originally like a regular punk rock song, but we slowed it all down and went wow, there's a really nice melody and chord change. And added the acoustic guitar, and of course at the time it was outrageous."

By the 1980s, at any rate, the Kinmans' music was growing beyond the boundaries of punk. "By that time, punk rock was devolving into hardcore. It became codified and a set of rules, like, to be a punk rock band you have to be this. We weren't really interested in that, and figured pretty much that the Dils had said everything that we had to say. It was time to move on musically." The final three-song 7-inch, it turns out, "was kind of a bridge into Rank & File, where we went totally roots."

More unexpected changes were on the way for the Kinman brothers. After playing in country/rock/folk band Rank & File for a few years, they went into quasi-industrial rock with a drum machine for Blackbird. Now they're playing cowboy music in Cowboy Nation, whose record was released two days ago, Chip tells me. Perverse? You betcha.

"Tony and I were always into going against the grain. When we played punk rock, it was against the grain. When we slowed down, it was against the punk rock grain. When we went country, it was against the punk rock grain. When we went noise, it was against the country grain. In almost all our changes, we completely grossed out whatever our audience was before."

Do they still hate the rich? It's fair to say they'll probably never *get* rich. "We're not very good at being corporate or any of that kind of stuff," says Chip merrily, without a tinge of regret. "Never have been."

Recommended Recording:
The Dils (1992, Damaged Goods, UK). This 29-song CD contains all seven songs from their three singles, along with a 1977 demo and 21 songs from various 1978–79 gigs, although the fidelity on the live material leaves much to be desired. Those who want to hear the Dils in a slightly better concert context may want to search for *Live!* (Iloki, 1987). Mostly taken from a 1980 tape, the vocals on that LP have considerably more presence than they do on the live cuts from *The Dils*.

The Raincoats

The Raincoats, from left to right: Gina Birch, Vicky Aspinall, Ana da Silva. Credit: Courtesy DGC Records; photo Eric Watson

"I think music has reached an all-time low . . . except for the Raincoats."
—John Lydon, *Trouser Press*, 1980

"When I listen to the Raincoats I feel as if I'm a stowaway in an attic, violating and in the dark. Rather than listening to them I feel like I'm listening in on them. We're together in the same old house and I have to be completely still or they will hear me spying from above, and if I get caught—everything will be ruined because it's their thing. They're playing their music for themselves. It's not as sacred as wiretapping a Buddhist monk's telephone or something because if the Raincoats really did catch me, they would probably just ask me if I wanted some tea . . .

"I really don't know anything about the Raincoats except that they recorded some music that has affected me so much that, whenever I hear it I'm reminded of a particular time in my life when I was (shall we say) extremely unhappy, lonely, and bored. If it weren't for the luxury of putting on that scratchy copy of the Raincoats' first record, I would have had very few moments of peace."

—Kurt Cobain, June 1993, in his liner notes to the CD reissue of the Raincoats' first album

It would be hard to think of another band that has inspired such glowing praise from the major figureheads of both punk and grunge. Confusing the matter is the realization that the Raincoats aren't truly a punk band at all. Their music eludes easy classification and ready imitation. Feminist punk? Post-punk?

Folk-jazz-dub-new wave? A bridge between the gentle side of the Velvet Underground and today's riot grrrls? Many take the easy way out, throw up their hands, and just describe them as "quirky"—an adjective that has never been as overused in rock criticism as it is in Raincoats reviews.

Despite the accolades from both underground fanzines and present-day grunge superstars, the Raincoats have never made music that found a ready home on the charts or the airwaves. That's especially true in the U.S, where two of the three albums they made between 1979 and 1984 were never even released until the mid-'90s; a live set from the same period only came out on cassette. But to their small cult, the group weren't just another weird British indie new wave band. They inspired almost familial feelings of devotion with their unpretentious eclecticism, inspiring scores of unseasoned musicians to record their own idiosyncratic music. Some of those unseasoned musicians, unlike the Raincoats, eventually became stars. Two of them were Sonic Youth's Kim Gordon and the late Kurt Cobain, who in the 1990s were instrumental in reviving enough interest in the Raincoats for the group to begin touring and recording again, after a layoff of a decade.

Playing music, however, was far from the minds of Gina Birch and Ana da Silva when they met as London art students. The climate of punk made uncompromising all-woman, or at least predominantly female, bands such as the Slits, X-Ray Spex, and the Au Pairs far more prevalent. The pair took the do-it-yourself ethos to heart by determining to form a band, although neither Birch (who bought a bass) nor da Silva (who ended up on guitar) were musicians.

"Neither of us would have dreamt in a million years that we would be doing anything like that if it hadn't been for punk," admits Birch today. "We really learned in public. We really, really believed in a kind of punk ethos. I think it became clear to us quite quickly that lots of people seemed to believe in it, but didn't really practice it. We didn't realize that so many of those musicians were actually fantastic musicians. We really believed the press, you know, that you just pick up an instrument and learn three chords and see what happens."

By the time they recorded their first album for the Rough Trade label in 1979, though, they didn't sound like run-of-the-mill bash-it-out three-chord wonders. Classically trained violinist Vicky Aspinall ensured that the Raincoats distinguished themselves from the typical punk (or indeed typical rock) band with her trills and drones, much as John Cale had lent a degree of sophisticated textures to the Velvet Underground with his viola in the 1960s. Drummer Palmolive came over from one of Birch's favorite bands, the Slits, to help establish the jerky, unpredictable time signatures that have served as Raincoats trademarks. Influenced by dub reggae, Birch used her bass to assertively carry the melody, rather than simply maintain the rhythm.

Birch and da Silva split the vocal and songwriting chores, and penned tunes that also stood pop clichés on their head. Instead of bluntly stating feelings or offering social comment, the Raincoats offered free-associative miniatures of sorts that didn't so much describe situations as evoke states of mind. While they did sometimes reflect quite feminist concerns (such as "Off Duty-Trip," which details a soldier's rape of a woman), the songs were elusive, requiring time to dig into. That in turn goes a long way toward explaining the rarefied nature of their following—Raincoats fans, by and large, have spent a *lot* of time with the records, and not as background music.

"Ana's stuff is more elliptical and poetic," remarks Birch. "You can savor it in your mouth, and get different tastes each time. You can have different feelings or images from it, and you can find your own meanings in it. Ana's got a doctorate in languages. I gave up languages far too early. I think what I write is much more on the nose. I'm more interested in kind of sharp, immediate, concrete, witty—I like tragicomedy a lot. I like things to be fast and immediate. I like things to have a resonance too. It's very important. But that's a very fundamental difference, I suppose."

All-woman bands still being somewhat of a novelty at the time (as they still are, to a lesser degree, in the 1990s), the Raincoats were often lumped in with other British female punk/new wave acts by critics. Birch concedes that one of the band's more distinctive traits was "the fact that we were women, and the fact that we had some inkling about what we wanted as women, I suppose. We wanted things to be different. We didn't want to have to wear short skirts and have fab legs in order to have people think what we did was great. Not that I've got anything against that either, but we wanted to be what we wanted to be.

"It's funny, there was a series of pieces about women in music at that time in glossy magazines. And they'd have pictures of all these all-girl bands, and they all looked terribly glamorous. And there was a picture of us in funny old jumpers, looking like what we'd just got out of bed and hadn't brushed our hair. It was a kind of precursor to what happened some years later, real kind of grungy riot grrl stuff. I suppose that's the look we had."

After the first album, Palmolive left (eventually becoming an evangelical Christian in Texas), leaving the band drummerless for a while. The band smuggled some unusual instruments that they'd purchased in New York through customs, and employed them to expand their sonic range on their second album, *Odyshape*. This set is perhaps the best illustration of the Raincoats' desire to record sounds and songs that arise out of the very process of creation itself. It's a quality that particularly endears them to fans like Kim Gordon, who described the group (in her liner notes to the CD reissue of *Odyshape*) as "ordinary people playing extraordinary music."

Elaborates Mayo Thompson, who helped produce the first Raincoats album, "It was about this element, this feeling, that drives one to make music in the first place, and the whole idea that music somehow soothes the savage beast, belongs to the organism, and has something to do with the way we are, the feelings. The Raincoats were not trying to convince anybody about who they were, or what kind of people they were, or those kinds of things."

Birch agrees that the Raincoats were unusual in how "we let ourselves be very vulnerable in a way. We were never really into a kind of idea of show business. [Watching us] was like watching a process, which the audience felt they were prvileged to kind of spy in on. I saw Tricky recently, and when he was on the stage, I just felt like there was this kind of invisible wall, and he thought he was in his rehearsal room. He was chatting away to the other members of the band. There's something really kind of unshowbizzy about it."

The Raincoats were canny enough to reject the limitations of straightahead punk and expand into all sorts of different directions. By the time of their third album, however, *Moving* (1984), recorded mostly with drummer Richard Dudanksi, their very eclecticism was threatening the stability of the band. "The formula, or lack of one, was stretched to the breaking point on this album," writes Vicki Aspinall in the liner notes to the CD reissue of the record. "Trying to contain influences as diverse as Chic, African music, Abdullah Ibrahim, funk, Cajun music, and the ever present reggae along with the continuum of guitar-based post-punk was a difficult act to pull off, and, in the end, pulled us apart." The Raincoats broke up after the album's release.

"We were all terribly egalitarian," says Birch now. "One of the things, I think, that we suffered from was that we all had the same amount of input and power, and we really, really tried to be democratic to the last nth degree. So it was actually quite painful a lot of the time.

"I remember when Green from Scritti Politti declared, probably about 1980, that he was going to be the leader of the group and the rest would do what he said. We all thought this was the most shocking piece of news ever!," she laughs. "We really endeavored to be incredibly democratic, which meant as we grew apart, or as our influences grew more and more diverse, that we ended up not really knowing how to censor ourselves. We were a group without any sense of censorship at all."

Birch went on to play in one of the many lineups of Red Krayola (led by her ex-producer Mayo Thompson), and formed a more pop-oriented band called Dorothy with Aspinall. Eventually Birch moved into film and videos (she has directed clips for the Pogues, New Order, and the Raincoats themselves). Aspinall started a dance label. Ana da Silva composed for dance theater and a British television film; when tracked down by *Option*'s Jason Cherkis in 1993, she was working at an antique shop a few blocks from Rough Trade headquarters. "The job leaves her uninspired," wrote Cherkis. "Da Silva . . . views getting [the Raincoats] back together as silly."

It was in that antique shop, though, that da Silva was found by Kurt Cobain and his wife, Hole singer Courtney Love. (Hole has covered a song from the Raincoats' first album, "The Void," as a B-side.) The first three Raincoats albums were reissued on CD; Birch and da Silva, together with violinist Anne Wood and Sonic Youth drummer Steve Shelley, celebrated by doing one reunion gig each in the U.K. and U.S. Then the Raincoats were asked to support Nirvana on a

British tour. The one-off reunion became a genuine re-formation of the band, who now have a deal with DGC Records.

Birch is still a bit taken aback by the resurgence of interest in the group. "It's very funny, because lots of people say, "We were influenced by the Raincoats.' But I can't really hear it in very many . . . in *any* groups, really.

"It's amazing that they saw those things in what we did, and felt so strongly about it. It makes me feel really proud. I suppose with Kim Gordon coming to see the Raincoats when she was just thinking about playing music . . . as a woman, if you're going to see a woman's band playing, you kind of feel pulled into it. I know, from my own experience, going to see women musicians play, I find it—particularly before I started playing—I found it really enabling, the fact that you might be able to try it after all, whereas you perhaps thought you never could. And I'm sure for Kim we provided a bit of that."

Looking in the Shadows, the first album by the reconstituted Raincoats, appeared in 1996. "When we first got together and played some of the old stuff, it just felt so right, and the stuff felt really fresh still," observes Birch. "Then we played a few dates with the old material, and we just began to introduce new material. So it was almost like it never stopped."

The album has more of a straightforward rock approach than their vintage releases. "We ended up making a record that was so completely opposite from what we had originally thought. But it was something that we really, really enjoyed the process of doing. I don't think when we started out, we realized quite what kind of record we were going to make. But we just went with our instincts. You get a group of people in a room, and you follow through what seems to be the best way of doing it under those circumstances. It kind of evolved in that way. I think we tend to kind of make things up as we go along, if you like."

Recommended Recordings:

The Raincoats (1979, DGC). The most jagged, angular, and (most importantly) *human* of the early British punk statements. It's also their most rock-oriented early outing, with ex-Slit Palmolive on drums, and a goofy cover of the Kinks' classic "Lola."

Odyshape (1981, DGC). Folk, jazz, and dub influences come more to the fore on their second effort, which might have alienated a few straightahead punk fans, but certainly made their work more accessible to a larger audience.

Moving (1984; DGC). The cauldron of influences within the Raincoats had boiled the lid off the pot by their third album, which sometimes sounds like the work of different bands on different tracks. It's certainly one of the most eclectic efforts of the early "post-punk" era. "No One's Little Girl" may be their best song, as well as the best illustration of their talents at conveying forcefully feminist sentiments with grace and subtlety.

Rocket From the Tombs

Rocket From the Tombs, mid-1970s. David Thomas, sitting in front, does his Elvis imitation; standing in back are (left to right) Gene O'Connor, Peter Laughner, Johnny Madansky, and Craig Bell. Credit: Courtesy Craig Bell

One of the most seminal American bands of the 1970s never released a record until a good 15 years or so after their demise. Cleveland's Rocket From The Tombs bridged early '70s hard/glam rock with the punk/new wave era. They wrote and sang about young adult alienation and modern dehumanization in explicit, confrontational terms while most of America was listening to the likes of Peter Frampton and Barry White. Singer David Thomas would go on to become the mainstay of Pere Ubu, one of the longest-lived and most respected experimental new wave bands. Cheetah Chrome and Stiv Bators, the latter of whom joined the group in their waning days, took guitar punk to its most lunkheaded extremes with the Dead Boys. Peter Laughner's slim body of work was enough to earn the singer-songwriter a cult of his own before his death in 1977, in his mid-twenties.

Yet even most punk/new wave devotees have never heard of this band, which only managed to lay down a few primitive home recordings and live tapes before imploding in 1975. Rocket's odd blend of the Stooges, heavy metal, Lou Reed, and brash experimentalism was both their greatest asset and their ultimate downfall. It was perhaps too much to expect such a diverse bunch of misfit talents to cohabit the same space for long. An even greater problem, perhaps, was that they played "alternative" music before the terms alternative, punk, or new wave really existed.

In a sense, it's surprising the band got as far as it did, considering that Rocket From The Tombs was originally considered as something of a joke band. David Thomas already had quite a reputation in Cleveland as critic for the local free music paper when he formed Rocket From The Tombs in mid-1974. Their first sets were filled with covers of '50s and '60s tunes, interspersed with comedy routines; "Hey Joe," for instance, would be changed to "Hey Punk." The band started to become more serious about their material with the entry of guitarist (and fellow rock critic) Peter Laughner, a singer-songwriter heavily influenced by Lou Reed.

Within a matter of months, in fact, Rocket From The Tombs had been totally revamped. Only Thomas remained from the original group; original bassist Kim Zonneville, aka Charlie Wiener, departed to form, of all things, a comedy Country Western band. Into the lineup came drummer Johnny Madansky, guitarist Gene O'Connor, and bassist Craig Bell (the last of whom had been playing in another underground Cleveland outfit, Mirrors). Gone was the comedy, replaced by abrasive, eclectic hard rock, with an emphasis upon original material. That at least would not be difficult to come by: everyone wrote songs in the band, with the exception of Madansky.

According to Thomas, "The common ground was the Stooges/MC5. We could all agree on that. The three of us [Thomas, Laughner, and Bell] were into the promise of rock and we were from the professional middle classes. Madansky and O'Connor (aka Cheetah Chrome) were into heavy metal, and came from the projects. The only common ground was the love of hard groove rock and overdrive dynamics. The tension of everything else yielded whatever originality we had."

Adds Bell, "I think the lineup of David, Peter, Cheetah, Johnny, and myself were the one and only true RFTT because we were the ones who really believed what we were doing and did not look upon the group as a joke or part-time plaything. When we got together we brought a lot of different ideas into the mix.

"Cheetah and Johnny were totally immersed in the KISS type metal of the day, while I was coming out of Mirrors, where we did the Velvet Underground thing along with liberal doses of Syd Barrett and the Kinks. David was very intellectual and stubborn, he basically didn't like anything! Peter was very in the middle. I admired him for his ability to go from Robert Johnson to Gene Simmons, and bring it all together into a cohesive manner that was the basis for what was the original RFTT sound." RFTT also got some lyrical assistance from Laughner's wife, Charlotte Pressler, herself a local poet/musician.

This was long before do-it-yourself indie releases were common, but it wasn't long before the band were recording a demo tape in the practice loft they shared with other underground Cleveland acts. Cut over the course of two nights in February 1975, this was never intended as a professional statement. Not that it would have been suitable for submission to CBS in any case: overmodulated distortion canceled any hope for a balanced mix or variegated frequencies.

Yet this is the music upon which Rocket's legend rests, for both the unusual nature of the material and the searingly raw spontaneity of the performances. The band had managed to synthesize their motley influences into something that had no easy reference point in 1975. The early Stooges, perhaps, but with a fiercer, more despondent bent on the nihilistic "Life Stinks," or with a touch of art-experimentalism on "Thirty Seconds Over Tokyo." "Final Solution" was the band's most ambitious thrust into the heart of human darkness. Both of these would become some of the most influential tracks in American new wave when they were re-recorded for early Pere Ubu releases; Rocket's versions are far more rock-oriented, and in some senses more powerful, though not as artfully produced as the remakes.

The less arty, more rocking sound of the band was represented by four songs that would later be redone by the Dead Boys—"Down in Flames," "What Love Is," "Ain't It Fun," and "Never Kill Myself Again" (the last of which the Dead Boys retitled "Caught with the Meat in My Mouth"). Overkill teenage angst? Perhaps. Yet the highlight of the set was not the meat grinder riff-dominated tunes, but the plaintive, almost folky "Ain't It Fun," with its very real sense of the waste and regret of youthful overindulgence. Co-written by Peter and Cheetah, this was perhaps Laughner's best attempt at matching the tender street tough ethos of his idol, Lou Reed, blow-for-blow. In retrospect it's doubly haunting, seeming to foreshadow Laughner's early drug-related death with a chilling realism. Nearly 20 years later, it reached a wide audience—though perhaps not in a way Laughner would have appreciated—when it was covered by Guns n' Roses.

The tape was broadcast on the popular local rock station WMMS, where Laughner opined that "most records today are made by formula," and urged listeners to form their own bands and make their own music. Some more material, recorded live at the Agora in Cleveland (and featuring Don Evans as a temporarily replacement for Madansky), aired on WMMS a bit later, introducing their most notorious number. "Final Solution," the ultimate teen frustration anthem, would again become one of the cornerstones of Pere Ubu's early repertoire in a less straightahead rock-oriented remake. Although these tapes far from approximated legitimate studio conditions, they remain the only documents of Rocket From The Tombs, preserved as radio broadcasts and circulated for 20 years among rabid underground rock collectors.

"When we made the loft tape we had no idea we were being a bridge from one style of rock to another," maintains Bell. "We were just putting down on tape what we felt was a strong rock and roll sound with lyrics that were not the usual 'baby baby wanna fuckya all night long.' We lived in Cleveland and our influence was that if you were gonna play rock music it had to hit hard and by god, we kicked ass as best we could. We had so many diverse influences that it was a battle sometimes to rein in ideas to complete a song."

If that was the case, it was no surprise that internal debates soon began to take their toll on the group. Thomas' unique vocals—with a strangled quality that could make him sound like a more atonal Captain Beefheart—were not unanimously appreciated by the rest of the band. Stiv Bators, a far more conventional rock vocalist, was recruited to take most of the lead vocal chores. Thomas, the band's founder, was reduced to playing organ, saxophone, and singing "Thirty Seconds Over Tokyo." In Thomas' view, this shakeup did not only alter the balance of power in the band, but acted as a detriment to the music itself.

"Thomas-Laughner-Bell-O'Connor-Madansky was the best lineup," he claims. "It was the one that wrote all the songs, including the ones later credited to the Dead Boys. It was the most balanced and it had potential. The versions of RFTT before this were transitional from a vanity band to that group. The versions after were a falling apart. Madansky left and Wayne Strick replaced him, and the balance began to go. Then I went through a crisis in confidence and we got Stiv Bators to sing, which was the end of the thing really. The balance was gone and it was getting ordinary. What was good about RFTT was the tension between what Peter, Craig and I were into, and what O'Connor and Madansky were into."

After supporting a then-unknown Television in Cleveland in mid-'75, Rocket From The Tombs broke up. Bators, Chrome/O'Connor, and Madansky formed the Dead Boys, who dumbed the RFTT aesthetic down into a trashy punk band that had a modicum of success and popular acclaim. Thomas formed Pere Ubu, who created a quick critical splash with their first two singles, artier, spookier remakes of "Thirty Seconds Over Tokyo" and "Final Solution."

Pere Ubu, in fact, are still going strong today, after several lineup changes and periodic hiatuses. Of the differences between the Rocket/Pere Ubu versions of songs from the RFTT repertoire, Thomas observes, "They were evolving. That's what happens when you explore. You like to look at things in different ways. Also, Pere Ubu had been together three weeks when we recorded 'Tokyo,' for example, while RFTT had been together a year or more when we made those recordings. The people in Pere Ubu were different and had different ambitions."

Laughner was in Pere Ubu's first incarnation, but left the band shortly before his death in 1977. Always one who lived as well as played the rock and roll lifestyle, he went too close to the edge he wrote about in his songs; partially as a result of some solo recordings, he's attracted a small cult following of his own.

"If I could go back in time and change anything I think I would have been more forceful in my feelings about deposing David as the lead singer and bringing Stiv in," says Bell today. "I did not agree with it at the time but said nothing, and I regret that. If we could have gotten through that problem and continued on the path we were on, we could really have made some music that would still be viable today. I think we would have pursued some of the areas that Pere Ubu did, but not on such a pure artistic level. We would have combined the power and attitude of the Dead Boys without the sophomoric ideas they were wont to lean to."

Thomas is dismissive of the idea that Rocket From The Tombs were too ahead of their time. "No one is ahead of time. We may have been of the moment. The band would never have lasted—the differences were monumental. Certainly once the balance of tension in the group was lost we were on borrowed time. The Thomas-Laughner-Bell-O'Connor-Madansky group could have survived two-three years before blowing apart, but Madansky left, so it's no use speculating . . . . It was not an exploratory group. Pere Ubu was built to explore and survive. RFTT would have blown apart."

Bell isn't so sure. "Were we too ahead of our time? We were completely *out* of our time. We only played out five times, but everyone was totally knocked out . . . so much so they didn't know what to make of it. We had great audiences at our shows and I think we could have had a long and successful run if we just could have realized what we had at the time. Which we did not. We were in a vacuum at that time and were classic self-doubters, which was the main reason we could not keep the band going.

"If we had some sort of support and encouragement at the beginning, I think we would have made a major impact at that time. We had all sorts of ideas floating around in that band, and at that time could have had the freedom to explore those avenues, because the market was not as restrictive as it has become. I think that if you listen to the existing recordings, you hear a band that was willing to take extreme risks, because we felt that we could pull it off and at the same time not leave our audience behind."

Part of the reason Rocket From The Tombs retains such a mystique is that the recordings themselves are so hard to come by. For years, they were available only as a tape, circulated among in-the-know collectors. Some were finally issued in 1990 on the 600-copy limited edition release *Life Stinks*, which is itself hard to locate these days; some also made it onto Geffen's Pere Ubu box set. Rocket From The Tombs is a fitting name for a band whose legacy has yet to truly even break the earth's surface.

Recommended Recording:
Life Stinks (1990, Jack Slack). This isn't much easier to find these days than the bootleg tapes of the group's demos and radio broadcasts, from which this small-press indie release is drawn. If you can find it, however (or the source tapes, for that matter), it's essential listening for anyone interested in the roots of punk and new wave, including different versions of a lot of material that ended up on early Pere Ubu and Dead Boys records.

X-Ray Spex

"Some people say little girls should be seen and not heard," Poly Styrene solemnly intones at the beginning of X-Ray Spex's debut single. "But I think—" and then the voice suddenly rises to a scream—"OH BONDAGE UP YOURS! 1-2-3-4!"

Then the band kicks in with all the immediacy of a custard pie in the face. Fuzzy power chords and careening saxophone bleats fight it out with Styrene's half-chanted, half-sung vocals, a mixture of glee and rage that periodically trails off into caterwauling shrieks. An audacious debut, to say the least—and, one would think, not very commercial, especially considering this was 1977.

Punk's taking off in Britain, however, and "Oh Bondage! Up Yours!" puts the band into the media spotlight almost immediately. A flurry of mid-size hit singles followed—"The Day the World Turned Dayglo," "Identity," and "Germ Free Adolescents." The debut LP make the U.K. Top 30, and X-Ray Spex played two weeks to enthusiastic audiences at CBGB's in New York, with fans like Blondie and Richard Hell in the audience.

Singing about consumerism, feminism, and the glossy sterility of the modern-day world with an exuberant cynicism and (literally) braces on her teeth, Styrene and X-Ray Spex were instrumental in broadening punk's range from simple rage to broader concerns. As a mixed-gender group unconcerned with presenting themselves as glamorous icons, they also defied the stereotypes of typical rock images. It all came to end shortly after that debut album, though, when the original X-Ray Spex split. Poly Styrene made a much quieter, jazzier solo album, and joined the Hare Krishnas in the 1980s. Only one EP (1986's *Gods and Goddesses*) appeared over the next 15 years. Strange rumors circulated that Styrene had all but vanished from the face of the earth, and retired from music to immerse herself in religion.

As it turns out, in early 1997 Styrene is alive, well, and making music in London. Not only that, she's never stopped making music in the intervening years. A second X-Ray Spex album, *Consumer Consciousness*, finally appeared in 1995, exploring lyrical concerns not all that different from the *Germ Free Adolescents* days. A recent legal dispute over the X-Ray Spex dampened Styrene's spirits somewhat. Yet she's still excited about her ever-growing catalog of unreleased songs, which she's worked on more or less uninterrupted, even when she lived in a Hare Krishna temple for about five years. A major label, she tells me, has shown some interest in some demos that are "a really spiritual, kind of cross between rock and new age tape."

Styrene's strange voyage from punk to rock-new age hybrids began in the mid-'70s. The daughter of a Somalian father and English mother, a teenaged Marian Elliott went to parties attended by members of Pink Floyd and Led Zeppelin; Brian May of Queen had actually been a schoolteacher of hers. Under the name Mari Elliott, she recorded a little-known reggae-influenced single in 1976. A poster on the Hastings Pier for a then-unknown band called the Sex Pistols changed that.

"I wondered what it was, so I walked over to the pier and watched the Pistols," Styrene remembers. "They weren't famous or anything—hardly anybody was in the audience. They were doing some covers of old, I think, Stones songs or some R&B songs; they might have had 'Pretty Vacant' then, but I don't think they had all their new songs that they later became famous for.

"That sparked me to kind of get out of that scene that I was a bit young for, and made me realize that there was something happening outside of that. There was something that was a little bit more of my generation. It was just a little bit different than the long hair kind of rock syndrome that had gone before. I thought, 'Oh, if they can get a band together, I should be able to do that too.'" After advertising in *Melody Maker* and auditioning a few musicians, Styrene ended up fronting X-Ray Spex, though the music didn't exactly end up sounding like the Sex Pistols.

How did X-Ray Spex distinguish themselves from the rest of the first generation of British punk bands? "I think the message was different lyrically," Styrene postulates, "because I was writing about things that at the time were a bit futuristic. Like 'Genetic Engineering' was just something that was sparked

Poly Styrene of X-Ray Spex, jolly punk rocker.
Credit: Courtesy Maharani Devi, © Falcon Stuart

off by me reading an article about genetics in *Time* magazine. Now it's a real thing, isn't it? Some people would even use genetic engineering seriously if they could . . .

Poly Styrene gets ready to do the shopping.
Credit: Courtesy Maharani Devi, © Falcon Stuart

"I was always interested in these kind of things, and consumerism, and things like that. The other bands were mainly writing about the dole queue. I mean, I had a bit of boredom in that song 'I Am a Cliché' [the B-side to 'Oh Bondage! Up Yours!"]. But generally speaking, they were going on about anarchy. And I wasn't really writing about things like that so much as modern-day consumerism."

One of the most distinguishing marks of X-Ray Spex's early tracks was the squealing saxophone of Lora Logic, a 16-year-old who cut nearly as unusual a figure in the male-dominated rock world as Styrene. By the time the *Germ Free Adolescents* album was finished in 1978, however, she'd been replaced by a more, er, conventional player, Rudi Thompson. Logic went on to form Essential Logic, and appears on the 1995 X-Ray Spex album, though she isn't playing with Styrene on a long-term basis.

"She was in school at the time, she was 16," Styrene explains when asked about Logic's departure. "She couldn't really [tour], she had to finish her education. And when we used to play live, she used to play the saxophone over all my lyrics." She laughs heartily. "I could never hear myself sing! I couldn't actually discipline her into playing in the spaces when I wasn't singing. Obviously, when I made the last album, she was a bit more easy to work with. Well, I actually told her, 'Don't do that again, like you used to! Otherwise this isn't going to work.' You know how it is when somebody—they want to be the front person, really. So what they do is they just blow all over your vocals so they have the voice. That used to happen a bit, and that was a bit irritating."

X-Ray Spex were at their best on their singles, which had a pop-punk abandon that didn't come through as well on the one album by the original incarnation of the band. Styrene feels this was because the tracks were recorded at different times over a twelve-month period and not always with the same saxophonist, which inevitably led to a loss of continuity. Unfortunately, due to the band's busy schedule, there was no other way that the album could be finished.

Although the album charted for a major label in the U.K., it wasn't even released in the States, where X-Ray Spex gigs were limited to a two-week stint at CBGB's in New York. (It was finally released Stateside, with bonus tracks from the early singles, on Caroline in 1992.) "When we played in New York, we felt like we were really well known," recalls Styrene. "I think we were in the *New York Times* the first day we arrived. For us at the time, we felt that everybody that we wanted to know [about us] knew who we were. When you're young like that, you've got a pretty naive approach to things. The fact that the place was packed out twice a night, we were happy with."

X-Ray's prospects for U.S. success became moot when the band broke up shortly after the release of *Germ Free Adolescents*. "To be perfectly honest, it came to a point where it was just like quit while you're ahead, or go down. The last single that we put out after the album really wasn't that well received. We'd had a lot of media attention and a lot of overexposure very very early on. My very first gig that I played, I was on the front cover of *Sounds*. Then I was always in the daily press over here as well. Dealing with that was one thing, being quite young. Musically, because you get in a touring situation, you don't really have that much time to write. I needed to take time off to write."

Styrene released a solo album, *Translucence* (1980), in an about-face from punk into cocktail jazz-like arrangements. She caused even more confusion among fans when she joined the Hare Krishnas. For over a decade, most alternative rock fans assumed that she'd vanished into religious cultdom. Although she no longer lives in a Hare Krishna temple, Styrene confirms that she's still "very much a devotee . . . it wasn't like a fad for me." She's even considering living in India part-time, in connection with her spiritual pursuits. But, she takes pains to clarify, this didn't mean that she ever meant to give up music.

"We had a recording studio in the temple, and I wanted to work in the industry, but I kind of got blacklisted because I was a Hare Krishna," she says. "At the time, it was just considered unhip. I wanted to make music. I was still *making* music. But I couldn't get a deal. And the minute they knew I was a Hare Krishna . . . I wasn't that subtle about being a Hare Krishna, 'cause I'd walk into EMI wearing a sari. I played at Glastonbury Festival, but in the Hare Krishna tent. Then later other people came along like Boy George and had hits with Hare Krishna songs. I organized the chanting on that record.

"Also, I was known to have had a bit of a nervous breakdown," she adds. "So that went around too, and that wasn't very helpful. Because then people thought, well, will she be able to really tour, or will she crack up? Or is she just going to go out there and just be a fanatic Hare Krishna? I got labeled as having schizophrenia, because I said that I saw a UFO in an article. I mean, I'm *not* schizophrenic," she notes emphatically. "But there is still rumor around the industry that I may have actually got schizophrenia. It's kind of hard to shake that sort of thing off sometimes, when it comes to getting contracts."

As a consequence, although X-Ray Spex's 1995 album, *Conscious Consumer,* was perceived as a "comeback," much of the material had actually been written about 15 years before its release. All the industry wanted, claims Styrene, was for her "to regurgitate *Germ Free Adolescents.* I never got the opportunity [to do other things], which wasn't interesting for me as a writer." But why fill an album with mostly old songs that Styrene would have recorded as part of X-Ray Spex back around 1980, had the original band lasted that long? "When I put out albums, I try to get rid of the old songs first before I put out my new ones, because I've got so many," she states. "So I try to keep some continuity."

Original X-Ray Spex members Paul Dean (bass) and Lora Logic play on *Conscious Consumer*; a member of Kula Shaker, which in 1996 would enjoy massive British chart success with the Indian-influenced "Tattva," contributes guitars under a pseudonym. Though somewhat more subdued than the late '70s recordings, it's a worthy effort that finds Styrene continuing to examine consumer culture on songs like "Junk Food Junkie," and get into more spiritual concerns on cuts like "Prayer for Peace" and "India." The languid "Crystal Clear," a relatively recent composition, may have the most pop appeal of anything she's recorded.

But when it came time to promote the record, the X-Ray Spex comeback died at the starting line. Styrene had assembled a touring band, but was hit by a fire engine, which put her out of commission for several months. By the time she was ready to hit the road, she'd fallen out with the band's agent, who managed to convince the other musicians to tour as X-Ray Spex *without* Poly. This ad hoc X-Ray Spex actually played a gig with a different singer, telling the audience "that due to circumstances beyond their control, I was unable to be there"— somewhat akin to, say, the Rolling Stones telling an audience that Mick Jagger was unable to make it tonight, so would you please welcome this anonymous stand-in instead? Styrene eventually had to initiate legal proceedings against the musicians to prevent them from using the X-Ray Spex name. When I speak with her in early 1997, it looks like the dispute will blow over, though Styrene's disillusionment with the experience means it's quite unlikely she'll work with this particular band in the near future.

Whether Styrene fronts X-Ray Spex again or not, she's determined to keep writing about anything that interests her, whether it's sparked by an advertisement, a newspaper article, or Hare Krishna consciousness. Currently she's all abuzz about her Flower Aeroplane project, which has stirred interest from a big label. "It was very nice for me to do, with a couple of friends of mine. One of them was a healer, and we decided to make a healing tape, but with some edge, with this rock influence. It's spiritual, it's healing, but it's pop and it's rock as well."

Healing music from the Germ Free Adolescent? More likely it's a case of Styrene continuing to say "Oh Bondage! Up Yours!," as an adult who wants to meet the record industry on her own terms, even if it's taken the better part of two decades.

Recommended Recordings:
Germ Free Adolescents (1978, Caroline). One of the seminal early British punk albums; the CD reissue adds several important early singles.

Conscious Consumer (1995, Receiver, UK). Probably not as outrageous as diehard punks would prefer, but this finds Styrene's eccentric songwriting muse intact, in a more straightahead rock context than the material recorded by the first incarnation of the band.

Post-Punk Hybrids

Post-punk **may be the most roundly abused,** if not even meaningless, term in all of rock. If we are to agree that the first wave of punk rock abated around 1980, does that mean that most of the underground rock in the ensuing 15-plus years falls under the post-punk umbrella? A ballpark definition might simply describe it as underground rock that emerged after the initial punk/new wave detonation had cooled off, combining said punk/new wave with an ever-diverse array of influences, from '60s pop and exotica to avant-garde jazz, cold electronics, dub, and hip-hop.

The acts that have been described as post-punk literally number in the thousands—combine the *Trouser Press Record Guide* and all the back issues of *Option*, and you probably only have half of them. To winnow them down to three, as I've done here, will probably be considered nothing less than sacrilege by those who faithfully trundle to the indie bins of their specialist record store every week.

My take is that many, maybe most, of the groups hailed as post-punk for their fusion of twelve or more flavors of hipness aren't nearly as interesting as their reviews might have you think. The three pieces that follow examine artists who really *are* as strange, versatile, and unclassifiable as their combination of influences would lead you to believe. And even within the world of alternative rock, their contributions have been relatively undocumented, their records rarely heard, even on non-commercial and college radio stations. Do they point to the future of rock? I hope not, actually—not because their music is unworthy, but because it defies easy imitation.

Aisha Kandisha's Jarring Effects

Walk through a large Moroccan city, and you're apt to hear the traditional sounds of shabee dance music. An intoxicating mix of Arabic and African influences, as well as trance-like Moroccan rhythms and rituals, is played on instruments such as the violin, mandolin, and lute, against the exotic percussion of the bendir and darabukka. At the same time, radios and cassette players might also be blasting the latest in American and European hip-hop, house, and techno. You might think that the combination of traditional Moroccan sounds with new Western technology would be the next logical step.

Aisha Kandisha's Jarring Effects, though, didn't so much tentatively tiptoe into the modern age as hurl a brick through the window. The intention was clear from the first notes of the first track on their debut album, as industrial-sounding tapes slow and grind to a halt, a robotic voice babbles indecipherably, gunshots fire, metal clangs, and glass breaks. Only when the haunting stringed instruments begin to strum and the clattering percussion starts do you have any clue that this is a Moroccan album.

For the next 40 minutes of *El Buya*, AKJE (as they often abbreviate themselves for convenience) take off on a hold-on-for-your-life ride that runs traditional Moroccan music through the cutting edge of electronic technology. Turntables are jiggled back and forth, and dub-like echo makes the percussion rattle like a tin can trapped in outer space. The haunting vocals and chants sometimes splinter into cut-up stutters and loops. Creaking anvils and mysterious rushes of industrial effects, crowd noise, and reverb are interjected unpredictably, sometimes traveling from speaker to speaker. Yet it never drowns out those traditional Moroccan dancing violins and guitars, as well as the achingly beautiful vocals, that remain the bedrock foundations of the tracks.

Released in 1991 (though recorded in 1988 and 1989), *El Buya* genuinely sounded like no other album that had ever been produced. Many African, Middle Eastern, and Asian groups had tried to update traditional world musics with state-of-the-art technology, usually ending up sounding more like tired disco with a slight twist than the gateway to the twenty-first century. Aisha Kandisha broke from this pack by using rap, dub, and club DJ techniques in the service of their own indigenous music, rather than approaching the issue from the other way around by smothering the non-Western elements in drum machines and funked-up bass.

It comes as something as a surprise, then, to learn that the forerunners of Moroccan avant-pop are unknown in their own country, where they have never played live or released a record. Even their name invites controversy in Moroccan culture, where Aisha Kandisha signifies a witch-like female spirit that can, the legend goes, so distract men as to drive them into madness and even suicide. Particularly among the older generation, even speaking her name aloud inspires fear. It's hard to draw a comparison to the situation in the U.S., where, despite those omnipresent parental advisory stickers, bands can call themselves Elvis Hitler or the Dead Kennedys without facing total ostracization.

So AKJE release their records in Europe, and have found their audience—although it remains small—in Europe, Japan, and the U.S. Given the collision of the West and Northern Africa in their music, it makes sense that one of the principal architects of the sound is Pat Jabbar, a Swiss musician who usually handles sampling and programming. Jabbar's Barbarity label has become a labora-

Aisha Kandisha's Jarring Effects, Moroccan mavericks. Credit: Courtesy Pat Jabbar

tory for several Moroccan acts exploring cultural fusions, also including Ahlam, Amira Saqati, and Argan (all of whom feature contributions from AKJE members). The English-speaking Jabbar, who is based in Basel, Switzerland, is also something of a liaison between the Western media and the Moroccan musicians, releasing their records for international markets, often handling the electronic end of the production, and promoting the records himself.

Jabbar was playing sax with ska and punk bands when he visited Morocco for the first time in 1985, when jams with, as he puts it, hip-hoppers from Marrakech began to lead to the songs that ended up on *El Buya*. The Moroccan musicians had already been exposed to rap, hip-hop, reggae, and black dance music on weekend radio programs, which were broadcast in Tangier and Casablanca. "They were maybe not yet really interested in trying to do a sort of crossover themselves at this time," explains Jabbar. "That was maybe my influence, unconsciously."

M.Y. Ahmed, at that time a singer with a traditional shabee band, became AKJE's lead vocalist after their unusual mix—"we were already in quite a noisy, industrial way" confesses Jabbar—piqued his interest. Seven musicians contributed to *El Buya* on violin, mandolin, darbukka, bendir, percussion, electric and acoustic guitars, and what are simply noted in the press releases as "noises." The final track—the enigmatically titled "Rooftop Suck 2," a mostly acoustic instrumental with a lo-fi, Walkman-recorded texture—gives an idea of how the basic tracks might have sounded before they were embellished by those "noises," which rate as some of the most seat-of-the-pants-generated sampling and mixing to be found on a 1990-era recording.

The mixing was done by Jabbar and Fido K. back in Basel, making the album a cross-cultural collaboration in fact as well as spirit. Jabbar points out that the relatively primitive state of recording technology in Moroccan studios would have made it difficult to record and mix all at once. "Most of the [Moroccan] people can't afford to buy any samplers or computers or any synthesizers. It's very hard to get good gear, good material and effects, whatever. The best things you only can find in bigger studios. You have to rent them, and it gets quite expensive. If you have a ten-day production, for instance, in Casablanca, it's more expensive than Fido's studio here in Switzerland.

"Most of the bands do like a two-track recording, everything on two tracks. They don't use even eight track, they record direct on two tracks. They do the mix *during* the recording—quite crazy. Now, with that new studio in Casablanca, they do like a normal recording in one day, and next day do mixing. They don't really get the time to do a lot of arrangements and try to play with the effects. It's more or less quite a very natural mix."

The taboo surrounding the Aisha Kandisha name, says Jabbar, is not as serious a barrier to AKJE's acceptance in the Moroccan market as the cold fact that their music is just too, well, far-out. "In Morocco, it's very hard to sell this kind of music, because it's much too avant-garde. Marrakech is still very popular, very traditional-oriented. Most of the people, either they listen to some heavy hip-hop and techno and pure European music, or they prefer pure Moroccan stuff, or Algerian or Moroccan rai [a form of North African vocal pop music]. This kind of experimenting might be too heavy for most of the people."

And, apparently, for the Moroccan music industry. "Young people, I think they would accept it if they could know that it exists. But a cassette label wouldn't take the risk of taking it in their catalog, because they think it's going much too far. They prefer some commercial rai, or some commercial shabee, or any popular stuff, even if it's quite modern."

So *El Buya* was distributed primarily to European and American alternative/underground audiences, which eventually resulted in a crucial contact for the band. They met Randy Barnwell of Sub Rosa Records in Tangier, at the home of famous author Paul Bowles (*The Sheltering Sky*). Barnwell, it turned out, was a good friend of Bill Laswell, the famous New York-based bassist and producer whose production credit seemingly graces every other experimental rock record (as well as more mainstream projects with Mick Jagger, Yoko Ono, Laurie Anderson, and the Ramones).

Barnwell, Jabbar remembers, sent a copy of *El Buya* to Laswell. After finding out that the group planned to do another album, Laswell altruistically volunteered his production services. He also played bass on about half of *Shabeesation*, which came out in 1993 (and was released Stateside by Rykodisc in 1995). Bernie Worrell of Parliament-Funkadelic and Umar Bin Hassan also made guest appearances on the record, which had a much more polished, dancefloor-conscious feel than the debut.

"He's really great," enthuses Jabbar about Laswell. "It's incredible how he never wants to hear a tape of them before a new production. He just says okay, you come, bring your reels, [and] listens once to the songs in the studio. The second time he plays a little bit bass. Third time he's recording, fourth time it's mixed already."

Shabeesation might be more palatable to dance-oriented audiences, but it also loses a good deal of the spontaneity and prominent traditional elements that were so crucial to the appeal of the first record, replacing them with rather typical rhythm sections and programming in particular. Jabbar seems to have become used to explaining the transition. "Maybe we might go a little more dancefloor somehow," he admits, "because it's more attractive, more easy to expose to European listeners, and to get some more airplay on the radios here.

"At the beginning," he elaborates, "there were no commercial intentions. It was music we did for fun, and we never even thought of having a label, or doing some other bands. The response was so good and there was so much heavy demand for that music that we thought okay, why not produce another album, another record. We don't think too much 'this song has to be techno, this song has to be reggae,' or something like this. It just comes automatically, somehow." Jabbar, in fact, gave up his studies to try to make a living from music with the Barbarity label. Of the handful of Barbarity releases, it is in fact the debut of Ahlam (*Revolt Against Reason*), rather than AKJE's own *Shabeesation*, that comes closest to matching the spontaneous feel and trad-electronic combustion of *El Buya*.

The entire Barbarity roster, like Aisha Kandisha's Jarring Effects, is more focused on international success than selling records in their homeland. It's not just because the music could be interpreted as being too avant-garde, or even because of the occasional controversial bent of some Barbarity lyrics. (Ahlam's "El Quods," for instance, is a call for peace between Arabs and Jews that could be interpreted as downright inflammatory in Moroccan society.) It's also because even the biggest Moroccan stars, says Jabbar, don't get royalties for their recordings. "Even a quite popular band might record for $10,000, and that's it. There are some bands, they sell like half a million cassettes. Most of the bands don't see a penny for that. Most of the artists get really ripped off, which is quite sad, I think."

That dampens the motivation to even record follow-ups, which to some degree explains why, as Jabbar observes, if the innovative Moroccan bands can gain acceptance on their own soil, "it's okay. If not, they don't care. For them it's more important—unfortunately, sometimes—to get [heard] out of Morocco."

Ironically, when AKJE were invited to travel to the U.S. as an opening act for rai singer Cheb Tati, they were told by the American ambassador in Casablanca that it would be nearly impossible to get visas (although the group have toured in Europe). Unwilling to play in Marrakech, unable to play in the States, Aisha Kandisha's Jarring Effects are almost underground by default—a "world music" band that has tried to bring together two continents, and is virtually unable to perform on either one.

Recommended Recording:
El Buya (1991, Barbarity, Switzerland). Still unavailable in the U.S., this is one of the most unheralded landmark post-modern recordings of the rock era. One of the very few times when world music and modern electronics have combined to take on exhilarating new forms—and, in view of the far more conventional Laswell-produced follow-up, perhaps the product as much of accident as inspiration.

F.S.K.

I've just told Thomas Meinecke of the German band F.S.K. that in my 15 years of music journalism, I've never come across an act as impossible to classify as his group. Other musicians might take the remark as an insult. Or panic: how are consumers going to find his CDs if Tower doesn't know where to put them? But if anything Meinecke, speaking on Christmas Day from his home near Munich, seems positively flattered. As he declares proudly, "Transatlantic misunderstandings are one of the main things we believe in."

Since their formation in 1980, F.S.K. seem to have taken a positive pride in being perverse. Their first records were typically dark, Teutonic post-punk. Just at the point where they had been labeled as, in Meinecke's words, "*the* intellectual German band," they donned jeans and flannel shirts, and began playing recombinant mixes of polka, Country Western, Cajun, bluegrass, drinking songs, yodels, and funk. When the label of "roots band" began to fit a little too comfortably, they junked their accordions in favor of cheap beatboxes and Japanese Yamaha electronic keyboards.

Upon further examination, the contradictions only multiply. Some of their left-wing lyrics attack the German left wing. Where other German rock bands sing in English to make their message more listener-friendly to the international audience, F.S.K. write their original material in German. They also write songs about Jane Fonda, Roxy Music, and German cult rockers Amon Düül. They deign to sing in English only on cover tunes, which are often obscure American Country & Western tunes written about—ironically—Germany.

Paging through the thick sheaves of bio material Meinecke has sent me, you'd find it hard to believe that F.S.K. were anything less than underground superstars. There have been several dozen releases since 1980, and dozens of raves in the British and American press from the likes of *New Musical Express*, *Melody Maker*, and *Rolling Stone*. John Peel, BBC's most revered rock DJ, has had them record live "Peel sessions" for his show more than any other non-British group. There's also a paragraph's worth of F.S.K. fans that reads like a who's who of alternative music: Michael Stipe of R.E.M., Michelle Shocked, and members of Dream Syndicate, Pavement, Palace, NRBQ, and "Madonna's sister Melanie Ciccone." And that's not even getting one-quarter of the way through the list.

But F.S.K. remain virtually unknown outside of an in-crowd of critics, musicians, and fanatical indie rock fans. In the 1990s, it's helped that David Lowery, the prime mover behind Camper Van Beethoven and Cracker, has taken an extensive interest in the band. He's produced their records at his home studio in Richmond, Virginia, and even joined them as a part-time member of sorts. But the famous associations with Lowery, Peel, and whoever else might become an F.S.K. devotee aren't going to change this hard reality: a band that composes a whole song around the titles of the albums by Amon Düül, or employs deadpan female vocals to cover male-to-female love songs, will never be a hot ticket with a wide audience.

F.S.K. are such committed, iconoclastic eclectics because they are, at heart, music fans who happen to play instruments. In fact, before they started the band, they helped produce a German fanzine entitled *Mode & Verzweflung* (Fashion & Despair). Admirers of oddball early punk/new wave groups like the Raincoats, the Swell Maps, the Contortions, Gang of Four, and Pere Ubu—as well as proto-punk cult groups like the Velvet Underground, Roxy Music, and the Monks—most of the members had little musical experience when they began playing together. "I still feel like a non-musician who just treats instruments," admits Meinecke, who now plays lap steel, guitar, cornet, drums, and more. "The ones who had been playing in bands since they were 12 or something, like Justin [Hoffman]—he had to reduce his virtuoso abilities to a mechanical new wave/punk thing."

F.S.K. is an acronym for Freiwillige Selbstkontrolle; translated as "voluntary self-control," this slogan was also the official title of an organization overseeing self-censorship in the German film industry. From the beginning, F.S.K. were determined to set themselves apart from the bulk of German bands, which by

F.S.K., German post-punk ironists supreme. Credit: Courtesy Thomas Meinecke; photo Bernd Hartwich

and large imitated American and British trends (as most of them do to this day). The group wore German Army surplus clothes, refused to talk onstage, and in general made little effort to consciously entertain the audience. They played their first live show in 1980 in Hamburg, Meinecke recalls, "in front of 600 hardcore punks who had just beaten the Clash off the stage a week before because they had signed to Columbia or something." It was a good thing F.S.K. were reasonably well-received by the audience, as "the band which played after us—it was like a festival—they were beaten off the stage immediately."

"We were always described as *the* intellectual German band," Meinecke continues. "Every gig we played was like a lecture in post-Marxism. People were just standing there watching us and applauding. In the very beginning, there were brawls all the time in the audience. But as soon as it had been written—*the* intellectual German band—it was very calm, and it was not very exciting. It was a *gig*, not a lecture. So we tried to blend musical elements in, which were supposed to be roots music."

This was not roots music in the sense of Bruce Springsteen trying to pretend to be Woody Guthrie, or Elvis Costello trying to impersonate George Jones. This was a time, Meinecke explains, when German bands were either trying to live up to the stereotypes of the soulless German new wave music seen on the *Saturday Night Live* parody "Sprockets," or trying their damnedest to sound like English-speaking underground groups such as Sonic Youth or Dinosaur Jr. "We felt the same dilemma, in a way. We started also to look for music we heard in the New World.

"What we found was country music. In country music we found a lot of roots of the country music styles or other bastard American music styles which we liked so much, like Tex-Mex, Cajun, bluegrass, polka bands from Chicago—the Polish ones," he clarifies. "Or the Czech polka bands from Texas or whatever. We found many elements which had been European music in the last century, but much less exciting over here. We learned from that way how Americans treat their heritage with not much respect.

"We liked that, and tried to learn from that. We took some of these Texas bohemian songs, which had been traditionals anyway, even here in Europe, and made other lyrics, which were still very political. We never really tried to give the impression that this is now roots music."

Critics, however, couldn't resist comparing them to the Pogues, Camper Van Beethoven, and especially the British underground band the Mekons for their deconstruction of folk music forms within a rock context. The Mekons comparison holds water to a certain degree (an F.S.K. EP of drinking songs was produced by a Mekon). But F.S.K. were weirder than any of those bands—which is to say, about as weird as any. The mesh of styles—Bavarian yodels meeting George Clinton-style funk, haunting Nico-ish tunes sung by bassist Michaela Melian (Meinecke's wife), drinking songs next to accordion-flavored polka-rock, and lyrics about free jazz guitarist Sonny Sharrock—defied easy audience identification. Even within the same album, it seemed as if you could be listening to several different artists. There was a sense of gleeful piecemeal extraction from everywhere that sounded akin not just to the Mekons, but also to pop experimentalists/absurdists like Frank Zappa.

"We never really wanted to express ourselves as individuals in the band, or really create one style which could be immediately identifiable, like R.E.M. or something," claims Meinecke. "Maybe that's why people call us a critics' band. 'Cause critics are working maybe in a similar way. It's like their record collection, or the way they put records in their CD during an evening or something." The end result has F.S.K. "quoting things, but never quoting things as a whole. Quoting parts of things and putting them into a totally different context, which makes it like a Weill-Brecht theater play in a way. We want to expose the brokenness of the material. We always glue things together which are not really meant to be together. So for the chorus, we take a bluegrass melody and the refrain or the verse from some house music from Detroit or something."

Is it all some kind of intellectual joke, perhaps? "It's kind of criticism, played on instruments. A lot of times [it's] also music about music. But it's still meant as *music*. It's not cabaret, not satire or something." Though Yankees wouldn't know it, the German lyrics often remain political in nature, criticizing German nationalism and the political compromises of the German left. Their latest album, *International*, also delves into gender studies. It's as if they've made their underground literary fanzine into records.

Why sing in German, when so many bands from non-English-speaking countries sing in English to reach a broader audience? "In Germany, most of the bands sing in English. [It] is kind of more disturbing and strange if it's suddenly in German," maintains Meinecke. "It's more like the *un*natural thing, to sing in German."

For those who can't grasp the subtlety of the German lyrics—i.e., well over 90% of the British and American audience—F.S.K. offer an assortment of fractured covers of tunes like "I Wish I Could Sprechen Sie Deutsch." The irony of throwing American bastardizations of European folk forms across the ocean yet again is not lost on Meinecke. The intent behind the English cover songs, he explains, is "to show English-speaking audiences how we put these scars into the musical material we play, through songs which they know in a different way. We started putting out these cover versions of GI songs, country songs about Germany." These songs, he notes with no visible regret, create a picture of Deutschland that's "as wrong as a Wim Wenders movie where you have a tumbleweed every 20 seconds."

It was an approach that won them a standing invitation to appear on John Peel's show whenever they felt like it (an offer, according to Meinecke, that is only shared by the Fall). But it wasn't a strategy that would win them many permanent fans, who had to constantly get used to a new style once they'd assumed they'd figured out what these wise guys were up to. In fact, Meinecke says that very few of the band's latter-day fans are over 30 (though most of the bandmembers are in their 40s), their original audience having lost interest in alternative music quite some time ago.

F.S.K.'s records were extremely difficult to come by in the U.S., a situation that changed to some degree when they picked up their most important fan of all. As the most crucial member of Camper Van Beethoven, which also combined roots music and post-punk into a goofy mix, David Lowery could have been expected to appreciate F.S.K. Meinecke, who also works as a radio DJ, met Lowery when he interviewed the musician during a European tour. "What we agreed was that using traditional music forms, like [Camper] with their balalaikas and mandolin and whatever, did not mean that this is now folk music. He was very much addressing the point that this is pop, with Camper Van Beethoven. I always thought about F.S.K. the same way."

When Meinecke sent Lowery a cassette of the interview, he also enclosed an F.S.K. CD. Lowery liked the disc so much that he offered to produce their next album. At the time he was somewhat at loose ends anyway, having disbanded Camper Van Beethoven and not yet formed his current group, Cracker. He invited the band to record with him in his hometown of Richmond, and ended up becoming a quasi-member of F.S.K. himself, playing some guitar and writing and singing the occasional tune. He also had F.S.K. tour with Cracker recently in the States, where the ironically titled *The Sound of Music* was issued on Flying Fish, a label usually associated with traditional folkies, not alternative rock weirdos.

"He's the first real producer we ever had," says Meinecke. "Before that, we produced our records on our own, and we were always democratically trying to get everything played at the same volume in the mix. It was like a flat picture. It's like remixing, what he did with stuff. We have learned from his way of producing that we *write* our songs like he *produces* them."

Tired of being pigeonholed as a maverick roots band, F.S.K. have recently moved back to a harder, "art-school" rock sound. Even Lowery—their producer and honorary bandmember—is getting confused. On their latest album, Meinecke reveals, "He had put this yodel, this Japanese-Swiss yodel sample into his mix of 'Eurotrash Girl,' which is his song anyway. He did not understand in the first place why we suddenly disliked having yodels on our records, since we had been so fond of our yodeling, or fake yodeling, before." Meinecke knows it's absurd to get upset about a Japanese-Swiss yodel sample, but it's apparent that he's still concerned he might have hurt his friend's feelings. "He was so proud to have found this Japanese yodel record in the public library!"

Recommended Recordings:

Bei Alfred (1995, ZickZack, Germany). The best (and only) condensation of the group's sprawling 1980–1989 discography, on two CDs and 44 songs. Drawn from 11 different discs, it's a roller coaster ride through the jungle of roots, punk, and electronic influences the group absorbed into their peculiar brand of German rock. Includes some of their more notoriously strange compositions, such as "Jodler für Sonny Sharrock," 'Ich Habe Migräne," and "Drunk," as well as oddball English covers like "My Funny Valentine" and "I Wish I Could Sprechen Sie Deutsch."

The Sound of Music (1995, Flying Fish). Their first widely available disc in the U.S., and the first to feature participation by David Lowery. It represents the group in their most Bavarian-polka-country fusion mood, though it isn't one of their most adventurous efforts.

Savage Republic

For a movement that was supposedly providing a lot of options to the mainstream, "alternative rock" of the 1980s sure produced a lot of bands that sounded pretty similar to each other. This led to a certain can-you-top-this desperation to be different as underground music looked for new fields to explore. Thus you might understandably be inclined to doubt Ethan Port's description of his band, Savage Republic (in a 1986 issue of *Option*), as a combination of "Tibetan Buddhist chants, a Ventures record, a Beatles record, a Pink Floyd record, Throbbing Gristle and Neubauten, test patterns on TV, and cement mixers."

It's not the most accurate (or appetizing) recipe. But the fact was, Savage Republic truly *didn't* sound like anyone else before or since. For those who wanted industrial rock without the nonstop jackhammer drill of bands like Einstürzende Neubauten and Throbbing Gristle, Savage Republic gave you more variety and more guitars. For those who worshiped at the Church of the Sonic Guitar and wanted a post-modern sort of 1980s psychedelic music, Savage Republic gave you that *and* industrial noise. The noise rock and the chiming guitars didn't always mix, meaning that you might have a hard time finding listeners—even dedicated Savage Republic fans—who found it easy to get through their albums without pressing the pause and skip buttons.

If nothing else, it's a tribute to the band's goal to, as guitarist Bruce Licher puts it, "make every song be as different as possible from every other song. So that we might have one song where we played two basses, drums, and percussion with no guitars, sticking one bass through a fuzz box. And then we might go ahead and write another song that had two guitars, drums, and keyboards with no basses at all. And then we had other songs that were just percussion and chanting. The idea was, let's keep it interesting. Let's keep exploring and trying to find new ways to put things together."

Actually, in time Savage Republic could get a lot weirder than that, with guitars that sometimes employed six identically tuned strings, or performances that saw guitarist-percussionist-bassist Port destroying bookshelves onstage. The hypnotic guitar drone of their instrumental pieces in the mid- and late 1980s, however, was a far cry from the music that former UCLA students Licher and Mark Erskine starting fooling around with in 1980. Banging on metal percussion in the utility tunnels below the university (for the good echo), the duo eventually evolved into Africa Corps, becoming Savage Republic just before their recorded debut in 1982.

Noise rock was a much bigger element on the group's early releases, as the musicians deployed oil cans, metal pipes, 55-gallon drums, and oddly tuned guitars in their search for places that no "rock" band had ever explored. To a large degree, they achieved their goal with their first LP, *Tragic Figures*. "I still go back and listen to *Tragic Figures* sometimes and think, there's nothing that sounds

Savage Republic live, circa 1986. Left to right: Ethan Port, Bruce Licher, Mark Erskine. Credit: Annabelle Port

like this before or since," claims Licher. "Every song on that record is completely different from every other song on that record too. I think that's one of the things that makes it so unique."

Savage Republic were also determined to avoid repeating themselves on-stage. Indeed, "onstage" is hardly an appropriate term to describe performances at a Kansas City factory (where Port destroyed that bookshelf he was using as a percussive instrument), a Great Peace March benefit, and a parking lot on Los Angeles' Skid Row, where the band played for an appreciative audience of prostitutes, junkies, and the homeless. The extroverted Port also did his best to break down barriers between staged rock performance and performance art by burning trash cans full of pampas leaves.

According to Licher, "When we first started out, every time we did another show, for like the first year or so, we would either play something that we'd never played before live or rework a song so that it was different than we had previously done it. We always wanted to have something new that we were doing every time we played a show." And, he might have added, to make records that physically *looked* different than anything else. Most of Savage Republic's releases were hand-letterpressed on Licher's still-active Independent Project label. Indeed, Licher's IPR artwork would eventually gain a Grammy nomination (for the first

Camper Van Beethoven album), as well as clients like R.E.M., who had IPR do one of their Christmas fan club releases.

By the mid-'80s, the band had started to pull in different directions, resulting in the departure of some original members and the development of a more accessible, instrumental, guitar-oriented sound. Far from being a sellout, this resulted in Savage Republic's most enduring work, as the layers of droning guitars created a hypnotic and seductive modern psychedelic music, with strong elements of surf and Middle Eastern sounds. *Ceremonial* (1985) is probably their strongest trance-rock outing.

Commercial success (even by alternative rock standards) was never a big concern for the band. They could always count on a reasonably busy live schedule on the underground circuit, and unexpectedly big audiences in countries like Greece, where they could sell out some of the nation's biggest rock clubs. But by the end of the 1980s, the band began to dissolve, as different members wanted to pursue different directions. Bruce Licher had really been the only constant presence in the group's many lineups, and his decision to move on effectively destroyed the continuity of the act.

Licher, who now plays instrumental experimental-rock guitar music with Scenic, explains, "Personally, my interests leaned more towards the instrumental stuff, as is obvious with what I've been doing since. On the first album, I was really into a lot of the industrial noise things at the time, Throbbing Gristle and that sort of thing. I think it was really important to get some aggressions out that you could do by banging on a piece of metal.

"Eventually I got to the point where I felt like 'no, I've done that, I don't need to do that anymore.' I felt like the longer, more instrumental pieces were things that could go a little bit deeper and get what I felt was some more mature emotions. That was one of the reasons that the band went through so many permutations, and why it eventually split, was because there were other band members who wanted to continue doing the aggressive stuff. I felt like I'd done that; I didn't need to do it anymore." Port and other bandmembers Greg Grunke and Thom Fuhrmann, Licher notes, continued to work together and "did want to continue using the name Savage Republic. I strongly advised them not to. I told them they should probably try to come up with something of their own. They got kind of pissed off at me for a while, but we're all friends now."

Current IPR bands like Scenic and Tone Sustain bear some resemblance to Savage Republic in their use of post-punk guitar crescendos in instrumental song formats. But as Licher proudly notes, it's not a sound that is easily imitated. "It's not like Nirvana or My Bloody Valentine, any of those other bands where there's a lot of people who are just like going, 'Yeah, it's a cool sound, we're gonna do that,' and you can obviously tell. It's a bit more subtle in terms of Savage Republic. Savage Republic didn't influence so much in terms of sound, but just in the fact that we were doing something really different, interesting, and unique."

Recommended Recordings:
By Savage Republic:
Tragic Figures (1982, Independent Project). The band in its noise-rock phase. More primitive than their subsequent work, with intimations of what was to come.

Ceremonial (1985, Independent Project). By a considerable margin, their most accessible effort, putting the Middle Eastern melodies and shimmering guitar instrumentals at the forefront.

Live Trek 1985-1986 (1987, Fundamental). A lengthy (80-minute) compilation of mid-'80s concert recordings that's less consistent than *Ceremonial*, but has more variety.

By Scenic:
Incident at Cima (1995, IPR). The debut by Licher's post-Savage Republic band, Scenic, puts the focus on guitar instruments with a snaky feel that's similar to his '80s work, but executed with a cleaner, more eclectic flavor.

The full lineup of Savage Republic, circa 1986. Left to right: Mark Erskine, Bruce Licher, Thom Fuhrmann, Greg Grunke, Robert Loveless, Ethan Port. Credit: Scott Sing

Lo-Fi
Mavericks

11

If mystique and eccentricity are the key factors in generating a cult following, the newly coined genre of lo-fi music would seem to be a likely breeding ground. These are artists who, after all, have often eschewed the conventional recording and distribution process entirely. They've made their records on home four-tracks, sometimes overdubbing all of the parts themselves. They've released their music on self-distributed cassettes or tiny indie record labels. The lo-fiers shun conventional publicity tactics with as much eagerness as Courtney Love embraces them. They are major label publicists' nightmares, and fanzines' fondest dreams.

After all that, it may come as something of a letdown to inform you that, when these shadowy figures are tracked down in person, they turned out to be regular, affable sorts, engaging in the kind of banter you'd find at the local cafe or pub. Perhaps that's not a surprise; their whole approach to music-making has been based on stripping away artifice and the whole industry image charade. In fact, many of them find the "lo-fi" label itself a laugh, being more of a media creation than an organic, self-generated category.

The lo-fi story is still very much in the process of being written, with acts like Sebadoh, Magnetic Fields, Palace Brothers, and others achieving unhoped-for levels of critical (and, in the case of Pavement, even commercial) success. The centerpieces of this section, however, are two of the movement's founding fathers, who have been paving the lo-fi trail for nearly 20 years: Martin Newell and Chris Knox.

Martin Newell

It was the beginning of the 1980s when Martin Newell—failed pop musician, skilled songwriter, menial restaurant worker, and all-around English eccentric—was blinded by the flash of a light bulb inside his brain. "You know that slogan, 'What if they had a war and nobody came?'" he asks. "Well, what if they started a record company and nobody signed?"

Newell was fed up with playing the rock 'n' roll game by the accepted rules. He would not sign with a record company—not that there were any clamoring at his door. He would not even make *records*. He and his buddy Lol Elliott would tape their wacked-out but exceedingly tuneful brand of pop on a home portastudio. They would distribute the music by cassette only, relying upon underground fanzine reviews and word of mouth for sales and publicity. Their business stance could not have been any more underground and anti-music industry.

The irony is that the music itself was not that underground at all. With Cleaners From Venus, the Brotherhood of Lizards, and as a solo artist, Martin Newell has crafted some of the most inventive, catchiest British pop-rock of the last couple decades. His songs burst with melodic exuberance and harmonies; his lyrics boast a wit akin to fellow U.K. zanies such as Robyn Hitchcock and Syd Barrett; his vocals are a fetching mix of charm and insouciance. While strongly indebted to such icons of the past as the Beatles, XTC, and Small Faces, it's not mere recreation, but contemporary in attitude, and fresh in execution.

It's music that, if packaged properly, might stand a good chance of making the international hit parade. But Newell isn't interested in the dehumanizing compromises that the music business asks in return for popularity. Thus he remains Britain's best-kept musical secret, known primarily to cult followings abroad, and virtually unknown as a musician on his home turf.

When Newell talks to me from his English village, it's a bit like being taken down to the local pub by Monty Python. This is, after all, the man who did a musical tour using a bicycle as his chief mode of transport, and called himself "The Hedge" at one point because of his passion for gardening. A poet of some renown in Britain (he's a regular contributor to the *Independent* newspaper), nothing seems to delight him as much as making self-deprecating light of his own music, or poking fun at his hippie-punk persona. Except, that is, for verbally raking the music business over the coals, which he does frequently, and with a vicious glee.

In the 1970s, Newell had his fleeting brushes with flame. He responded to an ad in *Melody Maker* to discuss forming a band that (he is fairly sure) would become known as London SS, which (despite never playing a gig) spawned future members of the Damned, the Clash, and Generation X. He played backup keyboards for vocalist Helen Terry, later of Culture Club. He had a 1980 solo single for Liberty Records, "Young Jobless," which later became a theme for the British TV series *Job Hunt*. He was working in a restaurant when his mum called to tell him that the record was causing a scandal of sorts in the *Daily Mail*, who objected to what they saw as a record "about dole and drugs."

"The British press are quite ruthless in pursuit of a story," shudders Newell today. "They'll tell any amount of lies, and they don't care who they sacrifice. It turned me into a druggy, paranoid little recluse. It helped me spawn Cleaners From Venus.

"I was one of the inventors of the cassette underground," he continues. "Being pretty much an average dumbshit *Spinal Tap* type-pop musician, I was interested in haircuts, girls, drugs, and quite a lot of music. I had no knowledge of politics. But I suddenly started reading anarchist tracts. I became a fully-fledged agit-prop anarchist.

"We said, 'Look, the equation is this: we want to make music, and there's people who want to listen to it. So how do we get our music out of our hearts, through our fingers, into people's ears, without this plethora of parasites interfering with it?' And I thought, I know. As the technology improves—they'd just invented four-track portastudios—we could have the same facilities in theory as the Beatles had, in our living rooms. And we could just mail it out to people."

Newell's first partner in musical terrorism was drummer Lol Elliott. The first tapes distributed under the Cleaners From Venus banner were lo-fi, murkily recorded affairs that couldn't hide the power of the melodies, or a wit that could be both tender and savage. It should also be noted that while tens of thousands of musicians are oiling the international cassette network with product today, there were relatively few acts recording and distributing their music from home in 1980. Cleaners From Venus were taking the DIY ethic to a more intense level, and pioneering the lo-fi sound (a catch phrase that wouldn't become widely known until the 1990s) in the bargain.

At this point, according to Newell, the band's attitude toward the capitalist economy was so vitriolic that they would have rejected financial rewards

Martin Newell, holding a mirror to the English psyche.

even if the possibility arose. "Lol, who was well-studied in anarchism, said, 'Look, do we have to take money for it? Can't we just do a direct swap—music for groceries?'" Newell snickers with sheer delight. "But obviously, the thing has a self-limiting factor inasmuch as if you start sending melons or oranges and stuff, there's perishables. We're vegetarians, so there wouldn't be any rotting meat being sent to us. It would have to be dried goods. I think somebody did actually send us some tea bags. But that's as far as it got. Then we realized that we couldn't swap tea bags for stamps, so we couldn't mail the stuff out. We had to modify it a bit. In the end, we just charged the lowest prices we could."

Primarily through fanzine reviews, the Cleaners were managing to sell a few hundred or so of their tapes—a remarkable figure considering there was virtually nothing in the way of self-promotion involved. The cassettes were being played by such diverse enthusiasts as underground Swiss radio stations and radio operators fighting for the British Army during the Falklands War. "It began to get quite successful, so I got in an argument with a businessman one day, who said 'Martin, this thing seems to be taking off for you. What happens if you become successful?' I said, 'We'll give it away.' He said, 'What happens if it gets really global?' I said, 'We'll pay people to take it with the money we've made.' He got really angry, and I had to leave the pub before he hit me."

Credit: Courtesy New Millennium Communications

The Cleaners were using radical politics to spread music with more mainstream pop appeal than almost anything else in the underground. R. Stevie Moore was using the same sort of home tape approach in the United States, but the Cleaners were more accessible to a classic pop-rock audience. And they were *way* more accessible to such an audience than DIY punk acts such as Crass, the famed anarchist British punk band that issued and distributed their music themselves. (Newell on Crass: "They did actually sound like two lathes buggering each other on an elevator in an aircraft hangar.")

"I wanted to make pushy little pop tunes with nasty lyrics, that's all," insists Newell. "And sometimes *nice* lyrics. I was very naive, really. I liked the Beatles and the Monkees and things like that. I wasn't interested in all those art statements. I like pretty tunes, verse-chorus, verse-chorus, a bit of psychedelic guitar, then that's the end. I leave it to the art-school boys to do all that noise."

As far as the band's mutation of their love for '60s pop, Newell declares without shame, "The people who played music in the '60s were quite good musicians. And we weren't, really. We were very *bad* musicians! Lol could keep a beat, but he was always fucking stoned or tripping or something. I was never a good guitarist, I couldn't play it that well. I always thought you should do things instantly. I believe that great pop was hatched by people fumbling around in the dark. I wasn't interested in getting things perfect. I just wanted it to be fun."

As the band improved in competence and upgraded their audio fidelity, their cassettes began to match the standards of the best pop albums of the day. *Living with Victoria Grey* (1986) in particular is one of the lost classics of the 1980s, presenting a set of cracking good tunes linked by Looney Tunes-like intrasong banter. Newell's lyrics combined a celebration of past icons (silent movie star Clara Bow, *Man From U.N.C.L.E.* hero Ilya Kuryakin) with an uneasy, wary view of the present. A committed eclectic, he crafted moody acoustic guitar ballads and a cappella Beach Boys–Turtles hybrids. The sound was planted in the '80s by a rich, slightly echoing guitar jangle; "Victoria Grey" and "Mercury Girl" had genuine hit potential, if '80s radio had been open to songs that emerged from the heart rather than the drum machine.

Living with Victoria Grey may be the most consistent of Newell's '80s efforts, but each of his tapes has its many small pleasures. Part of the delight of each one is how he constantly tinkers and experiments within classic pop structures—left-field glockenspiel pops, creepy echo effects, lounge organ, lyrics about being abandoned by American girlfriends, celebrations of "Christmas in Suburbia." The boxy drum sounds on many of the tapes are the only chief drawback (professional audio technicians, indeed, may shake in rage at both the percussive textures and the occasional hiss/distortion). The effect is often, as Martin wrote on the sleeve of one of his cassettes, like a 40-minute trip to England.

Song titles like "Song for Syd Barrett" and "I Was a Teenage Idiot Dancer" make it easy to categorize Newell as a standard-bearer of the sort of idiosyncratic British whimsy doled out by Ray Davies, Andy Partridge (of XTC), and the Television Personalities. "Well, I'm *English*," sniffs Newell, as though such critical observation is so obvious that it's barely worth noting. "Hemingway said, you should write about what you know, and not go that much off it. There's no point in me writing a song about Route 66, 'cause I've never been on it. I like writing about the little things that we know about. Bathos, where you go from the sublime to the ridiculous—a Monty Python kind of thing. That's the essence of my writing."

The record companies ultimately couldn't be fended off forever. Their 1984 tape *Town and Country* had already been issued on vinyl when the Cleaners released *Going to England* in 1987. By this time Giles Smith had replaced Elliott as Newell's collaborator, and although the album contained much of the same material as the *Victoria Grey* tape, it somehow sounded much flatter and more generic. Though he's not entirely dismissive of his '80s vinyl, Newell agrees that some of the Cleaners' special qualities were whitewashed in the studio.

"*It was not the same thing*," he emphasizes in a booming tone of voice. "The tapes had the spirit of it. When it was me and Lol mucking about, bashing bits of vacuum cleaner and overloading the copycat echo machine, it was good. Once we got signed by a record company, there were people like engineers and musicians to stop all that nonsense going on. 'Rock musicians having fun? Can't have that. Put a stop to it immediately!' I don't want musicians making me sound too good. The whole idea, the fun, the genius, the spark of it all—has got to be from experimenting, like boys building a den."

Despite some success in Japan, Germany, and France—as well as a small cult in the United States, where many of Newell's tapes were played on college radio and available through a U.S. distributor—significant financial success, and even a modicum of renown in the U.K., was not forthcoming. By the end of the 1980s, Newell and Smith had stopped working together. (Newell has also sometimes enjoyed an extra-Cleaners sideline writing songs with Captain Sensible of the Damned.) Smith, now a journalist, writes about his Cleaners experiences as part of his recent volume of pop music appreciation, *Lost in Music*. "He actually wanted to be a pop star!" exclaims Newell in disbelief, as if the very notion was as absurd as running for the U.S. Senate as a Socialist and expecting to win. "He wanted to be Green of Scritti Politti, George Michael, or Sting. I can't imagine anything worse!"

Newell, in association with one-named bassist Nelson, released some material as the Brotherhood of Lizards in a successful attempt to get back to the vintage Cleaners sound. "It was like a homemade log raft and a pair of underpants for a flag when me and Lol set sail into the shallows of the music business," he surmises. "By the time Giles had been on the ship for a couple of albums, we were a schooner, or something like that. And instead of the pair of tattered underpants as a flag, we've now got at least a pair of open-crotch panties up there. But I didn't like it being so slick. So we kind of went back to being a rowboat with me and Nelson."

Nelson was eventually lured away by the New Model Army, though, and Newell did a one-off album with XTC leader Andy Partridge producing. The partnership seemed logical enough, as XTC is one of the names that most frequently crops up when listeners are trying to provide ready reference points/comparisons to the Cleaners. Newell was by this point making some headway with his poetry career, but put that on hold "when I heard Andy Partridge wanted to do an album with me, 'cause I'd always really loved XTC. I got on with him really well, and we made this cracking album. It's probably the best thing I've ever done. Me and Andy were both at a loose end, and both in relationships that were breaking up. Not unlike Phil Collins and Sting, we didn't go to therapy or cry on each other's shoulders. We just got on with the bloody job, like the British chaps fucking do. Locked ourselves in a shed and made an album. And it's a cracker."

Positive coverage in *Rolling Stone* notwithstanding, the album did little to break Newell into the international mainstream. His combination of pleasure and disillusionment with the *Rolling Stone* review is typical: "Finally at age 41 I get one, and it's a good one. Does it make me any money? Does it matter any more? No." But in many respects, Newell is better off than Partridge, his far more celebrated partner. Partridge, it was recently reported, had to sign a subpar recording contract in the late 1980s in order to get his label to pay off legal bills amounting to 400,000 pounds. For several years, he was unable to record with XTC as they tried to wriggle out of their major-label deal.

By contrast, Newell's not in massive debt, is free to record as the occasion allows, and is finding a new level of success in Britain, where he's known primarily as a poet/humorist, not a rock singer-songwriter. Over the last couple of months, he tells me, he's done 5,000 pounds of business through his self-published poetry volumes—kitten feed in the record industry, but an astronomical amount by the standards of the poetry world. And he's just as set as ever on wagging his ears at the music establishment.

"I might make another album this year," he enthuses. "But I'm going to do it in a really bad, cheap studio. I'm probably going to play all the instruments, which means it'll definitely be crappy. But I maintain that our real fans actually like that quality in us. Record companies and musicians, for 15 years now, have tried to make me *so-o-o* good. And I've considered it a mission to fight them."

Recommended Recordings:

By Cleaners from Venus:
Living with Victoria Grey (1986, Man At The Off License, UK). The most pleasurable of Newell's many album projects, vastly superior to its rough vinyl counterpart (*Going to England*), but issued on cassette only.

Town and Country (1988, RCA, Germany). The Cleaners' best vinyl full-length. "The Beat Generation and Me," "I Was a Teenage Idiot Dancer," and the jubilant "Let's Get Married" (Martin must have woken up on the right side of the bed for once that day) are all among Newell's best songs.

By Martin Newell:
Martin Newell's Box of Old Humbug (Humbug, 1996, UK). All of Newell's recent solo records in one three-CD box: *The Greatest Living Englishman*, the slightly more baroque *The Off White Album*, and a four-track single. Hard to find and a bit pricey, but then if you've read this far there's a fair chance you're eager to check out anything by Newell. All the discs are available separately, and are consistent with his Cleaners ethos of carefully sculpted witty pop, with somewhat more considered (though not slick) production values.

Flying Nun Records

As a country of a mere three million people—less than the total population of the San Francisco Bay Area—New Zealand's influence on the mainstream international rock scene has been small. Go into the alternative rock community, however, and it's a much different story. For many underground music fans, New Zealand rock means Flying Nun Records, the Auckland-based operation that has been churning out neo-psychedelic-based pop since the early 1980s. Tall Dwarfs are just one of numerous New Zealand bands on the Flying Nun label that have established an international cult following.

Flying Nun was founded in 1981 by Roger Shepherd, manager of a record store in Christchurch. The imports passing through on heavyweight British indie imprints Factory and Rough Trade were inspirations of sorts to apply the same aesthetic to the South Island's burgeoning underground rock scene, which was particularly active in Christchurch and the university town of Dunedin. "It was a regional thing, much the same as I imagine other labels of that and following periods—early Sub Pop springs to mind—were," says Paul McKessar, Flying Nun's International Manager. "There was a definite DIY attitude born out of necessity."

Although the bleak post-punk of groups like Joy Division and the Fall (who actually had a Top 20 hit in New Zealand in 1982) is cited by McKessar as a formative influence, what actually came out on Flying Nun was a good deal cheerier and more melodic. Bands like Tall Dwarfs, the Clean, and the Chills did not seem as intent on breaking from classic rock traditions as transmuting them into a post-psychedelic aesthetic that valued home-spun production values, whimsical lyrics, actual tunes, and a determination to be quirky. This quirkiness was evident before you even played the records, which were enclosed in colorful sleeves, often hand-drawn, with swirling colors and lettering that screamed anti-slickness.

Syd Barrett's daft psychedelic pop seems to be cited as a reference point in over half the reviews of Flying Nun product. To some extent, the Flying Nun roster could be viewed as the collective expression of cult rock fans that eventually became musicians. "The '60s were a huge influence over all the key musicians in the Flying Nun scene," responds McKessar. "The whimsical edge is probably not exclusively Barrett-driven. A lot of people were listening to everything from the Byrds and Love to Skip Spence (the Kilgours [brothers David and Hamish, of the Clean] are huge *Oar* fans) as well. There's certainly a strong Celtic thing that seems to come naturally to the South Island bands, probably genetic and geographical. The strong, simple beat of the drums identifies the music for many listeners, and you could probably put that down to [Velvet Underground drummer] Moe Tucker filtered through [Clean drummer] Hamish Kilgour. I'd say the major '60s influence, though, is in the unfettered-by-commercialism free-spiritedness at the heart of most Flying Nun music."

While not every band embraced the DIY recording ethics with as much intensity as Chris Knox and Alec Bathgate of Tall Dwarfs did, studio polish was not nearly as much of a concern as getting across the feeling and the power with a minimum of fuss. "Most people found they could make the music sound the way they wanted to hear it by recording on relatively 'primitive' equipment. No one wanted to sound like all the awful synthesizer bands that came to prominence in the early '80s. Economically, that fitted the FN agenda rather well too, of course.

"Once people had been recording for a while, many artists came to want things in their sound that they couldn't achieve with the four-track. Chris and the Tall Dwarfs are an exception, I think, because most of the other bands were live three- or four-piece rock bands. It is difficult to record that live power (and most were incredibly powerful live bands) on a four-track and be consistently happy with the results."

Flying Nun's economics were also well-served by the DIY nature of the record covers, often drawn by the band themselves; the sleeves have also ensured that the releases remain perennial hot tickets among collectors. McKessar says the illustrations and sleeve design is always up to the bands, "unless they have absolutely no idea of what they want on a cover, then we have to find something else. That is a continuation of the artist-driven aesthetic. A lot of the bands seem to have at least one member with ability and interest in fine or graphic arts. Look at Knox—musician, artist, cartoonist, film and music reviewer, cultural commentator, etc. etc. There's quite a few where I have no idea what they're supposed to mean, but at least they don't look ugly or corporate."

Despite the label's anti-corporate stance, Flying Nun had a surprising amount of success for an indie label shortly after it launched operations. The Chills, Clean, Verlaines, Bats, and Double Happys all had chart entries in the first half of the 1980s with singles and EPs. That's one of the advantages of being a band in a country where (as of 1989) only 7,500 units of sales were necessary to qualify for a gold record. Also, points out McKessar, "We're a small country a long way from the international action and you don't see a lot of foreign bands touring through NZ, especially 'alternative' ones."

New Zealand's relative isolation from the heart of the international pop machines of London, New York, and Los Angeles may have aided the incubation of an original underground rock scene that wasn't as inundated with passing trends and pressure to conform to certain standards of hipness. Its isolation, of course, also worked against significant exposure in North America and Europe. Until the late 1980s, records on Flying Nun (or other New Zealand labels) were extremely hard to come by, even in specialist shops.

But by the mid-1980s, Flying Nun imports were picking up a following among devoted indie rock obsessives, even if at that point it might have been limited in the U.S. to a few hundred or so rabid fanzine readers. Aside from Tall Dwarfs, there were the Chills, perhaps the most accessible (and Syd Barrett–influenced) act on the Flying Nun roster; the

Verlaines, who dressed up their pop-rock with a poetic lyrical sensibility and references to classical motifs; and the Bats, whose guitar jangle fit comfortably into the thrust of college radio playlists in the late 1980s. Licensing deals in the U.K. and U.S. helped give these bands, and others like Straightjacket Fits and the Jean-Paul Sartre Experience, a much greater profile abroad.

Once many fans got into the Flying Nun aesthetic, they found it hard to stop, picking up FN titles by various lesser-known bands and side projects/offshoots, like Sneaky Feelings, the Puddle, Look Blue Go Purple, and the Cake Kitchen (most Flying Nun band names are nothing if not living-room friendly). Still, Flying Nun never enjoyed the commercial success and media attention of, say, Sub Pop. Most of the Flying Nun fanatics were concentrated around urban centers such as San Francisco, New York, and Chicago, as well as university towns.

In the 1990s, the Flying Nun roster seems increasingly static, populated by longtime stalwarts such as Chris Knox, or offshoots of acts that started with the label back in the 1980s. In early 1997, Roger Shepherd resigned from the label, which is now owned by the large, Australian-based Mushroom company. It's a development that's a bit worrisome for some who fear Flying Nun may lose some of its creative latitude, though no major changes seem to be in the offing as of this writing. "Flying Nun bands have continued to influence younger bands here," says McKessar. "We're definitely the old guys of the alternative music scene here. For the most part we're still ignored by the commercial radio music industry and suchlike, but there's a certain amount of respect and support that keeps us going."

What of the effect Flying Nun's had on underground rock *outside* of New Zealand? Observes McKessar, "Internationally, it seems that Flying Nun is synonymous with NZ music, which is probably not how it should be really, but at least we're waving the flag. There's constant wonderment at how so many amazing bands can come from a tiny place so far away. (And I don't know why that is either.) People have a fairly healthy respect for the label and I'm seeing bands get their due more and more—as the years go by, the Tall Dwarfs are cited or made a reference point for a lot of home-recorded stuff, and I think the influence of other bands, from the Chills, Clean, 3Ds etc. to Dead C (originally a Flying Nun band) can be heard in a lot of stuff.

"It is constantly amazing to learn of things like the Croatian Tall Dwarfs fan who ended up supplying a tape loop for the new Tall Dwarfs album *Stumpy*—that means the music has got a long way from NZ. I guess being a cult means you're getting a certain amount of respect for doing things your own way, which to me is healthier and more rewarding than the kind of respect someone like Clive Davis or David Geffen gets from their time in the music business for making millions of dollars."

Home Tapers

When Martin Newell set up his portastudio around 1980, he was following the path of thousands of other musicians around the world—who, for the most part, made their music in isolation, unaware of the level of similar home recording activity. Many, perhaps most, of these artists would be content to simply record music for their own pleasure, or use their home tapes as demos, for the mundane purposes of securing live work or recording contracts. Relatively few thought of the home-produced tape as a vehicle for bypassing the vagaries of the music industry entirely, as Newell did.

While cassette culture remains very much an underground phenomenon, trends in both technology and music would increase the ranks of the "cassette underground" exponentially in the 1980s and 1990s. To begin with, the cassette itself would not truly enter its golden era until about 1980, when the widespread presence of boomboxes—as well as the increased sophistication of home stereo equipment—made it a universal household item. Sophisticated musical technology—not just four-track recorders, but instruments of all kinds—were now more widely available to the average, and even poor, citizen than ever before. Yet the record industry was becoming increasingly rigid in its specifications of what was commercial or uncommercial, which ultimately determined who it would actually record. Increasingly large numbers of musicians felt frozen out of the pipeline of distribution, unless they were willing to incur the considerable expenses of studio recording and record manufacturing themselves.

Fortunately, the increased constriction of major record labels and commercial radio stations coincided with a spider web network of underground fanzines and college radio/noncommercial broadcasters. Fanzines were willing to review anything, including self-produced tapes; adventurous DJs were willing to play anything if they liked it. Listeners who liked what they heard, or were curious about what they read, could then order it directly from the source. It wasn't going to make anyone rich, but at least the home tapers would find an audience outside of their bedrooms.

By the standards of the music business, Martin Newell's early outings with the Cleaners From Venus were abysmal failures saleswise, shifting only several hundred "units." By the standards of the cassette underground, however, they were wildly successful. Lots, perhaps most, home tapes sold only in the dozens; even in those cases, they were often usually just given away to friends, or exchanged/traded with other home tapers. Those privy to the cassette community, however, often found a level of personal expression and experimentation that was unavailable on "real" records. It wasn't just a matter of "lo-fi" technology (see separate sidebar), although that was a part of it. It was also because, unencumbered by any commercial pressures or expectations, the musicians would do whatever they wanted. Which, often, just amounted to being themselves.

A corresponding problem, however, was that this led to an enormous amount of self-indulgence, as well as product by "artists" who were too untalented, undeveloped, or uninspired to have any business making music in the first place. Finding the gems among the dross required a Herculean effort, which often fell to overloaded editors of magazines such as *Op*, a principal source of information about home tapes in the early '80s. *Option* magazine (which was similar in format to *Op* in its early days) would pick up the ball in the mid-'80s by running extensive cassette reviews. These were curtailed and, eventually, virtually eliminated. But numerous other fanzines were around to pick up that slack, guaranteeing exposure both for companies that made sure to distribute cassettes (such as the K label) and individuals just starting out.

Inevitably, the cassette underground started to spawn its "stars." Martin Newell's closest American counterpart may be R. Stevie Moore, who's made dozens if not hundreds of eccentric rock tapes since the mid-'70s, though his work is on the whole more experimental, and less pop, in nature than Newell's. There were dozens of acts who, taking advantage of the ease of technology, seemingly blasted out difficult experimental music by the cartload, such as Psyclones and Minoy. Acts like Eugene Chadbourne and (to a lesser extent) Savage Republic put their most important work on record, but released tapes of live or extraneous material for devoted fans.

It's fair to say, though, that few artists used the cassette medium for uncommercial-but-melodic pop-rock nearly as effectively as Newell has. Some notable contemporaries of Newell worth checking out would include melodic folk-rocker Jeff Kelly, funnier-than-hell weirdos Walls of Genius, dainty miniaturist Linda Smith, and Dennis Carleton, who created a worthy cassette-length suite of bits and bursts of catchy pop tunes on *Color with Crayons*. On rare occasions, acts "graduate" from self-released cassettes to "real" record deals, such as Sebadoh, Throwing Muses, or (though he might hate to admit it), Martin Newell. The most celebrated examples by far are Liz Phair's *Girlysound* tapes, which landed her a record deal. The tapes have subsequently circulated to literally thousands of Phair fans, many of whom would put the songs and performances on the same level as her albums (which have been acclaimed as some of the best alternative rock of the '90s). The *Girlysound* material has even done brisk business on bootleg CDs, an honor accorded to few if any other rock home tapes.

A problem with finding out about home tapes years after the event, of course, is that they're all but impossible to find in stores. Unless you have the cassette packages themselves, it's also often difficult to find the addresses of the musicians themselves for direct ordering. Some (though probably not much) great music probably remains buried on home tape productions that were never fortunate enough to reach even a few hundred listeners. Don't be surprised to find rock archeologists of the future counting several home tapers of the '80s and '90s among their greatest "discoveries," decades after the equipment used to record them has faded into obsolescence.

Chris Knox
Tall Dwarves

"Haven't a clue, who follows who; haven't the foggiest notion of what I'm expected to do," moans Chris Knox on Tall Dwarfs' "And Other Kinds." It's only a song, but it could also serve as Knox's artistic manifesto. For 20 years, he's largely made records by learning the recording equipment—and, often, even the songs—as he's gone along. It's not a method you'll find endorsed in any book on how to succeed in the music business. It seems to have worked fine for Knox, however. It's an arguable point, but there may be no more influential figure in the history of New Zealand rock, even if few listeners outside of the international underground have ever heard him.

It was Knox who fronted the Enemy, which may have been the first punk band in New Zealand to play original material. He also sang for Toy Love, a more pop-oriented combo that became, for a brief period, the most popular new wave band in the country. But Knox didn't really find himself until he began making four-track recordings on his own, deliberately avoiding expensive, sterile, state-of-the-art studios. Valuing spontaneity and inspiration more than finished gloss, he was one of the principal fathers of lo-fi, a sub-genre which didn't even have a name when he and partner Alec Bathgate began releasing Tall Dwarfs records in the early '80s. By the 1990s, groups like Pavement and Guided By Voices would take lo-fi into the pages of the *New York Times* and (at least in Pavement's case) the charts; both acts, and several others in a similar vein, cite Tall Dwarfs as a primary influence. With only slight upgrades in equipment, he continues to work in much the same way today, both as half of Tall Dwarfs and on his own solo releases.

On the surface, the articulate Knox—now in his mid-forties, married, and the father of two children—bears little resemblance to the wildman who would paint his face, shave his hair into partial mohawks, and take to the stage in front of the Enemy in the late '70s. Knox formed the band in 1977 in Dunedin, the most southerly city of notable size in New Zealand (and thus the most southerly city in the world), inspired by early tremors of British punk from the Sex Pistols and the Damned. As to whether they were the very first Kiwi punk band to play their own material, Knox says, "I'm not sure whether we beat out some of the northern ones by a month or two or not. But certainly *one* of the first—definitely the *biggest*. And," he adds disdainfully, "the least concerned with *looking* like punks. None of us changed our names. All the Auckland punks changed *their* names."

Live Knox would rip a page from the Iggy Pop fan club book by engaging in bloody self-laceration. The Enemy never released a record, and had toned down somewhat by the time they evolved into Toy Love. Signed by WEA, their debut single, "Rebel," made New Zealand's Top Thirty. But after only one album, Toy Love were through. An attempt to start cracking the international market by moving to Australia for a few months had exhausted the band. And Knox wasn't satisfied with the LP, a rather cheery pop-new wave confection that is only impressive given that few New Zealand bands were even trying to do something in that direction.

"It was a horrible album," he states categorically. "It's so depressing listening to some of that stuff. The songs were coming from someone in a state of arrested adolescence. There were a lot of songs about sexual inadequacy, masturbation, and unavailability of anywhere to put your dick—pretty pathetic. The Enemy was much more straightforwardly punky than Toy Love. But that album really pushes the commercial side and loses the much rockier, nastier side we had. Other performances on demos and stuff are far superior.

"It got to the point we were so bored with what we were doing, and we were just getting sick of each other. The drummer wanted to play guitar, and

Massachusetts, 1994. Chris Knox on left, Alec Bathgate on right. Credit: Courtesy Chris Knox

the keyboard player wanted to play drums. Now, I think it was a great idea, but at the time, it seemed sort of ludicrous. So I just gave it up, much to the disgust and embarrassment of our record label."

Any discussion of Knox's career must give nearly equal weight to Alec Bathgate, who had played guitar in both the Enemy and Toy Love, and would form a musical partnership with Knox that endures to the present. "We were totally disenchanted with the music industry," says Knox. "We were absolutely sick of playing reams of gigs without any time to actually be creative. We were devastated by lack of money and lack of good health." When Toy Love scattered, Chris and Alec stayed in the same city and began making their own home experiments on Knox's newly acquired TEAC four-track recorder. "We just started mucking around with it and thought, we don't have to deal with the engineers. We can play exactly what we like; we can do what we like."

By choosing to work outside of professional studios, Knox and Bathgate were in a sense taking the do-it-yourself ethic of punk to a more intense level. To the surprise of some, however, the music they made on their own was not punk or new wave. It was more like a kind of '80s psychedelia that tried to shove as much experimental weirdness into melodic pop songs as possible. The results were as enigmatic and oppositional as the name they chose for themselves: Tall Dwarfs.

"We'd always been interested very much in the psychedelic stuff between '66 and '68, where a lot of interesting stuff was being investigated by even real mainstream bands, like the Beatles," explains Knox. "But we were both pop idiots. We love good pop melodies, and the idea of having odd musical sounds plus nice pop melodies really intrigued. Especially if those melodies were laced with nasty lyrics, or lyrics that actually made you think rather than just sing along. That sounds like we actually had a plan, but we didn't. We just recorded a couple of things and thought, this is wonderful. Somebody was silly enough to release them."

Although their 1981 debut EP was released on Furtive, with their 1982 follow-up the group began their still-running association with the Flying Nun label, the most creative and influential New Zealand record company of the 1980s and 1990s (see sidebar). The 1982 EP *Louis Likes His Daily Dip* actually cracked the national Top 20, a rather astonishing feat for a record that sounded like Syd Barrett's jolly uncle, featuring a protagonist whose "only turn-on is his wife." Just as importantly, Knox was helping other bands in Christchurch record on his TEAC four-track. Several of these, such as the Chills, Verlaines, and the Clean, would also be instrumental in establishing the Flying Nun aesthetic: neo-psychedelia that was personal and quirky, without sounding revivalist.

Not long into their partnership, Knox left Christchurch to settle in Auckland on the northernmost of New Zealand's two islands. For most two-man bands recording on their own, this would have been the end of the line. Knox and Bathgate, after all, were living in two separate cities (and islands) a thousand miles apart. Instead, they determined to continue the Tall Dwarfs project by recording—and writing—all of their material together in periodic three-day holidays of activity, whenever the two could manage to be in the same place at the same time. Complete songs—constructed from chords, tape loops, and vocal overdubs—were written and recorded virtually simultaneously. Knox has even done vocals *while* mixing the track. On a recent album, they solicited rhythm tracks via mail-order from other like-minded souls around the world, issuing a "You Too Can Be a Tall Dwarf!" invitation in their liner notes.

Tall Dwarfs' personalized recipe has gotten a lot of attention in the underground press, sometimes tending to overshadow the strength of the material itself. Over the course of about ten albums and numerous EPs and compilation tracks, their songs are habitually infused with a tension between pretty, acoustic-driven melodies and bursts of fuzzy noise. All manner of oddball sound effects and instruments, including clavinet, spoons, omnichord, and crumhorn, make the sonic textures ever-inventive. Like an amusement park ride through a house of horrors, there's a new and frequently nasty surprise awaiting round most of the corners. Despite the (by modern standards) primitive equipment used in recording, the actual fidelity is never amateurish, while avoiding the formica finish of most contemporary product. The overall approach varies fairly little from album to album; within each album, however, the approaches always vary immensely.

Knox and Bathgate like pure pop—check out the orchestral version of "Nothing's Going to Happen" on *That's the Short & Long of It*, which is something like a garage-psych take on *Sgt. Pepper*. The pleasant tunes and bursts of noise, though, can make one overlook the lyrics, which are not readily comparable to anything in either mainstream *or* underground rock. If this is psychedelia, it's reflecting inner turmoil rather than outer space bliss. It may use acidic imagery, but there's a nasty edge reflecting insecurity and uncertainty about self-image and sanity.

But as Knox notes with pride, "There's no room in Tall Dwarfs for love songs. It seems that a lot of Tall Dwarfs stuff is about people on the outside—I don't know whether through accident or design. The name Tall Dwarfs is indicative of that. As far as we're concerned, *everybody's* just a Tall Dwarf. It's my way of writing fiction. Because there's a great deal of fun to be had trying to get into someone's head that I don't get the opportunity to do in any other way."

Tall Dwarfs, as well as several other acts on the Flying Nun label, have drawn comparisons with Syd Barrett, the original Pink Floyd leader who painted pretty psychedelic pictures with a hint of madness that eventually came to dominate his writing. The difference, according to Knox, is that "I've still got 99% of my mental capabilities. I never listened to much Syd Barrett before starting to make music. I've listened to a lot since, and get a perverse and sad enjoyment out of listening to his disintegration. But what he does that is weird is because he *was* weird. What we do that's weird is because we *like* being weird. We can do stuff that's absolutely cohesive and beautifully structured. He's genuine—we're not. We just pretend at being weird, really."

Knox's repertoire is not totally devoid of love songs. He just saves them, as well as some of his more personal musings, for his own solo albums, which he's made off and on since 1983 (since about 1990, there have been about as many Chris Knox records as Tall Dwarfs ones). These are recorded in the same lo-tech (a label he prefers to the trendier "lo-fi") manner as Tall Dwarfs albums; *Polyfoto, Duck Shaped Pain & "Gum"*, his 1993 release, was recorded on a Walkman (though the fidelity is about as clear as anything else he's done on four-track). There *are* romantic songs in his solo outings, albeit not extremely conventional ones. More daring are Knox's frequent excursions into gender politics, sexual roles, and the impossibility of living up to social norms of self-image, on songs like "The Woman in Me," "Rapist," and "Young Female Caucasian."

"In my solo stuff, I can be completely personal, 'cause it's all just me," remarks the songwriter. "I don't feel I can speak for Alec in a love song. I can't understand people who write love songs and have bands, 'cause it's such an immensely personal thing to do. To share it with a bunch of people who don't love the person that you're talking about seems really odd to me."

As resistant as Knox might be to being lumped into the "lo-fi" trend written up in big periodicals, he's happy to find that Tall Dwarfs' aesthetic has spread around the international underground over the last decade. Due to the country's isolation, trends are slow to reach New Zealand; by the same token, it often took years for Tall Dwarfs' records to make an impact abroad. Underground audiences and musicians began picking up on the music by the late '80s, but as Knox remembers, "We had no idea for years. We knew that these recordings were going overseas, and we knew that [some people] were really enjoying [them] for one reasons or another. But it wasn't until some of these people starting coming over here, like Pavement—a couple of the guys would go, those early Tall Dwarfs records had a real big influence. It's very gratifying. I think the fidelity to what comes out of people's mouth and creativity is much higher on [lo-fi records] than on 48-track digital."

A cartoonist and writer by day, Knox will continue to maintain simultaneous solo and Tall Dwarfs careers for the foreseeable future. He and Alec have been fortunate, he thinks, in being able to regard music as a hobby, without commercial pressures to make a living at it. As far as their continued geographical separation, Knox agrees that it could actually work to the music's advantage. "The main thing it does is keep it really, really fresh. Every time we get together it's like being away from your sexual partner for a long time, getting back and having rabid sex for a few days. Every time I do it, I have to relearn the whole process, 'cause I've got a shocking short-term memory and [am] technically so inept. We really enjoy what we do musically, and I think that comes through. The only restriction is that you can't really do much that's really planned out in advance."

Knox doesn't exactly seem downcast about that particular inconvenience. "We've never worked with a finished song in mind. We've always just put down noise until we're satisfied that there's enough noise of some nature there that we can put a melody over, and then write the melodies. It's an adventure. It's wonderful!"

Recommended Recordings:
By Tall Dwarfs:
Hello Cruel World (1987, Flying Nun/Homestead). Every Tall Dwarfs album has something to appeal to adventurous tastes; by the same token, every one will most likely exasperate and annoy at some point as well. Keeping those factors in mind, the best introduction may be this compilation of tracks from the early and mid-'80s.

By Chris Knox:
Songs of You & Me (1995, Caroline). Knox's solo records, to most ears, are quite similar to those he makes with Tall Dwarf Alec Bathgate. It's a toss-up as to what his best overall effort is (he himself prefers 1990's *Seizure*), but this one contains some of his most thought-provoking songwriting, though at 21 tracks it can be hard to manage in one dose for the unconverted. The *Meat* CD on Communion, which combines *Seizure* and the 1991 album *Croaker*, is a suitable alternative.

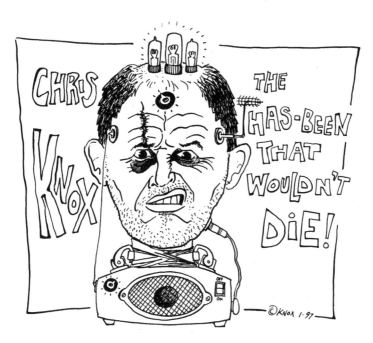

One of Chris Knox's not-so-flattering self-portraits. Credit: Chris Knox

Lo-Fi

Only a few minutes into my conversation with Chris Knox, it's time to drag up that label that neither of us really wants to refer to. "Your method of recording on four-track," I hem and haw, "was picked up by a lot of people who . . . as much I hate to use the label, now that it's been overused and abused so much . . . there's really nothing else to call it, though . . . LO-FI." Thank God that's over with.

Knox is eager to put us out of our misery. "Lo-tech is what I prefer to call it."

"Lo-fi" is the label, however, that has stuck with the media. That's a bit unfortunate, in the view of Knox and some others, because it implies a recording that is difficult to listen to, because of its lack of clarity or poor mix/balance. The lo-fi brigade is more accurately pigeonholed as performers who have determined that their music is best recorded via simple, often spontaneous, methods that rely more on inspiration than overdubs. Relative to state-of-the-art studios, their equipment may be less sophisticated, primitive even. The care and dedication they invest in their songwriting and recording, however, often exceeds that of musicians with much greater budgets at their disposal.

Rock groups working on four-track TEAC recorders in the 1990s may be perceived as defiant dinosaurs, but it's best to remember that only 30 or so years ago, four-track recording was cutting-edge technology. Only a little before that, the whole concept of overdubbing in the studio was all but unknown. Lo-fi artists are reacting against the sterility inherent in much modern music as records became eight-track, then 16-track, and so on. Musicians began to record their parts separately, sometimes without other members of the band present. The lo-fi groups are the counterweights to this excess, striking a blow for methods that emphasize the music itself, not the technology.

Throughout the history of recorded music, there have always been people working with the most primitive of methods. This is usually due to limited budget and resources, however, rather than deliberate choice—a factor which differentiates the garage and punk bands from the lo-fi acts. What the first "lo-fi" group was is a matter of debated opinion. Knox himself puts in a vote for Half Japanese, the idiot-savants from Maryland that released a seemingly infinite trail of demented primitivism, starting in the late '70s. Around the same time, scores, and then thousands, of musicians began to record at home as the affordability of basic recording technology for the average joe became something of a reality. A lot of these musicians, lacking an easy entree into the standard music business, used this technology to record and distribute their own home tapes (see chapter on Martin Newell, and sidebar on home tapers).

Lo-fi as a consciously defined aesthetic, however, didn't really start to penetrate the music community until around the beginning of the 1990s. Much of the credit (though they would be the first to pass the acclaim around) would go to the K label, which since the mid-'80s had distributed folksy, homespun rock and pop from around the globe. Beat Happening (featuring K founder Calvin Johnson on vocals), the Cannanes, and Mecca Normal were a few of the more high-profile acts with K affiliations. Pavement were probably the first so-called "lo-fi" group to break, even in a limited fashion, into the glare of mainstream attention and success, even making the *Billboard* album charts.

There was also a flood of attention on such acts as Sebadoh (who, at least in their initial efforts, lived up to lo-fi stereotypes by releasing material that was badly recorded by every conceivable definition of the phrase). There were distinct differences between the lo-fi "stars." The Palace Brothers, a vehicle for actor turned singer-songwriter Will Oldham, offered twisted Appalachian folk; Alastair Galbraith, from New Zealand, brought that country's Syd Barrett fixation to funkier extremes. Guided By Voices began attracting rave reviews for their cheaply recorded (and extremely frequent) updates of classic pop-rock, although they had been at it for almost ten years before suddenly being "discovered." Liz Phair was, probably inappropriately, lumped in the lo-fi camp by some because the singer-songwriter had attracted a wealth of underground attention with simple, home-recorded tapes before her official debut launched her into stardom.

More subterranean acts with the lo-fi tag, such as the Grifters, Silver Jews, and Superchunk, kept their sales figures low enough to withstand the inevitable backlash as lo-fi became a trend, rather than an adjective. Yet one act, Beck, took the lo-fi vibe to the Top 20 with his mixes of boom-box rap and creaky folk—his most acoustic outings, incidentally, bear an interesting similarity to those of late '60s acid-folk casualty Skip Spence. Beck ensured that his more primitive, less commercial, outings had a home by arranging to have his more lo-fi material issued by K Records, even as he maintained a simultaneous career on a major label.

While it may be dismissed as too trashy by audiophiles, lo-fi is doing a great deal to keep humanity in rock music as the twenty-first century approaches. The less-than-16-track equipment allows performers to record live in the studio (or, as the case may be, at home) with far greater ease; the occasional shiver in the vocal, or even click of the tape machine or wrong note, let us know that people, not machines, are behind the music. The songs themselves, similarly, are usually far more down-to-earth and straight-talkin' than what you'll hear elsewhere—not just on the charts, but on other underground rock records. Don't be at all surprised to see some of the names listed above tell stories of their own when cult rock retrospectives are assembled in the 2020s, as our kids and grandkids will be amazed to hear of the days in which you could record without computers, and distribute your music without using the Internet. Well, we hope not, but . . .

One Shot Was All They Got

The lifespan of the creative rock group is notoriously short—particularly when that act is making music that is so adventurous that it a) doesn't meet with commercial success, and b) demands a great deal of cooperation between diverse talents to succeed on artistic grounds. One-shot artists who produce only one album before falling apart have always fascinated me, particularly as very few of them lasted long enough to receive any press coverage. What is behind the creation of such an off-the-wall semi-masterpiece as Judy Henske & Jerry Yester's *Farewell Aldebaran*? How could groups as simultaneously brilliant *and* commercial as the Bluethings fail to last for more than one LP? What possessed major labels to sign uncommercial experimental acts like the Hampton Grease Band? How did the Monks—ex-American G.I.'s, singing nihilistic pre-punk polkas in English to German audiences—even come to exist, let alone record?

The reasons one-shot bands don't last longer are basically the same reasons that most bands break up: frustration at a lack of commercial success, record company hassles, musical differences, fights about girlfriends and boyfriends. It may be that such problems are intensified and accelerated in the case histories of bands with only one record to their name. Or, even, *no* records to their name: The Rising Sons never even had their album released, and would have been a "no-shot" group if not for a CD reissue of much of their material in the 1990s. The tragedy of obscurity is magnified for the one-shot groups, however, simply because they were unable to make even one additional album that could expand upon their previous achievement or develop their potential. Yet several of the one-shot artists I spoke with took pains to point out that it was something of a miracle that their bands made even one album, with an early split inevitable.

The selective nature of this volume means that many intriguing bands failed to make the cut. The stories of Clear Light, C.A. Quintet, the Lollipop Shoppe, and J.K. & Company were mentioned in the introduction to the Psychedelic Unknowns chapter. Other one-offs worthy of future investigation might include the Belfast Gypsies (raw British Invasion R&B formed by ex-Them members), the aptly named Unknowns (dark surf-influenced early '80s L.A. punk), the Wayfarers (a mix of '80s indie rock and '60s Europop music that was never issued in the U.S.), Thunderclap Newman (remembered for the exhilarating 1969 hit "Something in the Air"), Fapardokly and H.M.S. Bounty (both detailed in the Merrell Fankhauser chapter), and Fotheringay (Sandy Denny's post-Fairport Convention band). This isn't even mentioning one-tenth of the one-shots that might merit consideration—let alone the numerous legendary bands which never got to record. What follows are in effect testimonials—sometimes heartbreaking—to what might have been.

The Bluethings go psychedelic; Val Stecklein seated with guitar, far left. Credit: Courtesy Cicadelic Records

The Bluethings

Imagine a group that fused the best aspects of the Byrds and the Beau Brummels, with a singer/songwriter who tapped the most accessible elements of early Dylan and the mid-'60s Beatles. Like the mid-'60s Beatles, they also had a voracious appetite for change and experimentation, moving from Buddy Holly-flavored Merseybeat through folk-rock and psychedelia in a space of two years. Sounds like a fantasy, doesn't it?

There's precious little surviving evidence today, but this group *did* exist. From the Midwest hinterlands of Hays, Kansas, the Bluethings (also known as the Blue Things) released one superb folk-rock album on RCA in 1966, along with a few good-to-excellent singles in the mid-'60s. In Kansas, Oklahoma, and Texas, they're still legends of sorts, known as the first self-contained Midwest band to successfully follow in the path of the Beatles. Elsewhere, they're unknown, even in the record collector ghetto. A serious contender for the crown of finest overlooked American band of the mid-'60s, the crime is that this is not just a group that appeals to cultists. Like the Byrds and Beatles, they were one of those acts whose artistic innovations were also commercially accessible enough to rule the charts—if only enough people had heard them.

Val Stecklein, the group's guiding light as lead singer and principal songwriter, evidently didn't think so. "I haven't had any interest in the Bluethings since I went solo and I can't imagine why *anyone* would," he wrote in 1985, in a response to Michael Greisman's interest in reissuing vintage Bluethings material. "No offense intended, but it baffles me why you insist on pursuing this. I don't really want to get involved in it because I'm simply not interested in it anymore. It was over a long time ago."

Why exactly Stecklein held such a low opinion of his former group, as well as the acrimonious circumstances under which they split, may forever remain a mystery. Stecklein died in 1993, at the age of 52; the whereabouts of the other Bluethings are unknown. Luckily, we have the music, available on the reissues that Greisman's Cicadelic label was able to coordinate with Stecklein before the singer's death.

The roots of the Bluethings stretch back to the early '60s, when Stecklein, a Paul McCartney look-alike, was performing acoustic folk music with groups like the Impromptwos and the Hi-Plains singers. Stecklein's true heroes, however, were Buddy Holly and the Everly Brothers. Like many folkies across the country, he was exactly the right age to be bowled over by the Beatles and the British Invasion. By September 1964, he was recording rock 'n' roll demos as rhythm guitarist in the Blue Boys. Several of the demos were Merseybeat-Buddy Holly hybrids, somewhat in the mold of Bobby Fuller. But Stecklein compositions like "Silver and Gold" clearly looked forward to folk-rock, with their blend of the Searchers' jangle and hootenanny harmonies.

After changing their name to the Bluethings, the group began to release singles on the tiny Ruff label from Amarillo, Texas, in 1965. These and demos from the period show the band starting to arrive at a more original folk-rock style, with their blends of electric and acoustic guitars and Beatlesque melodic sense. Stecklein's foggy, earnest vocals were clearly becoming Dylan-influenced, but, like those of Byrds leader Roger McGuinn, were much easier on the ear for pop audiences. The mid-'65 single "Pretty Things-Oh" was a superb Beatle knockoff, and a regional hit. Soon they had signed a deal with RCA, quite a coup for a band that was far from the action on either coast.

The Bluethings on bridge outside of Lawrence, Kansas in 1966; Val Stecklein on far right.
Credit: Courtesy Cicadelic Records

Recorded in Nashville, the Bluethings' one album, *Listen and See,* may not have been all that the group wished it to be. Producer Felton Jarvis was far more experienced with country acts than rock ones. Indeed, at this point there were very few self-contained rock groups on RCA at all. Only half of the material came from the pen of Stecklein; although the cover tunes mostly suited the group's style quite well, the band were also lumbered with the corny ballad "Look Homeward Angel." Drummer Bobby Day once said (in the *Not Fade Away* fanzine) that RCA "buried the drums and mixed the tambourine too high. It wasn't representative of us as a live band."

In the end these were minor drawbacks, as *Listen and See* is a minor folk-rock classic, recommended to anyone who enjoyed the early Byrds albums. Twelve-string guitars and thick Beatlesque harmonies dominate tunes that are both melodic and lyrically forceful, especially "Doll House" (apparently about a prostitute) and "Man on the Street," which fit in well with the anti-conformist tone of late '65 folk-rock. Stecklein's vocals were hitting a most attractive midpoint between troubadour folk balladeering and yearning phrasing that recalled John Lennon in the *Rubber Soul* era. "Honor the Hearse" (written by minor rockabilly star Ronnie Self) showed a countryesque bent that foreshadowed Stecklein's later direction, and the cover of rockabilly singer Dale Hawkins' "La Do Da Da" showed that the group hadn't forgotten how to rock out hard.

The album wouldn't come out until September 1966, although it was prefaced by a couple of singles that showed up on the LP. "Doll House," issued as a 45 in May 1966, ran into trouble with radio programmers who found its lyrical content offensive. According to bassist Richard Scott, as quoted in one of the group's fan club booklets, "We could have had a hit by doing sure chart material, but we preferred to do original material and work at it more slowly."

At least they were getting lots of airplay on KOMA in Oklahoma City, a 50,000-watt station that had one of the strongest signals in the country. This ensured that the Bluethings were stars in the Midwest; they played Texas so often that collectors have sometimes erroneously assumed they were a Texan band. Live they had a devoted following throughout the Midwest states, mixing originals with obscure covers of songs by bands like the Who and the Yardbirds. Guitarist Mike Chapman could generate a violin-like tone with his fuzztone and pickups; the ambidextrous Scott used a saxophone strap that made it possible for him to switch from left-handed to right-handed playing (and back) during the same song. But national recognition seemed no closer than before the RCA contract, and it was difficult-to-impossible to find the album outside the Midwest.

In addition, by the time the LP came out, it was somewhat unrepresentative of how far the band had evolved by late 1966. Hot on the heels of *Revolver,* the Bluethings recorded three songs in Nashville in September 1966 that found them embracing psychedelia full-throttle. "The Orange Rooftop of Your Mind" was a Stecklein-Chapman composition about a mixed-up mod girl that introduced Chapman's violin-influenced guitar distortion with a vengeance. The Dylanesque wordplay was buttressed by a snake-charming psychedelic organ solo (played by Ray Stevens, famous for novelties like "Ahab the Arab" and "The Streak"), and an instrumental break that ground to a halt with a simulated nuclear explosion. Only mildly less adventurous was "One Hour Cleaners," with its backward vocals, science-fiction guitar effects, and more surrealistic lyrics about psychological confusion.

Scott offered this capsule summary of "Orange Rooftop" in the group's fan club booklet: "It is about a girl caught up in the rat race of today, she is trying to be like and do like everyone else and can't take the pressure so her mind is slowly snapping." "One Hour Cleaners," he added, "concerns a psychiatrist whose only hold on sanity is provided by his patients." Pretty far-out fodder for November 1966, when the single was issued by RCA. Another, similar cut from the same session, "You Can Live in Our Tree," was released on a single in May 1967.

By that time, however, Stecklein had left the group under circumstances that remain cloudy. The *Not Fade Away* article claims that Val, subsisting on a reputed diet of grape wine and vitamin pills, had suffered a nervous breakdown that required hospitalization. Stecklein couldn't have been happy that the Bluethings continued without their leader, continuing to play live and recording a horrid single for RCA in late 1967. Stecklein landed a deal with Dot as a solo artist, and his 1968 LP for the label, *Grey Life*, mixed remakes of Bluethings songs with new material. For anyone who admired his work in the Bluethings, the record was a major disappointment, consisting of lugubrious, orchestrated MOR-folk that sounded a lot more like a poor Jimmy Webb imitation than vintage folk-rock.

By the time Michael Greisman tracked down Stecklein in the mid-1980s, Val had completely reinvented himself as a Nashville-style country-pop songwriter, even taking a pseudonym, Oskar Solomon. He had placed material with Glen Campbell, Bobby Goldsboro, Waylon Jennings, and Hank Williams, Jr. Initially he was reluctant to talk about the Bluethings days, but in the course of spending several days with Stecklein, Greisman was granted some insight into what made him so bitter about his old band.

"It was my understanding, from what he said to me, that when he split the band, it was not under great terms," Greisman remembers. "You have to look at it in the perspective of the time period. They were putting out material with RCA, [but] they weren't getting national recognition. There's a point in time where the money and the energy being put out does not equal the right equation. It equals disillusionment. Especially when you get to the point where you've done 150%.

"The problem with the Bluethings, I think, is that they were a Midwest band at the wrong time. The songs he was writing and the things he was doing were as good, if not better, than the bands that were hitting the Top Ten—easily.

His music at the time was not commercially unacceptable. It wasn't far out—it was a commercially viable product. But they weren't getting the recognition.

"RCA, at the time, think about it—what rock bands were with RCA that you can recall?" He answers the question himself: "The Jefferson Airplane. The only reason they managed to do it properly was probably because they lucked out in getting a band from San Francisco at the right time. If you look at [the Airplane's] first album, it didn't do anything nationally."

Val Stecklein's mutation into Oskar Solomon, Nashville country writer, was apparently not simply a matter of commercial survival. "He was into pure hard country. I didn't think he was doing it because he was trying to keep up with the trends. After the '60s, I think he got to the point where he wanted to go back to his roots." Yet Stecklein not only consented to reissue the Bluethings recordings, along with a stockpile of unreleased tapes, but made unrealized plans for a newly recorded solo album that would mix new material with remakes of songs from the Bluethings days. That's proof enough to Greisman that Stecklein's convoluted feelings about group had more to do with frustration at their lack of success, and sour memories of their breakup, than the music itself.

"Everything he ever did, he dug up," states Greisman. "If he wasn't into the Bluethings, this would never have happened. So he had to have a good feeling about the Bluethings, except for the fact that they never made it that big, and split up with bad feelings. You can't keep going in a direction that's not getting you anywhere. But I think deep down, he really loved that period."

Recommended Recordings:
The Bluethings Vol. 1 & 2 (1993, Cicadelic). Almost everything the Bluethings officially released is contained on these two CDs, along with a wealth of interesting demos and previously unreleased tracks. Aside from the fact that much of it's excellent, it reflects—as much as any release by more widely known bands—the evolution of American rock in the mid-'60s, from Beatle imitations through folk-rock to early psychedelia.

The Free Spirits

"Can you imagine a group with songs that are as classic pop as the Beatles or Stones, with Hendrix playing guitar and Coltrane playing sax or something?" Drummer Bob Moses is talking about the Free Spirits, a mid-'60s New York group that could legitimately claim to be the first jazz-rock outfit ever. "C'mon! It would be something unbelievable, never heard before, and could have been incredibly successful."

As is so often the case with bold experiments, that never-before-heard blend was heard by only a select few people before the house of cards collapsed. The Free Spirits only managed to release one rarely seen album, circa late 1966, and a couple of even more rarely seen singles. And the music on that LP, according to Moses, "has absolutely nothing to do with how the group was . . . . Everybody [in the band] hated it." If the Free Spirits are referred to at all nowadays, it's because their guitar player was a very young Larry Coryell, soon to become one of the most influential guitarists in jazz and fusion.

Jazz-rock fusion wasn't exactly what the Free Spirits had in mind when they first assembled in New York's Lower East Side. Moses, Coryell, and saxophonist Jim Pepper were living in a musician-dominated building on Eldridge Street—"the most bombed-out, funkiest tenement, dangerous Lower East Side you can imagine," claims Moses. They were young—Moses was still in his teens, in fact—but they were very much of the *jazz* world, not the rock or pop one (Moses was, he admits, "somewhat of a be-bop snob"). Coryell, however, didn't think these worlds had to remain apart.

"It was really Coryell that got me over whatever prejudice I might have had about rock, much in the way it was Jim Pepper that kind of got me to look freshly at avant-garde-style playing," observes Moses. "Most of the white rock I heard really sounded like the people couldn't play. A lot of it today still sounds like the people can't play! But at least I don't judge it because of its genre. Larry, the first time I heard him, was playing jazz, and he sounded like Wes Montgomery or something. I said, 'Wow, this guy's a great guitar player.' And the next day I hear him playing a Bob Dylan tune, and I started really listening to Dylan's music, for example, Stones stuff, especially just seeing the whole guitar language that's separate from the jazz guitar language. And really starting to dig it. When it's good, it's *good*, it's like any music."

The Free Spirits lineup was completed by Chris Hills, a Charles Mingus-like player who made the transition from acoustic to electric bass. Columbus "Chip" Baker—the only Free Spirit not to come from a jazz background—came in on rhythm guitar, and would also write some of the band's original material with Coryell. "We started off basically playing jazz," says Moses. "But Larry, I have to say, was the instigator in terms of really turning us on to rock.

"There was these two separate playing scenes—Larry and Chip and his friends, and then more the jazz cats. Eventually we just decided to put it together and form a band, and see also too if we could be more popular and have more effect on people than just playing jazz music, which was pretty underground and still is, unless you happen to be one of the very few big stars that manage to get an audience. But once we got into it, we all got into it big-time."

To a large degree, the Free Spirits' reputation rests on their long-running residency at the Scene, one of New York's hippest clubs. Not only were they not going to get rich off this gig, they weren't even going to survive—the quintet was paid in the neighorhood of $10 per night as a *band*, to be split five ways. What the Scene did offer was a chance to be heard by listeners and musicians on the cutting edge.

Jazz-rock fusion, as practiced by the Free Spirits, was nothing like the oft-saccharine instrumental background music that it had devolved into several decades later. The Free Spirits may have had serious jazz chops, but they also had a formidable body of original material. Sometimes there were improv jams, but by and large their repertoire was built around actual *songs*, with lyrics and vocals, drawing upon rock, blues, psychedelia, folk-rock, and Indian music in addition to jazz.

"Not too many people knew about it, but the *musicians* knew about it," points out Moses. "A lot of people came to sit in with us, both in the rock world and the jazz world." He sees the Free Spirits' influence in early fusion acts that didn't properly get going until several years later, such as John McLaughlin, Tony Williams' Lifetime, Weather Report, and *Bitches Brew*-era Miles Davis. The Brecker Brothers, Gary Burton, and Dave Liebman are a few of the more renowned jazz artists who sat in with the group; none of them would go the vocal jazz-rock route as the Free Spirits did, but all of them took some elements of rock into their playing. The Spirits would also occasionally jam with straight rock musicians like the Rascals and Mitch Ryder's Detroit Wheels.

But a lot of rock musicians might not have wanted to get *too* close to the Free Spirits onstage, according to Moses. "We were all really well-developed, fairly virtuosic musicians, which really was kind of unusual in rock in those days. I remember playing some festivals opposite the Jefferson Airplane and some of these bands, and these cats couldn't tune their guitars! It was a whole other world.

"A lot of times, we'd be opening for [other groups], and after they'd hear us, they were like, frightened. They didn't even want to go on the stage, 'cause we were blowing them away. I'm not saying this like an ego thing, but this is a fact. Especially guitar players—they didn't want to *touch* it after Larry was playing. And we were doing some really radical stuff, considering it was a rock venue. We would often start our sets with a ten-minute unaccompanied sax solo, completely free, just wild Indian screaming from the deepest gut. People would be mesmerized. Probably just at the point where they were thinking, 'geez, what is this, I didn't come here for *this*,' we'd crank into some serious Chuck Berry groove, and people would just go nuts, man, they'd be screaming.

"A lot of the stuff that Jimi [Hendrix] got credit for, that crazy feedback on guitar [like] something from outer space—Coryell was doing a lot of that stuff before I heard Hendrix. I'm not saying Jimi wasn't either, but let's say he wasn't famous yet. I'd heard Larry doing very similar stuff. He used to rub the guitar against the amp, hump it like he was having sex."

The live energy generated by the Free Spirits at the Scene was going to prove hard to capture on a major label record, however. When Larry Coryell made his recording debut, it was not as some proto-Hendrix-type wildman, but as a fairly straightahead jazz guitarist, playing as a sideman on Chico Hamilton's *The Dealer* in September 1966 on ABC-Impulse. Not that Coryell himself was averse to traipsing between the jazz and rock camps. "When I'm playing with the group," he told *Jazz* magazine at the time, "I'm more interested in the singing aspect of it, and the guitar plays a secondary role . . . I think about my guitar when I play jazz, I don't think about the singing. That's the only way I can explain it. They're definitely different, but I get just as much a kick out of both styles."

Moses believes the Free Spirits may have landed their own deal on ABC as a result of Coryell's recordings with Hamilton. "There was kind of a buzz about Coryell," Moses remembers. "In fact, the business people *always* tried to separate him from us. They thought he was more the star, and they were always trying to say, 'Well, you're the one we want, I don't care about the group.' I think that [Bob] Thiele wanted to make a record with him." Coryell was committed to recording as a member of the Free Spirits rather than as a solo artist, though. Around late 1966 (Moses admits he is unsure of the exact date), the band entered the studio under the direction of legendary jazz producer Bob Thiele, with the equally legendary Rudy Van Gelder, who had worked on numerous jazz classics for the Blue Note label, as engineer.

It sounded like an inspired combination, but Moses has anything but fond memories of the sessions. "I never listen to the album. I hate it with a passion. I don't even know if I have one. Everybody wanted to kill Bob Thiele. They treated us like children." He has equally unpleasant memories of Van Gelder, who established an authoritarian atmosphere, says Moses, that inhibited the group in the studio. "Unlike, let's say, Blood, Sweat & Tears or something, we were very accomplished musicians, but weren't like studio kind of cats. We weren't perfectionist. We were very sensitive. And our mood, we could be thrown off." The drummer goes as far as to speculate that the many classic jazz albums that bear Van Gelder's credit sound as good as they do, not because of the engineer's skills, but because his studio had such a "warm, beautiful, kind of resonant sound.

"There was one tune—we were recording it, and I actually got lost or something, or I dropped a stick. I stopped playing—there's a pause in it where I dropped out. But somehow the band kept playing, and I picked up my stick, and I kind of recorded. I said, 'Well, I might as well finish the tune, it's practice anyway. Obviously we're not going to use this take'. And then we finished the tune. Bob Thiele said, 'That's the take.' I said, 'What are you, crazy? It was completely messed up. I stopped in the middle.' 'That's alright, it's good enough, I don't care, nobody cares, it's just rock.'" To the best of Moses' recollection, the muffed take was actually used on the final LP.

While Moses would just as soon use the self-titled album as a dart board as play it, he's perhaps being too harsh on the record. While not recorded under optimum conditions, it does stake its claim as the first jazz-rock album of any kind. Jazz-rock, albeit, that was firmly confined within three-minute vocal tunes; those wild ten-minute free sax solos would have to be confined to the stage for the time being. Engaging, if somewhat self-consciously hip, pop-rock tunes were dressed up in unusual arrangements and time signatures that were rarely if ever used within a rock context. A sitar was even used on "I'm Gonna Be Free";

"Blue Water Mother" employed the rarely heard device of two simultaneous vocal tracks singing entirely different sets of lyrics.

The weakest link was the vocals. Instrumental virtuosity may have been more of a concern for the Free Spirits than for most rock groups, but even so they could not compare in this department with acts like the Jimi Hendrix Experience or Cream. Whatever its flaws, the LP certainly argues a strong case for the group's eclecticism—in Moses' words, "we were playing all those things from tune to tune, not even from week to week or month to month, but from tune to tune, and very convincingly." Moses himself prefers a rare non-LP single, "I Feel a Song Coming On," to anything on the album—"we came in and nailed it, even though it was [done with] Bob Thiele."

The group never got a chance to perfect their songwriting craft, or smooth out their various production and business problems. In 1967, Coryell left the Free Spirits to accept the guitar slot in jazz vibraphonist Gary Burton's group. Moses also decamped for Burton's group a few months later. The Free Spirits kept on going for a while with other members, eventually changing their name to Everything Is Everything and releasing an album. But nothing could bring the band's original Spirit, if you like, back.

"The reason I left the Free Spirits was because, for me, I knew that it wasn't going to be the same without Coryell," declares Moses. "He was the main singer, he was the guitar player. Jim Pepper may in fact have been the deepest musician of all in a way. But Coryell was what gave it its special flavor.

"Now the question is, why did he leave? I have my own theory about it. He had a lot of ambivalence about being a rock star. On one hand, he really wanted it. I mean, who wouldn't, especially when you're young—money and success and chicks, and it's exciting, it's a rush, it's a high. But on the other hand, he had this almost Calvinist guilt trip about it too. Musically too, he had gotten a little attention for playing jazz with Chico Hamilton and Gary Burton. Burton had jazz credibility, was considered *the* up and coming jazz master on vibraphone.

"I think Larry wanted to prove that he was a serious musician or something, and that if he went with Gary Burton, he could develop the jazz side and get credit for being a serious player. Whereas if he went with the Free Spirits and became a rock star, he wouldn't have the same credibility or something like that." Moses points out that this dilemma, to various degrees, affected other members of the group as well. Several of them had been approached about playing in jazz outfits that offered more security and visibility than the Free Spirits, whose only album had flopped, and whose support from ABC was lukewarm (the record, long out of print, remains extremely difficult to find today).

The Free Spirits may have represented the road not taken, but the musicians themselves continued to be active in jazz, and even thrive. Within years, Coryell was acclaimed as one of the top guitarists in jazz; Jim Pepper, now dead, attracted a small cult following. Bob Moses continues to record eclectic, critically acclaimed jazz records for Gramavision; he has played and recorded with esteemed jazz players such as Jack DeJohnette, Pat Metheny, Jaco Pastorius, Steve Swallow, and Coryell. Currently he is on the faculty at the New England Conservatory of Music.

But Moses continues to harbor a good deal of pride for what the Free Spirits did—and disappointment about what they didn't do. "It's a shame we didn't get to make another record. I really do think that if [Larry] had stuck with the group, it would have happened. Because we were starting to get a buzz—Bill Graham was coming down, all these rock groups would come after the sets and get blown away. The melodies were hummable. People would come away from our gigs remembering the tunes, [the songs] had that quality. And yet we would start off with a ten-minute unaccompanied sax solo. What pop group could you think, even now, would do that?"

Recommended Recording:
The Free Spirits (1966, ABC). The only relic of the band is, according to drummer Bob Moses, a pale reflection of what the group could do onstage. But it's unlike any album of the era in its attempt to merge pop-rock song structures with jazz arrangements and improv-oriented sensibilities. For that matter, it's not much like any of the far more instrumentally oriented jazz-rock albums that would follow when the genre began to attract wide attention in the late 1960s.

The Hampton Grease Band

Legend has it that the Hampton Grease Band's *Music to Eat* was, at the time of its release in 1971, the second worst-selling album in the history of Columbia Records. The only title that undersold it, apparently, was a yoga record. "At the time, that's what we were told by the marketing people," says guitarist Glenn Phillips today. "They may have just been saying it to make us go away. I can't blame them for wanting to do that."

Both the band and the Columbia executives were well aware that *Music to Eat* was not the most unappetizing recipe, viewed purely in commercial terms. In fact, it was a bit of a marketing nightmare. Here was a band that was nearly unknown outside of their Atlanta base, offering not one, but *two* discs of experimental rock that made Captain Beefheart sound downright accessible. Three of the seven songs clocked in at nearly 20 minutes. The tracks alternated between frenetic rock-blues-jazz guitar jams and the lunatic shouts of lead singer Bruce Hampton, who declaimed lyrics straight off the back of a spray paint can, or read verbatim from an encyclopedia entry on Halifax. Unable to get to grips with the subtleties of the material, Columbia often marketed it as a comedy album to retail outlets, which would file the record in the section reserved for stand-up comedians.

Live audiences didn't know what to make of the band either. The Hampton Grease Band could be as much about performance art as music, throwing tables and chairs into the audience, swinging from water pipes, and inviting friends on-stage to watch TV, eat cereal, or do chainsaw-guitar duets. Hampton, writes Phillips in the liner notes to the CD reissue of *Music to Eat*, "would tape himself to the microphone stand while talking to the audience about the supposed Portuguese invasion of the U.S. through Canada." Once the group opened for Three Dog Night in Alabama, warming up a crowd of 10,000 with their obtuse brand of avant-rock. The audience, primed for AM radio hits like "One" and "Easy to Be Hard," was not amused, throwing cups of ice at the musicians on-stage.

"The thing that's really interesting about the band is we weren't attempting to do anything that aggressively," insists Phillips. "It naturally just came out this way, and it had that effect on people.

"The band was about this weird little effect that we had on people without trying to have it. It wasn't contrived. When we were writing really long songs we weren't thinking consciously, 'Let's go against the grain.' Genuinely, we had created a little insulated environment that was just encouraging to each other, and really exciting to be part of."

Whether you loved or hated them—and there were plenty who hated them—you'd have to admit that the Hampton Grease Band sounded like few other rock acts of the early '70s, although their fiercely improvisational dadaist sounds bore some ballpark resemblances to vintage Beefheart and Frank Zappa. The band's defiant inaccessibility may have been a direct result of the lonely trail they blazed as one of Atlanta's few "underground" acts when they started in the late '60s. Guitarist Harold Kelling had played Ventures-type instrumentals in his previous group, which sometimes invited Bruce Hampton onstage to ham it up as unplugged electric guitar wildman, while Kelling hid behind an amp and played the real leads. Kelling, Hampton, and teenaged Glenn Phillips were deeply into blues, country, and progressive jazz like John Coltrane and Ornette Coleman. Rehearsing in the basement of Kelling's parents' house, they developed an approach that sounded like nothing else in the South.

"I guess we all felt like outcasts—it was like a little sanctuary," remembers Phillips. "Then it got very kind of incestuous, in a healthy kind of way. We were very much just into each other; it was like a little clubhouse. We'd start bouncing ideas off each other and just building things. We just didn't seem to have any inclination, in any way, to try to sound like anybody else. That wasn't anything that interested anybody, or even came up."

The Hampton Grease Band, horsing around as usual. Left to right: Mike Holbrook, Glenn Phillips, Jerry Fields, Harold Kelling, Bruce Hampton. Credit: Courtesy Glenn Phillips; photo Bill Fibben

Adding Mike Holbrook on bass and Jerry Fields on drums, the group began to build up a reputation in Atlanta's small underground scene, perhaps as much due to Hampton's theatrics as the music itself. "Bruce was incredibly shy when we started off," reveals Phillips. "He used to not face the audience and sing from behind the PA cabinet. [When] the music started kind of exploding among the band, he just became much more aggressive a stage personality. *He* seemed to just kind of explode."

The band's chemistry was fueled by telepathic guitar duetting between Kelling and Phillips, who seemed bent on merging the fluidity of the Grateful Dead's instrumental jams with some of the angular dissonance of Ornette Coleman and Captain Beefheart. Certainly Beefheart's avant-rock classic *Trout Mask Replica* was a big influence on the band, particularly Hampton, who had never thought of himself as a rock singer in the mold of, say, Three Dog Night. What came out was a hoarse sing-speak that sounded more like a carnival barker on acid.

"The fact that he was very disconnected from the music, and not involved really with pursuing music, is what made it so neat and unorthodox," reflects Phillips. "It was obviously much more about attitude than any vocal expertise. It was pure self-expression. I don't think he cares, or has an interest in, what kind of singer he is, or ever did. He became this explosive presence that was a really neat catalyst for a lot of neat things in the band."

Despite some high-profile gigs such as the Atlanta Pop Festival, and sharing the stage with such major acts as Jimi Hendrix, Procol Harum, and B.B. King, the Hampton Grease Band maintained a militantly uncommercial stance. "There was a big show at the Atlanta auditorium, I can't remember, it was either with Fleetwood Mac or the Allman Brothers," recalls Phillips by way of illustration. "But it was a big show where we were opening up. It was sold out, not because of us, but because of whoever the name band was. Any other band would be going, oh, this is our big break. Jerry the drummer goes: 'Okay, we go out and we jam. No key, no nothing. I just count four, and we go.'

"And we were all *totally* into it. That's what we did. I'm sure if somebody had a tape of it, it would just be horrendous. We went out and played this half-hour jam. I don't know if it was good or not—I have no recollection of if it was good. But it was a big sold-out show in this place, and we were the opening band. We went out and improvised. We didn't even have a key. I'm sure that it was pretty disjointed," he laughs. "And for most people in the audience, just really horrendous."

The Hampton Grease Band were never one, however, to put much stock in audience approval, going as far as to a reprint a negative concert review on the cover of *Music to Eat*. "It talks about people wandering around aimlessly while we were playing," says Phillips with evident pride, "and that's literally what would happen sometimes. People would either be really into it or really *not* into it. When Jerry said, 'We just go out, I'm gonna count to four, and we just go,' it wasn't like an overt attempt to alienate the audience. It was just like, yeah, this'll be great. Obviously, I'm sure a lot of people in the audience thought, oh, these guys are just *trying* to be assholes and piss the audience off. But it was never that conscious."

Given the band's apparent lack of desire to even live up to psychedelic/underground audience expectations, and Bruce Hampton's gratingly hoarse vocal delivery, it's something of a minor miracle that the group landed a contract at all, let alone with one of the biggest companies in the business. Allman Brothers manager Phil Walden, however, helped put together a deal with Columbia Records. In late 1970 the band began recording, cutting an album's worth of material—including extremely intricate songs with numerous sections of complex guitar interplay, such as "Hendon" (with those notorious spray paint can-derived lyrics) and "Halifax," in two days. The shortest song on the tape that was sent to Columbia was 18 minutes long. "These little instrumental sections where the guitars are taking these solos, those are improvised," says Phillips. "Then there may be like a little signal, where we might look at each other to go to the next section. But the music is actually very structured and arranged."

Columbia came up with the idea of asking the band to record some shorter songs, and putting together the sessions for a double LP—an incredible strategy, in retrospect, for the debut recording of an unknown and uncommercial band. They did offer some shorter cuts on the subsequent sessions, but these yielded nothing that could be termed as remotely hit-bound, though the silly "Maria"— a sort of comedy-flamenco-rock piece—could have found a snug home on the Doctor Demento show. Columbia had tried to tame its investment by sending employee Tom McNamee to supervise the sessions; McNamee, as it turned out, was a fan of the band who had no intention of toning them down. When Columbia heard the supplementary tapes, McNamee was fired.

Oldies covers like "Rock Around the Clock" had gone down well in concert, and there was some thought of cutting songs such as those to make the album a bit more accessible, but the Grease Band were having none of it. "We weren't going to go into the studio and record anything that wasn't our own. We just didn't record anything commercially oriented, and we refused to. But it wasn't like we were thinking that the album was *un*commercial. Whatever we put on the record, its intent had to be pure. So when they'd try to get us to do something commercial, there wasn't an inkling of like, 'oh, should we do this or not?,' with me anyway. I remember having big fights, just [saying] no, if that's what they want us to do, then we won't go in and do it."

The group also got their own way with the cover artwork. In addition to reprinting the uncomplimentary review referred to earlier, they filled the sleeve with odd little doodles, cartoons, and unidentified photos. One showed four friends of the band loitering in front of soda machines, next to which a caricature of a lizard declared, "The 4 people (fraben) pictured here have complete control of the North American continent at this very second." Nothing that a Zappa fan, for instance, couldn't handle. But Columbia was unprepared to deal with such unrelenting strangeness, one executive quipping, "They were the straw that broke the camel's back, the most outrageous group anybody here ever had to deal with."

The album probably was *not* the second-lowest selling Columbia full-length of all time, but it made good anti-press of sorts. "Once again," laughs Phillips, "it's one of these times where we got a really bad quote, and started wearing it like it was like a little badge of honor." The record may have found its biggest (though not most appreciative) audience when Phillips' father took it into the main building of his company, Metropolitan Life Insurance, in New York. For an entire workday, the skyscraper's sound system grooved to the sounds of *Music to Eat*—anti-elevator music if there ever was such a thing.

Not everyone hated the group, though; fellow Georgian Duane Allman was a fan, and got Bill Graham to book them with the Mothers of Invention at the Fillmore East. Kip Cohen, who ran the Fillmore, was moved to write a letter to CBS chief Clive Davis praising the band, advising that "the Hampton Grease Band could become cult heroes with the right kind of publicity." But the sales were poor enough that the company dropped the act not too long after the record's release.

By this time, the group had become friendly with Frank Zappa, who helped get them signed to his Bizarre/Straight label. But the group's chemistry had been irrevocably altered with the departure of Harold Kelling. The band continued playing for a while with altered personnel, but broke up when Hampton quit in 1973 to unsuccessfully audition for a job as a vocalist for Frank Zappa. *Music to Eat*, in all its sprawling glory, would be the group's only release.

The chemistry, admits Phillips, "just got out of whack" with the absence of Kelling, who had always enjoyed a close repartee with both Phillips and Hampton. "There was a weird little connection between the three people. Without one of them, it's just not the same. Not that there wasn't anything neat musically happening in the band [after Harold left]; there was. But I think for Bruce, it started to get where it became a little more self-conscious. It wasn't as natural, I think it was harder for him to do things."

All of the members who played on *Music to Eat* would continue to be involved with music to varying degrees, especially Hampton, who made a couple albums with the Aquarium Rescue Unit, and Phillips, who has released ten instrumental records. With hindsight, Glenn doesn't regret that the band broke up when it did, because "it could have become a shtick. I love the early Mothers, and Zappa was a really incredibly nice guy, really supportive of us, much more than he needed to be, and helpful in a lot of ways. But I have no interest at all in [his] later stuff, because it just seems contrived and silly to me.

"I think that was the danger of something like the Hampton Grease Band. There was this love-hate relationship with the audience, and there was this kind of edgy aggression between what we were doing. But as soon as that starts to become a shtick, it loses any value. I think that's part of why the band died when it died."

Music to Eat itself, though, recently got a second lease on life when it was reissued on CD on Shotput, a Columbia subsidiary. Instrumental in bringing the reissue to fruition was Brendan O'Brien, producer of Pearl Jam and other current superstar acts. The band that Columbia once marketed as a comedy group may be, 25 years later, finally having the last laugh.

Recommended Recording:
Music to Eat (1971, Shotput). One of the most uncommercial—and, for the last 25 years, collectable—acts in all of 1970s rock is now widely available again, complete with witty, fascinating liner notes by Glenn Phillips crammed with stories that are as strange as the music itself.

Judy Henske
& Jerry Yester

Judy Henske, Jerry Yester, and family, from the cover of their sole album, 1969's *Farewell Aldebaran*.
Credit: Courtesy Herb Cohen

"**I had a strep throat,** an extremely high fever, and I was still nursing my daughter. I decided I'd try to read my way through the encyclopedia, and started looking in the encyclopedia under A. And I fell upon Aldebaran."

Judy Henske is remembering the genesis of the title track for the record that would become *Farewell Aldebaran*. "The thing that struck me was that Aldebaran was so big—this star was a red giant. If it rose over the earth, it would take up the whole sky; our sky would be red. Now when you've got a fever of 104 and a strep throat, you make it into something."

Recorded with her husband of the time, Jerry Yester, *Farewell Aldebaran* would not so much fill up the sky as drop off the face of the earth. Released in 1969 on Frank Zappa's Straight label, the record was comparable to nothing else on the psychedelic scene. Odd song-poems about mean-spirited churches, shooting stars, and medieval knights sat side by side with crunching blues-rock, warped country-folk, bubblegum satire, and early synthesizer experiments. Yester's arrangements deployed zithers, pipe organs, delicate strings, mandolins, and more to imbue the tunes with an off-kilter shimmer that matched the clashing psychedelic hues of the cover, with its ghoulish greened-over reverse negative of a Henske-Yester family photo. Pulling it all together were the incredibly versatile vocals of Henske, who swooped between low, bluesy moans, Nico-like gothic drones, and sweet, high harmonies with unpredictable grace. Despite the hummable appeal of many of the compositions, it was *way* too weird for the pop audience, and perhaps even a little too weird for the underground. When Frank Zappa himself is impressed by your record, you know you're onto something different.

There was little on the resume of either performer that would have led one to predict such a left-field gem. Henske had recorded several albums in a full-throated style that gained her a cult following, primarily among the folk audience. Her version of "High Flying Bird," released in 1964, was a precursor to folk-rock with its 12-string guitar and mild electric backing; the Jefferson Airplane would cover the song as one of their first recordings. Jerry Yester had been a member of the Modern Folk Quartet and (in their waning days) the Lovin' Spoonful, and had recently started a production career with work on albums by the Association and Tim Buckley. Confesses Yester, "We were beatniks, not hippies."

When Henske and Yester began writing songs together, what came out didn't sound like commercial folk-rock. "I wasn't strictly a folk singer," emphasizes Henske, who offers a nearly nonstop patter of stand-up comedy and low, hearty cackles as she talks from her home in Pasadena, California. "I did a mish-mash of stuff, because I liked all different kinds of music." She had done some rock-influenced singles with Phil Spector protégé Jack Nietzsche, and snuck a couple of songs by folk-rock enigma Fred Neil onto one of her most commercial albums. Yet even when Mercury Records was trying to market her as a nightclub singer, "I was the same person underneath. So it didn't work."

Henske was managed by Herbie Cohen, who also handled such eclectic artists as Tim Buckley and Frank Zappa. When Judy and Jerry moved to Los Angeles in 1968, Cohen and Zappa were just starting a new label, the ironically named Straight Records, for acts which were underground even by underground standards. Alice Cooper released their first LPs for the company; Captain Beefheart recorded his avant-rock masterpiece, *Trout Mask Replica*, there; and Tim Buckley made his journey from rock to jazz on Straight. The label even issued a piece of amateur-trash silliness by actual groupies, the GTO's. In this company, the duo of Henske-Yester fit right in. In fact, they were probably the most "normal" of the lot.

But they were a hell of a lot more far out than, for example, the Association or the Lovin' Spoonful, and Zappa was quick to appreciate their burgeoning experimental leanings. "The biggest encourager of me as a lyricist was Frank Zappa," states Henske, a bookworm who "grew up with poetry, right there in the middle of a table, like a big helping of mashed potatoes. He came up to our house one time, and I showed him all of these poems that I had written, and said, 'I don't know what to do.' He said, 'Every single thing I write I turn into a song. This is really good. Turn *these* all into songs!'"

Henske had a lot of help in this regard from Yester, who would provide the melodies for Judy's words, and who was getting a little far out himself as he stretched his wings as a producer. Jerry and his buddy Zal Yanovsky (whom Yester had replaced in the Lovin' Spoonful) were fascinated by Toni Fisher's 1959 single "The Big Hurt," the first pop hit to use electronic phasing (Henske: "We listened to this record five million times"). Yester co-produced Yanovsky's obscure solo album, in which the merry sonic travelers put a mike in a flushing toilet to try and emulate the sound of "The Big Hurt," the Small Faces' "Itchycoo Park," and other records built around phasing effects. "I think we spent like $7,000, trying to find that damn thing—'the sound'—before we just abandoned it," says Yester.

Yester and Yanovsky formed a production company, Hairshirt Productions, and would act as co-producers on *Farewell Aldebaran*. "I love that album because I love the *songs*," Jerry declares. "But I learned on that album how difficult it is to produce myself. It haunts me a lot because I'd love to get those tapes and remix it."

Yester's being too hard on himself; his inventive arrangements were chiefly responsible for the unusual allure of most of the record's ten tracks. "Snowblind," with brutal metallic blues guitar riffs from Yanovsky and bottom-of-the-soul wailing from Henske, was probably the album's most "normal" cut, with a sound described by Yester as "raw, dirty, ragged, and bitchin'" (indeed it was picked as the single, though outside of Seattle it saw little action). Any hopes for a Janis Joplinesque LP of hard rock were dashed by the next cut, "Horses on a Stick," with its helium vocals and merry-go-round pipe organ. "It's too icky, I hate it!" exclaims Henske today, though Yester is careful to point out that they were making fun of bubblegum pop, and not joining the merry-go-round of kiddie music.

But the merry-go-round of musical styles on the album itself was just starting. "Lullaby" was a spooky, somber incantation with a toy zither; "Rapture," "Charity," and "St. Nicholas Hall" were proto-goth with their counterpoint of hymn-like melodies that wouldn't be out of place in a church choir, and disquietingly somber lyrics, intoned by Henske in a thunder-of-doom voice that took Billie Holiday into purgatory. "St. Nicholas Hall" was especially wicked, with its pointed barbs at churches more concerned with milking their congregations' pockets than spiritual succor. The arrangement (except for the deliberate blast of off-key singing at the end) wouldn't have been out of place in any Sunday choir; the lyrics were sarcastic enough to get the choir banned from the Vatican for life. "That was kind of about Judy's and my background of Catholic schools," says Yester. "Any organized church, I know that they have to make a living, but the involvement with money really annoys us."

Yester assembled an all-star crew for "Raider," which sounds like a Neil Young hoedown gone awry (ironically, Young was recording an album in the next studio at the time, although Henske/Yester didn't hear any of it). Ry Cooder played rhythm mandolin, David Lindley bowed the banjo with a violin bow, and Elvis Presley sideman Jerry Scheff played bass; a friend of Lindley's added hammered dulcimer. The real treasure of the album, however, may have been "Three Ravens," whose lyrics Henske based on an old English ballad about, in Yester's words, "a knight who was struck down; a deer came along, fell in love with him, stayed to protect him, and was killed by the ravens." Married to music that Jerry had started as a cello piece in 1964, and embellished by gorgeous string arrangements, it boasted the most soaring melody of the record. It also has a stunning vocal by Henske (though she cannot even remember the melody today).

The limitations of late '60s recording technology forced Yester to be particularly resourceful at times, as on the piercing wobble of multi-layered backup voices on "St. Nicholas Hall," produced on a mellotron in the days before samplers were available. "It was an eight-second tape loop," remembers Yester. "You'd hold down the key, and this thing would play the tape of the violin, or voice, singing that note. You had to lift the finger before eight seconds had gone by, so the thing could snap back and rewind to the top so you could play it again. I deliberately played some wrong notes at the end," he adds with perverse pride. "Because they sang with such conviction!"

That was but a warm-up for the album-closing title track, bathed in washes of synthesizers and Frankensteinish Moog-treated vocals that eventually sound as if they're emanating from an underwater megaphone. "That voice at the end was like a piece of meteorite, coming from Aldebaran to burn up in the earth's atmosphere," explains Yester. "The voice of the star couldn't be just a singer. We needed the voice of a *star*.

"We got Bernie Krause, who was like the first synthesizer person working studios, and a Moog synthesizer. You *had* to hire this guy, because no one knew how to make the sound. You could spend six hours on the damn thing, and not even get a note out of it. Bernie would come around and set up sounds, and you'd do 'em note by note. He took Judy's voice and we ran it through ring modulators, which kept breaking her voice into overtones, and breaking that into overtones, and just kind of split it till it was this horrific gaggle of overtones. I sang bending over into a piano with Zally holding down the sustain pedal, so that the strings of the piano were the echo on the voice."

Yester felt the actual sound of the song never matched what he heard in his head. After a few passes at the mix, resulting in a desperate trip back to New York to get the engineer who'd worked on Yanovsky's solo album, it still didn't feel right. Jerry even had some recurring nightmares in which he'd "just painstakingly do it, in the dream, till by the time morning came, the thing was absolutely perfect." In the end he got John Boylan (later to produce Boston) to help him complete the mix in a mere hour and a half. "It got as good as it could be," says Yester, still obviously frustrated by the imperfections to this day.

The album, like virtually everything on Straight, was fated to be admired by critics, and barely heard by anyone else. Yester thinks it might have suffered from being one of the first releases on a label that was still learning how to sell its product. In almost the same breath, he admits that "it kind of 'eclecticted' itself out of existence. It's odd, too. My mother called up after I sent her a copy and said, 'What's wrong? Is everything alright with you?' And we're saying, 'What do you mean?' She says, 'God, the songs are so depressing.' I said, 'No they're not. They're great songs.' But I think it had that effect on a lot of people." He adds that "Lullaby" disturbed his mother the most, especially as Henske and Yester had a newly born daughter at the time. "I tried to make it as lonely and windy as some kind of eagle aerie . . . [my mother was like], gosh, what a frightening lullaby!"

I put it to Henske that "Rapture" was an especially gloomy song. "I had just had a baby, I had a big career and stuff," she replies. "I was thinking *deep thoughts*. Watch out for people who are thinking deep thoughts, 'cause sometimes they end up on a record. Then someone comes along 25 years later and says, gee, *that* was an especially gloomy thing!" She then breaks into a booming laugh that rattles the phone receiver.

Turning more serious, she elaborates, "I had, for the most part, a very weird turn of mind. Some of the lyrics had a very strange, surrealist kind of edge. But the music wasn't surreal. The music is really kind of pop, kinda up. It turned out to be a thing that was in the middle, and it felt like an amalgam of some kind that wasn't really working. I still think it was okay—I like it, I'm not ashamed of it.

"The eclecticness of it, I think, was my fault. I like too many different things. Then you have Jerry Yester, a completely different kind of artist. I'm like more with—" she breaks into a low growl—"and Jerry is"—she's off into a high trill. "He has a wonderful sense of melody, and he's more of a treble person. But I'm down there in the other level, on a darker side."

The very qualities that made the record special, it seems, made it impossible to market in its own time. Henske also points out that "there was no way on God's earth to reproduce that album on stage," although Yester counters, "I think if the thing became very popular, we'd find a way to perform it." Henske and Yester would give it another try, though not as a duo, in the early '70s as part of a group called Rosebud that boasted a fuller rock sound, and input from various other singers and writers. Yester remembers running into Warners executive Mo Ostin, "who said, 'we love the [Rosebud] album, we're going to give it a big push.' And I said, 'Judy and I have broken up, Mo.' He said, 'oh,' and drove off. That was, I think, the last time I saw him. It was just horrible timing."

As a bizarre footnote, as the sessions to *Farewell Aldebaran* approached completion, Yester and Yanovsky began to produce an album by, of all people, Pat Boone. Simultaneous work on two such wildly contrary projects seems like a feat beyond the capabilities of ordinary earthlings. But Yester—who helped select unlikely covers of Fred Neil and John Stewart songs for Mr. White Bucks, as well as enlisting musicians like Ry Cooder and David Lindley for the record—"really liked the album. We had a good time producing him. We had the best musicians in town. We really got to appreciate him as a singer." Adding some vocals to the project was Henske, who, by contrast, describes Pat as "the world's ickiest singer." Now you know why Jerry and Judy's marriage couldn't last . . .

The end of their professional and personal relationship had been foreshadowed by the sleeve of *Farewell Aldebaran*, which showed the couple and their baby, as Judy puts it, "sitting in a destroyed house. It was kind of a metaphor for what was going on at the time." Or, it could be said, for a record that was too unclassifiable to find a home—either in 1969, or in the 1990s, when it remains one of the finest records of the 1960s that has failed to make the transition to CD.

Recommended Recording:
Farewell Aldebaran (1969, Straight). One of the most inspired one-shot oddities of the psychedelic era, with one-of-a-kind songs, arrangements, and singing. Only available as an out-of-print collectible, and long overdue for reissue.

The Monks

When Eddie Shaw, bassist for the Monks, first heard that his old band had become a *cause célèbre* among aficionados of obscure cult rock groups, he called one of his young fans. Wendy Wild, singer for New York polka-punkers Das Furlines, was trying to assimilate Monks tunes into her repertoire. "She said, I thought you guys were GIs, and you went AWOL, and the Army found you performing on TV, and they went and arrested you in the TV station at the end of it," says a bemused Shaw.

"These are great stories. In some ways, I wish they were true because that'd be a heck of a great thing to write about. These myths are probably better than the truth."

Eddie's selling himself a bit short here. That particular anecdote may be more whimsy than fact, but the true story of the Monks is a stranger tale than any muckraking journalist could imagine. Picture this: five young American musicians formed a band while serving in the U.S. Army in Germany in the early '60s. After discharge, they decided to remain in Germany, guaranteed steady work on a rock 'n' roll circuit that had been thriving ever since the Beatles' legendary Hamburg stints. As the Torquays, they ground out the rock and R&B covers that were expected of a mid-'60s "beat" band.

When the Torquays became the Monks, the "beat" days were over. The good-time American rock was replaced with harsh, furious blasts of minimalist proto-punk. Lyrics, kept as simple and repetitive as possible to make the message clear, berated the madness of the Vietnam War, tormented love-hate romantic relationships, and drunken women. Titles like "Shut Up" and "I Hate You" ran counter to the spirit of just about every tune you might find in the Top 40 in 1966. Primitive guitar distortion fought it out with frenzied white-knuckled organ riffs, pounding bass, and electrified banjo.

To show that they meant business, the Monks dressed as real monks in robes and ropes, shaving bald patches on top of their heads. Crowds would part before them as if the musicians were walking through the Red Sea; women would touch the Monks' heads to see if the gimmick was real. Audiences would avert their eyes or stare at their shoes, not sure that this was really happening, or whether, if this was no illusion, they should even be *allowed* to watch something so sacrilegious.

Had these soldiers been stationed in the U.S. instead of Germany, it's doubtful they could have concocted such a strange brew. Bassist Shaw was into jazz, and prior to enlistment had played trumpet at a Carson City, Nevada, casino where teenage Wayne Newton was also getting his feet wet. Guitarist (later banjoist) Dave Day was an old-time rock 'n' roller; organist Larry Clark liked blues; singer/guitarist Gary Burger and drummer Roger Johnston were country fans.

But German audiences wanted to hear guitar-based rock in the mold of the dozens, if not hundreds, of British bands that were making Germany a second home. As the Torquays, that's what these expatriate Yanks tried to deliver, night after night, club after club, town after town, often working six to eight hours at a stretch. They released a limited-run 45 as the Torquays before boredom began to force their music to take on a life of its own.

"After you've done it for a while, you get so bored with the formulas," explains Shaw. "Sometimes it was just like a regular job. One could have been a mechanic or anything else, other than he was onstage. The only thing that would differentiate us was our show. As we played louder and louder, all of a sudden the feedback element started coming in. And we started discovering things to do with that feedback. The drums had to be louder and everything had to be overdriven. We just started having fun taking it to the extreme. Once we had hit on it, we couldn't stop. In the process, we got managers who were interested in what we were doing, and were convinced that we had hit on something."

As ex-American servicemen playing to Germans on a circuit dominated by British groups, they felt a sense of cultural displacement that seeped into their lyrics and arrangements. The Monks conjured what Shaw terms an *überbeat*—insistent, almost martial rhythms, a kind of polka you could pogo to. The lyrics would not be happy-go-lucky romances or rehashes of blues clichés. They were bleak, alienated, and basic, as they would have to be in order to be understood by a German-speaking population.

"It was really an experiment in overbeat minimalism," says Shaw. Without claiming to match Philip Glass in sophistication, he nevertheless sees some similarity between the Monks and the famous minimalist composer. "We started talking in a new vernacular, which was tension. We wanted to get the tension to a point where people just couldn't stand it anymore. Instead of doing 12 bars, we might do 15, we might do 17 before we'd change it. Of course, as we would find those tension points, we'd also feel uncomfortable, because at that point [the audience] couldn't stand us either."

The lyrics themselves, he points out, were severely edited from longer blueprints. "We would try to make [a song] into a three-word statement. Whatever that song was, was really based around three words. And the more words we had to add after that, we were in the process of destroying the song. There was something about it that felt like a sleeked-down sports car, in comparison to what else was going on."

It was years before Iggy Pop and the Stooges would introduce this approach in the United States, and seemed like commercial suicide in 1966. Or 1996, for that matter. In hindsight, it's kind of mind-blowing that the Monks were able to record an album at all. But they did, and what's more, they did it for one of the biggest record companies in the world, Polydor, which unleashed *Black Monk Time* onto the German market in March 1966.

Before the Polydor album, the Monks had recorded some demos that, according to Shaw, were even more minimalist than what was recorded for *Black Monk Time*. If that's the case, they must be primal indeed, considering that what survives on *Black Monk Time* is as close to the bone as just about anything recorded. That was apparent right from the leadoff track, "Monk Time": not ten lines have gone by before Gary Burger has delivered unhinged diatribes against the Army, the atomic bomb, and governments that send both American and Vietnamese soldiers to their death, backed by a cacophony of weird guitar explosions and carnival-from-hell organ. Two mikes were installed inside Dave Day's banjo to insure the instrument's unsettling presence in the final mix.

As their sacrilegious stage garb demonstrated, the Monks were never ones to do anything halfway. Left to right: Dave Day, Larry Clark, Gary Burger, Roger Johnson, Eddie Shaw. Credit: Courtesy American Recordings

Lacking in all but the most basic melody, and delivered with jackhammer finesse (Gary Burger's vocals can sound like Stevie Winwood caught in a cement mixer), the record was too crude to count as a classic on artistic grounds. ("For us, at that point, it seemed very sophisticated," laughs Shaw.) It does, however, sound like no other record from the mid-'60s, looking forward to the scabrous fury of punk a good decade or so before that term became commonplace.

The Monks did not just *sound* like no other band; they *looked* like no other, shaving their heads into monk tonsures during a time in which everyone was trying to look like the Beatles or the Rolling Stones. They may have lacked typical commercial appeal, but they did not lack in publicity. Their official photographer was Charles Wilp, one of Germany's top lensmen, who later became Ronald Reagan's official photographer during the politician's presidential term. They did interviews on Radio Luxembourg, appeared on German TV, and played on bills with Bill Haley, the Kinks, the Troggs, and Manfred Mann. In one misbegotten publicity stunt, they stayed in an actual monastery in Sweden. Thinking it was just another motel, the Monks smoke, drank, and entertained girls; the head of the facility was not amused, prompting a quick getaway. They played the legendary Top Ten club in Hamburg, where Roger Johnston got amphetamines from the same elderly washerwoman who had also supplied the Beatles, and where Tony Sheridan (whom the Beatles had once backed in Hamburg) would shout abuse to them from the audience.

"Hamburg was inundated with English groups," notes Shaw. "There was Duke Ellington's sidemen playing two blocks away in the off-season. The music was pretty intense and pretty sophisticated. So the people in Hamburg had pretty much heard everything. And they liked the Monks, because the Monks weren't playing anything that anybody else was playing. And we knew that. That's why we felt at home in Hamburg. If Hamburg would have been the world, the Monks would have been very, very successful."

In a less glamorous vein, they criss-crossed Germany on a series of endless one-night stands. "If there was a village that had 200 people in it, we probably played it. It was like a political tour, where the politicians just go from one town to another. We played in places where there would just be a little small bar and a little stage, and there might be 50 teenagers in the whole town." There was a not-so-faint tinge of absurdity to being billed as international stars while playing tiny German farming communities. If the Monks were to go to the next level, they'd have to conquer the American market. When Polydor told the group that an American release of *Black Monk Time* was imminent, the band were delighted.

As it turned out, *Black Monk Time* would not be released in the United States for over 30 years. Polydor, it seems, might have gotten cold feet at releasing a song that criticized the senselessness of the Vietnam War (and, it should be noted, criticized both the American *and* Vietnamese war machines). And there was the matter, in the same song, of that celebration of Pussy Galore coming down . . . even though the Monks meant Pussy Galore as in the character in the James Bond movie *Goldfinger*, without necessarily meaning to hint at more carnal pleasures.

"What we were told was, the American distribution companies wouldn't even touch it," says Shaw. "They just all turned it down, hands-down. They said no, we won't touch this one."

As for speculation about whether the Vietnam War references were the key obstacles, Shaw counters, "We felt that we did serve [in the Army], and we did have a right to say something. And we didn't want to be disloyal. But it could have been because of all the riots going on in the United States. One of the most horrible things that anybody could do is advertise ex-GIs as coming out of the Army while the Vietnam War is going on and saying that."

That said, Shaw has a hunch that the real reasons for the record's non-release in America may be more straightforward. "In the back of my mind, I thought, well, the music is just a little bit too strange and a little bit too loony for them. It would fall into the realm of novelty." What does he think the reaction would have been to the Monks in the U.S. if the group had been able to perform there? "Probably pure hatred," he laughs, without any real sense of remorse.

One place the Monks *were* appreciated was East Germany. Fan mail from behind the Wall began arriving after East Germans saw and heard the Monks on TV and radio broadcasts. "They felt that the Monks had that simple sort of explanation to everything that was wrong with the world," speculates Shaw. "They thought that we were saying something very important to them, and I suppose we may have expressed some idea of individualism that they really were not allowed to express. But, ironically, in some senses, we really weren't even supposed to do it over here either!"

By way of illustration, in 1967, the Monks were feeling pressure from Polydor to change their sound. In Shaw's words, the label told the group to move in a Lovin' Spoonful direction because "the hard beat is out, and it's never coming back." The Monks made some tentative moves in that direction with their third and final single in 1967, an effort that no one was really satisfied with. In a delicious irony, at the same time as the Monks were fighting record company politics, internal tension, and a general frustration at having worked so hard with so little to show for it in terms of material success, they supported an up-and-coming Jimi Hendrix at the Star Palast in Kiel in May 1967.

The Monks may have influenced Hendrix to add an important feature to his arsenal of effects. "We'd always buy the newest electronic stuff, because one of our premises to make the music was to experiment—the music of the Monks is really one vast experiment. In talking to Jimi Hendrix, we had the wah-wah pedals. And the only way to do them, is you had to move 'em from left to right.

They didn't go up and down, they went left to right, and Gary had to give his knee an awkward movement to do that. I used to stand down at the edge of the stage and make fun of him when he did it, and he used to hate it. But Hendrix was genuinely interested in it. And he didn't see anything humorous about it at all. I remember on break he was asking Gary, where'd you get that? And Gary told him that it was shipped from the States."

Shaw also felt a bit of kinship with Hendrix, not so much with in terms of the guitarist's particular sound (which was quite different from the Monks') as with his general approach. "When we played the Star Palast in Kiel, kids wouldn't look at us. If we walked through, people would move away. But Hendrix had the same problem. When I saw him sitting in the middle of the Star Palast to watch us, people did not sit around him. He was very much alone. Hendrix was the first person that I saw that I felt that there was something similar in our circumstances.

"It was that sort of hardness in the music. Hendrix was playing a lot harder than the other English groups were playing. On the other hand, I remember thinking, 'God, we're doing the wrong form of hard music. If we wanted to be successful, we're not going to be successful doing this, because it's not blues'. I didn't know that you could take blues and make it as hard as that, as Hendrix had done. We were taking [our sound] as far as we would go with it, even to the point where we were uncomfortable ourselves. And Jimi Hendrix seemed to be that kind of person. I felt that he was going to be successful, and we were not going to be successful."

The Monks weren't actually going to last that much longer anyway. Feeling that they had milked the German market for all it was worth, their management planned an Asian tour, including a lengthy stint in Vietnam. We'll never know how GIs and the Vietcong might have reacted to songs like "Monk Time," condemning the madness of the war in Southeast Asia and celebrating the delights of Pussy Galore in a crescendo of devil's-den noise-rock. The Monks were just hours away from boarding the plane by the time they found out that Johnston had fled back to Texas, writing in a note to Burger, "I can't take it any longer."

In retrospect, Shaw's relieved the band didn't make the trip, having heard that one of the members from a group that had just done the Vietnam circuit had been killed while doing their musical tour of duty. "Being an American rock 'n' roll band and playing in a war zone without the protection of the Army or anything else, we probably would have been setting ourselves up for some serious problems."

In ones and twos, the Monks slowly made their way back to the U.S. and years of culture shock, having felt caught between the Germans, Americans, and British for years. When Monks would play their record for their friends, they would be greeted with indifference or, worse, insults. Even when Burger played the record for Shaw in the late '70s, Eddie says he told his bandmate, "'Turn it off. It just makes me dizzy.' And I did feel kind of ill."

By that time, *Black Monk Time* was already beginning to gather a reputation as a one-of-a-kind artifact among collectors, original copies sometimes fetching several hundred dollars. In the early 1990s, the excellent fanzine *Ugly Things* tracked down Shaw and Burger for the Monks story; when Shaw called Burger to tell him that two young Monks fans had just interviewed him, Burger hung up, declaring that Shaw was either dreaming or drunk. Shaw was moved to play the album for his kids — "I was very surprised, because for the first time in my life as their dad, I had finally done something they liked. They couldn't believe it was me."

It didn't end there. A company took out an option for a feature film based on the Monks' story (the option has since been picked up by another outfit). Shaw, by this time a novelist living in his hometown again, wrote (with his German ex-wife) an absorbing 400-page autobiographical account of his Monks days, titled, naturally, *Black Monk Time*. Alternative bands have now started to cover Monks songs. Shaw's particularly pleased with the three covers by the Fall, a British punk institution since the late '70s. He thinks if Fall lead singer Mark E. Smith had been around the Monks in the '60s, "he might have been able to carry it off where we couldn't. I think he's got the same format that we do."

And in February 1997, American Records—a U.S. major label—released *Black Monk Time*, with bonus tracks. Seems that someone who works at American in the talent acquisition department has been a big Monks fan for years, and is finally fulfilling his dream of releasing *Black Monk Time* in the States. Is America finally ready for the Monks? It may take another 30 years before we have the answer.

Recommended Recording:
Black Monk Time (1966, American). The legendary, sole Monks album is finally available in the U.S., with seven bonus tracks from non-LP singles, previously unreleased demos, and a live cut. A zany, furious amalgamation of American '60s rock, British Invasion-influenced frenzy, and lyrics that are once spiteful and self-mocking.

Recommended Book:
Black Monk Time, by Thomas Edward Shaw and Anita Klemke (1994, Carson City Publishing). Even if the Monks' brand of minimalist proto-punk doesn't appeal to you, Eddie Shaw's memoirs of the group (co-written by ex-wife Anita Klemke) are riveting. The grinding tours, the groupies, the absurd image games and record company politics—it's all here, told from the perspective of a struggling band that never made it. Most poignant of all, however, is the sense of spiritual homelessness Shaw and the Monks felt as Americans playing dadaist rock in English before astonished German audiences.

The Rising Sons

For several decades, Ry Cooder and Taj Mahal have been acclaimed as two of the finest and most eclectic American guitarists ever to wield a pick. Both are masters of the blues, and blues-rock; both have also dabbled in just about every form of roots music known to man, especially calypso and reggae (Mahal) and Hawaiian, African, and Tex-Mex (Cooder). The idea of both axemen being in the same band is kind of mind-blowing. How could such a thing happen, and how could such a thing last?

Unbelievably, it *did* happen, well before either of those musicians had become famous. And no, it did *not* last—which is probably why you've never heard of the Rising Sons, the group that released just one single in the mid-'60s before dissolving in the aftermath of career frustration and record company politics.

In addition to Mahal and Cooder, the band also featured (at separate points) drummers that would rise to fame in subsequent groups—Ed Cassidy with Spirit, and Kevin Kelley with the country-rock-era Byrds. Also including singer-songwriter Jesse Kincaid and bassist Gary Marker, the Rising Sons were one of the first acts to play convincing blues-rock in the United States. With their blend of electric and acoustic guitar parts, as well as their fusion of roots sounds with early psychedelia, they anticipated some of the innovations of California guitars bands like Moby Grape and Buffalo Springfield by a good year or two. One would think that a group with so much talent couldn't possibly miss, but to the contrary, most people outside of Los Angeles never even knew they existed.

The Rising Sons were formed around the core of guitarists Kincaid and Mahal. Taj met Jesse, then playing a 12-string acoustic, in Cambridge, Massachusetts, in 1964. The pair formed an acoustic duo briefly before heading to Los Angeles, where they added teenage guitar phenom Ry Cooder, who had already accompanied early folk-rocker Jackie DeShannon. Completing the first version of the band were jazz bassist Gary Marker and jazz drummer Ed Cassidy, already into his forties and about to become the oldest stickman in rock (a position he retains to this day).

Like other pioneering California rock bands like the Byrds, the musicians had practically zilch professional rock experience. But like the Byrds, they knew that electric rock was the coming thing after the advent of the Beatles, and were determined to somehow make it work. It wasn't simply a case of folkies gone electric, however. "The goal was to play *blues*-oriented music," emphasizes Kincaid. "More specifically, what we called Delta, Mississippi-styled blues: a guitar-oriented thing, [with some] acoustic guitar, maybe a little harmonica. I was the songwriter, though, and I was always kind of interested in the Beatles. So I was always throwing a pop mix into the blues thing."

This tension between pop and blues instincts would soon become problematic, but the Rising Sons quickly made waves on the super-competitive L.A. club circuit. They were an interracial band at a time when such groups were nonexistent, pre-dating even Love. They played blues-rock at a time when virtually no one in L.A. had thought of the combination, with the arguable exception of the still-embryonic Captain Beefheart. They were a dynamic live act, inspiring

The Rising Sons, mid-1960s: the supergroup without an album. Left to right: Ry Cooder, Taj Mahal, Kevin Kelley, Jesse Kincaid, Gary Marker. Credit: Courtesy Gary Marker; photo Guy Webster

David Crosby, then of the Byrds, to jump on a table at the Troubadour club and lead the crowd in chanting, "Long live the Rising Sons!" Crosby relayed his enthusiasm to Byrds publicist Billy James; at James' urging, it would be the Byrds' label, Columbia, that would win out over several companies that were interested in signing the band.

Columbia was at that point experiencing its first true success in the rock band market with the Byrds, whose "Mr. Tambourine Man" was racing to #1 when the Rising Sons were signed to the label in mid-1965. The Rising Sons were assigned to the Byrds' producer, Terry Melcher, who was also hot with pop-rockers Paul Revere & the Raiders at the time. From a certain viewpoint, the logic was sound: Columbia was entrusting the group's fortunes to one of the few producers at the company with any feel for rock 'n' roll at all. The Columbia association, however, would prove to be something of a disaster for all considered.

"Prior to the Beatles and the English Invasion," notes Kincaid, "Columbia was a Mitch Miller kind of organization. It was all easy listening. They didn't really like rock and roll, and they didn't know much about blues either. When we started recording for them, the goal was to have a hit single. And once you had your hit single, you would release an album as a follow-up. It wasn't an album market so much as it is today. Certainly Columbia wasn't an album company as much as some of the folk companies of the time, like Folkways or Vanguard—they were interested in hit singles.

"And we got assigned a producer who was a top hit single guy. He was sort of like the wonderkid who was going to make the hits. And he just wasn't able to do it with us, because for whatever reason, we didn't get that hit single sound. So consequently, nothing got released; they didn't do an album on the band."

Almost nothing got released, to be precise. In February 1966, a flop single peeped out, pairing a Skip James song ("The Devil's Got My Woman") with one associated with Reverend Gary Davis ("Candy Man"). If Columbia was trying to find something commercial, the selection of these tracks in particular was somewhat peculiar; few if any other electric rock bands were covering pre-World War II blues classics at the time.

"Terry came in and we thought he was going to try and do a Beach Boys thing, or a Byrds thing," says Marker. "And he didn't. He kind of wanted us to be a blues band or maybe a pop band. He wasn't sure. We weren't sure. The band was so schizophrenic anyway. It was just possibly the worst possible combination to try to put together pop records that ever existed. 'Cause everybody had an opinion, and everybody had their own stuff to do.

"Ryland, even at that age, was really the musical timekeeper, the foundation of the whole band. If everybody else's amplifiers blew out, he would sit there and play the bass lines and everything else on one guitar. You could just cut out everything else, and the meter wouldn't waver, the energy wouldn't drop at all—he would be like throwing in horn parts and all that shit." Jimmy Page, then still a session guitarist in England, met Cooder while visiting California; Marker recalls that Page was impressed enough with one of the Cooder's 12-string acoustic arrangements to ask the L.A. guitarist to tape it for him. Cooder's transition to electric, in fact, was not an overnight thing, according to Marker: "Ryland was always breaking strings. He figured to get more volume, he had to play harder, instead of turning the volume up."

Meanwhile Columbia was sitting on almost an album's worth of material from late 1965, much of which showed the group to better advantage than their debut single. Kincaid made some tentative forays into Beatlesque pop with numbers like "The Girl with Green Eyes," but there were also blues-based rock adaptations of tunes by the likes of Sleepy John Estes and Willie Dixon. There was also a hard-charging rock version of an unreleased Bob Dylan composition ("Walkin' Down the Line"), a homey arrangement of the traditional folk ballad "Corrine, Corrina," and some quite competent bluesy numbers from the pen of Kincaid ("I Got a Little"). Throughout the tracks the guitar interplay was sparkling, achieving an unusual diversity of texture—acoustic picking, Cooder's bottleneck slide, hard rock jangle, even some mandolin and banjo. But in the days before the LP had achieved precedence over the 45 as the format of choice, the band's repertoire may have been *too* diverse for a mainstream company to deal with.

"Statesboro Blues," a Blind Willie McTell composition, was a particular favorite of the band, taken at a faster-than-light tempo that allegedly broke Ed Cassidy's wrist during one particularly ferocious onstage performance. Cassidy, in fact, was gone by the time the group began to record the late 1965-early 1966 material that was eventually issued by Columbia on a 1992 CD. His replacement was the much younger Kevin Kelley. "In our opinion, [Ed] had kind of a light feel, a jazzy kind of feel," explains Kincaid. "We were more interested in different kind of rock feel, a harder kind of feel. So we just swapped." There was another pragmatic consideration at work. "Kevin had a van, too. And we rehearsed at his mother's house, now that I think about it."

The quest for a hit single led Melcher to bring them a Carole King-Gerry Goffin tune, "Take a Giant Step." Recorded in March 1966, this was the group's shot at the Top 40 if they ever had one, with its interlocking bottleneck/hard rock guitar parts, sophisticated Byrds-Beatles harmonies, and clever lyrics. A friend the band's, Barry Hansen (later to become famous as radio personality Dr. Demento), helped with the arrangement. Even though it had arrived from an outside source, the group seemed to genuinely dig the tune; Taj Mahal liked it enough to record it again on one of his first solo albums.

"Whenever Jesse came up with guitar parts or other arrangements, there was a feeling that he was being humored," observes Marker. "Despite that, he came up with lots of neat stuff. For example, when it came time for a kind of mini 'raveup' guitar solo overdub on 'Take a Giant Step,' Cooder had absolutely no idea what to do. After an hour or so of diddling with overdubs, he was stumped. 'Give me that guitar,' Jesse said. He charged into the studio, tape rolled, and in two takes he had two wheezing, satirical psychedelic guitar solos put down on tape.

Ten minutes, end of story—break for dinner. Cooder was stunned. 'Well, I believe that sounds pretty fuckin' good,' he said, with an embarrassed shit-eating grin. His estimation of Kincaid went up a bit at that point, I think."

The song would become a hit, of sorts—but not for the Rising Sons. The Monkees, giving the song a far lighter treatment, placed it on the B-side of their debut (and #1 smash) single, "Last Train to Clarksville." The Rising Sons even got as far as lip-synching the number for Dick Clark's "Where the Action Is," but the single, mysteriously, was never released. Marker says the 45 made it to the white-label promo stage, and even got a bit of airplay in San Francisco, but re-members hearing that it was pulled because Columbia thought it was a "drug record." Columbia's commitment to the group seemed to be wavering, possibly because it just wasn't sure what to do with such an eclectic outfit.

"The thing about the Byrds was, they were all going in the same direction," comments Melcher in the liner notes to the *Rising Sons Featuring Taj Mahal and Ry Cooder* CD. "Here you had guys who should have been in two different groups. If I had it to do over, I would've found some Beatle-type group and put Kincaid in there, and had another group with Ry and Taj."

"Taj was the most salient performer in the group in terms of being a front guy," elaborates Kincaid. "And yet the songs that I was writing were very pop-ori-ented. But I don't particularly like my tracks very much because I wasn't much of a singer in those days, and even as a pop songwriter, I was just beginning. So it started to make a conflict. There were two pulses that were strong in the band. One was a pop music sensibility, and the other was a blues sensibility. I was basi-cally the pop guy— Taj was basically the blues guy, along with Ry. Terry didn't have the power to separate and make two bands out of it—that wasn't the issue. I think he was just pointing out that there were these two directions within the band that both seemed to be strong and working pretty well, but he couldn't ever reconcile any of those into any success.

"Personally, in retrospect, I think Columbia was just a big mistake. Because all they did really was try to make a hit single out of us, which we didn't have in us. And they never explored the acoustic textures in the band, in any kind of a way, until the very last session. We threw all the electric guitars out the window, and just did an acoustic session. Those were my favorites, actually. That was more like what Taj and I were doing before we even had this band around our neck, just a duo act, which I really liked."

Adds Marker, "We had all just made the switch from playing acoustic instru-ments. Once we got into that kind of rock format with the electrified instru-ments, that kind of interplay [Taj and Jesse] had really fell by the wayside. Taj didn't play guitar onstage—rarely if ever. Which is kind of sad, because he's a pretty fair guitar player."

The final tracks cut by the band in May 1966 (now available on the reissue CD) are indeed some of their best, most relaxed moments. "By and By" was a hammock-swinging cover of a Charlie Patton song; the supremely sad and folky "2:10 Train," written by local songwriter Linda Albertano, would be covered by Linda Ronstadt on her first album with the Stone Poneys. "Sunny's Dream," "Spanish Lace Blues," and "11th Street Overcrossing" are all classy Kincaid originals with superb slide and mandolin work, and an oh-so-slight spacy psychedelic lyrical influence. All were earmarked for a debut album that, although ready to be mixed, would never see the light of day. The Rising Sons, tired of working hard with nothing to show for it, disbanded in late 1966.

"We got caught, I think, in the politics of Columbia Records," offers Kincaid. "Terry [Melcher] and Billy [James] wanted to manage the band, and in the end basically strong-armed us to become our managers. We didn't want them to do it. That soured everything, and Terry just kind of dumped us pretty much, didn't want to work with us anymore. Wanted a piece of the action, I suppose. But we were kind of fighting over nothing, because we never *got* any action.

"The ending was a little bit unpleasant. We had Terry and Billy saying, 'Well, if you don't sign with us, you're not gonna work again.' Then Taj and Ry kind of drifted off into their own areas. It was pretty negative; from my point of view, it sort of dissolved away in a struggle of power. Which I wasn't ready for." Marker emphasizes that these sort of management-production deals were standard operating procedures in the music business at the time: "Sure, the ultimatum issued by Melcher and James may have been a catalyst that hastened our breakup. But I believe it was destined to happen anyway—and very soon."

Marker goes on to offer another take on the Columbia impasse. "Billy James kept trying to hype us as being the American Rolling Stones, because that's what they needed to hear. Once they kind of came out and got a look at us, they said, 'Shit, this is an integrated group. What are we gonna do with that big buck up front?' There was kind of an illusion that we were like four white boys backing a black dude. It's ridiculous to think about it now, but it was a real big issue back then. I used to hear these stories that the internal name for the Rising Sons was two WASPs, two Jews, and a conspicuous Negro. And they were all scratching their heads back in New York saying, 'How do we market this?' I said, 'Well, it's an All-American band.' When Taj heard that, he got hysterical. He said, 'Who's the conspicuous Negro?'"

Columbia finally released a Rising Sons album of mostly unreleased material in 1992, but despite the high quality of much of the music, Marker for one feels that it doesn't represent the band at their best. "I was really opposed to probably about 90% of that album being released. Much of it was live demos that we ran through just to see if there was anything worth working on later. A lot of stuff, [Taj] was playing piano and guitar parts you don't even hear because they're not even in the mix. They dropped it out, or couldn't find the original eight-tracks, or didn't know he was on there."

Taj Mahal would soon establish a career of his own at Columbia in a more defined blues-based style that had not always been apparent in his work with the Rising Sons. "I think that's why they released the single with me singing on it, as opposed to Taj singing," says Kincaid. "'Cause they were really trying to turn Taj into a pop singer [while he was with the Rising Sons]. As a matter of fact, they wanted Taj to be a pop singer on 'Take a Giant Step.' I can remember being in the studio with Taj when he was recording it, kind of like leading him, actually conducting his vocal. Trying to get him to do it this way, instead of the way *he* would do it. In the end, it kind of sounded strained to my ear. But they probably suppressed the blues element. We'd have been better off with Vanguard or something like that, or Elektra, somebody who was into the musical style."

Cooder, after briefly joining Captain Beefheart's band for the *Safe As Milk* album, was soon jump-starting his own career as in-demand session man, playing on *Let It Bleed* with the Rolling Stones (who had first checked Ry out live with the Rising Sons several years previously). By the 1970s he was reeling off a series of critically acclaimed albums; now he is also a respected film scorer, still managing to find time for innovative projects like his collaboration with West African guitarist Ali Farka Toure, *Talking Timbuktu*. Kelley joined the Byrds in time for their landmark country-rock album, *Sweetheart of the Rodeo*; Ed Cassidy was by that time a star as the drummer of psychedelic L.A. band Spirit. Marker made a jazz-rock album as part of Fusion, later working as an architect and journalist. Kincaid made a few singles for Capitol as a solo act (one of these, "She Sang Hymns Out of Tune," would be covered by Harry Nilsson). Today he lives in Mill Valley, near San Francisco, teaching music, competing in fiddle contests, continuing to write songs, and harboring no bitterness about the supergroup that never was.

"What we're looking at here is individuals, not a band," Kincaid concludes. "We were all different people, from different places and different backgrounds, with different points of view. The two strongest characters went on to be good recording and performing acts. I think it served its purpose to get these two guys up in the front and performing—not as a band necessarily. I think after a while, the constraints of band activities wore Taj and Ry out. They decided they'd be better off on their own. The band was successful enough to guarantee that Taj had a solo career, and Ry had a solo career. I think it did what it had to do."

Recommended Recording:
The Rising Sons featuring Taj Mahal and Ry Cooder (1992, Columbia/Legacy). Over 25 years after their 1965–66 sessions, the first and only Rising Sons album finally came out. This has their lone single, plus 20 outtakes. It's not the way the band might have preferred to arrange their record. But it's consistent, durable, innovative, and ahead of its time—and certainly would have been worthy of release back in 1966.

Tomorrow

The first half of 1967 was a heady time to be in London. The Beatles' *Sgt. Pepper* was merely the culmination of months of activity that found British rock breaking away from its blues/R&B-based roots into experimental psychedelic music. Bands played havoc with conventional pop song structures, infusing their music and lyrics with a giddy utopian yearning. An epicenter for this scene was the UFO club, ground zero for the exploding London underground, London and otherwise.

Of all of the emerging bands that played the UFO often, three were usually singled out as the most innovative. One—Pink Floyd—went on to become one of the biggest acts in the world. Another, the Soft Machine, would become leaders of rock's avant-garde over the next five years. Yet the third, Tomorrow, would only record one album, and is mostly remembered today for featuring future Yes guitarist Steve Howe. That's especially true in America, where Tomorrow never appeared.

Tomorrow, the best early psychedelic British group never to cross the Atlantic. Left to right: Twink, a pre-Yes Steve Howe, Junior Wood, and singer Keith West.

Of all the one-shot albums in the history of rock, Tomorrow's self-titled 1968 effort rates as one of the best and most fully developed. Fey, distinctively British story-songs about stuck-up colonels, dress shops, and dwarfs alternate with West Coast-influenced psychedelic numbers featuring stunning guitar riffs. "My White Bicycle" and "Revolution" summarize the period's naive hopes for social change and upheaval as well as anything else from the era.

Despite the group's identification with the psychedelic movement, all of the songs are tightly constructed, with airtight arrangements and no meandering jams. Those scared by the Steve Howe name should be assured that the material bears little relation to Yes, being far more pop-oriented and good-humored. By the time the album was issued, however, the moment had passed; psychedelia was receding, and the group themselves would soon be no more. For Tomorrow, there was no tomorrow.

Like most of the psychedelic bands, Tomorrow had their roots in surprisingly conventional British Invasion rock, R&B, and soul music. Howe and lead singer/principal songwriter Keith West had already recorded with little-known London bands by the time they teamed up in the In Crowd. The modish outfit enjoyed a strong live reputation, but their singles made little impact. Their transition to a psychedelic band was a swift one, brought about by necessity as much as invention.

Keith West, today marketing director for the Burns guitar company in England, saw the writing on the wall. "When Steve joined the In Crowd originally, the whole thing changed a bit because he was into jamming a bit more. He wouldn't play the same thing twice. We were bored playing the R&B stuff, we could see something else was happening. We thought it was time we started writing our stuff. I didn't think we were going to last otherwise."

The In Crowd missed an opportunity for wider exposure when they were briefly considered for a role as the band in a club scene in Michelangelo Antonioni's classic Swinging London film *Blow Up* (the Yardbirds ended up snagging the spot). By the time they changed their name to Tomorrow, though, they had their hands full as a house band of sorts for the UFO, especially when UFO stalwarts Pink Floyd were unable to keep playing the club regularly.

Asked to compare Tomorrow with cohorts Pink Floyd and Soft Machine, West reflects that the Floyd "were learning as they were going along, more or less; they weren't great musicians by any stretch of the imagination then. We had Steve Howe, who was the top guitarist, as far as I was concerned, in London. Soft Machine were a lot more avant-garde kind of band. We were more of a straightahead rock, fun psychedelic band. We did crazy things and had a good time.

"We didn't want to get *too* serious. The Doors were doing all that. We *were* serious about what we were doing, but we were kind of a 'let's lighten up a bit, let's have some fun' kind of band. We always used to like to have a good time. Why not? Why walk around trying to be so cool all the time?"

Inspired by a scheme in Amsterdam to provide free bicycles for citizens, "My White Bicycle" certainly epitomized psychedelia at its most fun and creative, with its clattering bike-pedal percussion, backwards guitar, police whistles, and insistent chorus. Work began on an album. Then the unexpected happened. A Keith West solo single—the grandiose "Excerpt from a Teenage Opera"—was released with little expectations, but rose to #2 on the British charts. A multi-part suite with fruity horns and a children's chorus that narrated the last day of the life of a "grocer Jack," it's been cited as an influence on the rock operas of the Who (*Tommy*) and the Pretty Things (*S.F. Sorrow*), although West doubts the connection.

The problem was that now the public was confused about Tomorrow's identity. Tomorrow played hard guitar-based psychedelic music, not twee pop operettas. The success of "Teenage Opera" (and a follow-up, "Sam," which became a moderate hit), and widespread media speculation of an entire opera that West would compose and perform with producer Mark Wirtz, may have delayed the release of the group's debut LP. By the time it finally emerged, it was already 1968, the psychedelic scene was waning, and Tomorrow were yesterday's flash.

"It was far too late coming out," concedes West. "By the time it was released, the thing was all over, more or less. We were at the forefront of that kind of era. I can't remember what happened, but I always think, that was crazy! Why didn't they just rush that thing out?

"I know John Lennon at the time got in touch with our office, and inquired whether Tomorrow was free, what we were doing, if the publishing was free. He liked 'My White Bicycle,' he liked our cover version of 'Strawberry Fields.' That would have been a great move for me, to have signed with Apple or something like that. But instead, I'd already got locked into EMI. They just signed me up on some bum deal. I'd never had a chance to try anything else out, I was always stuck at EMI. Which was really the wrong label for us."

By mid-'68, the band had broken up. Drummer Twink, one of the great practical jokers of British rock, went on to join the Pretty Things and the Pink Fairies, two bands with underground cults of their own. Howe and West did continue to write for a while in hopes that something might develop, but they soon went their separate ways, West to various solo and group projects, and Howe to eventually gain stardom with Yes. The Tomorrow album refuses to go away, reissued in various configurations over the last couple of decades.

"It was all over very quick," remembers West, with little apparent surprise or regret. "The original idea, what it was supposed to be all about, was all over. When the psychedelic thing came along, we got asked to play the UFO club, we'd say, 'This audience is fantastic, they actually really listen to the music.' And everybody was kind of really well behaved. Everyone thought that was really cool. We had a year or two of that, and we got spoiled. That affected me, that kind of thing. I thought we'd go on—music could change, politics could change. But of course that's never going to happen. It always goes back to square one. We were a bit naive at the time."

Recommended Recording:
Tomorrow (1968, Decal, UK). Virtually everything recorded by the band, including the B-side "Claremont Lake." For those who want even more, check out RPM's compilations of obscure '60s releases, featuring projects in which Steve Howe and Keith West had a hand. The Keith West compilation (*Excerpts From*) includes the two crude but interesting unreleased Tomorrow cuts that were considered for the *Blow Up* soundtrack.

The United States of America

Rock groups are supposed to be hatched in garages and inner-city lofts, not the upper reaches of academia. That wasn't going to stop Joseph Byrd, experimental composer and ethnomusicologist from the UCLA New Music Workshop, from devising a plan in 1967 to approach rock 'n' roll from the opposite direction.

Byrd, who had frequented avant-garde circles since hanging around with Terry Riley, LaMonte Young, and Virgil Thomson in the early '60s, used the United States of America to bring cutting-edge electronics, Indian music, and "serious" composition into psychedelic rock 'n' roll. The group's sole, self-titled album in 1968 was a tour de force (though not without its flaws) of experimental rock that blended surprisingly melodic sensibilities with unnerving blasts of primitive synthesizers and lyrics that could range from misty romanticism to hard-edged irony. For the relatively few who heard it, the record was a signpost to the future with its collision of rock and classical elements, although the material crackled with a tension that reflected the United States of America itself in the late '60s.

By mid-1968, the grand experiment was over. Conflicting egos, a drug bust, and commercial pressures all contributed to a rapid split. The United States of America may have had their roots in the halls of higher learning, but ultimately they were prey to the same kind of mundane tensions that broke the spirit of many a band that lived and died on the streets.

From the time Byrd founded the band in Los Angeles with colleague Michael Agnello, says singer Dorothy Moskowitz, "group dynamics were never a strong point in the USA." Moskowitz, Byrd's ex-girlfriend, had a background in writing and performing for musical theater. She moved from New York to California to join the group and, as she puts it, provide "the requisite schmaltz." Bassist Stu Brotman, one-time member of the stunningly eclectic L.A. psychedelic group Kaleidoscope, was also an early part of the group.

But he and Agnello were gone by the time the group began recording for Columbia. Agnello, a radical sort, was arguing with Byrd over leadership of the band, and was not sure the act should even be signed to a record label in the first place. "When you ask why the group broke up, well, why did the group even record *after* it broke it up?" points out Moskowitz.

Yet the lineup featured on the album brought impressive credentials to the table. Electric violinist Gordon Marron expanded his instrument's parameters with a divider that could raise or lower it an octave, as well as tape echo units and ring modulators. Rand Forbes played an unfretted electric bass, and drummer Craig Woodson tinkered with his sound in unusual ways, attaching contact microphones to his set and suspending slinkies from cymbals to get a musique-concrète effect. Ed Bogas added organ, piano, and calliope.

Most of the material was penned by Byrd and Moskowitz, the latter's alto delivering the lyrics—which are alternately evocative and foreboding—with a cool precision reminiscent of an icier Grace Slick. Byrd was chiefly responsible for the electronic textures that would provide the album with its most distinguishing characteristics. This was 1968, remember, when synthesizers had rarely been employed on rock records. What Byrd crafted were not simulations of strings and horns, but exhilarating, frightening swoops and bleeps that lent a fierce crunch to the faster numbers, and a beguiling serenity to the ballads. Byrd had crucial help in his endeavors from Richard Durrett, who designed the Durrett electronic music synthesizer used by the band, and from Tom Oberheim, who pioneered the use of the ring modulator employed by the USA.

The United States of America, plugging into state-of-the-art 1968 electronics. Singer Dorothy Moskowitz in front; Joe Byrd is next to her in striped shirt and glasses. Credit: Courtesy Dorothy Moskowitz

Nico, Moskowitz has recalled, tried unsuccessfully to join the band, after leaving the Velvet Underground.

Add to this mix a fascination with modal playing and Indian music. Byrd and Moskowitz were serious students of North and South Indian music, and had already made little-known contributions to a Folkways LP of Indian music by Gayathri Rajapur and Harihar Rao, recorded in 1965. Country Joe & the Fish, the Doors, and others were opening the gates for modal playing in rock 'n' roll, and the USA were one of the first ones through; Frank Zappa had also incorporated ideas from contemporary composition into a rock format. And then there was Byrd's application of concepts from Charles Ives, which simulated marching bands moving together from opposite sides of the stereo spectrum . . .

Was it all too much to fit onto one album? "As a whole, the album does not have a coherent, unified vision," declares Moskowitz, who now lives near Oakland, California, where she composes music for both adult and children's theatrical events in the San Francisco Bay Area. "Joe had vision, but by hiring all these interesting people, it had to be diluted. Everybody had to have their say. I'm told that someone took the album to Apple Records. The Beatles listened to it and asked, 'Which is the band?' If you listen to each song, it's almost like a variety show.

"Today you would say, it's a cultural blending of avant-garde music, of elements of Indian music. If you asked me back then, I'm not sure what we were doing. That might have been the basic charm of the group. We were charting territory for which their *were* no names."

Recording the electronics in particular proved a challenge for both the band and their producer, David Rubinson, who remembers, "The ring modulator and the volt-control oscillators and voltage control filters—they didn't come in a set, like they did in a Moog. You had to build each one—which they did—and actually hard-wire them together. It was an eight-track album. So all that synthesized stuff was painstakingly layered in, sound by sound, one oscillator at a time. Now you may get a bank of oscillators and you can run six, eight, twelve of them in a row, and make all kinds of wonderful waves, shapes, and it can be very complicated. But at that time, it was not possible.

"It had one oscillator, one ring modulator, one voltage control filter—that's it. It looked funny. It was like aluminum boxes, little knobs sticking out, and patch cords. And it was very exciting to me, because it was a marriage of a lot of what was happening in what people called classical music at the time. When people think about what Steve Reich was doing then, and Terry Riley was doing then, and what Joe Byrd was doing then, it was very, very similar in different areas."

Aside from the even more obscure San Francisco group Fifty Foot Hose, and the New York duo Silver Apples, the United States were virtually alone in their attempts to combine psychedelic rock with cutting-edge electronics. The very fact that the equipment was so primitive, however, lent a spontaneous resonance and warmth that has rarely been achieved by subsequent synthesizer technology. Listen to "Hard Coming Love," for instance, where the oscillations seem to be launching into outer space from an Olympian-sized swimming pool. Moskowitz's voice was also run through electronic filtering at times to give it a particularly eerie quality.

In Moskowitz's opinion, "Synthesizers in those days were so unpredictable—that was part of their appeal. You didn't *know* what was going to happen! So you'd turn on the volume—you'd get a 'squawk,' or you might get a 'bleep.' It didn't really matter, so long as you were playing in rhythm. And that was very exciting. So you'd go 'bling, bling,' and that became part of the rhythm track. Nowadays, you can pretty much pre-program the precise 'ping' or 'click' you want. Back then, the limited technology didn't allow for the kind of options we have now.

"In the mid-'60s, a synthesizer was considered an instrument on its own terms, not a means of duplicating the sound of something else. It expanded the palette and gave the music a dangerous edge. It certainly did lend a richness."

Columbia balked at a plan to use an album cover of, in Rubinson's words, a flag with blood dripping from it (Moskowitz doesn't remember the illustration as being quite so blatantly anti-Establishment). The LP was eventually issued with more standard band photographs, in a plain manila wrapper with a stamp that declared, "United States of America—Top Secret." Onstage, according to Rubinson, the band "reproduced the album exactly." So when it came time to go on the road and bring the USA to the *real* USA, playing the music was not the chief problem. The greater problem was finding a sympathetic audience for such an unusual act.

At such venues as Washington, D.C.'s Corcoran Gallery, the band felt in their element. It wasn't as easy playing for audiences that expected out-and-out rock 'n' roll, like the one that gave the group the thumbs-down on an ill-fated pairing with the Troggs. The USA also played once with the Velvet Underground, which seemed like a more copacetic match, although Moskowitz has related how the Velvets knocked over the USA's amplifiers as they were going offstage.

Tensions within the group escalated into a backstage fistfight between Byrd and Marron at one of their most high-profile gigs (at New York's Fillmore East). "Joe Byrd was one of the most insane examples of control freak that I've, to this day, ever experienced," observes Rubinson. "At that time, I was in my twenties, and I wasn't the easiest person in the world to get along with either, I guess. But he was really bizarre, and a very, very difficult person to deal with. So there were constant personality conflicts in and among the band. People quitting, people getting replaced, arguments, yelling about intonation, and so forth. They were very talented people, and I don't think they liked being dictated to. But he had a vision of what he wanted."

The final straw, as far as the lineup from the first album was concerned, was at a gig in Orange County, California, in which three of the members were busted for marijuana, leaving Joe and Dorothy to complete the show with help from the support act. And Rubinson didn't like the direction in which the United States of America were going.

"The band started off as a completely revolutionary, anti-authority, nihilistic group. Whatever they wore, whatever they wanted to do, it was the opposite of patriotic. It was supposed to be an anarchist kind of group, to do everything possible to rub the wrong way. To take no conventions seriously. They became less anarchistic and less different, and submitted material which was kind of ordinary."

In a letter to Richard Kostelanetz that was reprinted in Kostelanetz's book *The Fillmore East*, Byrd states that he started the band "as an avant-garde political/musical rock group," with the intention of combining electronic sound, musical/political radicalism, and performance art. "The idea was to create a radical experience. It didn't succeed. For one thing, I had assembled too many personalities; every rehearsal became group therapy. A band that wants to succeed needs a single, mutually acceptable identity. I tried to do it democratically, and it was not successful."

Moskowitz offers a different perspective on the clash between Byrd and Rubinson: "[David] didn't like the fact that Joe hired studio horn players, and that we all of a sudden lost our pure sound. He thought we were attempting a slickness, and he didn't like it. I didn't care either way, because the original album had syrupy movie theme music, if you notice. To me, the intent of the US of A was to pull from different genres. That was the excitement. If Byrd wanted to use horn players doing Motown licks—no problem!

"But Joe heard him grumbling. And his response was, 'Let's get rid of Rubinson.' Although I didn't agree with David aesthetically, I felt loyal to him. He was, after all, the one who had put us on the map. Joe might have been well-advised to step back and ask, 'What would you rather I do here?' But no, there was this arrogant angry reaction between the two of them."

The US of A split into two factions, one being Joe Byrd & the Field Hippies. Moskowitz's group was, in her words, "a very mild-mannered, non-electric band. Too mild." When the Field Hippies recorded their only LP for Columbia—which was a rather uninspired effort with the odd tune that was obviously aiming for a USA-type feel—there was one last chance to reunite the Byrd-Moskowitz partnership.

"I got a call about three months later, after the breakup, from Joe's producer," says Moskowitz. She remembers being told, "'The instrumentation is wonderful, the songs are great, the singers are not [that good]. And we listened to your demo, and the singing is really nice, but the people you put together are just sub-standard. Why don't you come back, and work again together?'

"I was too angry. I was too leery. I had been with Joe romantically in the early '60s, and I had been with him professionally in the mid-'60s, and I was tired of dealing with tension and being the moderator. I was on his side aesthetically. I was not very happy with the way he conducted his personal affairs. In terms of fame and fortune, it might have been the wrong decision. But the fact that I'm sitting here in this lovely suburban house, with a fine family . . ." She pauses, and smiles. "I guess I'm glad I got away from it, more or less intact."

Recommended Recording:
The United States of America (1968, Columbia/Legacy). Now on CD with two extra cuts, this remains one of avant-rock's greatest moments. But not at the expense of good songs, whether driving rockers ("Hard Coming Love," "Garden of Earthly Delights") or ethereal ballads ("Clouds," "Where Is Yesterday," and the wonderfully titled "Love Song For the Dead Che").

Young Marble Giants

In Chris Marker's classic classic 1962 short film *La Jetée*, the protagonist is given a glimpse of a post-nuclear future populated by cool, remote beings who resemble statues more than breathing humans. Asked to escape to this tranquil future, the hero rejects the invitation in favor of traveling into the more turbulent, but more passionate, past. Had the film made the journey into the future, there may have been no more appropriate soundtrack than the sole album by Young Marble Giants, *Colossal Youth*.

Naming themselves after a book about classical statues, the trio emanated a cool elegance with their carefully crafted miniatures of troubled love and romantic desperation. In an era in which rock was struggling to maintain the momentum of punk and new wave, Young Marble Giants defied convention by turning their amps down instead of up. Lonely, reverbed guitar lines, spooky organs, funk bass, tinny drum machine clicks, and Alison Statton's restrained, lounge-lizard vocals created a spacious sound that bounced around like balloons in a rubber room. Even the sleeve—which showed all three members in unsmiling half-shadow, like a post-punk version of *With the Beatles*—projected a postmodern formalism. They looked like those ancient classical statues come to life—or, more disquietingly, like those icy futuristic characters in the final scenes of *La Jetée*.

Young Marble Giants, smothered in half-shadow on the cover of their only album, 1980's *Colossal Youth.*

Young Marble Giants only managed that one album in 1980, plus a few stray EP and compilation tracks, before dissolving undramatically shortly afterwards. More than almost any other rock record of its era, *Colossal Youth* has exuded a powerful mystique over the subsequent decade-and-a-half. Influential alternative bands that came of age in the 1980s—such as Beat Happening, Barbara Manning, and Lois—were devoted fans. All would eventually collaborate with Young Marble Giants guitarist and principal songwriter, Stuart Moxham, in the following decade.

If you take the aura surrounding the group seriously, it may come as a letdown—or, more likely, a relief—to find that Stuart Moxham is hardly a cold fish at all. The soft-spoken Welshman is now a family man with three children, able to concentrate on his songwriting and solo career more than ever now that a couple of overseas superstars have covered his compositions. Being able to make music for a living, after all, seemed like a pipe dream when he formed Young Marble Giants in the late '70s in Cardiff with his brother Philip (bass) and Alison Statton. The Moxhams were playing as part of a cover band; Alison began a relationship with Philip after she had auditioned for a position as backup vocalist. When the band broke up, the trio determined to continue with original material, drawing from influences like Devo, Kraftwerk, early Ultravox, early Roxy Music, and Iggy Pop's *The Idiot*. Moxham's songwriting also betrayed the less obvious (and less hip) traces of early heroes such as Neil Young, James Taylor, and Joni Mitchell.

"We wanted to make a body of work that was exceptional, that was really gonna stand out," states Moxham today. "We were all kind of desperate to make it and get out of Cardiff. Cardiff wasn't on the musical map at all until recently. The music had to achieve a lot for us. It had to get us a record deal, which nobody we knew had ever done."

Cardiff, Moxham adds, was at that time—and to a degree still is—an industrial town far more interested in heavy, rootsy rock than arty experimentalism. "I can remember one night doing gigs in Cardiff before we'd made any records or anything, and someone shouting out, 'Play rock and roll!' I kind of went into this Chuck Berry riff, then stopped and said, 'Look, anyone can do that. They're doing it all over town. But *we* want to do *this*.'"

This was music that was deliberately constructed to sound unlike the local competition. "My whole idea was, let's just turn our backs on that, and see what else there is to do. Being quiet was one thing, and being very minimal was another. We thought, 'We'll go against all the grains and see if we can come up with something.' As somebody once said in Rough Trade, basically it's rock and roll. It's basically 12-bar blues. It's just sort of chopped up a bit."

Rough Trade, probably the most influential indie British label of the time, signed the band up after hearing a couple of cuts on a compilation LP, *Is the War Over*. (Previous to that, Moxham sold tapes of home recordings at the Cardiff branch of Virgin Records, where he worked.) Asked by the label whether they wanted to make a single or an album, the group—now fortified with plenty of quality originals—opted for an album.

Colossal Youth was recorded in a mere five days; the mix was completed in 20 minutes. The group's drum machine effects—used far more tastefully, and less obtrusively, than they were (and are) in most electro-pop acts—had been condensed onto one cassette for use in their live gigs. The same cassette was used to make the drum machine sounds on the record, on which, according to Moxham, "We did exactly the same thing in the studio as we did live. I think we did about two or three overdubs on the whole album. The whole idea was to keep it very simple. Since then, I've got fucked into the way of working [like] everybody else works. Endless overdubs, multitracking, mixing, and remixing, I've done all that business. At times I just think to myself, God, I got it right the first time around. Why am I doing all this? It's crazy!"

Minimalism was indeed the order of the day on the record, which backed Statton's coolly assured vocals with Philip Moxham's rumbling bass and Stuart's haunting, mildly reverbed guitar licks. Occasionally Stuart injected some lean, sad keyboard licks that sounded halfway between synthesizers and conventional organs. The songs were moody and mysterious, in the manner of nineteenth century romantic poets, but the coating of modern electronics made it sound oddly futuristic at the same time. Stuart Moxham admits to being a bookish, solitary sort in his youth, and without a doubt the record's principal appeal is to other bookish, solitary adolescents and post-adolescents throughout the world. This is the kind of record that such an audience will want to play alone, in their rooms, over and over—which accounts to a large degree for its unwavering cult appeal over the years.

The album may have been recorded in a phenomenally fast period of time by modern standards, but Moxham insists there was a lot of deliberate calculation on the group's part, in both material and arrangements. "My songwriting before the Young Marble Giants was kind of organic; it's just whatever came to mind. It wasn't styled in any way. The Young Marble Giants stuff was very rigidly written for [a] kind of formula: very stylized, very molded, for a purpose. We were very, very strict about how we wanted to do it when we went into the studio to do *Colossal Youth*. It had to be stripped right down. I've always been a reverb freak, so we had that. But I mean, there were no frills, really."

An important fourth member of sorts was Pete Joyce, a cousin of the Moxhams who "was a telephone engineer at the time, and a bit of a gearhead. He built our drum machine and a few other things. We were very excited by the early techno thing of drum machines and synthesizers. He was quite a big influence in that he supplied all the technical know-how, and all the gear we used." The strange organ effects—not sterile enough to be a modern synthesizer, not warm enough to be a genuine organ—were produced by Joyce's Stylophone, an early synthesizer built into a briefcase (most famous for its use on David Bowie's "Space Oddity"). "It had a shiny metal keyboard that didn't move, and a pen with a wire which attached it to the main body of the instrument," remembers Moxham. "It just made this nee-nee-nee-nee noise. It's quite naff."

Colossal Youth posted quite respectable sales for an indie release in Britain, as well as some exceptionally verbose praise in the rock press. (*Sounds* magazine: "*Colossal Youth* acts as a commentary, a remote and assured mirror to the contemporary hysteria for the safe, the predictable, the emotionless.") There was enough interest for an American tour, which found the band in such unlikely settings as an outdoor concert in San Francisco with the Flamin' Groovies; a Hell's Angel-run club in Palo Alto; and a Czechoslovakian community center in Los Angeles. There was a folk club in Vancouver with an unplugged policy that, says Moxham, "allowed us to plug in, but with the amps on, like, 1. And it was just great, a lively atmosphere." But after a couple of weeks in New York, the band broke up. *Colossal Youth* would turn out to be their only statement, aside from a single and an EP, *Test Card*.

Sudden early success, as well as some mundane interpersonal tension, had caused an equally sudden split. "If I had an ounce of common sense, I would have said, let's have a break, let's keep this thing together," laments Moxham. "We would have been absolutely massive. I'm sure we would have made a couple more really good albums, at least. I don't want to diminish the input that Phil made musically, and of course the impact of Alison's singing. But at the time, I was sort of cheesed off. I thought, I'm doing sort of 80% of the work here anyway, writing the songs and melodies and everything, the lyrics, half the drum machine stuff, even some of the bass lines. Also I was managing the band as well. I just thought, well, I can do this on my own. Typical kind of *Spinal Tap* ego trip."

Had the group continued, Moxham thinks they might have pursued the more "open-sounding arrangement" of some of their later cuts, such as "Salad Days." "Maybe we would have diversified our sounds a bit, but still have really tight, poppy songs. We would have used different instruments for a start. I think we had an excellent formula which had, as I say, at least another two albums in it. Maybe with less of the scratchy guitar, perhaps a better drum machine sound, and different keyboard sounds. I think the quality of the songs was so good that it almost wouldn't have mattered, really, if we even just kind of ploughed the same furrow. Even some basic production techniques would have made the albums different enough from [*Colossal Youth*]."

In fact, Moxham did attempt to reunite the band a few times over the next couple of years, making some tapes with Phil and another brother, Andrew (on drums). Although these were passed on to Statton to see if she wanted to add vocals, nothing came of it. Admits Moxham, "Funny enough, I've recently listened to the tapes all the way through, 'cause I just got a digital eight-track and [was] kind of archiving all my analog tapes. I didn't bother to keep *any* of that stuff. It seemed great at the time, but in retrospect it's not too good."

As a side note, in their early days the band made tapes of their music on a reel-to-reel as they were writing it. When we speak in early 1997, Moxham is hopeful that some of this material will be assembled for a Young Marble Giants release in the near future. "We like a good gap between albums," he deadpans.

Statton would go on to pursue a much smoother pop-jazz-inclined direction with Weekend, and as a solo artist. Moxham carried on for a while as leader of the Gist, who made one album for Rough Trade (about which "the least said the better," he chuckles). For almost ten years, he released hardly any product at all, although he continued to write and record at home. (Also an animator, at one point he worked as a cell painter on Disney's *Who Framed Roger Rabbit?*) Eventually "I just decided I could go solo and be a minstrel with my acoustic guitar. Skip right back to where I started before the Young Marble Giants, just somebody who was a singer-songwriter."

Moxham began his solo career with 1992's *Signal Path*, and has released several records since then that have a folkier, more fully arranged sound than his Young Marble Giants recordings. He produced an album by indie lo-fi fave Lois, and worked with such indie hepcats as Mekon Jon Langford and former X-Ray Spex saxophonist Lora Logic. Indie cred doesn't feed the family, and a 1994 feature in *Option* painted a grim picture of an unemployed musician, reduced to living in state housing, selling all his equipment to finance his solo debut, and borrowing money from his American record company to keep from starving. In order to play his music in England, he had to suffer the indignity of performing "pay-to-play" gigs in small venues.

Over two years later, things seem much sunnier. Hole's cover of "Credit in the Straight World" on their multimillion-selling *Live Through This* album has brought Moxham unexpected royalties, as has a French pop superstar who's recorded a couple versions of a Gist tune. Moxham seems happiest, though, about the new material he's writing and recording, and the new album he's making—"I really feel that I'm back on the case again, totally, for the first time since the Young Marble Giants. I can't wait to finish this."

As to the enduring appeal of *Colossal Youth*, Stuart puts it down to two factors. "All great albums are immensely atmospheric. The other thing is detail. If you listen to the bass line, or the sound of a kick drum, it's still absolutely sublime in its details. The songs are good, the riffs are great, and somehow, just by the fact that it's extremely simple, it's very atmospheric as well. It's the quality of Alison's voice. There's lots of minor chords, and a lot of the songs are very sad. Everyone goes on about how there's a darkness about it as well. I think mystery is always a great selling point."

Recommended Recording:
Colossal Youth (1980, Crepuscule). One of the earliest and most seminal albums that could be termed "post-punk." The 1994 CD reissue on Crepuscule is the definitive document, assembling all 25 tracks the group ever released—the entire original *Colossal Youth* LP, plus the *Test Card* EP, a 1979 single, and a compilation-only song.

Laws Unto Themselves: Rock Enigmas

Contrary to the impression you might have received after the previous barrage of one-shot artists, the life of a cult artist doesn't necessarily have to be a short one. A select few musicians have been able to work at a low level of commercial success for decades on end, without particularly selling out or conforming to passing trends. Every musician interviewed for this book was extremely dedicated to his or her art; few, however, were even able to maintain a regular release schedule for more than a few years, let alone cultivate a devoted following that spanned generations.

None of the artists profiled in this section fit comfortably into categories. It's rather convenient to use that as an excuse to lump them all together into a category of their own, of course, but there's more behind this cluster of names than a mini-genre tag. Part of the reason that superstar vets like Eric Clapton remain superstars is because of their adaptability—they've found a format and stuck with it, modifying it as necessary to maintain a certain level of popularity. The reason that Mayo Thompson and Robert Wyatt, to use the most outstanding examples, have maintained an underground following for 30 years is exactly the opposite. They have made their mark by resolutely *not* following trends; eventually, the trends passed, and listeners caught up with those musicians, although in not nearly large enough numbers for the artists to afford those houses on the Riviera.

It's hard to say what has enabled them to build longlasting careers where others gave up or vanished. Persistence, perhaps. Or a long-standing belief that there's always room for improvement; Robert Wyatt, perhaps the most beloved underground musician of all time, insists that he's *still* trying to get it right. There's also the firm conviction that age doesn't matter, the musicians continuing to work when most of their peers have retired from the music business or settled into a formula. Not all of these veterans, of course, are as cutting-edge as they once were; Doris Troy is content to sing in Las Vegas and elite supper clubs, Merrell Fankhauser's search for the lost continent of Mu in the Hawaiian Islands has been put on hold while he returns to the California desert in which he was raised. But all—as well as many of the artists detailed in previous chapters—are proof that cult artists need not be shooting stars; they can grow as artists and people as they age.

The Coyne-Clague band, 1969. Kevin Coyne third from left; Dave Clague third from right
Credit: Courtesy Dave Clague.

Kevin Coyne

Kevin Coyne, 1969. Credit: Courtesy Dave Clague.

When I track down Kevin Coyne in Nürnberg, Germany, I find nothing of the "bad-tempered, dour nightmare" that, according to his own press release, the singer could be to journalists in the old days. "I'm glad someone remembers me," he rasps into the phone. How, I think, could I *not* remember that unhinged voice which yelped, "Good boy, go-o-o-od boy!" over and over on one of his early album tracks? When I heard the song as a 12-year-old on the local FM station in 1974, I thought the DJ had gone temporarily mad.

It was not an entirely atypical morsel from the Coyne songbook, and plenty of critics assumed that this abrasive folk-blues-rocker was as mad as his music. It's doubtful that any madman, however, could keep up the hectic pace of work that Coyne maintains to this day. In addition to the 30 or so albums under his belt, he's published acclaimed collections of short stories, plays, and poems, and has exhibited his paintings in German and English galleries for decades. His sardonic vocal delivery and black-comic portraits of maladjusted misfits made him a critical favorite in the 1970s. John Lydon (nee Johnny Rotten), always grudging in his praise, even admitted Coyne as an influence. Never more than a hazy underground favorite in the U.S., Coyne's work has all but disappeared from stateside distribution since his relocation to Germany in the 1980s.

But for Coyne, success has always taken a back seat to unbridled personal expression. "I write books, and have a concern for language, the written word. But when I do songs, I tend to be very spontaneous. I like to mirror the moment and the time. That all sounds very idealistic, but I'm a great believer in that. I think at best it really works. It doesn't sound so manufactured as some pop music efforts. I learned something from the bluesmen, and this kind of attitude. Very open-ended and responding to whatever the day brings, really. Or life at that time."

At the time Coyne began recording with the low-key blues-rock outfit Siren in the late '60s, life consisted of fitting in his artistic pursuits around a job at a mental hospital. The horrors that the recent art school graduate saw at the asylum, he stresses, "were very much on my mind. I was very concerned about what went on. I guess I do have an affection for outsiders, but I got much of it when I was working, just over three years, in this hospital. A lot of the things were to do with the day-to-day events that I was dealing with in the hospital. I like to use music and whatever I do as a source of therapy as much as anything else, to get some of this out, and it was a good opportunity."

As a blues-rock band, Siren—which also included ex-Bonzo Dog Band member Dave Clague on guitar—were also-rans of the late '60s British blues boom. Far more compelling were the tunes in which Coyne let loose with his brand of folk-cum-poetry, extemporizing in a manner that reflected, and seemed to sometimes identify with, the mental disorders of his charges at the asylum. The approach remained essentially unchanged when Coyne went solo on the independent Dandelion label, run by John Peel (Britain's top alternative rock DJ). "It was very spontaneous, really," says Coyne of his stream-of-consciousness songwriting method. "Some of it works, some of it doesn't. I tend to work on that principle to this day."

Coyne's burgeoning cult reputation was enough to attract the interest of the manager of Elektra Records in Europe, who had a somewhat grisly proposition in mind. In mid-'71, as Coyne remembers it, Jim Morrison had been dead for a few days at most when Coyne was approached with the idea of becoming the new frontman for the Doors. "I didn't show too much enthusiasm, and nothing more was heard about it. Maybe I should have shown more enthusiasm, maybe I would have gotten the job. Probably [Elektra] thought I was an ungrateful swine or something. But I really didn't fancy it anyway."

So Morrison had barely settled into his grave before a search was on for his replacement? "Such are the machinations of the record industry," replies Coyne, with the even tone of a veteran who's seen it all. "No sentiment or taste anywhere. There wasn't any question of, you know, poor old Jim, let's give him a bit of a rest now. It was like, got to keep the money wheels turning, keep the cash registers going."

Coyne would enter the world of big-label record company politics soon enough, when he became the second artist to sign with the fledgling Virgin label in the early '70s (Mike Oldfield was the first). Far from being the industry giant it is today, Virgin at that time was an alternative-minded start-up. The singer would remain with Virgin throughout the 1970s, when "I think I was at my very best. I was wild and idealistic and younger, and I thought there was a great passion in what I did. A little misguided on occasion, but I'm very proud of the records I made."

Coyne had already firmly sketched out his territory on the Dandelion re-lease *Case History*, which, as the title implies, drew upon the harrowing experiences at the mental hospital, rendered starkly and with compassion. In the eyes of many critics, Coyne's first Virgin release, *Marjory Razorblade* (1973), was his finest hour, especially "House on the Hill," in which Kevin takes the role of a drugged-out institutionalized patient. Coyne's vocal style was deemed too unsettling for the U.S. market, where the double album was truncated into a single disc (a fate that would also befall the 1977 double live LP, *In Living Black & White*).

"I think [Elektra Records founder] Jac Holzman somewhere along the line—somebody like him—said he's too English or something for the American market. I think these are all clichés developed to support the commercial aspect of the music business. They make up these rules which they change periodically. Sometimes it's good to be English, sometimes it's not good to be English. But it's a very sort of vacuous thing to say."

Coyne has recorded so prolifically that his discography defies capsule summarization. (A best-of/career survey is long overdue.) Generally, it's fair to say that if you've acquired a taste for his blend of disturbing realism and black humor, you'll find something to like on all of his '70s albums. At times his producers edged him more toward a full-band sound, but he's at his best when the arrangements are at their sparsest, emphasizing acoustic or slide guitar and his cutting vocals. A pre-Police Andy Summers played with Coyne in the mid-'70s, but Kevin agrees that "what I wanted to avoid more than anything was a mainstream rock sound."

"Kevin's way of working is very fast," says guitarist Brian Godding, who played and wrote with Coyne on several albums in the early '80s. "When I said we wrote songs together, what I mean is I'd go in and start playing something, and he'd just start singing. You'd only do it once, and he'd go, yeah, I like that, we'll keep that. He's brilliant at improvising songs. It does work. Probably with a lot of people it wouldn't.

"If he picks up a guitar, he plays it in a very unusual opening tuning. His guitar is tuned to chords, as opposed to standard fourth tuning on the guitar. He doesn't use his fingers at all—he plays with his thumb over the neck. He's basically playing like a blues player, who'd use a slide, except he doesn't use a slide or his finger like that, he just puts his thumb over it and plays like that.

"Some people think he's crazy. But if you know Kevin, you *know* he's not crazy. You know that he's just reflecting craziness in his lyrics. He's actually a very intelligent person. You could almost say he has sort of a jazz quality in his approach to music. He's happy to try things out on the spot, and very capable of doing it."

Coyne's anti-commercialism was hailed by Johnny Rotten/Lydon of the Sex Pistols, who's expressed his admiration for Kevin's work. Coyne receives the praise with a mixture of pride and reservation. "I think the Lydon thing was all right at the time, I rather appreciated it, but he's gone to really carry on doing the same thing over and over again. I don't seem to have influenced *him* that much in the end. He's still can't really sing properly! He's still wailing away pointedly."

A much more unlikely admirer was Sting, though it's a lot tougher to detect traces of Coyne in the Police than in the Sex Pistols. "I can remember Police coming in rehearsal rooms near to where I was rehearsing, and all of us laughing, because we thought, this is Andy's [Summers] last chance to make something. They all looked rather old to be punks. They didn't look like punks at all anyway! But I was very impressed by the early Police. Now I find it all rather naive, but at the time, I thought they were rather good. So Sting said whatever he said in his interview, which is true, he did say something to the effect that it moved him. Maybe just a passing fancy on his part, but it seems to have hung around in press releases ever since."

In the years following the advent of punk, Coyne produced some of his most ambitious projects, such as a theatrical song-cycle with German chanteuse Dagmar Krause (*Babble*), an album with support from Robert Wyatt and the Ruts (*Sanity Stomp*), and, most unusually, an album of one-minute songs by famous non-musicians like psychiatrist R.D. Laing and cartoonist Gerald Scarfe. By the early 1980s, though, alcoholism and a rough divorce were taking their toll on the artist. Some accounts of this period implied that the singer who once sang about mental patients was now a loony himself. "I didn't actually enter a hospital for treatment, but I came pretty close to it," he admits.

Coyne turned things around in the mid-1980s after relocating to Germany, marrying a German woman, giving up the booze, and finding consistent opportunities to record for German labels. He does regret, though, that "a certain rigidity creeps in" to his albums from the period, due to the way records are made in Germany. "It's very hard to make it sort of loose here. They have a great respect for the machines, and the guitars all have to have six strings on them," he sniffs, as though unconventional guitar models should be a given. "Everything has to be in order. It doesn't suit my way of going about things. The most important thing is to get what they call a good studio sound. What the hell that is, I've never known, and I've never found out."

Coyne's best recent work is to be found not on disc, but on the printed page. Even if you despise his music, you may well find yourself absorbed in his short stories, dark vignettes with a comic bite that often mercilessly satirize the experiences of the touring rock band—the neglected sidemen, the has-beens undergoing cosmetic surgery, the one-shot wonder being milked dry by greedy relatives. If a musical play based on squabbles in rock 'n' roll heaven between Sid Vicious, Janis Joplin, Bob Marley, Jimi Hendrix, and Jim Morrison strikes you as tasteless, you may be better off giving it a miss. If you like your rock 'n' roll fiction with both savage wit and a dose of all-too-true realism, however, Coyne's your guy. The *Show Business* collection, published by Serpent's Tail, may be the best starting point.

Coyne allows that his stories are sometimes drawn from actual rock 'n' roll road experiences, reflecting "the British musician's overriding sense of cynicism about everything. A lot of it comes from mid-'70s touring and things said, in vans and in dressing rooms. A lot of people seem to think it was done out of bitterness, which it certainly isn't. It's done with a sense of horror, really. It was meant to amuse, but certain people didn't like it, maybe because they saw something of themselves in it. I don't care, really. All I know is that the musicians who've read it have laughed their heads off. I must be reaching somebody and doing the right thing."

Lest you get the impression that Coyne is an incurable curmudgeon, he adds that he's pretty pleased with his last three albums, on which his voice, whether due to age or increased mellowness, has become considerably less scratchy. He's just finished an album with some guitar by Gary Lucas, veteran accompanist to Captain Beefheart, Jeff Buckley, Joan Osborne, and others. The upcoming European gig list is full, a big consideration for the singer, who considers himself a performer, not a chronicler of social woes.

"I very early on cottoned on to the idea that people like to be entertained and amused and shocked. The theatrical aspect of what I do has been very much ignored by people who haven't seen the gigs. The records reflect part of what I do, but live performances are very different. The lyrics from the records are often forgotten, and tunes are changed round. Everything's turned upside down, depending on the venue and the time. It can be almost a comedy show some nights, and very serious another night. But I regard myself as an entertainer as much as anything."

Recommended Recordings:
Case History (1971, Dandelion/See For Miles, UK). Coyne at his rawest and most disquieting. Reissued on CD in 1994 with bonus tracks.

Marjory Razorblade (1973, Virgin). Somewhat (though not much) lighter in tone than *Case History*, if only because of the diversity of material necessary to fill up a double-album release.

In Living Black & White (1976, Virgin). In the absence of an anthology of Coyne's 1970s work, this double live album (edited to a single disc for the U.S. market) is the closest one might come to a best-of, the backing musicians including future Police guitarist Andy Summers.

Recommended Reading:
Show Business (1993, Serpent's Tail). Engrossing vignettes, musical and otherwise, that detail peculiarly British character neuroses with both menacing humor and subtle compassion.

Merrell Fankhauser

If the Rock and Roll Hall of Fame held elections for artists most highly esteemed by collectors of rare records (don't hold your breath), Merrell Fankhauser would be one of the first inductees. What's all the more remarkable is that he's generated rabid cult followings among aficionados of not one, but several different styles, from surf to folk-rock to psychedelia to progressive. To those who have never pored over the fine print in record collecting magazines, he's nothing more than an entry in the funny band name contest, having led such outfits as Fapardokly, HMS Bounty, and MU (pronounced "moo," not as in cow, but as in the lost Pacific Ocean continent).

What's the link, you might ask, between the teenager who wrote and recorded the first surf song called "Wipe Out" in the early '60s, and the cosmic rocker who, decades later, was working on songs about getting picked up by a spaceship while walking through the jungle? Only, perhaps, that the sea, the desert, and islands have been constant themes in the Californian's work, whether he's churning out instrumental surf rock, some of the most overlooked folk-rock of the '60s, or mystical heart-of-the-tropics weirdness with MU. You could add that, for all his weirdness, Fankhauser's music is about as accessible as a "cult rocker"'s can be. That's gotten him close to commercial success numerous times—and into fleeting contact with celebrities like Nilsson, Captain Beefheart, and George Harrison. But Fankhauser's name has never clicked with more than a few thousand devoted fans. And many of them may know only one Merrell Fankhauser—the folk-psychedelic rocker from the '60s, the Beefheartian cosmic rocker of the '70s, or a footnote to early surf music—but not all three, or even two, of his musical personalities.

Fankhauser's closest shot at the brass ring, oddly enough, may have occurred at the start of his 30-plus-year career. In the early '60s, the teenage guitarist was learning his craft in Pismo Beach, California, on the Central Californian coast. Recruited while working at a gas station by a bunch of local surfers, the Impacts, he got the group to drop their slide trombonist and start playing instrumental rock. When they recorded a bunch of sessions for Del-Fi in Hollywood in 1962, one of the tunes was the Fankhauser-penned "Wipe Out." The following year, a similar song by a group called the Surfaris would drench the airwaves to become one of the biggest instrumental hits of all time.

To this day, Merrell claims that the Impacts demoed another version of the song that served as the prototype for the Surfaris' hit. The dispute's never really been settled among surf authorities, particularly as the Impacts' own rendition of "Wipe Out," which served as the title track for their sole LP, was dominated by a steel guitar and saxophone, and was *not* too similar to the more familiar drum and guitar-based arrangement employed by the Surfaris. The Impacts broke up; Fankhauser formed another band, the Exiles, and began writing and singing average pop-rock in the mold of Ricky Nelson, Buddy Holly, and early Mersey-beat. For most such musicians with a minor controversy to their credit, the curtain would have dropped there.

Except that the Mojave Desert—a landscape that, for the most part, is as barren of cultural innovation as it is of water—had this odd tendency to breed eccentric geniuses in the '60s. Perhaps the lack of stimulation cultivated originality, but both Frank Zappa and Captain Beefheart did stints in the region in the '60s while honing their music. So did Fankhauser, who was now recording on the tiny Glenn label, run by the eccentric Glenn MacArthur, whose true love was gold mining. In the mid-'60s, Fankhauser's songs began to take on a folk-psychedelic hue that was, well, strange.

Although working for Glenn Records largely limited sales to a few thousand copies in the desert area, it may have given Merrell a little more latitude than he would have had if he'd been swallowed by the Hollywood machine to the south. Recording Merrell's vocals in a plastic military surplus jet cockpit, MacArthur would, in Fankhauser's words, "put echo in the room that wasn't even there." The Glenn tracks had a sound heavy on both the high-end shimmer and a thick bottom, and Fankhauser began to craft supremely melodic Byrdsian pop with an astral, almost goofy edge. Merrell's Exiles went through a variety of complicated

MU in concert; Merrell Fankhauser is guitarist on left. Credit: Courtesy Merrell Fankhauser

personnel changes, but it's for certain that two of the musicians, guitarist Jeff Cotton and drummer John "Drumbo" French, would end up in Captain Beefheart's band later.

Some of the better Glenn singles, like the Americanized Zombies-like "Tomorrow's Girl," were combined with some of the newer material on the inimitably titled *Fapardokly*. The group had briefly changed its name to the enigmatic Fapardokly as well, which probably helped doom the LP to instant collector status. Which is a shame, as it had some true wacko gems, like the "Eight Miles High" rip-off "Gone to Pot," and songs addressed to a cuckoo clock and a glass chandelier (the drugs were most likely truly starting to kick in).

"I got into that folk thing for some reason, because I always liked the Kingston Trio," says Fankhauser. "They did these ballads that told stories, and I just took that to a more far-out approach with songs like 'Lila' and "Super Market.'" Nobody would confuse those dreamlike tunes with the Kingston Trio's clean-cut catalog, however. "Lila" was a 12-string guitar folk-rocker worthy of the Byrds at their best, and "Super Market" was a hazy blend of airline commercial melody (complete with son-of-Herb-Alpert trumpet lines) and psychedelic incantations to the singer's girl, urging her to close her mind and leave her luggage behind.

The album's 12 tracks spanned several years' worth of material, contributing to a schizophrenic quality that makes the group seem weirder than they actually were. One moment they're imitating Ricky Nelson and oozing teenage heartbreak, the next they're moaning about astral travel (quite literally, in "Gone to Pot"); the guitar lines range from brisk rockabilly to some of the best haunting 12-string raga guitar lines this side of Roger McGuinn. Only 1,000 copies were pressed; by the 1980s, the album had become one of the prime collectibles of '60s rock, commanding over $500 for mint copies.

Fapardokly didn't find an audience in their own time, though. By 1968 Fankhauser was leading a new band, HMS Bounty, which decided to make an assault on Hollywood, landing a contract with the Uni label. One self-titled album resulted, and fell into a pattern that would become all too common for Merrell's projects: enthusiastic praise from those who heard it, almost nonexistent distribution, and quick ascendance to semi-legendary rarity. It was actually quite a decent pop-psychedelic affair, its best moments featuring the group leaning toward the psychedelic side of the equation. While still capable of crafting rather standard commercial California rock, Fankhauser's true muse seemed to lie with spacy, lyrically elusive tunes, given a human dimension by his wistful, airy vocals. "A Visit with Ashiya" (with sitar) and "Madame Silky" in particular are two of the better overlooked Indian-influenced rock tunes of the era, and "Ice Cube Island" demonstrates the blossoming of Fankhauser's unusual matches of lyrical images.

It wasn't enough to keep HMS Bounty from splitting up in 1969, though. Fankhauser took a crack at the commercial market by cutting an odd, mariachi-flavored single of "Everybody's Talkin'" with the A-team of L.A.'s session players, but his friend Nilsson's version creamed it in the marketplace. By this time, though, Merrell was getting into much freakier, bluesier sounds. An intimation of this can be heard on the HMS Bounty's final single, "I'm Flying Home." More crucially, he'd begun hanging out with Captain Beefheart, and recruited the mad genius' equally colorful guitarist, Jeff Cotton.

At Chez Beefheart, remembers Fankhauser, "We'd just sit up all night writing crazy songs and playing wild, weird music. He locked various members of the group in the house. At different times [they] would try to flee. Because they would stay in the house recording constantly under Don's control. And they would start looking very pale. People would go visit 'em, and they didn't quite recognize them anymore."

So when Fankhauser and Cotton began playing together in their own band, "It kind of bugged Don. He was having a hard time keeping the band together in those days, because things would get so wild. They'd fly off to Belgium or somewhere and do a concert, and then come back and stay in the house for six months, work on another album, and things like that. A couple of them didn't even know who the President of the United States was. It's like they were in suspended animation there."

Both Fankhauser and Beefheart coveted Cotton for his unusual swooping bottleneck slide sounds. Cotton, a non-drinker, would even go to liquor stores purely to test the whisky bottles with his little finger in his search for bottles that would yield the best slides. So the good Captain, admits Fankhauser, "got a little disturbed when Jeff wanted to go back and play with me again. He said, 'The guy's a rock phenomenon. He's probably at least the third best guitar player in the world right now for his particular style.' What Jeff did with slide guitar, I still haven't heard anybody do. He could play harmony notes, and more than one note, and picks up stuff like a photographic mind." According to Fankhauser, it took a lengthy session of negotiation in Beefheart's "Magic Bathroom" before the Captain relinquished his claims on Cotton's talents.

With former Exiles Larry Willey (bass) and Randy Wimer (drums), MU was formed, taking as their inspiration the mythic sunken continent of the Pacific. As you might guess, the band's philosophy was becoming more mystical and spiritual in nature by this time. Fankhauser and Cotton wrote prolifically. The only album released by the group in its lifetime (*MU*, 1972) was a sort of collision between Beefheart, the Grateful Dead, and Crosby, Stills & Nash. Such name-dropping doesn't really do justice to the unclassifiable character of the music, which incorporated Cotton's biting slides, tribal rhythms, unpredictable shifts from straight verses into jazzy jams, tropical ambience, and exuberant harmonies. The clarion calls to hippy unity might provoke sneers in this post-punk age, but musically, MU were among the most sophisticated and unusual acts of the late psychedelic era.

Few people outside of the L.A. underground heard the *MU* album, and the group took their cosmic beliefs seriously enough to relocate to Maui after its release. More material was recorded at the band's jungle house with equipment left behind by Quicksilver Messenger Service, a generator supplying the electricity. The group unexpectedly fragmented when Cotton and Wimer decided to become Christian ministers and return to California. The tapes were virtually forgotten by Fankhauser until the 1980s, when he hacked his way through the jungle with a machete to find them in the abandoned, decaying house, just a few inches from a puddle that would have made them unusable. Much of the material, which was in a mellower, even more tropical mode than the official MU LP, was issued for the first time on various collector labels in the 1980s.

Fankhauser by this time had imbibed great deal of the Maui vibe — indeed, MU were quasi-celebrities there, performing what Merrell believes was only the second rock concert on the island (the first was by Jimi Hendrix, in 1970). With his girlfriend of the time, violinist Mary Lee, Fankhauser returned to California in the mid-'70s to record a solo LP in a sort of updated, more interesting Crosby, Stills & Nash mode. Although the producer was interested in placing the record with George Harrison's Dark Horse label, it ended up as another small-press independent item. By the late '70s,

Merrell Fankhauser, Maui rocker.
Credit: Courtesy Merrell Fankhauser

Fankhauser may have at any rate been more interested in furthering his search for evidence of the lost continent on the Hawaiian Islands, as well as his studies of Tibetan Buddhism (in 1975, he was anointed as a Buddhist monk by a Tibetan lama).

Time has a way of catching up with rock enigmas, though, as the songwriter found in the early '80s, when he was tracked down on Maui by devoted German record collectors eager to issue some of his material. Unbeknownst to Fankhauser, a cult had sprung up around his work, especially in Europe. A bootleg of the Fapardokly LP appeared in Britain in the early '80s, followed in the next several years by legitimate reissues of most of his recordings from the 1960s and 1970s. An onstage heart attack in the late 1980s hasn't stopped him from issuing periodic albums (primarily for the benefit of his small legion of fans). In 1996, he was working on a double-CD rock opera, *Return to MU*, about the lost continent he's never given up trying to find.

Sitting in Hollywood in 1985, far away from MU or what remains of it, Fankhauser gives me a clue as to both his failure to reach a mass audience, and the longevity of his best music. "I was always one of not wanting to listen to the radio. Because you get too
sucked into the radio, pretty soon something gets you and you're unconsciously doing something that's already been done. That's what Captain Beefheart would do in his own way. He would try to get everybody outside of everything else, to where you got something different. Well, I do the same thing. You know, living in the desert, living by the ocean, going to Maui, just trying to get outside of it, so you're not pumped full of it subconsciously."

Recommended Recordings:
By Fapardokly:
Fapardokly (1967, Sundazed). Possibly *the* great overlooked folk-rock album, including both 12-string lovelies and off-the-wall early psychedelia.

By Merrell Fankhauser & His HMS Bounty:

Merrell Fankhauser & His HMS Bounty (1968, Sundazed). More consistent than *Fapardokly*, although the high points aren't as eccentrically inspired. Nonetheless, anyone who wants to hear poppier takes on Buffalo Springfield, the Byrds, and other such L.A. bands of the '60s will like this.

By MU:
MU (1972, Sundazed). A psych-progressive rock near-masterpiece, with a fusion of blues, hippie mysticism, and jungle rhythms that sounds like little else from that era or otherwise. The Sundazed CD reissue is the definitive MU collection: the double-CD includes the entire *MU* album and all of the more subdued 1974 MU material that came out on various compilations in the 1980s.

The Red Krayola

The first time that Lelan Rogers, owner of the Texas-based International Artists label, saw the Red Krayola in 1966, they were playing at a shopping mall. Not the most appropriate venue, one would think, for a band that was working up songs like "Hurricane Fighter Plane," "Vile Vile Grass," "Transparent Radiation," and "Pink Stainless Tail." "He couldn't believe that we were serious," remembers guitarist and singer Mayo Thompson, who over the last 30 years has been the constant source of the guiding vision for the band (and indeed, their only permanent member). "He thought it must be comedy."

Rogers, the older brother of country-pop superstar Kenny Rogers, recalled in the liner notes to the *Epitaph for a Legend* compilation, "There was this group of kids, three of them, up on a stage that had four or five different kinds of instruments and they could not play a note. They were just making noise and they were really putting the people on. I figured anybody that was able to put on a crowd like that—there's got to be a market. I went over and I said, 'Hey guys, give me a call.'"

Red Krayola, late 1960s; Mayo Thompson, center. Credit: Courtesy Drag City Records

No doubt some listeners think that Red Krayola are still "just making noise" 30 years later. Mayo Thompson's lyrics are still free-associative patterns with little in the way of narrative, anthemic slogans, or, god forbid, feel-good romanticisms. The music is still an admixture of catchy pop tunes and incongruous chords, delivered in ever-shifting arrangements that sometimes seem to owe more to chance than planning. And Thompson's still singing in his gentle whine, like an off-kilter, slightly off-key Texas cousin of Ray Davies.

Truth to tell, Thompson couldn't care less what mainstream *or* underground critics might think of his discography. For one thing, at the moment he's as busy as ever with another edition of the Red Krayola, collaborating with members of noted alternative rock bands Tortoise and Gastr Del Sol, and experiencing a greater level of success in his native U.S. than he's ever attained since 1967. He's up from southern California to open for Palace in San Francisco, but it's not a "comeback." Unlike just about any other "underground" rock musician you could name who began recording in the 1960s, Thompson's gone from psychedelia to punk to post-punk without missing many beats. Whether with the noise-psychedelia of the '60s Red Krayola, the scratchier-than-fingers-on-a-blackboard guitars of his late '70s English edition of the band, or a current lineup that falls somewhere between those extremes, he's remained resolutely outside of both pop and "counterculture" trends.

Speaking in his San Francisco hotel room before his soundcheck, Thompson is hardly the disheveled weirdo you might expect from listening to those old Krayola albums. In a sport coat and neatly pressed pants, he's more like a leaner, professorial version of Spaulding Gray, given to user-friendly theorizing about pop music and his place in it (or lack thereof). And, in fact, he is a professor of sorts, having returned from years of residence in Europe to teach art in Pasadena, California.

"We set out from the beginning to mark our difference from everybody," he proclaims. "We wanted to eliminate everybody, and we wanted to tighten the logic. We wanted to say, is there logic in pop music? And, if there is, if there's a claim for a certain kind of progressive logic or certain kind of developmental logic, well, let's see where it goes. Our strategy was totally informed to some extent by art and avant-garde traditions and those kinds of things. But, our aim was to shut everybody else up. 'Cause we hated everything everybody did, just about, with the exception of a few things"—some of those few things being guitarist John Fahey, the Legendary Stardust Cowboy (who was responsible for the lunatic blast of cowpunk, "Paralyzed"), Country Joe & the Fish, and baroque pop composer Van Dyke Parks.

The first lineup—which had even included future acclaimed country singer Guy Clark at one point—settled into a core trio of Thompson, Steve Cunningham, and drummer Rick Barthelme (who is now an acclaimed novelist). "We also did not see ourselves as *part* of what everybody else was doing. We were not hippies. We weren't involved in the worldview that informed counterculture."

But the original Red Krayola was certainly unusual enough to find a small but interested audience in the counterculture with their two International Artists albums, especially the first, *The Parable of Arable Land*. Thompson's tunes—odd little folky ruminations that had a vague kinship to the surreal sort of ditties being penned by Syd Barrett around this time—were augmented, or even smothered, by the noisy waves of clattering dissonance provided by the band's numerous friends in the studio, including fellow Texan Roky Erickson. From a pop standpoint, Thompson's early material is better served by the sparse demos that surfaced on the *Epitaph for a Legend* compilation. There's no question, however, that *Parable of Arable Land* anticipated some of the elements that would appear in industrial rock over a decade later.

"We were counted as outsiders somehow, weirdos," notes Thompson. "Weirder than people who were *professional* weirdos. Not Frank Zappa, not Beefheart. Zappa is like an analogue for us in a certain sense. He also, I think, thought hippies were stupid and foolish, and kidding themselves, and congratulating themselves on how hip they were, but only by keeping their eyes closed, not noticing what anybody else was doing. At the same time, he recognizes that humor was one of his most powerful devices. But it ate at him to the point that he wanted actually to be taken seriously. So that became more important to him than anything."

Thompson's reputation as a weirdo could have only been enhanced by a performance at the 1967 Berkeley folk festival in which the band played to the amplification of an ice block melting and dripping onto aluminum foil. Local alternative paper the *Berkeley Barb* labeled the group the "Bummer of the Festival." "Our music," says the eminently quotable Thompson with a touch of pride, "was informed by steering a course through those things that we saw as landmarks, and various things that we saw us piles of dogshit in the street."

The Berkeley trip brought about more long-term damage when the band cut some material with John Fahey, drawing the ire of International Artists. The label threatened to not bring the group back from California to Texas, although, according to Thompson, they had illegally used the Red Krayola's publishing royalties to fly the group out there in the first place. That led to the demise of the original Red Krayola. Thompson hung around California for a few months, doing a bit of work with the avant-electronic-rock band the United States of America, and briefly considering working with Nico.

A 1970 solo album for the short-lived Texas Revolution label was (until its recent reissue on Drag City) one of the top collectibles of its era. It was also Thompson at his most accessible, deploying more "rootsy" folk and rock sounds than was his wont, although at its core the material remained irreducibly strange. "I had a friend who lived in a commune in New Mexico," recalls Thompson. "He'd get up and put that record on and people would throw things at him—'Don't put that goddamn record on again!' They hated it." But he retains fond memories of Texas Revolution's unrealized goals: "We were going to make records of the news. We were going to put the newspaper to music, and sell it on street corners. Like make it in one day, press it, and sell it the next week. Topical songs, sold out of the back of a truck. All the things that we've later come to see—indie music, the DIY scene, all that stuff."

In the early '70s Thompson, while not severing his connection to music entirely, became more involved in art and political discourse, moving to New York to work with *Art & Language*, a journal of conceptual art. "Maybe a year before I left New York, I had a conversation with a guy I was working with. He said, 'That Red Krayola stuff, that's shit. Nobody cares about that. Nobody knows about it. Nobody *wants* to know about it. You're a joke.' He was mad at me about something else, but he lit into me about this. It rang in my ears for a while, I thought about this. But then when I got to England, I found it was absolutely the opposite. There was a whole bunch of people who, ten years later, so to speak, knew those early records, who thought that they were groovy records, and liked them. I began to find out that they had some resonances in Britain. They gave me a kind of entrée."

Moving to England in the aftermath of the punk explosion, Thompson became an expatriate pillar of the British post-punk scene, doing A&R and press for

the pioneering British indie label Rough Trade. He also did production for Stiff Little Fingers, the Raincoats, the Fall, Scritti Politti, and other acclaimed U.K. underground bands. And he formed a new version of the Red Krayola that was heavy on the discordant, scratchy guitars and discursive, non-linear lyrics.

It wasn't pop radio's cup of tea—which was, in essence, the reason Thompson was able to move into the post-punk world without weathering accusations of hippie irrelevancy. "People like Gang of Four would take us seriously and invite us to go and open for them on tour, because it made sense given the kinds of things that *they* were investigating.

Mayo Thompson, mid-1990s. Credit: Courtesy Drag City Records

The same things that were [said] about the music then are the same things that people [say] about it now—'jazzy, broken, dada, blah blah.'"

"Fragmented," I offer.

"Fragmented," he nods. "I didn't fragment the world—I just happened to notice that it *is* fragmented."

Thompson's jagged, off-kilter sensibilities appealed to leading U.S. new wave band Pere Ubu, resulting in an invitation to join the band for a while in the early 1980s. For Mayo it was a simultaneously rewarding and frustrating experience, as he couldn't play some of his favorite Pere Ubu material with the band due to leader David Thomas' Jehovah's Witness convictions, which had led Thomas to disown previous Ubu faves like "Final Solution." "I got a reputation for being difficult," says Thompson, "because I went in there and had an alliance with nobody. David saw me as an ally, and as a force for driving the band in a certain kind of direction. He wants to order things, he wants to control things, he wants to make things happen in certain kinds of ways."

When Pere Ubu broke up for an extended period in 1982, Thompson did a few more records with Krayola, and then drifted more into production, working with groups like the Chills and Primal Scream, and producing the soundtrack for acclaimed filmmaker Derek Jarman's *Last of England*. His musical activities became more sporadic after a spell in Germany in the late '80s and early '90s. Some demos with Gastr Del Sol's David Grubbs, however, led to a contract with the Chicago-based Drag City label. When his mother became ill, and teaching opportunities arose, Thompson began, for the first time in nearly 20 years, to spend much of his time in the United States. For the first time since 1970, his principal musical concentration, in terms of both albums and live performances, is now on the American market.

Listening to the Red Krayola's recent output on Drag City (which includes three albums released in the mid-'90s alone), one has to admit it fits comfortably into whatever state of entropy the alternative rock world finds itself in as the twentieth century ends. That's a long-winded way of saying that Thompson continues to sound both remarkably contemporary and remarkably uncommercial. There's still the tug-of-war between whimsical, rather endearing pop and inaccessible lyrics, odd time signatures, and unpredictable production flourishes.

That may be why Grubbs and other musicians with impressive alternative rock resumes, such as Jim O'Rourke, Tortoise's John McEntire, and Overpass' Tom Watson, want to record with a musician who's just passed his 50th birthday. "The luxury I have is that I don't have a huge baggage of a certain kind of success to carry around," speculates Thompson. "People expect certain kinds of things of you if you have a certain kind of success. I've been a failure from the beginning, no problem, in conventional terms."

What's the similarity between the numerous Red Krayola lineups, then? "I would say that the continuity between them is that I find that we deal, pretty much, with the same kinds of problems. Our attitude remains fairly much the same. It's defined by experimentation—a will to experiment, and a will not to repeat, and a will not to reproduce."

But why have so few musicians from Thompson's generation been able to span eras of underground rock? "I met a lot of people over the years, like Country Joe, who were heroes of a certain period. They've become trapped in a period that functions for them, where they know where they are. I mean, I don't mind a bit of insecurity. I don't mind a little instability, a little quicksand. I *like* it. More fire, more danger, please. Because otherwise I get bored to death.

"For some reason, I cannot stop making music. And believe me, I wouldn't mind. Somehow, it remains an interesting problem. It's also a challenge to find out: Am I irrelevant? Has history passed me by? I don't think so. I think I'm still ahead of the fucking curve!" he laughs.

Recommended Recordings:
By the Red Krayola:
Parable of Arable Land (1967, Collectables). A noise-freakout exercise which finds the first edition of the Krayola at their most extreme. Gentler, but less innovative, material is found on their second album, *God Bless the Red Krayola and All Who Sail with It*; five demos on the various artists *Epitaph for a Legend* compilation let the songs rely on their inherent strengths rather than odd arrangements.

Amor and Language (1995, Drag City). Kinder, gentler post-punk might seem like a contradiction in terms. But if you're looking for music where bits and pieces of all kinds of styles, rhythms, and words rub against each other without being unduly grating on the nerves, this may be what you're looking for. More of the same, with mild variation, is on tap on the Krayola's two other mid-'90s Drag City albums, *The Red Krayola* and *Hazel*.

By Mayo Thompson:
Corky's Debt to His Father (1970, Texas Revolution). "Acid-folk" is perhaps an inaccurate designation, given Thompson's avowed distance from the hippie counterculture. But it *does* fit the skewed, witty miniatures on this record to some degree. It may also be the most accessible thing Thompson's made, with or without the Krayola.

Doris Troy

She's sung on sessions for a clientele that would fill up an entire wing of the Rock and Roll Hall of Fame. She's written songs with two of the ex-Beatles, Stephen Stills, Billy Preston, and the famous soul songwriting teams of Nicholas Simpson and Valerie Ashford, and Kenny Gamble and Leon Huff. She's made an album for the Beatles' label, Apple Records. She's played venues from the Apollo Theater to London's fabled 100 Club. At the same time, she's also fit in stints with the highest-paid female singer in Las Vegas, and toured with a musical based on her life story for over a decade.

Yet Doris Troy still remains known to much of the public as a one-hit wonder for her 1963 Top Ten single, "Just One Look." Should there ever be a contest for the one-hit wonder with the longest resume, this soul singer and prolific songwriter might win it hands down. And there have been few other African-American performers who have proved their mastery of so many styles—girl-group pop, stone cold soul, gospel, hard rock, and more. If her eclecticism brought her few rewards in terms of hits, it certainly helped bring her a longevity that few of her peers could match.

When Troy entered the music business in the early '60s, it was as a backup singer on the New York pop-soul scene. With fellow up-and-comers Dionne Warwick, Dee Dee Warwick (Dionne's sister), and Cissy Houston (mother of Whitney), she did sessions for the likes of Solomon Burke, Chuck Jackson, and the Drifters. Unlike many female R&B singers of the time, she was also a songwriter, teaming up with Gregory Carroll under the name Doris Payne. A March 1963 demo of "Just One Look" was issued by Atlantic. With its stuttering piano and Brill Building-savvy melody, it made #10—her first and last chart hit.

End of story? Not exactly. Not only did the hit give Troy the chance to support herself through live work for years, but she also recorded a wealth of material (mostly original) for Atlantic and other labels in the mid-'60s that qualifies as some of the most criminally neglected early soul music. There was a bit of bossa nova, straight girl group pop, blues ("Draw Me Closer"), and wrenching ballads ("Heartaches" in particular stands as one of the great lost classic slices of orchestrated soul angst), all soaked with Doris' expressive, gospel-drenched vocals, delivered with an uptown New York sophistication. And there was a rousing uptempo dance-soul number, "I'll Do Anything," written and recorded with Kenny Gamble and Leon Huff, years before that duo had established their Philly soul production empire with the likes of the O'Jays and Jerry Butler.

What made Troy's work so unusual in the context of the era was its incorporation of more or less equal parts R&B and pop, with some blues, gospel, and jazz thrown in. Troy herself thinks that "Just One Look" stood out from the crowd "because it was very basic and very clean. It was different. Because every other song had a lot of strings, big-time arrangements. We had only four pieces."

A career lifeline came to Troy from unexpected quarters. Over in Britain, "Just One Look" became a big hit for the Hollies in 1964. The Hollies covered another of her tunes ("What'cha Gonna Do About It"), Lulu did "Just One Look," and other acts covered Troy material. "I'll Do Anything" became a huge hit on the British Northern soul circuit, populated by a band of fanatical soul aficionados that have ensured continued sales and popularity for many an obscure American R&B artist. One of whom was Doris Troy, who made her first visit to the U.K. in 1965, recording a storming rock song, "You'd Better Stop," in London with a guitar break that sounds a hell of a lot like the young Jimmy Page (then Britain's top session axeman).

In the second half of the 1960s, Troy was concentrating more on singing than songwriting, "because when I realized that I wasn't getting the money that I should have gotten, that kind of stopped me from writing for a little while. I decided, if I go to work, the man has to pay me. So when I found out the man was keeping 90% and giving me 10%, and I had to fight for that instead of a 50-50 which we agreed to, that put me off for a little while. I knew I could work anywhere, I knew I could sing any style of music, and that's what I did."

And by the end of the 1960s, she was doing most of that in England, where a session with newly signed Apple artist Billy Preston led to a contract with the label run by the biggest group in the world. "When I got there, I met Billy Preston for the first time, and George [Harrison, who was producing the session]. George said he had everything I ever did. I couldn't believe that. And then he picked up his guitar and started playing 'Just One Look' and stuff like that, and I thought it was so hip, you know?" At the end of the session, Harrison asked her if she wanted to record for Apple as a solo act; a few days later, she was getting a recording, writing, and production deal together with Apple. That's how fast things could happen in those days; today, a year's worth of marketing meetings might have been necessary before Troy even got a phone call.

Troy began recording for Apple in early 1970, at precisely the time the Beatles were on the verge of breaking up. Apple itself was in the midst of a financial chaos that took literally decades to get sorted out. But Troy has little but fond memories of her Apple days. "Before there was all the problems, man, it was fun, it was very creative. The business part, that wasn't a cute part at all. The musicians and the artists, they had a good time together.

"We really got into taking care of business and writing good tunes. Some of the stuff we did in the studio, I'd be messing around on the piano and somebody would walk over and say, what is that? I'd say, this is what I got so far. And they'd so, okay, try this, try this, and that's how come on the [songwriting credits] you see Ringo on some of it, Stephen Stills on some of it, and George. Nobody stopped to say, well, you can't do this or you're signed to this company or you're signed to that company. We were all just doing it."

Several of the songwriting credits on her self-titled Apple album bear the

Harrison/Troy byline, but Doris is careful to point out that George's principal role was as a polisher rather than a co-composer. "He was like a perfectionist. He wanted every note to be exactly right. To me, he didn't have to take that long. We could have knocked it out and just went for the feel of it, you know? But he would take into a solo, man, and take hours to get the solo right. I'm not knocking him or anything; it's just that that's the way he was." Harrison's mother died while the sessions were still in progress, "so that made it really difficult. I was left to finish up the project because he couldn't handle it."

The album had something of a surfeit of supersession guests, featuring instrumental contributions from not only Harrison and Stills, but from Peter Frampton, Eric Clapton, Leon Russell, Delaney & Bonnie, and Billy Preston. Troy also had something of a musical chairs' worth of songwriting collaborators, including Harrison, Ringo Starr, Stills, fellow Apple artist Jackie Lomax, and bassist Klaus Voormann (an intimate of the Beatles and a member of John Lennon's Plastic Ono Band). Perhaps as a result, the soul-rock-gospel fusion of the LP got top-heavy at times; the best tracks tend to be the more sparsely arranged ones.

The Apple record was followed by less visible efforts for Polydor and Island. But Troy was gaining most of her celebrity for her work with many of the top British rock acts of the time, capped by her vocals on Pink Floyd's *Dark Side of the Moon*—a creation about as far away from her New York early '60s roots as could be imagined. "They can call me up three o'clock in the morning, and I would come do sessions. That's how

Doris Troy, live in 1962. Credit: Courtesy of Showtime Archives and Bill Millar

I did 'You're So Vain' with Carly Simon. They [weren't] getting their harmonies together. Somebody called me up and said that Paul McCartney wanted me there, and Mick Jagger was there. I got 'em all together and we got that 'You're So Vain' down to a nice little sound."

Troy has made few recordings as a soloist since returning to the States in the mid-'70s, but it's not as if she's had trouble keeping busy. There was work with Lola Falana (according to Doris, "the highest-paid female singer in the whole of Las Vegas"), and a starring role in the musical *Momma I Want to Sing*, which she's played since 1984 (and which was written by her sister, Vi Higgensen, a top New York soul disc jockey). If she has any regrets about not adding any more hit singles to "Just One Look," they're not evident. For one thing, she's busier than ever before. When I catch up with her in late 1996, she's just returned to her Las Vegas home from a lengthy stay in London, where she sang at the 100 Club, the Soho Jazz Festival, and Mezzo (one of the largest restaurants in Europe), and is getting ready to go to Los Angeles to participate in a "Legends of Rock and Roll" show. The key to the constant call for her services? "Because I'm doing gospel, jazz, blues, soul, pop stuff. It just keeps me rounded."

Recommended Recordings:

Just One Look: The Best of Doris Troy (1994, Soul Classics). Definitive compilation of her 1963–65 sides, including her sole Atlantic LP and various non-album singles. Some of the best overlooked, wide-ranging soul of the era.

Doris Troy (1970, Apple). While Troy's sole Apple effort screams "1970" with its heavy rock flavor and rotating cast of famous session guests, her vocals—more gospel-inflected than on her '60s sides—are always accomplished and emotional. The CD reissue adds five bonus tracks from non-LP B-sides and outtakes.

Robert Wyatt

"I'm still trying to do the same thing, only get it right!" laughs Robert Wyatt when I ask him what direction he'll be moving in next. "The appearance of variety is a complete illusion. It's like somebody who's got a dart board in his room, a large dart board, and there's darts all over it. You think, wow, you've got a lot of different directions you throw your darts. And you say, well yeah, but all I was trying to do was hit the board. That's all I've ever tried to do."

That's a pretty modest summary of a 30-year career that started with him holding down the drum chair in the Soft Machine in the 1960s, playing alongside the Pink Floyd in small underground clubs at the birth of British psychedelia. Then it was on to American tours supporting Jimi Hendrix, and pioneering largely instrumental jazz-rock with later editions of the band, before founding the short-lived Matching Mole in the early '70s. A drunken fall from a fourth-floor window paralyzed him from the waist down in 1973. End of the line?

More like a new beginning. Switching his focus to voice and instruments that he could play with his hands alone, Wyatt released increasingly personal solo albums. He became one of the few musicians to play his hit single on television in a wheelchair. He was one of the few card-carrying communists to be found in the British entertainment business in the 1980s. He released quirky, almost experimental cover versions of both Chic's "At Last I Am Free" and a

Robert Wyatt, elder statesperson of progressive rock, mid-1990s. Credit: Kladaradatsh, Brussels, Belgium

gospel song about Stalin. He had a small hit with a cover of Elvis Costello's "Shipbuilding." He guested on innumerable rock and jazz albums by the cream of the international avant-garde.

When he speaks to me by phone from his home in Lincolnshire, England, in autumn 1996, he seems on the brink of resuming a more active profile than he's held in recent years. He's planning to do some recording next week at the studio of ex-Roxy Music guitarist Phil Manzanera, and has recently contributed to an opera by contemporary composer Mike Mantler. Punctuating his thoughtful comments with frequent laughter and self-deprecating remarks, one would have little idea of the high esteem in which he's been held in the rock underground since the late '60s.

"What keeps me going," he muses, "is a constant sense of disappointment with what I've already done." He's gotten it right, though, enough times to make a difference. If there's been any constant to output that's gone from psychedelia

Robert Wyatt (standing on right) with the Soft Machine, 1969. Credit: Courtesy Cuneiform Records

to the most avant of avant-jazz, it's that voice—a strange, raspy, sad instrument that radiates humility, compassion, and soul, albeit of an intellectual sort.

That voice was first heard in a mid-'60s outfit called the Wilde Flowers, in Canterbury. Raised in a highly intellectual environment, Wyatt and his friends couldn't resist the pull of the British Beat boom, leaving Coltrane and Stockhausen for the moment to grind out rock and soul covers on the local dance circuit, as well as increasingly idiosyncratic original material. Several future members of the Soft Machine and Caravan passed through the Wilde Flowers' lineup. A recent Voiceprint CD unearthed crude but fascinating early recordings, although Wyatt tends to "prefer the mystic clouds of nostalgia to the real thing, to be honest."

Wyatt and various Canterbury chums formed the Soft Machine, which began making a name on the London underground circuit in 1967 with their whimsical, jazzy take on pop-psychedelia, crammed full of odd time signatures, unexpected chords, and lyrics which could verge on the surrealistic. Early demos (which have circulated officially under various names) show a surprisingly accessible outfit that began to tackle jazzier, more difficult directions by 1968, when they supported Jimi Hendrix on grueling American tours. Wyatt's busy drums and vocals, apt to break into jazzy scatting as much as soulful balladry, were key elements of the band's appeal. They were also one of the artiest of "pop" groups, if any band that sang the alphabet backwards (as Robert did on their second album) could be considered a "pop" act.

The Soft Machine ran through about one lineup an album, and had adopted an almost wholly instrumental approach by the time of 3rd, which actually made the British Top 20. They briefly expanded into a septet in an effort to truly fuse the energy of rock with the improvisational verve of jazz. Yet in 1971, Wyatt was dismissed from the band due to disputes over musical direction, a move somewhat equivalent to kicking Brian Wilson out of the Beach Boys.

Asked if he preferred any phase of the group's development to others, Wyatt replies, "That's difficult, because it's like talking about a marriage after a bad divorce. If it's a bad divorce, then it kind of spoils the whole thing in your memory. So in fact I have *no* happy memories of that band at all now, because of the humiliation of being thrown out at the end of it. I never quite got my confidence back from that.

"I'm happy that, if people enjoy it [the Soft Machine], that's good. Because that means it wasn't a waste of time. But for me, the overall experience—I came out of it without much self-respect, without any money, without anything, really. So I haven't dwelt on it too much."

Wyatt played rather haphazard art-rock with Matching Mole for a couple of albums before the June 1973 accident that left him bedridden for months, and permanently confined to a wheelchair. The music, however, continued to flow almost interrupted, as Wyatt shifted into a solo career.

"In theory, I'd like to work in a group," he declares. "But the group I'd like to work in, all the musicians in them are long since dead. The classic Charlie Mingus quintets, I wouldn't have minded working with!" That being an impossibility, Wyatt views his evolution in the following terms: "I would divide it into when I was basically a drummer. Then, when I lost the use of my hi-hat and bass drum legs, I became basically a singer who did a bit of percussion. Certainly I would say that I would like to think that the singer is the butterfly, and the drummer was just the little grub in the ground, working to become a caterpillar."

Wyatt's first solo LP, *Rock Bottom* (1974), was an art-rock summit meeting of sorts, also including old Soft Machine bandmate Hugh Hopper, guitarist Mike Oldfield, and eccentric British spoken word artist Ivor Cutler, and was produced by Pink Floyd's Nick Mason. Its abstract lyrics, emotional singing, and lengthy compositions (all six tracks clocked in at five to eight minutes) guaranteed that its acclaim would be more critical than commercial. Yet Virgin, for all its extensive art-rock catalog, was looking for a hit single. And Wyatt delivered, sort of, with a cover of the Monkees' "I'm a Believer," which had been written by Neil Diamond.

"I thought, 'Well, what should I do that's just like the most unhip thing you can possibly think of? But that's really nice?' I thought of the Monkees doing 'Last Train to Clarksville' or something like that. But then, I couldn't remember the title, and I did 'I'm a Believer.' I'm not full of malice, but I do dislike Neil Diamond a lot, and I'm sorry that I've done a Neil Diamond song. If I lived my life over again, I would leave them to the master," he laughs.

Was the British underground shocked to hear Robert Wyatt covering the Monkees? "But I've always liked pop music," he counters. "There was a bit of a misunderstanding with the avant-garde rock scene, because I think I was sort of swimming the wrong way, really. A lot of the rock thing came out of people who'd started out doing covers of versions of the English scene and the American scene, the Beatles and Dylan and so on, and then got more and more involved in instrumental virtuosity and esoteric ideas.

"I was really going the other way. I was brought up with esoteric ideas and modern European music and Stockhausen, Webern, avant-garde poets, and all the kind of avant-garde thing in the '50s, before pop music—the beat poets, the avant-garde painters at the time, and so on. To me, the amazing thing was to discover the absolute beauty of Ray Charles singing a Country & Western song or something like that.

"So my actual journey of discovery was I discovered the beauty of simple, popular music. And it was much more elusive, really, than people who put it down realize. Anybody who thinks pop music's easy should try to make a pop single and find out that it isn't."

In the early '80s, Wyatt made the leap from prog-rock to post-punk, recording a series of interesting singles for Rough Trade, perhaps the leading British rock indie of the era. Somewhat to the surprise of some observers, his focus had shifted from original material to unexpected covers, including Chic's "At Last I Am Free," the Cuban national anthem, and Billie Holiday's "Strange Fruit." The most successful of these, "Shipbuilding," was an anti-Falklands War protest by Elvis Costello; Wyatt's rendition gave him another left-field minor chart hit.

Wyatt doesn't see a big difference between singing original material or interpreting the work of others. "I was very influenced by painters and artists, more than musicians, when I was a teenager. I don't think it's necessary for a painter to invent the things that he paints. If you paint a tree, it's your painting of the tree, it's your choice of color, what you put in and leave it. If you really work it through—interpreting something—it's you. People are quite shocked when you remind them that Elvis Presley and Frank Sinatra never wrote a song that they recorded in their lives, as far as I know. Because people associate those songs by (Otis) Blackwell and Big Mama Thornton with Presley. They don't say, well, he just did cover versions. They think of them as his songs, and quite rightly so, because they're no *better* than the originals, but they worked as Elvis Presley songs. So they're his songs, because of his voice."

In the 1980s, Wyatt's work was often informed by left-wing politics; he also espoused the most unfashionable cause of communism (although he left the Communist Party in the late 1980s). He recorded songs by Chilean folk singer Victor Jara, and contributed to a benefit album for striking miners. He did a whole album of what he termed (in the Wyatt biography *Wrong Movements*) "un-misusable music: music that couldn't be appropriated by the Right," addressing such concerns as CIA activity in East Timor. Even on his 1991 album of poems by his wife Alfreda Benge (*Dondestan*), he found time to reflect concerns about Marxism and international relations. Wyatt's brand of political music often succeeds because for him, the political is also personal—and because the politics never subsume the music.

"I think artists can be overestimated in the amount of control they have over what you do," answers Wyatt, when I ask whether he prefers to present political or personal concerns. "You sort of do something, and what you do, what you are, comes out. I wouldn't write about anything because I thought, gosh, I ought to write about this, or I ought to write about that. Those times when it comes out as politics for example, or whatever, it's because that's really something buzzing in my gut at that time. And it's just as strong and personal, as emotional, as being in love or anything else. They're not arguable things.

"I'm open to the criticism of that, which is, you know, love is blind. My politics has been too. I think you can fall in love with ideas, and you can fall in love with people. It's a very subjective experience. And I'm loyal to that experience."

Wyatt continues to work at his own pace, recording with such artists as Ultramarine or ex-Henry Cow members Peter Blegvad and John Greaves. After a six-year gap between solo releases, he came out with the well-received *Shleep* in

1997, an album that included guest appearances by Brian Eno, top British jazz musician Evan Parker, and most surprisingly, British pop superstar Paul Weller (formerly of the Jam). He confesses that he's not really cut out for this pop business. "I mean, if you go to a shop down the road and buy something from the shop, it doesn't have to be the most successful shop in the universe. As long as he makes enough money selling his stuff that he can eat too, he's happy.

"And I'm like that with my music. I don't want to have to do the things you have to do. I don't want to live the life. It just doesn't mean anything to me, very much, the high-profile, big money side of things. I just want enough to live on, and to be able to get on with what I do, and hang around my friends. This constant pressure from record companies to come up with a hit single or something like that, I find completely tiresome. I just find that there's no understanding, really, of what the industry is.

"And I find the same problem in the studio, even with engineers who don't like scruffy noises. They like to clean it up and get everything sounding really pristine clear because this is going to go in their CV, and they don't want another engineer to hear them on a record which doesn't sound all clean and tidy. And my music isn't clean and tidy. That's always been a difficult to me—just not being in tune with the industry."

Part of the problem of working with that industry, of course, has been his refusal to stay within easy categories. It's a long way from the Monkees and Elvis Costello to the Cuban national anthem and avant-jazz opera, after all. "In the end, there are notes and intervals and chords and rhythms. Some I like, some I don't. But actually very often, in all these different kinds of musics, all these musicians from different styles are actually picking and choosing from the same tiny little bunch of notes, and the same little bunches of possible rhythms, and so on. Underneath the kind of superficial differences of style, the kind of music's haircut, if you like, or the current clothes the music is wearing, when you're actually working on a piece of music with at least one good idea in it, that good idea is not really fixed or tied to a style or an idiom. There's no field of music which doesn't have good ideas. So anybody who has a good idea and I can deal with it suits me fine."

And why has he, unlike most of his generation, maintained his stature in the rock underground for 30 years? "Although I like pop music and I love rock and roll, I've never been in the commercial world, never swam in the business end of it, really. I think that pop, and to some extent rock, are like sport and fashion industry in that they're about the exuberance of youth. That's the sort of subliminal ideology, really. Whereas the things that I draw on, and the world that I feel part of, aren't particularly youth culture.

"My heroes are—not people that I hope to emulate—people like Picasso and Miro and people who at last really reach something in their old age, which they absolutely couldn't ever have done in their youth. I feel I'm more like in one of those kind of art forms, than in a youth-orientated art form. I think the people who did well, or are happy, in a youth industry, where their youthfulness was part of the act, obviously, by definition, they define themselves out of the business after a decade or so.

"If I say I'm disappointed in what I've done—and I can think of more wrong with it than right with it—maybe the good side of that is, it sort of keeps me hungry, you might say. It gives me a motive. People say, oh it's a shame, you're not nostalgic about the '60s. Well actually, it's quite good, when you think of it. Wouldn't it be sad if I was sitting here wishing it back? And I don't. So at least you can turn those things around. It's quite healthy, I think."

Recommended Recordings:
By the Soft Machine:
Jet-Propelled Photograph (Charly, UK). The 1967 Soft Machine demos show the group at their most pop-friendly, though with more than a hint of the weirdness to come.

Vols. 1 & 2 (1989, Big Beat, UK). A combination of the Soft Machine's first two albums, both released in the late '60s, that plot their progression from psychedelia to instrumental-oriented jazz-rock.

By Robert Wyatt:
Rock Bottom (1974, Virgin). Progressive rock mood music, with some of Wyatt's more eerie, haunting, and melancholic pieces.

Compilation (1990, Gramavision). Combines *Nothing Can Stop Us Now* (a compilation of his Rough Trade singles) and 1985's *Old Rottenhat*. The best view of Wyatt as he enters a more eclectic, internationally flavored, and political worldview.

Recommended Book:
Wrong Movements, by Michael King (1994, SAF, UK). "A Robert Wyatt history" by Michael King that provides a chronological record of the musician's recording and professional activities. Includes numerous quotes from Wyatt and his associates, as well as a discography that makes some sense of his numerous recordings and appearances on dozens of releases by other artists.

Bibliography

One of the questions that kept coming up again and again while writing this book was: "How did you even *find out* about these bands?" Not on the radio, certainly. But it's not as if obscure great rock bands of the past are closely guarded state secrets. Given the curiosity and the will to make a little effort beyond the usual chain stores, a wealth of information about rock unknowns reveals itself. Some of the books about specific performers profiled within these pages have already been noted as "recommended reading" choices within the chapters themselves. Listed below are some of the best general reference books with valuable coverage of little-known pioneers. More are sure to be written in the next few years—if there's a market for a 400-page autobiography by a member of the Monks, anything's possible.

Books

Brunning, Bob. *Blues: The British Connection*. Blanford Press, Dorset, Poole, UK, 1986. Fine collection of profiles of British blues-rockers of the '60s by the original bassist of Fleetwood Mac, ranging from biggies like, well, Fleetwood Mac to foot soldiers like Graham Bond and the Groundhogs.

Dix, John. *Stranded in Paradise: New Zealand Rock'n'Roll 1955–1988*. Paradise Publications, Wellington, New Zealand, 1988. The bible of New Zealand rock, with 350 pages of Kiwi rock history from its earliest days to the late 1980s, with glossy photos worthy of art books. Covers mainstream pop, but there's plenty of attention paid to New Zealand '60s garage, '80s indie rock, and the legendary Flying Nun label.

Frame, Pete. *The Complete Rock Family Trees Vol. 1 & 2*. Omnibus Press, New York, 1980/1983. Vastly entertaining family trees of just about every notable British and American group of the 1960s and 1970s, with plenty of juicy little-seen quotes and anecdotes to enhance the branch graphics. A lot of this focuses on star groups, but since so many star groups emerged from barely-heard littler ones, you'll find a lot of detail on the likes of the Creation, Fotheringay, and (as you hoped) Frumious Bandersnatch.

Heylin, Clinton. *From the Velvets to the Voidoids: A Pre-Punk History for a Post-Punk World*. Penguin, New York, 1993. A history of the roots and early years of US punk, with lots of reminisces from heavyweights like the Velvet Underground and Patti Smith, all the way down to fascinating footnotes from Cleveland like Rocket From the Tombs, the Electric Eels, and Mirrors.

Juno, Andrea. *Angry Women in Rock, Vol. 1*. Juno Books, New York, 1996. Mammoth interviews with assertive female rockers of the late twentieth century. Some of these are superstars (Chrissie Hynde, Joan Jett), but most are candidates for inclusion in studies of cult rockers of the 1990s, like Jarboe, Lois, and Kendra Smith; there's also a talk with June Millington of Fanny, one of the first all-women rock bands.

Ryback, Timothy W. *Rock Around the Bloc*. Oxford Press, New York, 1990. Thoroughly researched history of rock behind the Iron Curtain, from the mid-'50s to the late '80s. Somewhat dry, but this is just about the only book to offer deep research and analysis of rock from Czechoslovakia, Hungary, Romania, Bulgaria, Poland, East Germany, and the former Soviet Union.

Savage, Jon. *England's Dreaming*. Faber & Faber, London, 1991. The best history of British punk. Lots of coverage of the Sex Pistols, of course, but once that story gets started, there are plenty of side digressions to the likes of X-Ray Spex, the Adverts, Eater, etc.

Sculatti, Gene & Seay, Davin. *San Francisco Nights: The Psychedelic Music Trip 1965–1968*. St. Martin's Press, New York, 1985. The birth and peak of San Francisco psychedelic rock. Stories about well-known bands like the Jefferson Airplane dominate, but there's also a fair amount of ink devoted to some of the best bands that didn't get a national audience, like the Charlatans, Mystery Trend, and Great Society. You can also find some of that same territory covered in Joel Selvin's *Summer of Love* (Dutton, 1994).

Tosches, Nick. *Unsung Heroes of Rock 'n' Roll*. Charles Scribner's Sons, New York, 1984. Not for the prudish, this takes a salacious view of the roots of rock 'n' roll, with 25 brief profiles of hillbilly and R&B performers who were instrumental in converting country and blues into rock music. Some of these musicians are famous, but most are not; even if you don't appreciate Tosches' leering prose, it's one of the few places to learn about important rock ancestors like Hardrock Gunter and Skeets McDonald.

Vale, V. & Juno, Andrea, eds. *Incredibly Strange Music Vols. 1 & 2*. RE/SEARCH, San Francisco, 1993 & 1994. This doesn't just cover rock music—it covers every kind of strange recordings imaginable—but many intriguing rock oddities whose following is too small to even be called a cult are discussed in these hard-to-put-down volumes. They consist mostly of fanatic vinyl collectors (including Jello Biafra and the Cramps) talking about the most amazing rarities in their collections, as well as a few interviews with performers, although those musicians don't tend to be from the rock world.

Magazines

The artists in *Unknown Legends of Rock 'n' Roll* represent a tiny fraction of the stories of the thousands of acts that didn't "make it." The following magazines are the ones in the trenches doing most of the crucial detective work, month after month, year after year. They're doing more than anyone else to physically locate the mysterious men and women who have been mere faces and names on record sleeves; getting them to tell their stories; and documenting their lives and recordings in a coherent fashion, before all traces vanish. Also keep in mind that many of the best articles on cult rockers appear in fanzines that publish irregularly, often available only by mail or at specialty record shops. These magazines also carry advertisements for the best specialty mail-order houses that carry reissues of records by the artists in this book, as well as many more.

Record Collector (43/45 St. Mary's Road, Ealing, London W5 5RQ, UK). Superb British monthly, averaging over 200 pages of reissue reviews, articles, and interviews with acts encompassing both superstars and unknown bands from the past who make the ones in this book seem like media sensations in comparison. Much stronger on British artists than American ones, but all kinds of rock from all eras are covered well.

Goldmine (700 E. State St., Iola, WI 54990). The premier rock collector periodical in the US isn't as sharp or wittily written as *Record Collector*. There's also a considerably higher ratio of ads to content, but the scope of coverage is still impressive. For every Kiss article, or millionth Rolling Stone retrospective, they'll throw in an immense piece on somebody like Merrell Fankhauser.

Ugly Things (3707 Fifth Avenue #145, San Diego, CA 92103). Appearing on a roughly annual basis for the last 15 years, this is packed with Torah-length interviews with obscure '60s British Invasion groups, '60s garage bands, and '60s Eurobeat artists, with a level of detail that is truly spectacular. If your interest is piqued by the previous chapters on the Outsiders, the Monks, the Music Machine, or the Creation, make this your next stop.

Ptolemaic Terrascope (37 Sandridge Road, Melksham, Wiltshire SN12 7BQ, UK). You might be able to tell by the title that this British publication is psychedelically-inclined, although they do cover a good deal of modern-day variations on acid rock, as well as just plain ol' alternative rock. The real highlights are the long interviews with cult enigmas of the psychedelic era. It's one of the only places where you can find mini-books on the likes of the Blossom Toes, the Hampton Grease Band, H.P. Lovecraft, the Nazz, and Pearls Before Swine, all exhumed with a passionate intelligence.

Forced Exposure (PO Box 9102, Waltham, MA 02254). Renowned underground rock scribes Jimmy Johnson and Byron Coley have been publishing (and writing much of) this filled-to-the-gills magazine of way-off-the-beaten track music and record reviews for over a dozen years. As of now it's on an, ahem, irregular publishing schedule of every few years or so, but many of the back issues remain available. These are stuffed with interviews with punk and post-punk icons like Lydia Lunch, Diamanda Galas, and Big Black, along with names that you won't find in college radio rotation, like MX-80, Divine Horsemen, and Copernicus. Lots of psychedelic/garage/experimental/reissue coverage in the reviews, too.

The Disc

You've read the book; now you can hear the music! It usually doesn't work that way, but we're talking music that you probably can't even find in the stores, let alone hear on the radio. The CD compilation accompanying this volume features tracks by twelve of the artists covered in these pages. Most of the songs are either out of print or available only on hard-to-locate reissues; many were never even released in the United States. It touches upon some of the most intriguing and unclassifiable sounds discussed in this book, from lost psychedelia and garage rock to Moroccan-dub-rap fusion and quirky independent cassette releases. Let the ride begin . . .

1. John's Children, "Smashed Blocked." "Please . . . I'm losing my mind!" declares Andy Ellison at the outset of this 1966 single, and as the psychedelic mayhem builds and builds over the next thirty seconds, there's no reason to doubt him. Just before the track freaks itself out into oblivion, it glides into an off-kilter, moony adolescent ballad, punctuated by more strange spaced-out vocals in the periodic choruses. "Nobody had ever done anything like that—ever," claims Ellison today. Recorded well before Marc Bolan (aka T. Rex's) brief stint in the band, it was certainly too strange for the hit parade of the day, though it did make #98 in the US charts and pave the way for the group's legendary banned *Orgasm!* album. But that's another story . . . Available on CD through Cherry Red Records, Bishops Park House, 25-29 Fulham High Street, London, SW6 3JH, UK.

2. The Music Machine, "Point of No Return." More mid-1960s experimentation on this early Music Machine track, recorded before they signed a deal and crashed the Top 20 with "Talk Talk." An oblique anti-war statement by leader, singer, and songwriter Sean Bonniwell, whose growling vocals are supported by squealing, strangled guitar leads that were quite forward-looking for the era, although the group's folkier roots are detectable in the acoustic guitar part. This song was available only briefly in the mid-1980s on a flexidisc in an obscure German fanzine, where Bonniwell's spoken introduction obscured the first few bars of the track; this compilation marks the cut's first appearance in its entirety.

3. Cleaners From Venus, "Clara Bow." This paean to the silent film star Clara Bow is among the best work by Cleaners mainstay Martin Newell: witty, nostalgic, British, and instantly hummable, decorated by airy harmony vocals. From their

1986 cassette-only release *Living With Victoria Grey*, which is full of such mod pop gems.

4. The Rising Storm, "Frozen Laughter." While this Massachusetts prep school band usually played stomping garage rock, this haunting acoustic-flavored original, somewhat in the mold of their heroes Love, revealed versatility and songwriting acumen well beyond the scope of the typical 1960s teen group. From the odd spoken opening "Honey, is that you?" to the hazy organ, forlorn harmonies, lyrical quotes from T.S. Eliot's "The Wasteland," and snatch of backward tapes that brings it to a close, the cut oozes mystery and an impenetrable sense of loss. It's the highlight of their sole album, originally pressed in minute quantities for themselves and their schoolmates in 1967, and now available as a CD reissue from Arf! Arf! Records, PO Box 465, Middleborough, MA 02346.

5. Savage Rose, "A Girl I Knew." When Savage Rose was founded in the late 1960s, recalls keyboardist Thomas Koppel, they strove to create "a new kind of music that had it all—elements from classical and folk and jazz and rock and soul and all of it in one go, as one style, not as a mix of a lot of styles." This mysterious, sad cut from their self-titled 1968 debut was one of their most successful attempts at realizing this ambition, anchored by lead singer Annisette's odd lead vocals (which somewhat foreshadow Kate Bush's approach), characteristic swirling keyboards, and an ominous surprise ending of funereal bells that seemed to announce the Grim Reaper itself. This is its first appearance on a US release, though the album has been reissued on CD in their Danish homeland. Available on Polydor, Denmark.

6. The Mystic Tide, "Frustration." One of the truly great 1960s garage classics, this leaps out of the speakers and grabs you from the word go, then proceeds to turn the heat up yet several more notches with a supercharged guitar break that was unbelievably unhinged and over-the-top by 1966 standards. Dig also the dueling vocal parts, which find the lead singer and backup dudes delivering totally different sets of lyrics simultaneously—an approach rarely employed to this day in rock music. Real-life "frustration" over the group's lack of success led Mystic Tide leader Joe Docko to throw out most of his copies of the group's rare, locally released 45s many years later, but luckily some survived, and "Frustration"—as well as all of the group's other records—are now available on the *Solid Sound/Solid Ground* compilation on Distortions Records, PO Box 1122, Bala-Cynwyd, PA 19004; Fax 610-394-6953.

7. Fapardokly, "Super Market." In a far sunnier mode is this breeze of a psychedelic pop tune, its Son-of-Herb Alpert trumpet lines meshing pleasurably with flamenco guitar runs and sweetly spacy lyrics. Few artists mix commercially accessible elements with such idiosyncratic weirdness as Fapardokly leader, singer, and principal songwriter Merrell Fankhauser; the melody was as appealing as the Byrds or the Mamas and the Papas, yet the execution was too oddball to reach a wide audience. This mid-1960s cut closed Fapardokly's self-titled (and only) album, which was fetching about $500 on the collector's market twenty years later; the LP's contents were finally reissued in the US in the 1990s as a CD on Sundazed Records, PO Box 85, Coxsackie, NY 12051.

8. The Outsiders, "Sun's Going Down." Not to be confused with the "Time Won't Let Me" Outsiders from Cleveland, these moody beat punkers of the same name from Amsterdam released dozens of fabulously eccentric tracks in the mid-to-late

1960s. "Sun's Going Down," the B-side of their 1965 debut single, is the high and lonesome sound Dutch style, centered around its high, eerie Aeolian vocal refrain. Outsiders singer Wally Tax describes it as "more or less like a Russian folk melody with a bluesy lyric," typifying the group's blend of R&B with Continental European music. While a few Outsiders cuts have appeared on vinyl compilations of dubious legality, this is the first Outsiders track to be reissued on CD Stateside. Available on CD through Pseudonym Records, PO Box 2078, 3140 BB Maassluis, The Netherlands.

9. Penelope Houston, "Qualities of Mercy." Although this may be the most "normal"-sounding selection on this compilation, such tunes were considered sufficiently uncommercial at the time of its early-1990s recording that Houston found herself without a deal in the US. This was leagues above most of the singer-songwriter competition, which may have been the problem: it was too dark and complicated to make inroads into the commercial market, and not angry or loud enough to be considered hip at the point when grunge was gaining ascendancy in the alternative rock world. Times have changed since then, but the success of Liz Phair, Aimee Mann, Kristin Hersh, and other moody melodic female folk-rockers hasn't helped Houston escape her cult status yet. Available on CD through id Records, PO Box 422163, San Francisco, CA 94142-2163.

10. Savage Republic, "Ceremonial." An apt title (from the mid-1980s album of the same name) from a group whose largely instrumental songs resembled ceremonies or rituals, their oddly tuned guitars, clanging percussion, and insistent riffs building into trance-like states. It's not quite the same without watching Ethan Port burn trash cans of pampas leaves or destroy bookshelves onstage, but this is one of their most effective studio tracks, and representative of their facility for building and maintaining tense momentum. Available on CD through Independent Projects, PO Box 1033, Sedona, AZ 86339.

11. The Deviants, "Nothing Man." The most far-out experiment of their 1967 *Ptooff!* album is not so much a "song" as a musique concrete composition. Its thundering, rattling percussive effects, distant ghostly choirs, and electronic blips underscore the somber spoken lyrical indictments of the "Nothing Man," a soulless contemporary archetype who can think, but cannot love. "I keep getting these fanzines in the mail where they're cross-referencing it with lo-fi industrial music by bands that I've never heard of," admits Farren of the *Ptooff!* album, released by the Deviants in 1967 and periodically reissued over the years, though never easy to find at the local chain store. Available on CD through Alive Records, PO Box 7112, Burbank, CA 91510.

12. Aisha Kandisha's Jarring Effects, "Sankara." One of the less jarring, if you'll forgive the pun, cuts from this Moroccan group's astonishing 1991 album, *El Buya*. Opening with a brief fanfare of mutant rap, the track quickly settles into a trancey groove not far removed from traditional Moroccan music. Halfway through the song, however, post-modern elements begin creeping in with searing distorted electric guitars and increasingly dub-echoed vocals. By the end it sounds far more like psychedelicized African music than a folk tune, deftly illustrating the band's skill at making familiar ingredients over into something new, even post-modern. The sound of the twenty-first century? Available on CD through Barbarity Records/Barrak El Farnatshi Productions, PO Box 140, 4020 Basel, Switzerland.

Index